CAMBRIDGE
UNIVERSITY PRESS

The History of the USA, 1820-1941

for Cambridge International AS Level History

COURSEBOOK

Pete Browning, Tony McConnell & Patrick Walsh-Atkins

Series editor: Patrick Walsh-Atkins

CAMBRIDGE
UNIVERSITY PRESS

University Printing House, Cambridge CB2 8BS, United Kingdom

One Liberty Plaza, 20th Floor, New York, NY 10006, USA

477 Williamstown Road, Port Melbourne, VIC 3207, Australia

314–321, 3rd Floor, Plot 3, Splendor Forum, Jasola District Centre, New Delhi – 110025, India

79 Anson Road, #06–04/06, Singapore 079906

Cambridge University Press is part of the University of Cambridge.

It furthers the University's mission by disseminating knowledge in the pursuit of education, learning and research at the highest international levels of excellence.

Information on this title: www.cambridge.org/ 9781108716291

© Cambridge University Press 2019

This publication is in copyright. Subject to statutory exception and to the provisions of relevant collective licensing agreements, no reproduction of any part may take place without the written permission of Cambridge University Press.

First published 2019

20 19 18 17 16 15 14 13 12 11 10 9 8 7 6 5 4 3 2 1

Printed in Malaysia by Vivar Printing

A catalogue record for this publication is available from the British Library

ISBN 978-1-108-71629-1 Paperback

Cambridge University Press has no responsibility for the persistence or accuracy of URLs for external or third-party internet websites referred to in this publication, and does not guarantee that any content on such websites is, or will remain, accurate or appropriate. Information regarding prices, travel timetables, and other factual information given in this work is correct at the time of first printing but Cambridge University Press does not guarantee the accuracy of such information thereafter.

Exam-style questions and sample answers have been written by the authors. References to assessment and/or assessment preparation are the publisher's interpretation of the syllabus requirements and may not fully reflect the approach of Cambridge Assessment International Education. Cambridge International recommends that teachers consider using a range of teaching and learning resources in preparing learners for assessment, based on their own professional judgement of their students' needs.

....

NOTICE TO TEACHERS IN THE UK
It is illegal to reproduce any part of this work in material form (including photocopying and electronic storage) except under the following circumstances:
(i) where you are abiding by a licence granted to your school or institution by the Copyright Licensing Agency;
(ii) where no such licence exists, or where you wish to exceed the terms of a licence, and you have gained the written permission of Cambridge University Press;
(iii) where you are allowed to reproduce without permission under the provisions of Chapter 3 of the Copyright, Designs and Patents Act 1988, which covers, for example, the reproduction of short passages within certain types of educational anthology and reproduction for the purposes of setting examination questions.

Contents

How to use this book

This book contains a number of features to help you in your study.

Each chapter begins with a set of **Learning objectives** that briefly set out the points you should understand once you have completed the chapter.

Learning objectives

In this chapter you will:

- understand how the US Civil War fits into its geographical and chronological contexts
- find out about the short-, medium- and long-term causes of the US Civil War
- investigate to what extent the attempts to address the issue of slavery in the decades prior to the Civil War were effective
- understand the rise in sectional tension, and breakdown of consensus, in the 1850s.

Before you start

Examine the Constitution of the United States to identify the powers given to:

- the president to manage the economy
- Congress to manage the economy
- individual states to manage the economy
- the Supreme Court to limit the states, Congress and the presidency.

How much territorial expansion took place within the United States in the period between the end of the Civil War (1865) and 1914? Did it acquire any colonies overseas?

Before you start activities are designed to activate the prior knowledge you need for each chapter.

The **Timeline** provides a visual guide to the key events which happened during the years covered by the topic.

Timeline

Sep 1873 The Panic of 1873

May 1893 The Panic of 1893

Jul 1890 The Sherman Anti-Trust Act

Sep 1901 Theodore Roosevelt becomes president

Jun 1906 The Pure Food and Drug Act

Oct 1907 The Panic of 1907

Nov 1912 Election of Woodrow Wilson as president

Feb 1913 16th Amendment to the Constitution

Apr 1913 17th Amendment to the Constitution

Dec 1913 Federal Reserve Act

Aug 1920 US women win right to vote

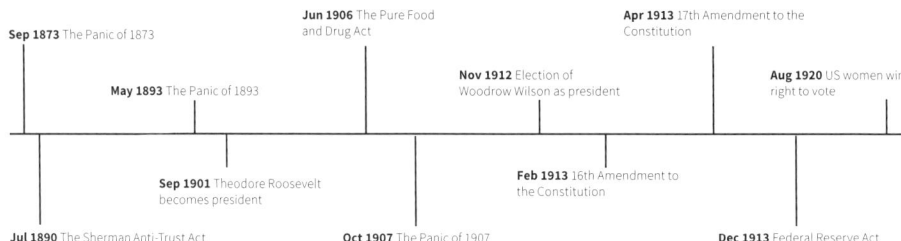

Each chapter contains multiple **Activities**. These are a mixture of individual and group tasks to help you develop your skills and practise applying your understanding of a topic.

Reflection boxes are included throughout the book so that you have the chance to think about how your skills are developing and how you can enhance your independent learning skills.

ACTIVITY 2.12

Using the information and interpretations you have gathered so far about the aims of Reconstruction, construct a case that Johnson performed well and was unfairly blocked by Congress.

Reflection: In what ways did you and your partner agree or disagree when discussing the sources? How far were you able to persuade one another? Were there points where you felt you needed to know more before forming an opinion?

Key terms are important terms in the topic you are learning. They are highlighted in black bold and defined where they first appear in the text.

KEY TERM

Upper South: the most northerly Southern states, adjacent to the Mason–Dixon line, as opposed to the Lower or Deep South

Key Figure boxes highlight important historical figures that you need to remember.

HENRY FORD (1863–1947)

Ford was a pioneer of the motor industry who revolutionised car production by developing the assembly line. He had an enormous impact on technological development and the US economy as a whole.

Key Concepts boxes contain questions that help you develop a conceptual understanding of History, and how the different topics you study are connected.

KEY CONCEPT

Change and continuity

How much changed in the lives of black people in the South in the second half of the 1860s, and how much stayed the same? Work in a small group to look at the various different ways in which life changed (or failed to). Share your ideas and prioritise them in two ways:

- Where were the biggest changes to be found? What were the biggest differences?
- Where were the most significant changes or continuities to be found? What mattered most?

Think Like a Historian boxes contain prompts and questions requiring that you apply your skills in evaluation and analysis. They go beyond the syllabus to help you understand how these skills apply in the real world.

THINK LIKE A HISTORIAN

Many historians think that the impeachment of President Johnson was more about personal politics than the Constitution, or his 'high crimes and misdemeanours'.

What examples of recent leaders can you find who have been, or are being, investigated for political reasons which are dressed up legally or constitutionally?

Learning summary

After working through this chapter, make sure you understand the following key points:

- the causes of what might appear to be an inevitable Northern victory in the US Civil War
- the ways in which political culture and daily life changed in the United States during the Civil War
- the changes and continuities in the lives of black and white Southerners in the Reconstruction period
- the causes of the rise and fall of the Radical Reconstructionist wing of the Republican Party.

Each chapter ends with a summary, Exam-style questions and a Sample answer.

The **Summary** is a brief review of the main points in the chapter to help you revise.

v

Exam-Style Questions provide an opportunity to relate your learning to formal assessment and practise writing longer answers.

a Compare and contrast Roosevelt's attitude towards business in Sources A and D.

b 'Roosevelt was determined to expand the role of the Federal Government.' How far do Sources A to D support this view?

The First New Deal, President Roosevelt's policies between 1933 and 1935, has had both supporters and critics. His supporters argue that he restored confidence in the American economy, ended the crisis of 1931–33 by his actions in the First Hundred Days, and made a start on dealing with the problems that faced America. These ranged from mass unemployment, poverty, an unsound banking and stock market system, a weak farming system and a system of government which was unsuited to dealing with major national problems. He proved to be successful in these areas. However, he had many critics who argued that he was not successful. Some argued that his government interfered too much in the economy and slowed recovery. Some argued that he did not go nearly far enough in dealing with poverty and unemployment, and the New Deal failed too many of the American people. Americans had different views on whether it was successful or not.

This is a good-quality beginning. The opening paragraph does not waste much time on background but gets straight to the point. It shows thought about what 'success' means in context. The main areas of discussion are set out in this paragraph and there is balance in the awareness of a case 'against'.

The **Sample answer** to one of the exam-style questions is a realistic student response, annotated with explanations about what makes it successful and commentary on how it could be improved.

Further reading

Kenneth Stampp makes the case in favour of the Radical Republicans for their noble aims and the real achievement of the 14th Amendment in *The Era of Reconstruction* **(New York, Vintage, 1865)**.

Eric Foner's seminal *Reconstruction: America's Unfinished Revolution* **(New York, Harper & Row, 1988)** has dominated recent historiography. He tells the story of Reconstruction as a tragedy of missed opportunity. Foner has recently concentrated on Lincoln's attitude to slavery, and telling the story of Reconstruction from the point of view of black Southerners.

David Blight paints a picture of Reconstruction as a cultural meeting of minds, undermined when white Northerners and white Southerners each conceded that the other had a point: *Race and Reunion: The Civil War in American Memory* **(Harvard University Press, 2002)**.

The **Further Reading** section suggests additional resources where you can explore the topic in more detail.

Introduction

Aims of the coursebook

Cambridge International AS Level History is a revised series of three books that offer complete and thorough coverage of the Cambridge International AS Level History syllabus (9489). Each book covers one of the three AS Level options in the Cambridge International syllabus for first examination in 2021. These books may also prove useful for students following other AS and A Level courses covering similar topics. Written in clear and accessible language, Cambridge International AS Level History – The history of the USA, 1820–1941, enables students to gain the knowledge, understanding and skills to succeed in their AS Level course, and ultimately in further study and examination.

Syllabus

Students wishing to take just the AS Level take two separate papers at the end of a one-year course. If they wish to take the full A Level there are two possible routes. The first is to take the two AS papers at the end of the first year of the course and a further two A Level papers at the end of the following year. The second is to take the two AS papers as well as the two A Level papers at the end of a two year course. For the full A Level, all four papers must be taken.

There are four topic ares to be studied within the American option:

- The origins of the Civil War, 1820–61
- Civil War and Reconstruction, 1861–77
- The Gilded Age and Progressive Era, 1870s to 1920
- The Great Crash, the Great Depression and the New Deal policies, 1920–41

The two AS Level papers are outlined below.

Paper 1

This is a source-based paper which lasts for one hour and 15 minutes and is based on one of the four topics listed above. Schools and colleges will be notified in advance which topic it will be. The paper will contain at least three sources and students will have to answer two questions based on them. The questions will be based on one of the four key questions set out in the syllabus. **There is no choice of question**. Students are be expected to have the ability to understand, evaluate and utilise those sources in their answers, as well as having sound knowledge of the topic. In the first question (a) students are required to consider the sources and answer a question based on one aspect of them. There is a particular emphasis on source comprehension and evaluation skills in this question, but contextual knowledge is important as well. In the second question (b) students must use the sources as well as their own knowledge and understanding to address how far the sources support a given statement. The relevant knowledge is provided in the appropriate chapter in this book.

Paper 2

This paper lasts for one hour and 45 minutes. It contains **three** questions, and students must answer **two** of them. There will be one question on each of the three remaining topics which have **not** been examined for Paper 1. So for example, if the topic covered in Paper 1 is the Civil War and Reconstruction, 1861–77, Paper 2 will contain a question on each of the following three topics:

- The origins of the Civil War, 1820–61

- The Gilded Age and Progressive Era, 1870s to 1920

- The Great Crash, the Great Depression and the New Deal policies, 1920–41

Each question has two parts: part (a) requires a causal explanation; and part (b) requires analysis. All the questions will be based on one of the four key questions set out in the syllabus. The focus of this paper is on assessing the students' knowledge and understanding of the specified topics and their analytical skills. The syllabus makes it clear what specific skills are being assessed in each paper, and how marks are allocated.

Acknowledgements

The authors and publishers acknowledge the following sources of copyright material and are grateful for the permissions granted. While every effort has been made, it has not always been possible to identify the sources of all the material used, or to trace all copyright holders. If any omissions are brought to our notice, we will be happy to include the appropriate acknowledgements on reprinting.

Thanks to the following for permission to reproduce images:

Cover Image: *Glowimages/Getty Images*

Chapter 1: Historical/GI; Bettmann/GI; duncan1890/GI; Fine Art/GI; Herbert Orth/GI; Bettmann/GI; Hulton Archive/GI; Fotosearch/GI; Kean Collection/GI; MPI/GI; Kean Collection/GI; UniversalImagesGroup/GI; **Chapter 2:** joe daniel price/GI; Hulton Archive/GI; Buyenlarge/GI; Buyenlarge/GI; Stock Montage/GI; Ed Vebell/GI; MPI/GI; Historical/GI; Print Collector/GI; The Frent Collection/GI; Bettmann/GI; Photo 12/GI; Bettmann/GI; **Chapter 3:** SuperStock/GI; Heritage Image/GI; Hulton Archive/GI; Hulton Archive/GI; Museum of the City of New York/GI; Bettmann/GI; Bettmann/GI; Universal History Archive/GI; PhotoQuest/GI; Paul Thompson/GI; Historical/GI; Transcendental Graphics/GI; Tony Essex/GI; Ken Florey Suffrage Collection/Gado/GI; Fotosearch/GI; **Chapter 4:** Bettmann/GI; Hulton Archive/GI; PhotoQuest/GI; Mary Evans Picture Library/Epic; Bettmann/GI; Mary Evans/Sueddeutsche Zeitung Photo; Bettmann/GI; FIA/Epic/Mary Evans; Bettmann/GI; Bettmann/GI; UniversalImagesGroup/GI; Mary Evans/Sueddeutsche Zeitung Photo; The Frent Collection/GI; Fotosearch/GI; Mary Evans/Sueddeutsche Zeitung Photo; Universal History Archive/GI; Fotosearch/GI; **Chapter 5:** Caiaimage/Sam Edwards/GI; Library of Congress/GI; Print Collector/GI; Department of Defense.

Key: GI = Getty Images

Chapter 1
The origins of the Civil War, 1820–61

Learning objectives

In this chapter you will:

- understand how the US Civil War fits into its geographical and chronological contexts
- find out about the short-, medium- and long-term causes of the US Civil War
- investigate to what extent the attempts to address the issue of slavery in the decades prior to the Civil War were effective
- understand the rise in sectional tension, and the breakdown of consensus, in the 1850s.

Timeline

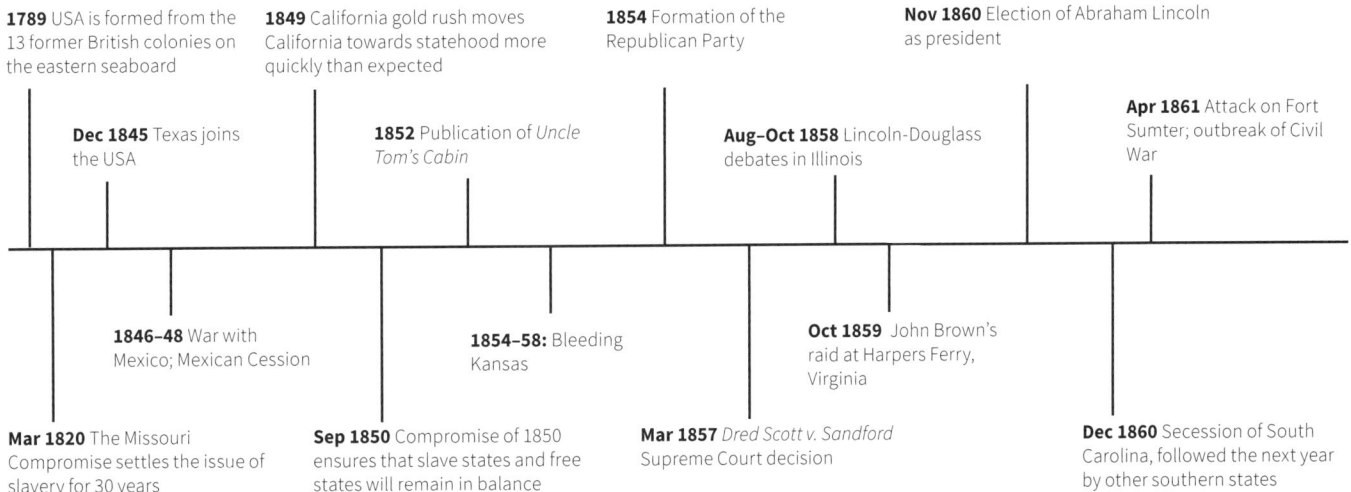

1789 USA is formed from the 13 former British colonies on the eastern seaboard

1849 California gold rush moves California towards statehood more quickly than expected

1854 Formation of the Republican Party

Nov 1860 Election of Abraham Lincoln as president

Dec 1845 Texas joins the USA

1852 Publication of *Uncle Tom's Cabin*

Aug–Oct 1858 Lincoln-Douglass debates in Illinois

Apr 1861 Attack on Fort Sumter; outbreak of Civil War

1846–48 War with Mexico; Mexican Cession

1854–58: Bleeding Kansas

Oct 1859 John Brown's raid at Harpers Ferry, Virginia

Mar 1820 The Missouri Compromise settles the issue of slavery for 30 years

Sep 1850 Compromise of 1850 ensures that slave states and free states will remain in balance

Mar 1857 *Dred Scott v. Sandford* Supreme Court decision

Dec 1860 Secession of South Carolina, followed the next year by other southern states

Before you start

The issue of slavery is often cited as a major cause of the US Civil War. What do you understand by the term 'slavery,' both in general and in its US context?

Look at the map, which shows slave states (where slavery was permitted) and free states (where it was not). 'Territories' were lands which belonged to the United States but had not yet become states. (When they did, they had to choose whether to become slave or free states.) What do you notice about the numbers and locations of slave and free states? Would new states be more likely to be slave or free states? What might that have meant?

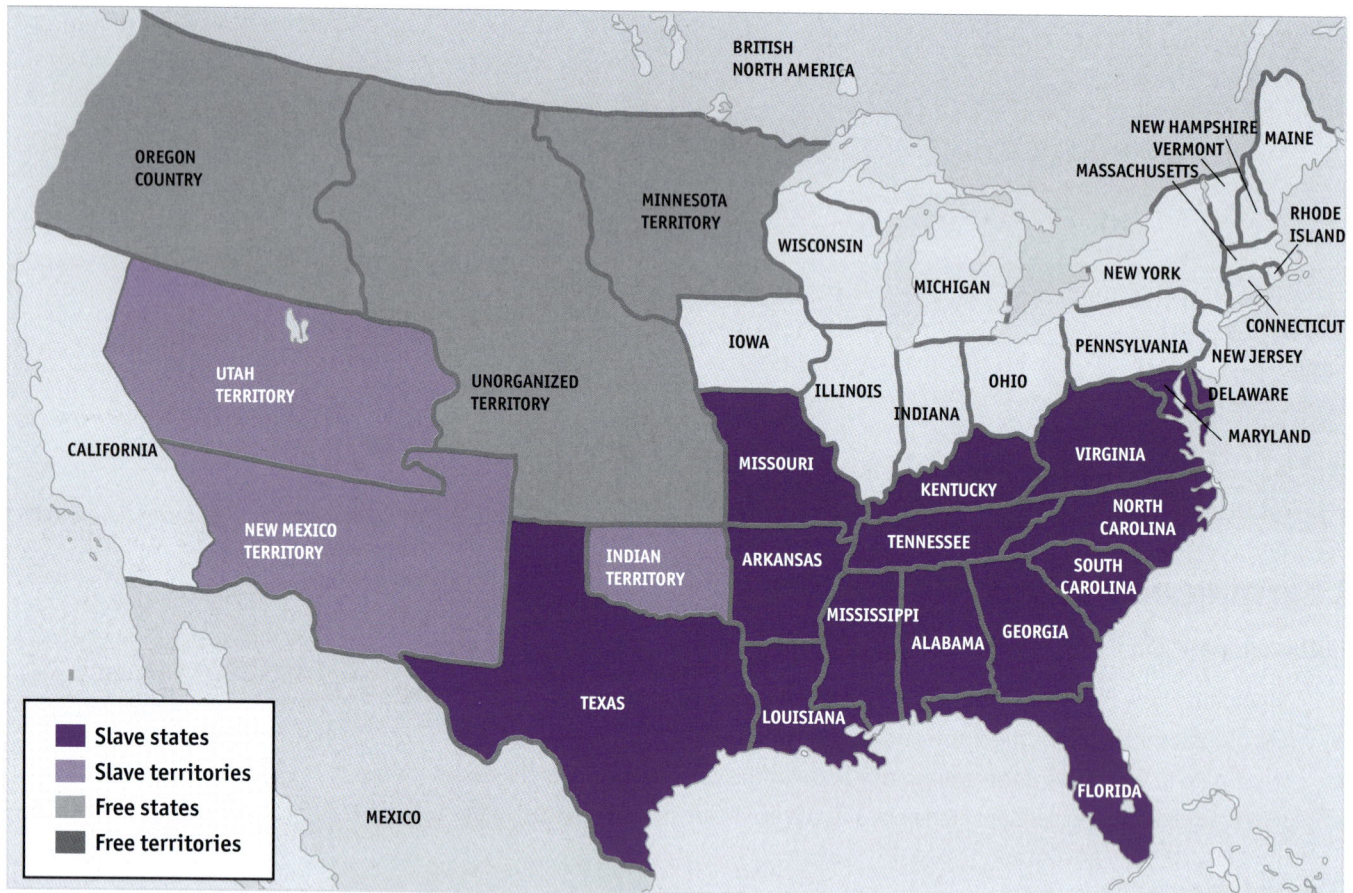

Figure 1.1: Slave states and free states in the USA, after the accession of California in 1850

Introduction

The 13 states which created the original USA, in a process beginning in 1776, covered a distance of thousands of kilometres along the eastern coast of the USA. The differences of climate and land from north to south were considerable. Most Americans in the early years worked on the land, and, because of the variety of climate, different forms of farming had developed. In the subtropical south, farming began mostly to depend on slaves of African descent. This included large-scale farms called plantations which produced cash crops, mostly but not only, tobacco and cotton. In the milder north, farming was smaller scale with individual families using paid workers to produce crops for themselves and local markets. So, despite being united in politics and government within the USA, the country was divided in economic structure and society.

The North and the South developed into two distinct political sections. In the first years of the USA, a balance between the two was achieved, but that balance was not fixed. Each watched the other carefully to make sure it did not dominate the government of the USA and advance its own interests.

The changing relationship between the two sections is key to understanding the events which led to the Civil War between them in 1861. In a long process, the two sides competed politically but agreed compromises. War began when the political process couldn't solve conflicts and when the compromises were considered inadequate.

1.1 How was the issue of slavery addressed between 1820 and 1850?

The political system and the balance of sectional interests in 1820

The question of North and South needs to be understood in the context of the wider political system. Although the question of slavery and the continual issue of the North–South balance was important in US politics, this never resulted in the formation of a 'northern party' and a 'southern party'. Everything to do with this political conflict happened within, as well as between, parties. It also influenced, and was influenced by, the tensions between the federal and states governments, and between the judicial and political structures.

The federal government and the states

The USA was a union of states which had agreed to set up a national, or federal, government. The capital was located on land between the slave states of Virginia and Maryland, on the Potomac River, Washington, District of Columbia. The capital was built around two key buildings representing two key institutions of federal government. The physical separation of these buildings symbolised their constitutional separation:

- The White House was the home of the US president: head of state and head of government, who decided national policy. Elected indirectly by the people, directly by an **electoral college** of state delegates, the president had the power to approve or **veto** new laws created by –
- The US Congress, which drew up US laws, in the Capitol.

The US Congress itself comprised two distinct institutions:

- The House of Representatives represented the people. It was directly elected by adult white male citizens on a state-by-state basis: the greater population a state had, the more representatives it had. In 1819, there were 156 representatives. They had to stand for re-election every two years. Article 1, Section 2 of the Constitution is important here. This allowed states to include in their population 60% of their slave population. This gave these states a greater proportion of representatives.

- The Senate represented the states. Each state, however large or small, had the same number of senators: two. Thus, in 1819, there were 44 senators. They were chosen by the assemblies in each of the states. Each senator was appointed for six years. The Senate was seen as the defender of the rights of the states as distinct from those of the US people. In practice, the Senate was more important in protecting the rights of the slave states than the House of Representatives was.

For a proposal to become US law, the approval of both Houses was needed. This would prove significant during the lead up to the Civil War. This political system is based on two key concepts:

- the separation of powers
- checks and balances.

The first maintains a distinction between the different branches of government. The second makes them work together. The intention was to insure that government was responsible and accountable, and could never become a tyranny. It could, however, (and still can) make the decision-making process long and difficult when there are entrenched and opposing views.

> **🔑 KEY TERMS**
>
> **Electoral college:** This system appoints the president and vice president. The voting tally, or count, in a presidential election in each state determines how that state's representatives will vote in the electoral college. Because different states send different numbers of representatives and, while some representatives vote for their state's winning candidate others vote proportionally according to the proportions of the votes for different candidates, the vote in the electoral college can be different from the popular vote in the election itself.
>
> **Veto:** To reject a decision or proposal. A president can use the right to veto to stop a bill passed by Congress from becoming a law. However, Congress can overrule this if two-thirds of both Houses wish to.
>
> **Supreme Court:** The highest court in the USA, which had constitutional right to annul any law passed by either Congress or a state legislature which it felt went against the principles of the US Constitution.

The Supreme Court and the practical application of the US Constitution

Of the three federal institutions of government in the 19th century, the US **Supreme Court** was the least noticed. It had been formed to decide whether the decisions and policies of the other parts of the government (Congress, the president, and the states and state governors) kept to the Constitution. If the Court decides that they are not, the only way around this is to change the Constitution, which is very difficult to do. It also interpreted the Bill of Rights, the first ten amendments of the Constitution, which protected the rights and freedom of the individual. There were nine Supreme Court judges, including one Chief Justice. They were nominated by the president and approved by the Senate. The president usually chose someone from his own **section** as Chief Justice. Once approved, they could stay in office for as long as they wished, usually for life. In theory, they could be dismissed, but, in the history of the Supreme Court, this has never happened.

While the Supreme Court had great legal authority, it had little practical power. Enforcing its judgements depended on the other branches of government. These had to accept that the rule of law was superior to politics.

> **KEY TERM**
>
> **Section:** In the context of the United States of the 1850s, the two sections were the geographical north and south; in practice this meant the free states and the slave states.

Slavery and the American South

In the 1830s, Southern politicians began to refer to slavery as 'Our peculiar institution'. They did not mean they thought slavery was odd or strange. They meant it was unique to the South. By then, slavery had existed for almost 200 years in the British colonies which had formed the USA in 1783. These slaves were transported from west Africa, but their masters had mostly come from west Europe. As Alexis de Tocqueville wrote in *Democracy in America*, first published in 1835–40: 'In modern times, the insubstantial and temporary fact of slavery is most fatally combined with the substantial and permanent difference of race.' (Penguin, 2003)

Though all slaves were black, it is worth noting that not all blacks were slaves (though most were) and not all slave-owners were white (though again most were). By 1860, there were about 4.4 million black people in the USA, and 3.9 million were slaves. More than half of the half-million free blacks lived in the South. Many free blacks did what they could to help emancipate slave blacks. It was also possible for free blacks to buy and own slaves themselves.

In 1783, slavery was legal in all of the original 13 American states. By 1800, six had abolished it. Many, in the South as well as the North, expected the gradual decline of slavery to continue, especially after 1808, when the overseas slave trade was banned. By the 1820s, all Northern states had banned slavery.

In reality, in the states south of the **Mason–Dixon Line**, slavery actually increased. As the USA expanded into new territory, new slave states were formed and the slave population grew. This was especially the case in what became known as the Lower South, the region around the lower Mississippi. This was well-suited to the rapid development of cotton production and to the use of slave labour. An internal slave trade replaced the abolished external slave trade. This moved slaves from the old slave states to meet the growing demands for slaves in the Lower South. The shortage of slave labour caused the market price of a slave to double between the 1820s and the 1850s from $200 to $400. In the early 19th century, slavery was becoming more important to the South and to the USA, not less. In this way, the issue of slavery became symbolic of the differences between North and South; any attempt to either end slavery in one state or to expand it into new states created a difference in the balance of power between the two sections.

The defenders of slavery were as determined as the opponents of it. Both sections had a range of arguments – geographical, economic, social, cultural, moral and racial – to support their cause.

Slavery was not the only problem facing the balance of sectional interests. The questions of tariffs (taxes) on imported goods, a national bank, public investment in canals and railroads and the power of federal (national) government over the states were all equally important in causing debate and division across the nation. Slavery, however, gradually emerged as the principal issue dividing North from South. From the 1830s, more people in the North wanted to abolish slavery, which they saw, in addition to any moral or religious misgivings, as an insult to the US Constitution and a threat to the employment prospects of free people. These were known as **abolitionists**. In the South, leaders wanted to expand slavery in order to protect the South's position within a US Constitution founded on liberty.

A range of solutions were proposed to try to solve the problem as complex as the existence of slavery in a free country.

> **KEY TERMS**
>
> **The Mason–Dixon Line:** A line on a map drawn by two men surveying colonial America in the 1760s. It separated Pennsylvania and Maryland, north and south, and then turned a corner to separate Maryland and Delaware, west and east. The line became the symbolic dividing line between free states and slave states. Dixon is one possible source of 'Dixie', the popular name for the slave-based south.
>
> **Abolitionist:** Someone who argued that slavery should be banned and slaves should be freed, usually for moral or religious reasons. Abolitionism was a rising force in 1850s America.

Sectional interests and the defence of slavery

On one side, defenders of slavery could maintain things as they were by using the constitutional rights of slave-owners to regain slaves who escaped to free states and/or take their slaves, as personal property, to any of the states, slave or free. Alternatively, they could have certain states identified as slave states. If slavery were limited to those slave states which had agreed the original constitution (six of the original 13), slave states would be outnumbered as new free states were formed, upsetting the sectional balance between North and South. This became impractical early in US history.

So, maintaining the existing balance meant slavery supporters had to find new lands to become slave states by expanding the USA to the south-west, or even separate from the USA as an independent country: a bold move known as disunion or **secession**. Most Southerners thought new lands to the south-west would allow for the expansion of slavery and so the formation of more slave states. Rather surprisingly, some argued the opposite case: that diffusion of the slave population to new states might lead to the gradual emancipation of slaves in the old southern states, such as Virginia. They reasoned that slaveholders and their slave property would move to the relatively empty lands to the south-west, reducing the number of slaves in the old states of the South. Emancipating the few slaves in many states would be easier for whites to achieve than emancipating the many in a few states in the Old South. Secession was frequently threatened by slave-owners, especially at times of crisis. Slave owners often quoted parallels with the 13 colonies breaking away from British control in 1776–83 to form the USA.

> **KEY TERM**
>
> **Secession:** leaving an organisation or federation, as when the Southern states left the USA and formed the Confederacy. According to most Northern political thinkers, it was constitutionally illegal.

Sectional interests and emancipation

On the other side, opponents of slavery believed they could get rid of it by the following means:

- Peaceful emancipation. Slavery could be abolished by agreement of key bodies, such as state assemblies and/or Congress. Emancipation could be gradual and local.

This had happened in the free states of the Northern section in the late 18th century, with each state making their own decisions about timescales. However, what compensation would slave-owners receive for the loss of property, and who would compensate them?

- Military emancipation. Slaves might be freed as a strategy to defeat a rebellion, either by slaves or by their owners, in the context of a civil war. The international laws of war were not the same as the national laws of peacetime. However, freed slaves might encourage or provoke a wider rebellion.

- Violent emancipation. Slavery could be abolished by force, perhaps in a revolution led by slaves. This had happened in modern-day Haiti between 1791 and 1804. US slave-owners feared something similar would happen in the USA. The most obvious examples are Nat Turner's short-lived rebellion of 1831 and John Brown's raid on Harpers Ferry in 1859 (see 'Growing strength of abolitionism' in 1.3).

In the end, as new lands were acquired from France and Mexico in the early 19th century, slavery expanded. It helped to maintain the crucial balance of free and unfree states. The 11 slave states and 11 free states in 1819 had grown to 15 and 15 by 1846. They formed a new status quo.

Although slavery was a key difference between the North and South, at this time, the issue was seen as a matter for sectional politics rather than a national concern. Supporters and opponents of slavery could be members of the same political party, for example.

In between these two groups of supporters and opponents, there were many, perhaps even the majority, who were neither pro-slavery nor abolitionist. They wanted to continue the political compromises which had established the USA and ensured its successful development. They looked to their political leaders in Washington DC to find these compromises as the USA expanded westwards. That expansion, however, made the compromises harder to agree on.

> **ACTIVITY 1.1**
>
> Divide a sheet of paper into two columns and list the arguments presented by defenders of slavery and its opponents. Which do you think was the most important argument on each side, and why?

5

The impact of territorial expansion: westward expansion and absorption of Texas

Manifest Destiny and the absorption of Texas

In December 1845, a journalist called John O'Sullivan wrote about: 'The right of our manifest destiny to overspread and possess the whole of the continent which Providence has given us for the development of the great experiment of liberty and self-government.'

In his article, he continued that: 'Other nations have undertaken [to check] our manifest destiny to overspread the continent.' This statement indicates the interference by other countries – especially great European powers, such as Britain – in the 'overspreading' process. This was notable in the annexation of Texas, which created a major change in the land area of the USA.

Texas had been part of the Spanish Empire, and then of Mexico when that country became independent in 1821. The area had a low population and the settler population was vulnerable to attacks from Native Americans. When more settlers did arrive, many came from the USA. By the mid-19th century, the majority of Texans were of US descent, and Mexicans were a minority. Some of the newly arrived immigrants brought slaves with them, despite the fact that Mexico had outlawed slavery.

In 1836, Texas declared itself an independent republic. The new country looked to the USA for protection, not least against the British. Britain, as an imperial power with interests to defend, thought of intervening in the region. The American government offered to annex Texas. The people of Texas decided to accept. They were partly aware of their state's mounting debts and the threat of bankruptcy, which influenced this decision.

The original plan of the US president, John Tyler, had been for Texas to follow the usual path to statehood by first becoming a US **territory**. This in turn meant that Texas would be placed under the control of the US Congress. There was talk in Washington DC of dividing Texas, which was far larger than existing US states, into four or five smaller states, mostly slave. In the end, and most unusually, Texas was allowed to join the USA directly as its 28th state. This meant its borders could not be changed without its consent. However, as it wanted to remain a slave state, it had to agree to one change. This was to give any land north of a latitude of 36° 30' to the US government (see 'Louisiana Purchase' in 'Attempts at compromise', below).

(see 'Louisiana Purchase' in 'Attempts at compromise', below).

KEY TERM

Territory: The differences between a state and a territory were important to mid-19th-century America. Territories were areas under the rule of Washington DC before they became states. For a territory to become a state it had to go through a minimum of three stages. It needed: a minimum (white) population of usually around 60 000; to devise its own draft constitution in line with the US Constitution; the approval of Congress.

The Wilmot Proviso and the Mexican Cession

The new western border between Mexico and the USA, now including Texas, was disputed. The gap between the claims was some 160 km. The new US president, James Polk, a Southern Democrat and keen expansionist, had promised to annex Texas if elected. He ordered troops into the disputed land. Mexico responded, a clash occurred and the US Congress declared war. 'Mr Polk's War', as some called it, was not universally popular. Critics included two future presidents, Lincoln (already in politics) and Grant (currently a soldier), as well as the leading African American of the time, the former-slave **Frederick Douglass**. At the same time, O'Sullivan's concept of Manifest Destiny was controversial. Most Americans agreed that the USA was a special country with a special mission. Some, however, thought that the willingness to gain more land by going to war undermined that claim to be special.

Douglass had escaped from slavery and became a leading abolitionist. His work was particularly important not only because he campaigned powerfully for an end to slavery, but because he was able to give first-hand testimony to oppose those Southerners who tried to minimise how appalling the practice was for the slaves. He travelled widely and lectured internationally. He helped to bring the problem of American slavery to a wider audience. It is hard to assess how much pressure such international campaigns put on slave-owning states.

FREDERICK DOUGLASS (1817–95)

As the war got underway, politicians were already considering its likely consequences. A US victory would enable the USA to take territory from Mexico. Such lands could become slave states, disturbing the sectional balance in favour of the South. **Slave power**, as Northern critics called the politically powerful plantation owners of the south, had to be curbed.

One such critic was David Wilmot, a Democratic member of the US House of Representatives from the state of Pennsylvania. (As we examine pre-war politics in more detail, it is useful to remember three things about leading politicians: their party, their state and their section. Wilmot was a Democrat. Democrats were usually pro-slavery. However, he was from Pennsylvania, which was part of the North and had abolished slavery as early as 1780.) In 1846, he introduced what became known as the Wilmot **Proviso**. He proposed that: 'As an express and fundamental condition to the acquisition of any territory from the Republic of Mexico by the United States, by virtue of any treaty which may be negotiated between them … neither slavery nor involuntary servitude shall ever exist in any part of said territory, except for crime, whereof the party shall first be duly committed.'

> **KEY TERMS**
>
> **Slave power:** The term came into use to describe the political and economic power held by the South, in opposition to the free-labour ideology of the North, during the 1850s. The phrase did not imply any power was possessed by the slaves themselves.
>
> **Proviso:** A limitation to be imposed on another item.

The Proviso was an attempt to prohibit slavery in lands expected to be acquired from Mexico. This paralleled the 1820 attempt to halt slavery in Missouri (see 'The Missouri Compromise', below).

However Wilmot's proposal was never passed by Congress, and was rejected twice, in 1846 and 1847. This rejection was the first instance of politicians dividing along sectional rather than party lines. The voting split for the Wilmot proposal highlighted the growing sectional differences between members of the same political party, a sign that these differences were starting to become more important to politicians.

Mexico was invaded following a clash between US forces and Mexican troops at the Rio Grande, inside the disputed territory. Mexico's capital was occupied.

Then a peace treaty was negotiated and Mexico was obliged to surrender areas of its northern provinces to the USA. The Treaty of Guadalupe Hidalgo, signed in February 1848, saw what became known as the Mexican Cession incorporated into the USA. This was a vast area, covering more than a million km^2, including modern-day California. A few months after California was ceded by Spain, gold was discovered and the 1849 gold rush began.

Territorial expansion

John O'Sullivan was writing in 1845, fewer than 60 years after the USA became independent. During those years, the USA expanded with great speed, acquiring lands from each of the European empires based in North America. The USA in 1789 was 13 former British colonies of about 930 000 km^2 on the eastern seaboard. Then the country steadily added other lands in the west:

1783 Britain handed over the North West Territory, totalling 670 000 km^2.

↓

1803 The Louisiana Purchase of lands from France gained another 2 million km^2.

↓

1819 Spain agreed to hand over Florida, another 186 000 km^2.

↓

1840s USA signed treaties with Britain to settle its northern borders, especially in Oregon.

↓

1845 Texas, by then an independent state itself, agreed to join the USA, adding another 1.8 million km^2.

↓

1846–48 Following the war with Mexico, the Mexican Cession totalled over 1 million km^2.

↓

1867 After the US Civil War, Russia sold Alaska and its 1.7 million km^2 to the USA.

ACTIVITY 1.2

The USA gained new lands by three different methods:
- negotiating for them (diplomacy)
- buying them
- fighting for them.

Use the map in Figure 1.2 to decide how often the USA used these methods and which was the most important.

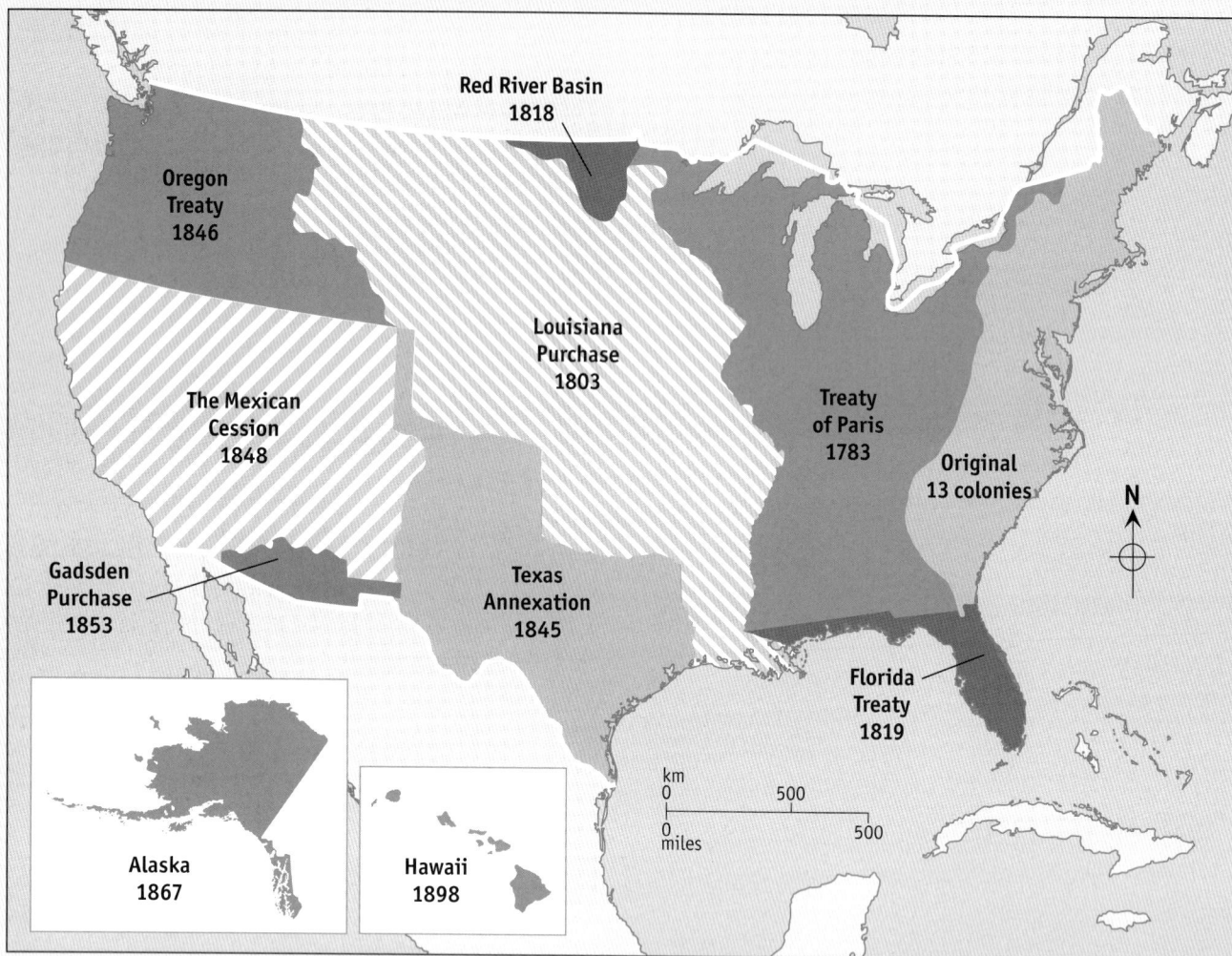

Figure 1.2: A map of the USA westwards expansion, 1789–1853

Within 70 years up to 1850, the USA had increased in area more than six-fold. Most new areas were sparsely populated, either by settlers from Europe or by Native Americans. The more fertile parts of these relatively empty spaces attracted many who wanted to make a new life in pursuit of the happiness that the Declaration of Independence declared their right.

This was a huge amount of land to be absorbed into the USA. How were these lands to be divided between slave and free, territory and state?

Impact of population growth and movement

During the period that the area of the USA grew, the country's population also grew very rapidly:

In these 40 years, US population more than trebled. In the 1850s alone, more than 2 million people came from Europe.

An important cause of this unprecedented growth was immigration from western Europe into the free states of the North. In the 1830s, large numbers of migrants started arriving from Britain and from other parts of Europe. There were both push and pull factors in this process. Factors pushing people to leave Europe were economic, social and political. These included the catastrophic crop failure which led to the Irish Potato Famine (1845–49) and the failed revolutions which took place in several countries in 1848. Factors pulling people to the USA included greater political freedom and economic opportunities, such as jobs in the towns and cheap land. From 1849, the discovery of gold in California was also a magnet.

This increased flow of immigrants produced a reaction in 'nativism', a political movement to favour people born in the USA over those who had migrated there (see 'The party system', below).

Immigration tended to affect the North more than the South as the opportunities the new arrivals were looking for were more likely to be found there. As a result, the Northern population was growing much faster. In wartime, this difference in population size and speed of growth would acquire a new significance.

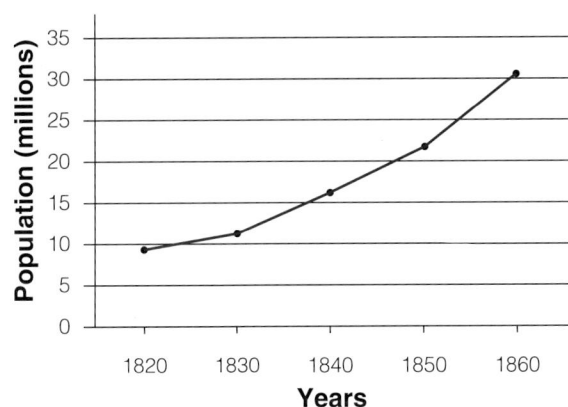

Figure 1.3: Population growth in the USA, 1820–60

A major consequence was the movement of peoples into the new lands west of the Appalachian Mountains. People in the South were also keen to move westwards, but for different reasons. In the South, plantation farming of the Old South to the east had exhausted the soil. Slave-owners went west to find new fertile lands on which to grow the new profitable crop of cotton.

These new lands and peoples needed law and order, and government. To provide this, by 1860, the USA had created another 20 states together with another six territories. They covered all the modern-day states apart from Alaska and Hawaii.

These issues could cause great problems, especially when it came to deciding whether the proposed state become slave or free. The two sections needed to keep in balance, to avoid either North or South becoming more powerful.

Each time a territory converted into a state that balance came into question as politicians calculated how the changing population numbers would affect the balance of power in Washington.

The wealth of the USA

There is one other major aspect of US history it is important to consider during this period and that is the country's wealth. Using **Gross Domestic Product** (GDP) as a measure, America's wealth grew as follows:

Year	GDP ($ millions)	2012 equivalent ($ millions)
1790	189	4568
1820	710	16352
1850	2581	56252
1860	4387	93146

Table 1.1: The growth of US GDP between 1790 and 1860, and its adjusted size in 2012 dollars

Figures from www.measuringworth.com/datasets/usgdp/result.php

KEY TERM

Gross Domestic Product: the annual value of a country's products and services (not including overseas investments).

So, in the 60 years to 1850, while the population of the USA grew rapidly, national wealth increased some 12 times, a huge amount. That economic growth was based upon many factors. Perhaps the most significant factor was the increased cotton production by the slave plantations of the South and its export via Northern ports to factories in Britain. According to Sven Beckert (*Empire of Cotton*, Penguin, 2014): 'More than half of all American exports between 1815 and 1860 consisted of cotton.' Slavery became more important to the wealth of the whole country.

As a result, the Southern states became increasingly prosperous, even though that prosperity was very unevenly distributed. Historians have debated how Southern and Northern states compared for economic success. A longstanding view was that, with the exception of a minority of wealthy slave-owning landowners, many white people and almost all black people in the mid-19th-century USA were poor or very poor. For some time now, however, there have been those willing to argue that, in fact, the South's economy was in a good shape overall, certainly as far as its agriculture was concerned. They concede that the North was more advanced in industrial manufacturing. This proved important in the Civil War, where the better-established industrial sector would take up the task for supplying armaments. One reason why there was a widespread assumption of Southern poverty is likely to have been that there was such poverty after the Civil War. However that was created partly by defeat and partly by the destruction of a socio-economic structure.

One cause for relative poverty in Northern states and relative wealth in the South is likely to have been immigration. With fewer immigrants, the South had a more established (white) population which had had the chance to accumulate wealth. With more immigrants, the North held more people who owned only what they had carried with them. This was often very little since they had often migrated specifically to escape poverty. In wartime, however, with the need to recruit soldiers as each battle results in casualties, this imbalance would favour the North.

Attempts at compromise

Between 1820 and 1860, there were seven attempts to resolve the issue of slavery within a rapidly expanding democracy with clear constitutional rules to live by. They differed in form.

The Missouri Compromise of 1820

In the first, which came in 1819–20, two political parties, the Democrats and the Whigs, worked together. The repercussions of the crisis it attempted to avert were still being felt when the Civil War broke out more than 40 years later. It formed the context within which the outcomes of the war with Mexico in 1846–48 can be understood.

In December 1818, the citizens (in this case all white men) of the US territory of Missouri petitioned Congress to become a US state. Missouri was the first territory wholly west of the Mississippi river to apply for statehood. Whether it was free or slave would form a precedent for other territories in the Louisiana Purchase region acquired from France. As Missouri already had some 10 000 slaves in 1810 – half its total population – it was expected that Missouri would become another slave state. It soon became obvious that this was far from certain.

In February 1819, the bill to allow Missouri to apply to become a state was blocked by the House after a New York representative, James Tallmadge, proposed an amendment preventing the expansion of slavery in Missouri.

This clause reproduced part of a document passed before the USA was finally established, the Northwest Ordinance of 1787. This was presumably deliberate. This Ordinance was a set of articles which described the principles for governing the territories which the British had surrendered to the USA in 1783.

Article 6 of the Ordinance stated:

> There shall be neither slavery nor involuntary servitude in the said territory, otherwise than in punishment of crimes whereof the party shall have been duly convicted; Provided, always, that any person escaping into the same, from whom labour or service is lawfully claimed in any one of the original states, such fugitive may be lawfully reclaimed and conveyed to the person claiming his or her labour or service as aforesaid.
>
> *Article 6 of the Northwest Ordinance, passed by Congress 13 July, 1787*

This meant that all states created from these lands – and six states were later created, starting in 1803 with Ohio – would be free. The House of Representatives supported James Tallmadge's proposal, but the Senate did not and so the bill could not become law. Arguments raged back and forth. Arguments became heated. Both sides used the Constitution to support their arguments.

ACTIVITY 1.3

a   The Tallmadge proposal has three elements in its short clause, quoted below. Identify each and explain their significance.

> That the further introduction of slavery or involuntary servitude be prohibited, except for the punishment of crimes, whereof the party shall have been fully convicted, and that all children born within the said state, after the admission thereof into the Union, shall be free at the age of twenty five years.
>
> *From the Tallmadge amendment, proposed on 13th February 1819*

b   Explain in your own words the section of the Ordinance Article 6 which was *not* in the Tallmadge amendment.

Abolitionists argued that the acceptance of slavery, never mentioned by name in the Constitution, was only a concession to a part of the USA and never intended as national policy. They argued that slavery was incompatible with the underlying principles of the US Constitution and that Congress had the right to impose conditions on any new state joining the USA. Supporters of slavery argued, however, that the Constitution did not give Congress the right to decide on the constitutions of individual states. Only the states had the right to do so. Here was the concept of **states' rights**, which was to become an important element of US politics.

> 🔑 **KEY TERM**
>
> **States' rights:** This is an important concept in US politics to this day. The argument is that the individual states retain certain political powers which they did not surrender to the federal government when the original 13 British colonies came together to form the USA, and that in some circumstances for Washington to issue orders to them is tyranny.

The anti-slavery group had other concerns too. One was political. They argued that the Constitution already gave special rights to slave states, such as the three-fifths clause. This clause stated that three-fifths of the slave population of a state was included in the population count used when allocating representation in Congress. Allowing the expansion of slavery would further tilt the balance of federal power towards slave states. The other concern was moral. Many argued that slavery was wrong, and that it offended the idea of the rights of man, upon which the USA was founded. These arguments, and others, were heard again and again over the next 40 years as the US people considered what to do about slavery in their country.

By skilful leadership, mainly by Henry Clay, the leader of the House of Representatives, in the Congress of 1819–20, the two sections agreed the following compromise:

- Missouri would be admitted as a state without any restrictions on slavery.
- Maine, in the north-east, keen to become a state, would be admitted at the same time as a free state, thus ensuring the balance of free and slave states.
- With the exception of Missouri itself, there would be no slavery in US lands gained via the Louisiana Purchase above the 36° 30' line of latitude.

The dividing line of 36° 30' north was not a new idea. When petitioning for statehood, Missouri had proposed its southern border would be 36° 30'. The line of latitude was already the border between several states to the east of the Mississippi river. This line of demarcation was an amendment to the Missouri bill made by a Northern senator from Illinois, Jesse B. Thomas, himself an advocate of slavery. The line would compensate the anti-slavery group for their acceptance of Missouri being a slave state. All new states created from Louisiana Purchase lands north of 36° 30' would be free states. This demarcation was accepted by the pro-slavery group because it meant they had secured Missouri as a slave state.

The president, James Monroe, from Virginia and himself a slave-owner, thought of vetoing the compromise bill on constitutional grounds. He argued that Congress did not have the constitutional power to impose limits on new states. He eventually decided that such a move would risk civil war. He signed the bill in March 1820.

11

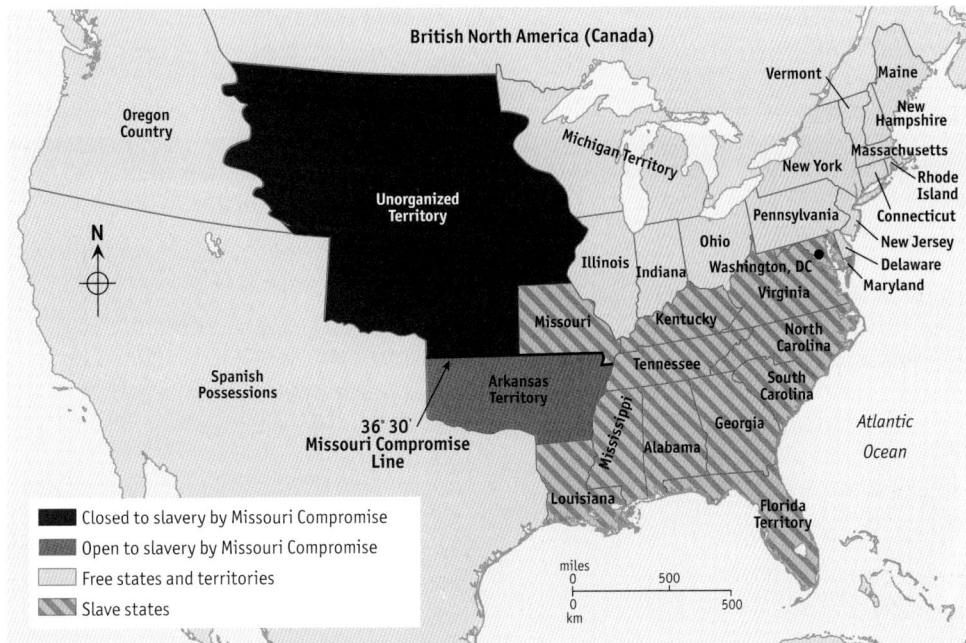

Figure 1.4: A map showing demarcations made under the Missouri Compromise, 1820

There was a second Missouri Compromise, often overlooked, specific to Missouri and its becoming a state. The slave constitution it devised was unacceptable to Congress. It took all of Henry Clay's skills to gloss over the differences and thus achieve the necessary compromise in 1821.

The party system

In 1819–21, politicians compromised over the expansion of the USA ensuring a balance of free and slave states. The balance was sustained in the 1830s, when Arkansas and Michigan joined, slave and free.

In the 1840s, maintaining the balance became a problem once more as a result of the annexation of Texas and the Mexico Cession. In Washington, national politicians grappled with the consequences of further American expansion. This time it took two years for them to come to agreement. They were finding it harder to agree.

By the 1840s, the USA had two national parties, each representing groups from both North and South, the Democrats and the Whigs. They had different visions of how the USA should develop.

ACTIVITY 1.4

'That any person escaping into the same [territory], from whom labour or service is lawfully claimed, in any state or territory of the United Sates, such fugitive may be lawfully reclaimed and conveyed to the person claiming his or her labour.'

a   Put the clause of the Missouri Compromise quoted above into your own words. What future problems can you foresee this law might create?
b   What important principles about the expansion of the USA had the Missouri Compromise established? Which section do you think gained more from the Missouri Compromise, slave or free?

The Democrats	
Important people	• Built up in the 1820s by Andrew Jackson, one of the great figures of US history. • A former general, Jackson was elected president in 1828 and again in 1832. • Once Jackson stood down from the party, leading Democratic politicians of the 1840s included Martin van Buren from New York and John Calhoun from South Carolina.
Potential points in favour	They believed the USA was essentially a rural, agricultural society. They placed great importance on states' rights: the freedom of states to govern themselves free from federal government interference.
Potential points against	They were opposed to expanding the power of the national government, but were prepared to use that government to expand the USA to the west, thereby gaining more farmland.

The Whigs	
Important people	• Leading Whigs of the time included Henry Clay from Kentucky and Daniel Webster from Massachusetts. • Of the same generation as John Calhoun, both died in 1852. There were no leaders equal in skill and talent to replace them.
Potential points in favour	Whigs wanted to develop the industrial power of the USA, using the national government to do so, via tariffs to protect new industries from foreign competition, by national support for building canals and railroads across the country and by re-establishing a national bank, which Andrew Jackson had abolished.
Potential points against	The Whigs emerged in the 1830s, in part to oppose the success of 'King Andrew', as President Jackson had been labelled by his critics.

Table 1.2: Comparisons between the Democrat and Whig parties

It is important to realise that these two parties were national, representing voters from both North and South. They were able to do so because, in the 1830s and 1840s, slavery was seen as a sectional matter, not an issue for national political differences. Thus the Whig Party of the 1840s consisted of two main groups: from the North, the Conscience Whigs and from the South, the Cotton Whigs. Not everyone was satisfied with the two-party system, so other parties were formed. In the 1840s and early 1850s, they included:

- Liberty Party, to support the abolition of slavery.
- Native American Party, to restrict large-scale immigration from Catholic Europe, such as Ireland and Italy. The word 'native' in its title meant people who had been born in the USA as opposed to moving there from another country. They were nicknamed the 'Know Nothings' because of a secret wing: when asked whether they were members, supporters were supposed to say that they knew nothing.
- Free Soil Party, to limit the expansion of slavery into western territories in order to defend paid free labour against competition from unpaid slave labour.

None of these lasted very long.

ACTIVITY 1.5

The Liberty Party, the Native American Party and the Free Soil Party were all short-lived. In each case, suggest some reasons why. Did they fail for similar reasons?

Does the failure of these parties reflect an actual failure, or did they simply achieve their aims rapidly and therefore cease to exist?

The Compromise of 1850

The best policy for dealing with the complex problems raised by the institution of slavery was an issue which perplexed mid-19th-century America. This happened continuously at state level and occasionally at national level. After the Missouri Compromise, it was almost 30 years before national actions were needed to address the peculiar problems of slavery. The failure of the Wilmot Proviso, however, and concerns following the start of the war with Mexico raised anxieties surrounding the issue of slavery and on how the balance between sections was to be maintained. Slavery was becoming a national, rather than a purely sectional, issue.

The Missouri Compromise involved just two future states, Missouri and Maine, and the latter only as a counter-balance. The 1850 Compromise involved four new states or territories: the status of California, New Mexico and Utah, and boundary changes for Texas. In addition to addressing potential sectional problems, Congress also agreed to two further changes concerning slavery: one concerning the national capital, Washington DC, and the other the treatment of fugitive slaves.

Senator **Stephen Douglas** was a leading Northern Democrat. He made a speech to a large audience in Chicago in October 1850, just weeks after the Compromise had been finally agreed by Congress, and listed the six key points of the Compromise. The first two were:

1 The admission of California with her free constitution

2 The creation of a territorial government for Utah, leaving the people to regulate their own domestic institutions.

The third was the creation of a territorial government for New Mexico. These were the lands acquired from Mexico. California came straight into the USA as a state in 1850. Utah and New Mexico became US territories. Utah allowed slavery in 1852 and became a US state in 1896. New Mexico never allowed slavery and didn't become a state until 1912.

Douglas explained their membership in terms of what he called 'the great fundamental principle that every people ought to possess the right of forming and regulating their own internal concerns and domestic institutions in their own way'. This is the principle which became known as **popular sovereignty**, a doctrine Douglas was to make his own in the next few years and which would be adopted by the Democrat Party.

KEY TERM

Popular sovereignty: Broadly, this means that sovereignty (power or authority to govern) resides with the people, rather than with, for example, a monarch or other institution of government. In the USA in this period before the Civil War, it meant specifically the right of the people in a territory to choose their own method of government for the state they would become, and even more specifically whether theirs would be a free or a slave state.

13

STEPHEN DOUGLAS (1813–61)

Douglas is a fascinating figure in American history. His career was intertwined with that of Abraham Lincoln. Both were politicians based in Illinois. In their youth they courted the same woman, Mary Todd, whom Lincoln would marry. In the 1840s, Douglas supported the Mexican war while Lincoln opposed it, and, in 1850, as a leading Democrat in the Senate, he negotiated the Compromise. He believed that the populations of individual states should decide on the issue of slavery, and worked hard throughout the 1850s to prevent the USA from falling apart because of it. In 1860, he was defeated by Lincoln in the presidential election. He died soon afterwards of typhoid fever.

Point 4 of the Compromise dealt with the adjustment of the disputed boundary with Texas. Texas agreed that its northern border should be the 36°30′ parallel. In return, the USA paid off the public debts which Texas had acquired when independent.

Point 5 was the abolition of the slave trade in the District of Columbia. Slave markets in the District of Columbia, in which the capital Washington stood, were banned, but only for those bringing slaves in and selling them for transfer to another state. Abolitionists had campaigned for the end of the slave trade, but slave-owners were concerned this would set a precedent for banning slavery in Southern states. Slavery as such, however, remained legal in DC.

The final point Douglas highlighted was the Fugitive Slave Bill. This bill, which would later become an act, strengthened the powers of those wanting the return of their slaves who, after running away, had been recaptured in another state. By 1848, 12 Northern states had passed laws known as Personal Liberty Laws, which aimed to help slaves escaping from Southern states. Slave-owners in the South argued that these laws undermined their constitutional right to have their slaves returned to them, and had demanded a new Fugitive Slave Act to enforce this. The new bill gave more power to federal government officials to help slave-owners regain what they saw as their property. The act was seen as necessary because of a Supreme Court judgement of 1842 in the case of *Prigg v. Pennsylvania*. The case dated back to 1832, when slave-catcher Edward Prigg forcibly took a black woman named Margaret Morgan from Pennsylvania to Maryland, where she had formerly been a slave, and returned her to her one-time owners. Since 1780 Pennsylvania had forbidden free blacks being taken from the state and enslaved and so Prigg was convicted of abduction by a Pennsylvania court. As there had been a federal law about the returning of run-away slaves since 1793, Prigg's lawyers appealed to the US Supreme Court on the basis that the 1788 Pennsylvania law had been rendered void by the 1793 federal law. The Supreme Court agreed, adjudging the Pennsylvania laws unconstitutional.

Completing the deal had taken Congressional leaders many months to negotiate. Henry Clay, the leading Whig, came out of retirement to help ease the passage of the Compromise though Congress. He failed, but Douglas took over and made a series of deals to see the Compromise through. The Compromise was supported by both Whig and Democrat parties in their **party conventions** of 1852.

The compromise was an example of Congress working to resolve national tensions relating to slavery. Once they had agreed the Compromise of 1850, most politicians returned home from Washington believing that it would last. After all, the Missouri Compromise had lasted for more than a quarter of a century. Senator Douglas assured his audience: 'The South has not triumphed over the North, nor has the North achieved a victory over the South.'

KEY TERM

Party convention: A decision-making rally or large meeting of the members of a political party, often part of the process of selecting candidates.

In the years 1820 and 1850, the issue of slavery moved from being a point of local disagreement to being a point of major dispute in national politics. Despite this, a policy of compromise was maintained, though it was one which required the presence of talented negotiators to make it work. New lands and new immigrants were absorbed into the state system, and still the spirit of compromise was sustained. The principle of popular sovereignty had managed to make the compromise projects seem fully democratic and in keeping with America's national values. The basic assumptions that there had to be dividing lines and a maintenance of balance held up. How many of the legislators that voted through the latest compromise foresaw how quickly it would unravel? Were its changes to the legal status and treatment of runaway slaves expected to become a new point of dispute quite as dangerous to the USA as the issue of territorial expansion?

●●● THINK LIKE A HISTORIAN

With hindsight, the Compromise of 1850 looks to have been entirely doomed to failure. It did not seem that way at the time – certainly not to Stephen Douglas. Which political compromises of the modern world seem to have worked so far? How can we tell if they are holding?

ACTIVITY 1.6

Figure 1.5: *Union*, an 1852 engraving of the key legislators responsible for the Missouri Compromise, by H.S. Sadd

Is this source more useful for the historian studying the Missouri Compromise, or the one studying the Compromise of 1850 which inspired its creation?

ACTIVITY 1.7

a What were the implications of popular sovereignty for the future admission of states into the USA? Which previous rules of membership did it call into question? Which groups might be opposed to popular sovereignty?

b Why did the 36° 30' parallel become the northern border of Texas?

c Explain why the abolition of the slave trade in the District of Columbia was almost a perfect compromise within the Compromise.

d Consider the six reforms in turn and consider which section of the USA gained more from each change. Then make an overall judgement about the Compromise of 1850.

ACTIVITY 1.8

Figure 1.6: A cartoon from late 1850, responding to the Fugitive Slave Bill, part of the Compromise. Bo-Peep represents the Union. She watches as seven of her sheep flee into a forest with wolves. (The palmetto trees represent South Carolina, the leading secessionist state.) The wolves wear crowns and represent the European powers. Their caption reads: "If we can only get them separated from the flock, we can pick their bones at our leisure".

Some of Bo-Peep's remaining flock are labeled Virginia (closest to her) and Kansas. An old dog "Hickory" lies dead in the grass while another, named "Old Buck," is seen towards the left. Bo-Peep calls: "Sic 'em Buck! sic 'em! I wish poor old Hickory was alive. He'd bring 'em back in no time."

'Buck' refers to president James Buchanan, while "Old Hickory" was the nickname of former Democratic president Andrew Jackson, seen as a champion of a strong federal union. .

What does this cartoon suggest about the reception of the Compromise of 1850 in the South?

Reflection: Compare your understanding of the source (Figure 1.6) with that of another student. How did each of you decide how the Compromise was seen in the South?

1.2 How and why did sectional divisions widen between 1850 and 1856?

Problems arising from the implementation of the Compromise of 1850

The calm of 1850 was short-lived. The Missouri Compromise had lasted for more than 20 years, but the Compromise of 1850 broke down within five. On the surface the agreement of established party leaders concealed some important changes in American attitudes towards slavery, especially in the North.

Most of the Compromise of 1850 was implemented without too much dispute: California did become a free state, the slave trade in Washington DC was abolished, and Utah and New Mexico did eventually made their own choices between freedom and slavery.

One part, however, became more and more contentious: the new Fugitive Slave Act. The problems which it created revealed the extent to which attitudes towards slavery had hardened in both sections. Its impact was reinforced by the publication in 1852 of **Harriet Beecher Stowe**'s *Uncle Tom's Cabin*, a fictional attack on the practice of slavery and especially on the Fugitive Slave Act. The novel became a bestseller in both the USA and Europe, and was highly influential. Indeed, when Stowe met President **Abraham Lincoln** in 1862, he is believed to have greeted her with the words, 'So you're the little woman who wrote the book that made this Great War!'

The application of the 1850 Fugitive Slave Act

Throughout the 1850s, the new Fugitive Slave Act provoked many local disturbances, all in the North. However, local newspapers made sure that by using the new invention of the electric telegraph, Southern readers knew of Northern hostility to the Fugitive Slave Act.

There was already a Fugitive Slave Act, dating from 1793. Dealing with escaping slaves was even part of the Constitution, although slaves were not named as such. Article 4, Section 2, Clause 3 stated: 'No person held to service or labour in one state, under the laws thereof, escaping into another, shall, in consequence of any law or regulation therein, be discharged from such service or labour, but shall be delivered up on the claim of the party to whom such service or labour may be due.'

This 1793 Act detailed how this clause was to be implemented, but it did not compel states to enforce the

HARRIET BEECHER STOWE (1811–96)

Stowe was a New England writer, political campaigner and abolitionist. This is a rare photograph of her. She is best known for her 1852 authorship of *Uncle Tom's Cabin*, an anti-slavery novel. It was considered by some to be rather patronising of black people, but it revealed the everyday horrors of slavery in an accessible way and sold millions of copies in the North. It was more popular for its political views than any particular literary merit.

ABRAHAM LINCOLN (1809–65)

Lincoln was the 16th president of the United States (from 1861 to 1865), the first Republican to hold that office. Born in Kentucky to a poor background, Lincoln was largely self-educated, and, always a diligent and conscientious worker, qualified as a lawyer. He started in politics as a Whig, but became a member of the anti-slavery Republican Party early on. Shortly after this image was produced he grew a beard, apparently in response to the advice of a young girl that it would soften his features. Lincoln would become a key figure in the abolition campaign, and one of US history's most influential figures. He was assassinated, while president, in 1865.

17

law and thus its effect was limited. The much stricter 1850 Act included the following clauses:

- A slave-owner's claim that a slave was a fugitive was sufficient for the slave to be arrested.
- Fugitive slaves could not ask for trial by jury nor legally represent themselves in court (in place of a lawyer representing them).
- Any federal official who failed to arrest a known fugitive slave, even in states where slavery was banned, would be fined $1000.

The act also created new federal officials to ensure the law was properly enforced.

At a time when federal interventions in state laws and lives were rare, the act caused much resentment in the North. The act limited the rights of the escaping slaves. It punished those who were found to help escaping slaves. It also stated that Personal Liberty Laws passed by certain states were illegitimate interferences with slave-owners' rights. Many free African Americans were arrested and became slaves in Southern states due to the act, as they could not defend themselves in court. As the Fugitive Slave Act applied to both Northern and Southern states, abolitionists and their supporters had to decide whether to support the law (and indirectly support slavery), or to resist the new law, either secretly or publicly.

Underground Railroad

Fugitive slaves escaping their southern homes often used the **Underground Railroad** to do so. 'Railroad' implies an organised, even centralised system, but this was an informal series of networks of those willing to help fugitive slaves evade capture and make their way to freedom. It was not centralised and the links between different groups involved were disjointed. No one planned it. It just developed at the local level from around 1840 onwards. There are understandably few records of its work. Even in the North, it had to remain partially secret, especially in the later 1850s. The most contemporary account was an 1872 book called *The Underground Railroad*, the title page of which stated that it was: 'A Record of Facts, Authentic Narratives, Letters & C. Narrating the hardships, Hair-breadth Escapes and Death Struggles of the Slaves in their efforts for Freedom as related By themselves and Others or Witnessed by

the Author, William Still.' Some 800 pages long, it is more a series of individual narratives than a history. Harriet Tubman was much better known for her work on the railroad and was much more significant. She was a fugitive slave who, in the 1850s, kept returning to the South, and so risked everything, to help others escape from slavery. As a result she became known as the Moses of her people.

KEY TERM

Underground Railroad: Only sometimes underground, and never an actual railroad, this is a term referring to the network of smugglers and safe houses dedicated to removing slaves to Canada or Northern states where they would be free.

How many slaves travelled to freedom on the Underground Railroad is impossible to say with any accuracy. Estimates suggest that, between 1830 and 1860, somewhere between 1000 and 5000 people each year travelled the Underground Railroad. Even if these numbers are overestimates, these figures show that a considerable number of slaves were prepared to take great risks to gain their freedom. On a small but significant scale, slaves were already taking freedom for themselves.

ACTIVITY 1.9

Conduct independent research on Harriet Tubman. What can you find about her which suggests that she was the 'Moses of her people'? Moses famously led his people out of slavery but did not reach the promised land of freedom himself. Write a short piece about how appropriate you feel the label is.

Implementing the Fugitive Slave Act caused much resentment across many Northern states. This new law made escaping from slavery even more difficult, but it probably helped to strengthen the Underground Railroad. When cases did come to Northern courts, they often provoked mass demonstrations in support of the fugitive.

Two early examples of Northern opposition to the act came just a year after it passed into legislation.

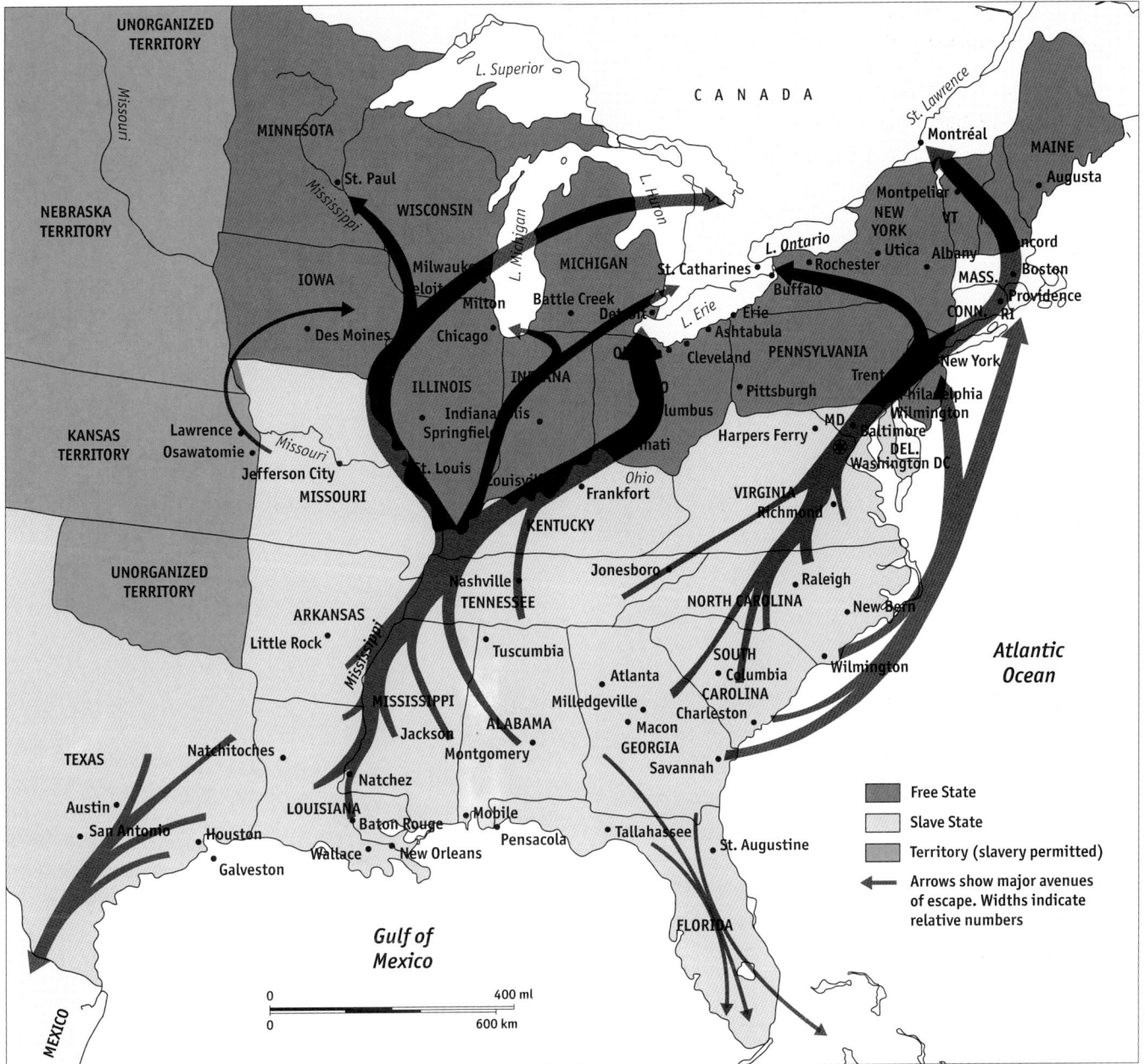

Figure 1.7: A map showing some of the routes of the Underground Railroad

The escape of William Parker, 1851

One example of resistance came in Christiana, Pennsylvania, in September 1851. Edward Gorsuch was a Maryland slave-owner who crossed state lines to recover his escaping slaves with some slave-catchers. He was met with resistance led by a former slave called William Parker. Shots were fired and the slave-owner was killed. Parker escaped via the Underground Railroad. US marines were called in to restore order. Those suspected of being involved in the resistance to the slave-owner were rounded up. Only one was tried, and he was acquitted.

The Jerry Rescue, 1851

A second example of opposition, which occurred in Rochester, New York in October 1851, became known

as the Jerry Rescue. Jerry was the preferred name of William Henry, arrested under the Fugitive Slave Act. The anti-slavery Liberty Party was holding its state party **convention** at the time of Jerry's detention. A large crowd assembled, determined to free him. The demonstrators' protests were so threatening that Jerry was handed over

🔑 KEY TERM

Convention: A convention is a special group of voters called for an extraordinary reason. South Carolina called a convention to ensure that its decision to secede would be legitimate in 1860. This is different from a party convention, which is a decision-making rally.

THE CHRISTIANA TRAGEDY.

Figure 1.8: A print of another anti-Fugitive Slave Act protest, the Christiana Riot, which took place in September 1851. The print is from *The Underground Railroad Records*, a description of the underground railroad written by abolitionist William Still and based on secret records he kept as he helped slaves escape to the North. How would you asses the reliability of the image as a description of the Christiana Riot?

to the crowd before travelling the Underground Railroad to Canada. The authorities then attempted to prosecute the ringleaders of the demonstration. The case lasted two years. Just one person was found guilty.

Frederick Douglass, a former slave himself and a leading abolitionist, later commented that the Jerry Rescue led to the act becoming a 'dead letter', as slave owners realized that the Act failed to return escaped slaves and also led to anti-slavery protests.

Anthony Burns and the Boston Slave Riot, 1854

In fact, the act did not become a 'dead letter' as Douglass wrote. Prosecutions continued. Demonstrations took place. Troops were called out to keep order. Not all fugitive slaves got away. One of the most significant cases involved Anthony Burns, a former slave now living as a free man in Boston, Massachusetts. On 24 May 1854, he was charged under the Fugitive Slave Act. The events which followed

were also labelled a riot, this time the Boston Slave Riot. It too saw a defender of law and order die. This time, however, the protestors did not succeed in freeing Burns before his trial. This outcome was a result of intervention by the president, Franklin Pierce. He was determined to enforce the Fugitive Slave Act. Hundreds of federal troops lined the streets of Boston to control the thousands of protestors.

A Massachusetts businessman gave a more concise summary of the impact of the Burns case and wrote: 'We went to bed one night old fashioned Compromise Union Whigs and woked up [sic] stark mad abolitionists.' (James M. McPherson, *Battle Cry of Freedom: The American Civil War*, Penguin, 1990, p.120.)

The case of Anthony Burns became a national, not just a local issue, perhaps because it took the force of federal government to return him to his owner. Feelings were slow to cool. Burns did eventually regain his freedom.

ACTIVITY 1.10

Yesterday the United Sates Commissioner surrendered the fugitive slave Burns to his master. He was immediately conveyed on board a revenue cutter which without delay set sail for Norfolk [Virginia]. The militia lined the street from the court house to the place for embarkation, where fifty armed policemen were stationed and the fugitive was escorted by one hundred and forty five regular troops, including a detachment of artillery with a nine-pounder [gun] loaded with grapeshot. Business was generally suspended and many of the buildings were draped in black. An immense throng assembled in the streets, which greeted the military with groans and hisses but ... there was no violent exhibition of the deep and intense feeling which evidently prevailed. The law has been vindicated, the irresponsible designs of the abolitionists have again been thwarted, order preserved. ... We sincerely hope the example will not be lost sight of wherever rebellion finds an advocate. But much remains to be done – the end is not at hand by any means.

From the New York Herald newspaper, 3 June 1854

Compare and contrast the sources about the removal of Anthony Burns (The NY Herald extract and the print in Figure 1.9). How far do they support each other? What attitude towards the Fugitive Slave Law is taken by the *New York Herald?* Why might this attitude be seen as surprising? What do you think is meant by 'much remains to be done'?

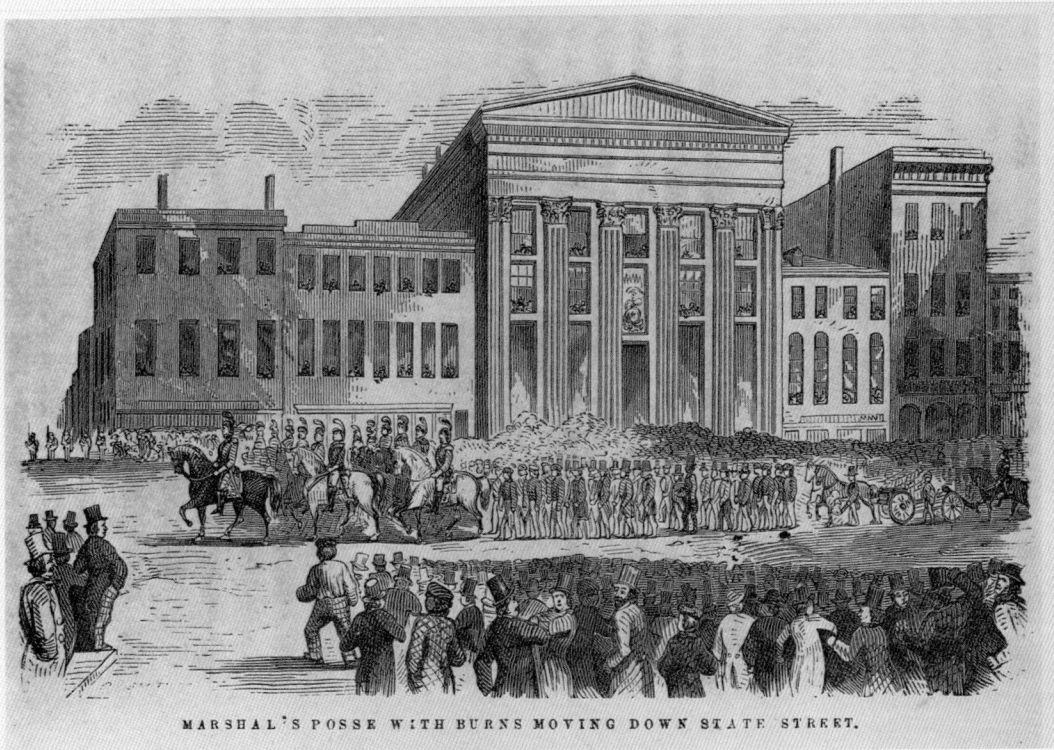

MARSHAL'S POSSE WITH BURNS MOVING DOWN STATE STREET.

Figure 1.9: A contemporary illustration of the Boston Slave Riot, entitled 'Marshal's Posse with Burns moving down State Street'. Published in *Anthony Burns, A History* by Charles Emery Stevens, 1856.

William Lloyd Garrison, 1854

Just a month after the Boston Slave Riot, the annual rally of the Massachusetts Anti-Slavery Society was held in Framingham, a few miles west of Boston. The day was 4 July, Independence Day. The 1854 rally attracted many leading abolitionists: Sojourner Truth, a former slave and a powerful speaker addressed the crowd, as did the leading abolitionist, William Lloyd Garrison. He had founded the abolitionist newspaper, the *Liberator,* some 23 years previously, in 1831.

21

The Fugitive Slave Act, which had been intended to form part of a compromise, only served to widen sectional differences. It supported property rights by empowering slave-owners to have runaway slaves returned to them. However, it weakened states' rights by overruling state laws which had been intended to protect slaves who had escaped to free states.

ACTIVITY 1.11

How useful to historians is the following *Liberator's* report of the 1854 rally against the Fugitive Slave Act? How far would you regard it as reliable?

Mr Garrison said he should now proceed to perform an action which would be testimony of his own soul to all present of the estimation in which he held the pro-slavery laws and deeds of the nation. Producing a copy of the Fugitive Slave Law, he set fire to it and it burnt to ashes. …

Then, holding up the US Constitution, he branded it as the source and parent of all the other atrocities – 'a covenant with death and an agreement with hell' – and consumed it to ashes on the spot, exclaiming 'So perish all compromises with tyranny! And let all the people say Amen!' A tremendous shout of 'Amen!' went up to heaven in ratification of the deed, mingled with a few hisses and wrathful exclamations from some who were evidently in a rowdyish state of mind, but who were at once cowed by the popular feeling.

From The Liberator newspaper, 7 July 1854

The issue of Kansas and its impact

The implementation of the Fugitive Slave Act was causing problems so severe that dealing with them required the president to send in the army. At the same time, another political problem appeared – or recurred.

Westward territorial expansion had not ceased and the political challenges the process created had not gone away either. In 1820, Missouri had been the problem. The Missouri Compromise stipulated that Missouri was the only slave state which could be established within the Louisiana Purchase above the 36° 30′ line. In the early 1850s, the **unorganised lands** in the Midwest called Nebraska became the focus of attention. An area much larger than the current state of that name, this stretched up to the Canadian border and across to the foothills of the Rockies. It had formed part of 'Indian

territory', with a population of Native Americans. Some of them had relocated from other parts of the country further to the settled and organised east. The proposal before Congress was to convert these unorganised lands into an organised US territory (see the maps in Figures 1.1, 1.2 and 1.4). This represented a vast area of potential farmland and offered the possibility of further railway development. Newly settled areas created new customers and there had been talk for some time about a national railway that would run across the USA from the east coast, through Chicago to the west coast, unifying the country.

KEY TERM

Unorganised lands: These were areas of the country where no governmental structures had been formally agreed. They were thinly populated.

The Kansas–Nebraska Act, 1854

In 1852 and 1853, Congress considered various proposals for Nebraska to become a US territory. But while legislators might have been happy to support the extension of the railway, they could not reach agreement on an old question which had returned in a new form: would the Louisiana Purchase lands west of the Mississippi become slave states or free?

During 1853, Stephen Douglas and others, mindful of the possibility of a transcontinental railway, decided to take the lead in persuading Congress to pass a bill. The Democrats had a comfortable majority in both Houses of Congress. The president, Franklin Pierce, was a Democrat. That dominance was indeed enough to pass any other kind of legislation, but the slavery issue was not a party question; it was a sectional one. The Nebraska Bill would only pass in the face of fierce opposition from Northern representatives, both Whig and Democrat. The vote saw both parties split along sectional lines, with votes for and against the bill based on section, rather than party.

Douglas understood that he would need the support of Southern politicians to push through any legislation. The bill he proposed at the beginning of 1854 would divide the area, cutting roughly a quarter from Nebraska's south to form the separate territory of Kansas. This was sensible in itself, as establishing government infrastructure would have been difficult across such a vast area. In addition, each of the new territories could vote on whether to become slave or free states. This was again the principle of popular sovereignty on which he had stood four years earlier. To Douglas, letting the local people decide was a sensible democratic move. It had been accepted in 1850 for Utah and New Mexico. Why not in 1854 for Nebraska?

However, the Nebraska Bill turned the calm into a storm in both Congress and across the country by reopening the question of slavery which the Compromise of 1850 had temporarily settled.

The bill explicitly replaced the Missouri Compromise guidelines for establishing whether a new territory was slave or free with those guidelines of 1850. The geographical line of 36° 30′, which had proved so important in 1820, would be replaced by the political principle of popular sovereignty.

Opponents quickly replied that it was unacceptable because:

- Nebraska was part of the Louisiana Purchase, to which the 1820 line applied
- it was never agreed that the popular sovereignty could replace the Missouri Compromise

- Douglas himself had accepted the continued existence of the Missouri Compromise until the Nebraska Bill
- removing the Missouri Compromise line would allow the expansion of slavery into the Midwest.

This last point united what became known as the Anti-Nebraska Movement. It meant that the Nebraska Bill was very different from the Missouri Act of 1820 or the Utah Act of 1850. Both of these had been achieved by the two sections working together. In 1854, it seemed that the Democrats were working on their own to impose their bill on other parties and interests. The one group which would benefit from the bill were the slave-owners. To its opponents, the Nebraska Bill was clear evidence of 'slave power'.

There was bitter opposition across the North, in newspapers and in many Christian churches. Anti-Nebraska supporters held rallies across Northern states, protesting the pro-slavery and pro-Southern changes to the Compromise of 1850. Even the proposed split of Nebraska into two states, Kansas and Nebraska, which would probably have reduced the area which might vote for slavery, did not help.

The Kansas–Nebraska Act: Vote in the House of Representatives							
	For				**Against**		
Section	Democrat	Whig	Other	Total	Democrat	Whig	Other	Total
North	44	–	–	113	42	45	4	100
South	57	12	–		2	7	–	

Table 1.3: Number of votes for and against the Kansas–Nebraska Act, 22 May 1854.The four 'Other' representatives who voted against the bill belonged to the Free Soil Party.

Figures taken from Allan Nevins, *Ordeal of the Union, Volume 2: A House Dividing 1852–57* (New York, Scribner, 1947), pp.156–57

After lengthy and bitter debate, Congress approved the Kansas–Nebraska Act, but the vote showed how divided the Whigs were over the issue. The president signed the bill on 30 May 1854. In a speech Lincoln gave in October 1854 on the subject of the act, he demanded, 'Could there be a more apt invention to bring about collision and violence on the slavery question than this Nebraska project?'

William Lloyd Garrison's inflammatory act on Independence Day 1854 had been in protest against the Fugitive Slave Law. But it came at a time when Congress had just passed the Kansas–Nebraska Act. This act was the second main development which made the Compromise of 1850 so hard to implement and which revealed the growing divisions between South and North. The mixture of fact and comment in the *Liberator* of 26 May 1854 (Activity 1.12) shows us how abolitionists viewed the new bill.

ACTIVITY 1.12

The Nebraska Bill passed – Another Triumph of Slave Power

The deed is done – the Slave Power is again victorious. On Monday [22 May] the US House of Representatives took up the Nebraska Bill … after several ineffectual attempts to defeat or delay it on the part of its opponents. It was read a third time at 11 o'clock at night [and] was passed by the following vote – yeas 113, nays 100. And so, against the strongest popular remonstrances, against an unprecedented demonstration of religious sentiment … and the rights of universal man – in subversion of plighted faith, in utter disregard of the scorn of the world and for purposes as diabolical as can be conceived of – the deed is accomplished. A thousand times cursed be the Union which has made this possible!

From The Liberator newspaper, 26 May 1854

In the source above *The Liberator* describes six main points of opposition to the passage of the Nebraska Bill. Explain each of them, using a dictionary to understand unfamiliar words where necessary. What do these points of opposition have in common?

Bleeding Kansas, 1854–58

In the new US territories of Nebraska and Kansas, there was a rush by both sides, slave and free, to gain the upper hand as a consequence of the passage of the Kansas-Nebraska Act. This led to what is called Bleeding Kansas.

Stephen Douglas's idea of popular sovereignty meant that whoever occupied a territory would decide its status. Kansas was virtually empty of white men, who were the only recognised citizens and voters. Thus both pro- and anti-slavery forces encouraged people to move to Kansas.

Anti-slavery supporters came by train from the East, funded by the New England Emigrant Aid Society. Meanwhile, pro-slavery supporters came across the border from the adjoining slave state of Missouri. The latter were soon labelled Border Ruffians, presumably by their opponents. Both sides were armed. Even clergymen wanting to end slavery argued for the use of guns. The Reverend Henry Beecher, brother of the author of *Uncle Tom's Cabin*, argued that the new breech-loading rifles were the moral equivalent of a hundred bibles. Clashes soon occurred. Some men died. Some people, then and since, have described the politically inspired violence in Kansas as a civil war, even if only a small one. Among the key events in a series of sporadic conflicts between two disorganised groups were:

- The Sacking of Lawrence, May 1856. Lawrence, a small, new free-state town, was attacked by some 800 'border ruffians', who destroyed the printing presses of free-state newspapers as well as the Free State Hotel.
- The Massacre of Pottawatomie, May 1856. In reaction to the destruction of Lawrence, a leading white abolitionist, John Brown, led an attack on a couple of family households. The attackers killed five men, on the assumption that they had taken part in the sack of Lawrence.
- The Battle of Osawatomie, August 1856. Osawatomie was another free-state town attacked and destroyed by a band of border ruffians.

Though fighting continued in Kansas for two more years, the time when these events had their greatest national impact was 1856, a presidential election year.

Significance

Why did Bleeding Kansas matter?

Copy and complete the diagram below using evidence from what you have learned so far, and thinking about the significance of the events known as Bleeding Kansas.

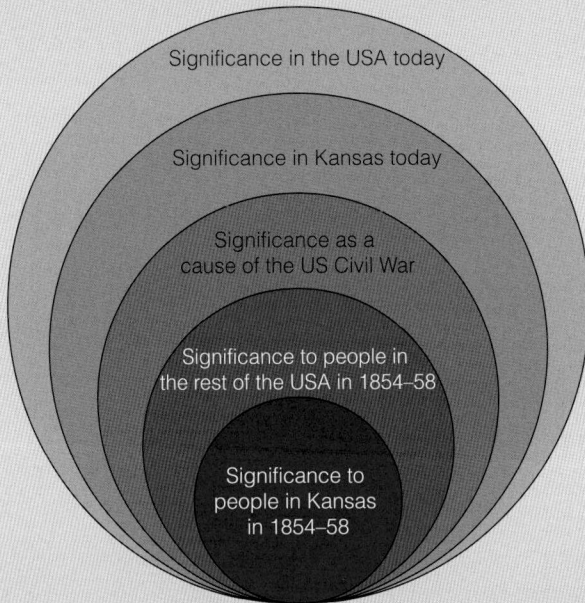

Significance in the USA today

Significance in Kansas today

Significance as a cause of the US Civil War

Significance to people in the rest of the USA in 1854–58

Significance to people in Kansas in 1854–58

Events might be historically significant for different reasons. Come back to this diagram later. What new evidence or new pieces of the story prompt you to add to the diagram? What is the overall significance of Bleeding Kansas? You might need to conduct some independent research, to make a full judgement.

The Caning of Senator Sumner, 1856

The impact of events in Kansas was reinforced by violence in another, unexpected place in May 1856 – the chamber of the US Senate. In a long speech about Kansas, Senator Charles Sumner, a leading abolitionist, criticised one of his opponents in very personal terms. Two days later, as he sat at his desk, he was attacked by Preston Brooks, a Southern Democrat who was a relative of the man Sumner had insulted. He beat him senseless with a stick in an incident which became known as the Caning of Sumner. Sumner took many months to recover. The incident provoked protests and demonstrations in both sections: in the North they protested against the attack, in the South against Sumner's insult. From Boston, via Kansas to Washington DC, political violence was spreading across the USA.

This violence caused anti-slavery supporters, alarmed by such events, to turn to the party most closely linked with opposition to slave power, a new party just two years old, the Republican Party. The events of 1854–56 can help to explain the sudden emergence of a party which just four years later was to provide the US president.

The Kansas question had made a major impact on the country's politics and people. The admission of the State of Missouri in 1821 had been negotiated peacefully. The lands acquired from the war with Mexico were accommodated, albeit more fractiously. The issue of Nebraska and then Kansas had led to the formation of a new dynamic and strong political party – one which would move quickly to win the presidential election of 1860. The issue had also, as we have seen, started both something approaching a local civil war in Kansas and an assault on a legislator in the nation's capital.

Much of the emancipation movement was as committed to a peaceful resolution of the problem of slavery in 1860 as it had been in 1840 or 1820. But with each crisis, suspicions grew on both sides, the willingness to compromise grew weaker and the willingness to turn to violence grew stronger. Events in Kansas and Brooks' attack on Sumner might have seemed like isolated departures from a political norm, but they were signs pointing the way to an approaching war.

Define a civil war. Consider what elements are needed to describe violence between two groups as a civil war. 'Civil' refers to the fact that the two sides are within one country. Can 'Bleeding Kansas' be described as a small-scale civil war? What are the defining features of a war, whether civil or between nations?

Reflection: Compare your definition with that of another student. Did you decide on different definitions and if so, why was this? How would this change the conclusions you reached about 'Bleeding Kansas'?

Changes in the party-political system

The rapid decline of the Whig Party

In 1854–56, the two-party system in US politics underwent a major change. The Whig Party quickly disappeared and the Republican Party emerged as quickly. These changes were a result of slavery becoming a national issue, as the combination of the controversy regarding the Fugitive

Slave Act and that over the Nebraska Bill provoked an upheaval in the US party-political system.

In 1854, the Whig Party was 20 years old. Historian Sean Wilentz has claimed, with challenging precision, that it was on 22 May 1854 that the National Whig Party died. The key word here is 'national'. As already detailed, on 22 May 1854, the US House of Representatives approved the Nebraska Bill. It had already been approved by the Senate. The divisions of the Whigs in that vote were clear to see. Further evidence of the death of the Whigs soon came about. In early 1853, the US president was a Whig, Millard Fillmore. In late 1856, the Whig Party did not put up a presidential candidate. Why did the Whig party fade so quickly? Given that the Kansas–Nebraska Act was a Democratic Party bill, the Whigs should have gained the anti-Nebraska vote. In the 1854 mid-term elections, the Democrats certainly lost seats – some 75 out of 156, and mainly in the North – but the Whigs also lost seats.

In the North, the anti-Democratic vote switched from the Whigs to several small parties. The most successful was the American Party (formerly the Native American Party), which represented the strong anti-immigrant feeling of the early 1850s. Others went by various names, usually with an anti-Nebraskan reference somewhere in the title.

These smaller parties gained from the Whigs because many voters saw the Whigs as partly to blame for the Nebraska Act and also for the Compromise of 1850. Aspects of these deepened sectional tensions by causing Northern opposition. When William Lloyd Garrison burned copies of the Fugitive Slave Act and the US Constitution, he also burned a copy of the court judgement against Anthony Burns. Wendell Phillips, another leading abolitionist, also linked the two issues, Nebraska and slavery, when, speaking to a mass meeting in Boston. Following the arrest of Burns he said: 'Nebraska I call knocking a man down, this [the arrest of Burns] is spitting in his face after he is down.' (See 'Anthony Burns and the Boston Slave Riot, 1854', above.)

In the mid-term elections a few months later, all 11 Whigs representing Massachusetts in the House of Representatives lost their seats to American Party candidates. Following the Nebraska Bill, the Whig Party, unable to maintain unity over the issue of slavery, split in two:

- Southern Whigs, who had voted in favour of the Bill, joined the American Party
- Northern Whigs, who were firmly opposed to any expansion of slavery in the new territories, joined the new Republican Party or left politics altogether.

The rise of the Republican Party

One great consequence of the passage of the Kansas-Nebraska Act was Bleeding Kansas. A second was that its opponents, who had been divided among several parties, came together and quickly formed a new party, the Republican Party. It broadly replaced the several other abolitionist parties, and drew substantial strength and leadership from Northern former Whigs. Within two years, it emerged as the main challenger to the Democratic Party.

'Free Speech, Free Press, Free Soil, Free Men, Frémont and Victory' was the chorus of a Republican rallying song in the 1856 presidential election. To the party's main aims it added the name of its candidate, John Frémont. The opening statement of the party's 1856 platform (proposed programme of action in government) gave more details. It was aimed at all 'who are opposed to the repeal of the Missouri Compromise; to the policy of the present Administration; to the extension of Slavery into Free Territory; in favour of the admission of Kansas as Free State; of restoring the action of the Federal Government to the principles of Washington and Jefferson'.

Frémont was an explorer more than a politician and was so well known that he was likely to attract votes. He was leading a very new party, still being born state by state.

The creation of the Republican Party began in the states of the Midwest – Wisconsin and Michigan – in the spring of 1854, even before the arrest of Burns and the passage of the Kansas–Nebraska Act. The new party was called Republican to show a link with Thomas Jefferson, one of the founders of the USA and a president whose party had been the Democratic-Republican.

Those in other Northern states opposed to slavery followed the examples of the Midwest and set up their own Republican parties. Conscience Whigs, Free Democrats, Free Soilers and some American Party members joined because they all agreed on the need to contain the advance of slave power and prevent the expansion of slavery. Abolitionists joined even though the Republican Party was not an abolitionist party. Their joining shows the tendency of US party politics to move towards a two-party system: better to be part of a large party with some chance of gaining power than remain a small party with little or no chance.

By early 1856, Republican parties had been formed in enough states to establish a national organisation. One of the last states to form a state Republican party, Illinois, did so in May 1856. One of the speakers at the conference was a lawyer called Abraham Lincoln. At the

Republican National Convention the following month, he was nominated as the party's vice-presidential candidate. He was a rising star of the new party but he did not win that nomination. After many years as a Whig, Lincoln had come to realise that the only chance of containing the slave power was in the Republican Party.

For a new party, the Republican Party did well in the 1856 elections. For example in Congress, in Massachusetts, it replaced the American Party in all 11 seats. For the presidency, Frémont came second to Buchanan, the winning Democratic candidate. In the North, he polled more votes than Buchanan did. Although Buchanan won states both in North and South, the split of five Northern states to 14 Southern states showed that voters, in addition to political parties, were beginning to separate along sectional lines.

Significance of states' rights

The concept of states' right was common to the arguments about both the Fugitive Slave and the Kansas–Nebraska acts. The USA was formed in a process that culminated in 1787–89, when 13 states agreed on the form of national government they wanted. That government and its rules were explained in the US Constitution, which the member states agreed to abide by. Thus there were two levels of government, state and federal. The Constitution identifies the roles and responsibilities of the new federal government, so each level has its defined responsibilities. The Constitution, however, is a brief document, written in the late 18th century and needed clarification to take account of changing circumstances. Who has the final say? How far could a state ignore a decision or law of federal government? Conversely, how far could federal government tell a state what to do?

Those who advocated states' rights wanted to give individual states the right to opt out of federal, country-wide laws – and even the right to leave the USA, if a state decided it was necessary. Indeed, it was seen that it might be necessary if the careful relationship between the two sections became imbalanced. Thus states' rights became identified with the South, especially as its slave-based way of life was criticised more and more from Northern abolitionists.

Every ten years, the census (an official survey of the population) showed the disproportionate growth of the free states. That change was then reflected in the distribution of seats in the US House of Representatives. Southerners cheered in 1845 when Texas joined the Union as a slave state. They were downcast by the inclusion of a California as a free state in 1850. They watched the increasing immigration from Europe into the free labour North with growing alarm. Slowly but surely, the balance of US politics would shift to the North. In this respect, time was not on the side of the South.

Southerners became determined to protect their position. They based their argument on the assertion that states which had given up their sovereignty in 1787 could take it back whenever they chose to. Unionists replied that the 13 states which had surrendered their sovereignty had done so unconditionally. Certainly the Constitution had nothing to say about the question of secession. The difference was deep. By the mid-1850s it was growing wider as the anxieties of the South increased.

> An article in the *Washington Sentinel* of 19 February 1856 felt it necessary to outline the concept of states' rights in relation to the Democratic party:
>
> What then, briefly, are the leading, cardinal, inherent principles of the Democratic State Rights party? We say State Rights because we consider Democracy a sham which does not assert the absolute sovereignty of the States of this **confederacy** and the unqualified rights of each and all of them under the Constitution. Indeed, this may be termed the leading and dearest principle of our party: the rights of the States and steady resistance to every act of the Federal Government which may limit their rights. What else? A strict construction of the Constitution, interpreting it to mean only what it says and only to have said what it meant. To interpret it otherwise would be to open the door to federal power that would soon grow (for there is no plant more rapid in its growth than power) to such an extent that the true theory of our Government would soon be lost sight of and the sovereignty of the States absorbed in the great and onerous central Government.
>
> *From the Washington Sentinel, 19 February 1856*

KEY TERM

Confederacy: The states which left the Union bound together and called themselves the Confederate States of America, or Confederacy, or CSA. Their president was Jefferson Davis and their capital was in Montgomery, Alabama and then Richmond, Virginia.

An important feature of the article is that it makes no mention of the South – even though the concept of states' rights was almost entirely used by Southerners opposed to the Kansas–Nebraska Act. Could the concept also apply to a Northern state opposed to the Fugitive Slave Act? The article was the interpretation of a journalist. The *Washington Sentinel* was very confident in its assertions about the US Constitution. The organisation which had been given – or, more accurately, which had taken – the interpreter's job was the US Supreme Court. In 1857, it entered the debate about state rights and slavery in a very dramatic fashion, making the issue even harder to resolve.

The balance between the power held by the federal government and states' rights was a fault line in American politics in the period up to 1860. Northern states had refused to comply with fugitive slave legislation. In its 1842 ruling on *Prigg v. Pennsylvania*, the US Supreme Court ruled that the Fugitive Slave Act was law in Pennsylvania, and that state's own personal liberty legislation could not be pleaded as a defence or in rebuttal. This was a declaration of the superior authority of federal over state government. States' rights would later be pleaded as the driving force behind the secession of Southern states. At the time, however, Northern states were equally likely to adopt a states' rights view and Southern states were equally right to argue for the rule of law and the authority of the federal government. Later South Carolina voted to secede and set out its Declaration of the Immediate Causes with reasons in imitation of the 13 former British colonies' original Declaration of Independence. It pointed to the failure of the federal government to enforce the Fugitive Slave Act.

1.3 Why did the Republicans win the 1860 presidential election?

The new Republican party did well in the 1856 presidential election, but, the Democrat James Buchanon won. The states he won were mainly in the South, but he did have some success in the North. Aged 64, from Pennsylvania, he had been chosen by the Democratic party over the younger, more energetic, but more controversial, Stephen Douglas. Buchanan had a great deal of experience, both in Congress and in federal government. In his **inaugural address** of March 1857, he asserted that the territorial issue had been settled by means of popular sovereignty. As a result, he hoped that the slavery agitation of the past 20 years might now come to an end. He was quickly disappointed.

> **KEY TERM**
>
> **Inaugural address:** A president's inauguration is the formal ceremony at which they are sworn into office as president. The speech which they make at this time, setting out their plans for the term, is known as the inaugural address. In the 19th century, there were four months between the election and the new president's inauguration.

The emerging notion of 'slave power', including Dred Scott 1857

Just two days after Buchanan's inauguration, the US Supreme Court issued its ruling on a case brought by a freed slave, Dred Scott. The president had hoped that the Supreme Court would settle the issue of slavery in the territories. However, this did not happen.

The *Dred Scott v. Sanford* case took years to come to a conclusion, and brought into play concepts of freedom, citizenship, ownership, states' rights and ethnicity. Dred Scott had been born a slave in slave-state Virginia, but was sold and moved to free-state Illinois with a new owner. Following the owner's death, Scott was moved to slave-state Missouri with the man's widow (Eliza Sanford). Scott, who had earlier tried to buy his freedom, made a legal case that residence in Illinois had freed him, since slavery did not exist in Illinois, and, having been free, he could not be returned to slavery.

The case went to the US Supreme Court. In the 1850s, it was accepted that the Supreme Court could review polices to decide whether they fitted with the Constitution. Presidents tried to appoint Supreme Court judges with political views similar to their own. In 1857, when the *Dred Scott v. Sanford* case reached it, seven of the nine judges had been appointed by Democratic presidents and five of them were from the South. The Chief Justice of the US Supreme Court was Roger Taney, from slave-state Maryland, appointed by southern Democrat president Andrew Jackson.

In announcing the court's majority judgements on the case, Taney posed the key question: 'Can a Negro, whose ancestors were imported into this country and sold as slaves, become a member of the political community formed and brought into existence by the constitution of the United States?' The court's answer was:

- An African American could not be an American citizen.
- Dred Scott had no right to bring his case to court.

ACTIVITY 1.14

Conduct your own research to fill in this table. What patterns do you notice?

US presidents 1841–61					
Dates/terms	President	Party	Background, e.g. politician, soldier, lawyer	State	Section
1841					
1841–45					
1845–49					
1849–50					
1850–53					
1853–57					
1857–61					

- Slave-owners could take their slaves anywhere governed by US federal law.
- Congress had no authority to restrict the rights given to people by the constitution.

The court's judgements in the case were not unanimous. The split was seven to two. The majority consisted mainly of judges from the South. The two judges who did not agree were from the North.

The Supreme Court thus overturned the Missouri Compromise of 1820 and the popular sovereignty concept of the 1850s – the work of politicians over 40 years. According to the Supreme Court, there could be no limits on the constitutional right of individuals to transport property, including chattel slaves, anywhere in the USA. In the struggle between the sections, the South had won.

It was not just the judgements which angered the North, however. Many Republicans believed that the way that the judgements were reached was itself unjust and that there had been a conspiracy involving the new Democrat President Buchanan and Chief Justice Taney. The Dred Scott rulings were announced two days into the Buchanan presidency. This was seen by them as evidence of growing 'slave power', especially as five of the judges were from slave states.

Dred Scott and politicians

The Supreme Court's ruling had great consequences for political leaders, who struggled to adapt their policies to the new judgement. They had to be seen to uphold the rule of law, including laws they disagreed with, so how were they to respond to the Dred Scott judgement? This dilemma caused tensions and strains within parties as well as between them.

Three politicians in particular responded in ways which affected the national debate about the slavery question:

- Democrat president James Buchanan supported the Dred Scott ruling. He decided to apply the judgement to the continuing, complicated problem of Kansas. By 1857, conflicts in Kansas were as much political as violent. Two territorial governments, slave and free, had been established there and were fighting for power, trying to impose their own constitution. Buchanan supported the pro-slavery group and its constitution, known as the Lecompton Constitution, even though its democratic flaws were plain to see.
- Democrat senator Stephen Douglas opposed the Supreme Court judgement because it had overturned his solution to slavery in US territories: popular

ACTIVITY 1.15

Figure 1.10: *Frank Leslie's Illustrated Newspaper's* front-page coverage of the Dred Scott case, 27 June 1857

Look at the illustrations and layout of this New York newspaper front page from 1857, reacting to the decision in the Dred Scott case. Discuss with your classmates how the newspaper seeks to show its sympathy for Dred and his wife Harriet.

sovereignty. According to the court, territorial voters had no right to overturn the Constitution. Douglas quarrelled with Buchanan in private while challenging the Supreme Court judgement in public. The Douglas–Buchanan divide was to persist in the Democrat Party with great consequences for both party and country.

- Republican politician Abraham Lincoln was opposed to the judgement that the constitution enabled slave-owners to take their slaves anywhere in the USA. A lawyer himself, he accepted the supremacy of the Supreme Court, but he challenged the historical and philosophical bases of the Dred Scott judgement. This was the start of his campaign to become a senator for Illinois, where he lived and worked.

The Lincoln–Douglas Debates, 1858

The Dred Scott judgements deepened anxieties across the USA regarding the issue of slavery. By allowing every state government the ability to decide on slavery without federal intervention, slavery could now expand across the USA into the new territories and eventually the North.

'A house divided against itself cannot stand,' declared Lincoln in a speech in June 1858, using a quotation from the New Testament which he knew his audience would recognise. The speech followed his nomination as Republican candidate as senator for Illinois. Lincoln continued: 'I believe this government cannot endure, permanently, half slave and half free. I do not expect the Union to be dissolved. I do not expect the house to fall, but I do expect it will cease to be divided.'

His opponent in the campaign was Stephen Douglas, up for re-election. The contest between them in front of large crowds in Illinois was to become the focus of the national debate over the future of slavery in the USA and the very future of the USA itself.

Douglas quickly disagreed in a speech he made a few weeks later, with Lincoln in the audience. Douglas quoted Lincoln's view of the future of the USA in order to argue that Lincoln was advocating 'boldly and clearly a war of sections, a war of the North against the South, of free states against the slave states – a war of extermination to be continued relentlessly until one or the other shall be subdued and all the states become either free or become slave'.

The two men took their disagreements to the voters of Illinois. Between August and October 1858, there were seven open-air debates between the two men across the state – Douglas, already a two-term US senator and leader of the Northern Democrats, versus Lincoln, a one-term Congressman and runner-up to be the Republican Party's vice-presidential candidate in 1856. Each debate lasted for several hours and the most popular debate attracted about 15 000 people.

Douglas accused Lincoln of having abolitionist sympathies and of believing in racial equality. Lincoln accused Douglas of being part of a Democratic Party conspiracy to 'nationalise' slavery. Each accused the other of saying different things in different parts of Illinois. In terms of the Declaration of Independence of 1776, Douglas said it applied to white men only, while Lincoln argued it applied to all men, irrespective of colour. Lincoln accepted that slavery was wrong while Douglas refused to do so.

The Republican Party was united in its response to the Dred Scott judgements, but the Democrats were divided, with some (mainly Southern) members supporting the ruling. This left Stephen Douglas in a difficult position during the 1858 debates. He could not fully support the Dred Scott ruling due to its pro-slavery views, as that would cost him votes in Illinois, a free Northern state. At the same time, he could not reject the judgements either, as he would lose the support of Southerners in his party.

Douglas's challenge took the form of what became known as the **Freeport Doctrine**. He argued that the implementation of Supreme Court decisions rested upon local law enforcement and that those local laws had to be decided by local people, not the Supreme Court. Only local people properly understood the local situation. It was his old idea of popular sovereignty in a new guise and it meant in practice that slavery could not be imposed on any territory or state. Douglas even began to work with Republicans to oppose the Congressional bill establishing the state of Kansas based on the Lecompton constitution. The Democrats were now as divided over the issue of slavery in the territories as the Whigs had been in the early 1850s. Some Northern Democrats even left the party and joined the Republicans.

KEY TERM

Freeport Doctrine: The idea that slavery could be (and perhaps should be) banned via a series of local decisions rather than a central federal decision to do so. It was not Stephen Douglas's idea, but he was its most famous promoter. It was named after Freeport, Illinois, a town in which Lincoln and Douglas held one of seven election meetings in 1858.

US senators at this time (and until 1913) were chosen by the state assemblies and thus only indirectly by the people. In the Democrat-dominated Illinois assembly, Lincoln lost to Douglas, but had the consolation of winning more votes than the Buchanan Democrat candidate.

The campaign and its debates attracted attention across the USA, helped greatly by detailed newspaper coverage. This made Lincoln, previously little known, a national figure. Over the next year he travelled widely across the North to widen his support with a view to the 1860 Republican National Convention. During that time, an event occurred which greatly affected the national debate about slavery: the raid on Harpers Ferry.

The growing strength of abolitionism, including John Brown

The willingness of some on both sides of the debate over slavery to pursue armed violence had been shown during the Bleeding Kansas crisis of 1854–58. Later in the 1850s, feelings hardened. One veteran of that period of raid and counter-raid began to lay plans to start a slave uprising, something which had long been a nightmare for the white South.

Harpers Ferry in the state of Virginia housed a federal arsenal and armoury, making and storing US army weapons. It has been estimated that 100 000 rifles and muskets were stored there. Abolitionist John Brown, who had taken part in the Kansas violence and was a friend of Frederick Douglass, formed a plan to take control of the armoury, lead a slave revolt, arm the slaves and overthrow slave power. Douglass viewed the plan as a suicide mission doomed to failure and refused to take part or endorse it.

Nonetheless, with a force of 21 men, Brown seized the armoury, but no slave rebellion followed. Within two days, local militia and federal troops (led by Robert E. Lee, later the leader of the Confederate armies in the Civil War) regained control of town. Ten of Brown's men died along with seven civilians. Brown himself was injured.

He was put on trial, found guilty of treason and sentenced to death along with six of his fellow conspirators. Shortly before he was hanged for treason in December 1859, he wrote: 'I, John Brown, am now quite certain that the crimes of this *guilty land* will never be purged *away* but with *Blood*. I had, *as I now think vainly,* flattered myself that without very much *bloodshed* it might be done.'

The failure of the Harpers Ferry raid suggested that slavery was well established and still well supported in the South and that slave rebellions were unlikely. It showed the 59-year-old Brown to be a romantic idealist but not a revolutionary leader. Yet the raid and its leader had a great impact on US politics.

In the North, Brown became a martyred hero to many, both black and white. His reputation rested less with the physical force he used at Harpers Ferry and more with the moral courage he showed in attempting a revolt then facing imprisonment, trial and death. He sacrificed his life for his beliefs; beliefs which many Northerners saw as admirable. Their Republican leaders, Lincoln and William H. Seward, were more cautious, and distanced themselves from Brown's actions and arguments. Seward was a former Whig and a US senator from New York. He had declared himself in favour of emancipation and was supportive of immigrants and Catholics, thus earning the hostility of the American Party.

In October 1858, Seward made a speech in which he argued that America faced 'an irrepressible conflict between opposing and enduring forces and it means that the United States must and will, sooner or later, become either a slave-holding nation or entirely a free-labour nation'.

He saw the conflict in peaceful, political terms as an argument between the Democratic and Republican parties. His speech was similar in argument to Lincoln's 'A house divided' made earlier that year. Democrats, North and South, argued there was a direct link between Seward's inflammatory language and the raid on Harpers Ferry. He was seen by many, especially in the South, as inspiring Brown to action, so Seward was advised to tread carefully on the issue of Brown. His speech received a good deal of attention as he was expected to be the Republican Party's presidential candidate in 1860.

The connection between Seward and Harpers Ferry seemed stronger when it was revealed that John Brown had received sympathy and support from a New England group which was dubbed the Secret Six, all of them keen abolitionists. Finally, the fact that Brown's raid was against Virginia, always part of the South, was said to show that the North's commitment to respect slavery where it already existed could not be trusted.

Brown's raid failed, but it showed that abolitionism was a growing force in the land. Moreover, although Brown himself might have been an extremist, the existence of the Secret Six revealed that moderates were becoming increasingly willing to support violence. As with other crises, it drew attention to the divisions within the country. For politicians such as Lincoln, Douglas, Seward and others, a significant question was whether these shifts in views would make the 1860 presidential election different from that of 1856 and, if so, in what ways.

Increasing confrontation within and between the North and the South

By the late 1850s, both sides of the slavery debate had their own conspiracy theories to explain the pressure they were under. The North believed in the menace of the slave power, the South in Black Republicanism. How to defeat these conspiracies became the key issue for both sides.

In the South, a vocal and growing minority, known as the Fire-eaters, believed the only way to protect slavery against the supposed black Republican threat was by breaking away from the USA. The group warned that, because the population of the North grew more rapidly than that of the South, the political balance in

ACTIVITY 1.16

Figure 1.11: Engraving of John Brown's raid on the Confederate arsenal at Harpers Ferry

Examine this illustration of the raid on Harpers Ferry. How can you tell which one of the characters is John Brown? What do you assume to be the sympathies of the engraver? Did he approve, or not, of Brown's actions? Why do you believe this? In what ways could Brown's actions in 1859 be described as successful and in what ways as unsuccessful?

Congress would inevitably tip towards the North and the abolitionists. However, most Southerners still had faith in the Constitution and the Supreme Court's ability to defend their way of life. They began to push for the international slave trade, banned to Americans since 1808, to be reopened. They also proposed a federal slave code – sets of special laws concerning slaves – to protect slave-owners rights in non-slave states and territories.

In the North, most people wanted the end of slavery to come about by political, constitutional means. No one wanted the South to break away. As the balance of economic wealth and political power did shift towards the North, the North could gradually introduce measures to contain and eventually remove slavery. This was a strategy of gradualism. Some considered returning free African Americans to Africa and this plan was partially put into effect. However, careful consideration soon showed it to be impractical on a large enough scale to change the political situation in the USA.

John Brown's raid on Harpers Ferry indicated that direct action against slavery was also unrealistic. The situation seemed to have reached a road block. There was no way forward that would carry enough of the country to solve the problem without splitting the North from the South. This threat began to seem increasingly realistic.

As these issues were discussed, another presidential election approached. All elections tend to bring one or more critical issues to a head, as the candidates and the parties have to decide what they stand for and against, and the electorate for what and whom to vote.

The election campaign of 1860 and the divisions of the Democratic Party

In early 1860, the process of choosing presidential candidates began. Many expected the contest to be between Douglas and Seward. The process of choosing party candidates was to provide several surprises.

The 1860 Democratic National Convention

Stephen Douglas was a well-respected Illinois Democrat senator and negotiator, an architect of the 1850 Compromise and the passing of the 1854 Kansas–Nebraska Act, and a veteran of the 1858 debates with Lincoln.

John Breckinridge, a Kentucky senator, who was Lincoln's wife's cousin and was personally on good terms with the Republican candidate, had supported Douglas's candidacy in the 1856 Democratic convention and served as Buchanan's vice president from 1857 to 1861. The

outgoing president himself backed Breckinridge, who became the candidate of the Southern Democrats.

Like Douglas, Breckinridge argued that when a territory became a state, its voters should decide whether or not to allow slavery. Unlike Douglas, however, the Kentucky senator publically committed to a federal slave code. Several states had drawn up slave codes, which put into law the status of a slave and the rights of their owner. They guaranteed the owner's power and the slave's powerlessness. The codes tended to ban slaves from learning to read or write, owning a weapon of any kind, engaging in any kind of trading with other slaves, or travelling without permission. The punishments specified were harsh. If such a federal slave code replaced state laws, it would secure the place of slavery in the United States.

In the event, the Democratic Convention broke down and Southern delegates left in disgust. Northern Democrat Douglas was consistently topping the poll but didn't gain the majority support needed to become a winning candidate, in a convention which had already turned down the idea of including a federal slave code in its platform.

The Democratic convention split along sectional lines and in two different gatherings chose two different candidates: Northern Democrats elected Douglas; Southern Democrats chose Breckinridge.

A party so deeply divided that it put up two candidates is unlikely to succeed in a contest as it divided its own support among voters into two.

In addition, a fourth, Southern, candidate was contesting the election. The Constitutional Union Party, a one-off centrist grouping composed mainly of old Whigs with former American Party members, hoped to gain support by avoiding the divisive issue of slavery. The party's candidate, Senator John Bell from Tennessee, argued that the status of slavery should remain guaranteed by the US Constitution, but that it should not spread beyond the existing slave states in order to avoid the risk of war. The intention was both to save the Union and to minimise the role of emancipation in the election.

Accordingly, Mississippi senator Jefferson Davis, the future president of the Confederacy, put forward a proposal for not just Douglas and Breckinridge, but also John Bell, to all stand down to allow a compromise candidate to be chosen. This would allow a unified approach to the election to avoid the fear that Northern votes would send Republican Lincoln to the White House. Breckinridge and Bell agreed, but Douglas and his supporters refused and all three men went into the election as presidential candidates.

The 1860 Republican National Convention

The 1860 Republican Convention was held in Chicago and was only that party's second such gathering. The favourite in a crowded field of candidates was widely assumed to be William H. Seward.

Seward was a New York lawyer. Once a prominent Whig, he had become perhaps the best-known member of the new Republican Party until Lincoln started attracted attention. Despite being the front runner and having many supporters, Seward also had enemies. His support for Catholic immigrants alienated some delegates, particularly former American Party supporters; his role in the abolition debate had alienated others. Seward, who had been known to use the word 'revolution' in speeches, became identified with Republican radicals. Knowing this, he attempted to conciliate the centre ground, but this tactic angered the radicals without convincing the centrists. When ballots started being cast, Lincoln came a close second to Seward in a result with no overall winner. By the time of the third ballot, many of the other candidates had been eliminated, which meant that supporters had to pick an alternative. Seward's support held reasonably firm but remained unchanged. Having fewer committed enemies meant that Lincoln's support doubled, with enough delegates switching for him to win the nomination.

The vice-presidential nominee was Hannibal Hamlin, the governor of Maine with a background in farming, law and journalism. He had supported the Wilmot Proviso and opposed the 1850 Compromise and the Kansas–Nebraska Act. Originally a Northern Democrat, he left over the issue of slavery to join the Republican Party in 1856 and so it was thought he could atrract disaffected Democrat voters. His dark complexion led hostile Southerners to claim that he was of part-African descent.

Representation at the convention was dominated by Northerners, with several Southern slave states sending no representatives, and was thus more unified. By contrast with the Democrats' struggle over their proposed programme, the Republicans adopted their draft platform unchanged and unanimously. Therefore they committed their future president to promoting an economy of opportunity in which talent, work and enterprise would win their rewards. This was seen as a contrast to the perceived wealth and power of the Democrats.

There was no proposal to abolish slavery. The institution was protected by the Constitution and should be left untouched:

- runaway slaves should be returned to their owners;
- states' rights should be preserved, but there should be a move to limit the power of slavery to existing states while new states would be built up as Republican-supporting 'free soil'
- Western expansion should favour free farmers
- a transcontinental railway should be constructed.

The 1860 presidential election campaign

There were three particularly unusual features to the 1860 presidential campaign.

- Douglas toured the country, North and South, in an effort to maximise support for his candidature. This broke with the tradition of the times that presidential candidates did not actively campaign. Lincoln stayed at home in Illinois, coordinating the Republican campaign.
- In three states – New Jersey, New York and Pennsylvania – there was a fusion **ticket**. In attempt to stop Lincoln's apparently 'inevitable' victory, the three anti-Republican candidates agreed to combine their popular vote. It did not make any significant difference to the final vote in each state, but it shows how anxious pro-slavery candidates were to stop a Republican victory.
- A new political movement emerged to influence the outcome of the election. This was dubbed the Wide-Awake movement.

The *New York Herald*, a Democratic-leaning newspaper, explained thus:

> The greatest feature of the campaign of 1860 has been the introduction of a vast Republican group, semi-military in character, political in purpose and daily increasing in strength and influence to an extent unparalleled in the political history of our country. We refer to the organisation known as the Republican Wide Awakes, who made their first New York demonstration on 13th September. The sleepy New York politicians were startled by the sudden brilliant illumination of our streets and the appearance of large bodies of men, bearing blazing torches and marching in fine military order. Each man carried a thin rail with a large swinging lamp and a small American flag bearing the names of Lincoln and Hamblin. The uniform of the privates was a black enamelled circular cape and a military fatigue cap with a brass or silver eagle in front. The captains were distinguished by an overcoat with black cape and an undress military cap. The measured tread and unbroken lines spoke of strict attention to drill and the effective manner

in which the various bodies were managed by their officers showed conclusively that men of long military experience controlled their movements.

New York Herald, 19 September 1860, *Chronicling America website, Library of Congress*

When Lincoln secured the nomination, the Wide-Awakes' energy and enthusiasm turned to helping his campaign and probably increased turnout in Northern states. Some 100 000 men are thought to have taken part in Wide-Awake marches. Their effect on voters' choices is impossible to measure, but, if nothing else, the Wide-Awakes were a sign of unstable times.

KEY TERM

Ticket: A 'ticket' refers to two or more politicians who run for office together. In particular, presidential and vice-presidential candidates run on the same ticket. Since 1804, they have either both won, or both lost.

••• THINK LIKE A HISTORIAN

The Wide-Awake clubs seem to have had some effect on the 1860 presidential and congressional elections, although it is difficult to be sure which of the various factors affected the results. How far do youth-oriented mass-movements affect modern election results? Do you think that the existence of such movements is a good thing, or dangerous?

The New York Wide-Awakes were just following a model which had been developed in Connecticut earlier in the year and was soon copied in many other Northern cities. In particular the Wide-Awakes attracted men in their 20s and 30s. According to a recent analysis of the Wide-Awakes, the 'strange movement electrified the presidential election' (Jon Grinspan, *'Young Men for War': The Wide Awakes and Lincoln's 1860 Presidential Campaign, Journal of American History,* September 2009).

The movement came from the grassroots. Seward was enthusiastic and in touch with the movement and addressed its rallies. Lincoln handled the movement cautiously, which helped him seem to Republican members as the more moderate of the two candidates and thus more able to bring in a wider range of voters.

In the South, the sudden appearance of the Wide-Awakes was viewed much less positively. On 22 September 1860, the *Nashville Union and American* newspaper, in Tennessee, reported the Wide-Awakes were 'the forces by which the South is to be whipped into submission to the rule of Abraham Lincoln'.

When the election came, the excitement and strongly held views meant that there was a high turnout of over 81%. Lincoln's support nationally was only 40% and depended entirely on Northern states – no slave state voted for him. In many states south of the Mason–Dixon Line, he did not even appear on the ballot. Nevertheless, he was the most successful of the candidates and the distribution of his popular vote meant that he was easily able to win the electoral college, this is shown in Table 1.4.

Presidential election result 1860							
Candidate and party	**Electoral college**		**Popular vote**		**States**		
	Votes	**%**	**Votes (in millions)**	**%**	**North**	**South**	**Total**
Bell, Constitutional Union	39	12.8.	0.59	12.6	–	3	3
Breckinridge, Southern Democrat	72	23.8	0.85	18.1	–	11	11
Douglas, Northern Democrat	12	4.0	1.38	29.5	–	1	1
Lincoln, Republican	180	59.4	1.86	39.8	18	–	18
Total	303	100	4.68	100	18	15	33

Table 1.4: Breakdown of results for the four candidates in the 1860 US presidential election

This success owed something to the split in the Democratic vote between Douglas and Breckenridge. Breckinridge too won purely in the section that had nominated him, and he would go on to serve as a Confederate general. John Bell of the Constitutional Party, who won only the support of his home-state of Tennessee in the election, would vote for its secession in a close-run referendum in June 1861.

Unlike the other candidates, Douglas won votes in both slave and free states, but his support was spread too thinly and despite coming second in the popular vote, his result in the electoral college was poor. Generous in defeat, he encouraged the South to accept the political fact of Lincoln's election and once again characteristically looked for a compromise. When fighting broke out at Fort Sumter (see 'Fort Sumter and its impacts', below) in what are often called the first shots of the American Civil War, Douglas supported Lincoln's response. Within months, Douglas died.

ACTIVITY 1.17

Use the evidence and information in this section to create a mind map of the reasons why Lincoln won the 1860 election. Remember to include reasons why he was a deserving candidate, as well as reasons why his opponents were not.

ACTIVITY 1.18

Read the aims set out in the opening statement of the Republican Party's 1856 platform, in 'Changes in the party-political system' in 1.2. Write one sentence commenting on each statement in turn. How far had the Republican Party's aims been met by 1861?

Reflection: What other types of historical evidence would you look for to help you answer the above question? Would certain types of evidence help you to support your answer more than others?

1.4 Why did the Civil War begin in April 1861?

Two schools of historical thought about the causes of the American Civil War emerged in the 20th and 21st centuries.

One school of thought argues that it came about from economic and social reasons, most easily summarised as:

- slave labour versus free labour
- industry versus agriculture
- urban versus rural
- North versus South.

A modern, industry-focused society was fast developing alongside a more traditional agricultural society. Between the two, differences of interests were bound to occur – and widen. This argument also stresses the class nature of North–South conflict: Northern middle class versus Southern plantation owners. As the 1850s progressed – and despite the financial panic of 1857 – the two sections were both confident of their growing wealth but were also increasingly fearful that the rival section threatened their future. For the North, the Dred Scott judgement was a severe blow. For the South, John Brown's raid on Harpers Ferry was probably more alarming.

The great difference between the two sides was that the North, with its increasing population, wanted to prevent the nationwide expansion of slavery. Meanwhile, the South, a shrinking proportion of the national population, needed to expand to the west and south-west – or indeed into the Caribbean and Central America – to maintain its position in the USA. This school of thought puts the economic interests of white men, North and South, before any moral concerns for the wellbeing of Southern slaves. It also sees civil war as an eventually inevitable outcome of this clash of economic and social blocs.

A different school of historians focuses on **political processes** and leaders, whom they blame for bringing about an avoidable war. The language of politics in the 1850s was more divisive than consensual. Whether over 'Bleeding Kansas', the Fugitive Slave Act, the caning of Senator Sumner or the raid on Harpers Ferry, language was emotional and extreme. Lincoln's 'A house divided' speech was not the language of compromise. Previous generations of politicians had been sufficiently pragmatic to compromise, albeit after a fierce debate. In 1861, a last compromise, proposed by Senator John Crittenden (see 'The Crittenden Compromise', below), was quickly dismissed. The political processes which had kept the USA together had finally and catastrophically failed.

KEY TERM

political processes: the formulation and administration of public policy usually by interaction between social groups and political institutions.

ACTIVITY 1.19

Prepare a debate in a group of four. One pair should argue that the political processes which had kept the USA together had failed because the forces ranged against them were too great. The other should argue that the processes failed because they were too weak.

Reactions to the 1860 presidential election results

Reaction to Lincoln's victory was swift and varied.

Secession required immediate responses from the sitting president, James Buchanan, Congress, and from **President-elect** Lincoln. The president mentioned by the *New York Herald*, however, was Buchanan. In his long annual address to Congress just a week later, on 4 December, he made many points about the slavery / states' rights / secession issue, including:

- The slavery question was the fault of the North's 'incessant and violent agitation' for 'the last quarter of a century'.
- The question had passed its peak of controversy.
- The election of a president (Lincoln) by proper constitutional means did not justify secession even before he took office.
- The USA was a permanent union. Although as the president, he lacked the means to prevent secession by a state.

- Congress and the states should agree an amendment the Constitution which would clarify the property rights of slaveholders throughout the USA.

The speech pleased neither South nor North.

The South believed that, once Lincoln took office, slavery would be banned in the Southern states, despite the absence of any such proposals on the Republican Party platform. During the five months between the Republican victory on 6 November and the new president's inauguration on 4 March, the southern states debated whether to secede, to leave the Union. South Carolina led the way. Four days after Lincoln was declared winner of the election, a specially elected convention of South Carolina was convened to decide whether to leave the USA.

KEY TERM

President-elect: In the period between their election and their inauguration, the incoming president has no formal power. When this period corresponds to a major national emergency, as it did in 1860–61, they are forced to use any informal powers of persuasion to achieve the agenda.

ACTIVITY 1.20

Look at the bullet points summarising Buchanan's attempt to calm the mood of the nation on 4 December 1860. Write a response outlining your objections to his claims. Try to arrange groups so that some students work from a Northern point of view, and others from a Southern point of view.

ACTIVITY 1.21

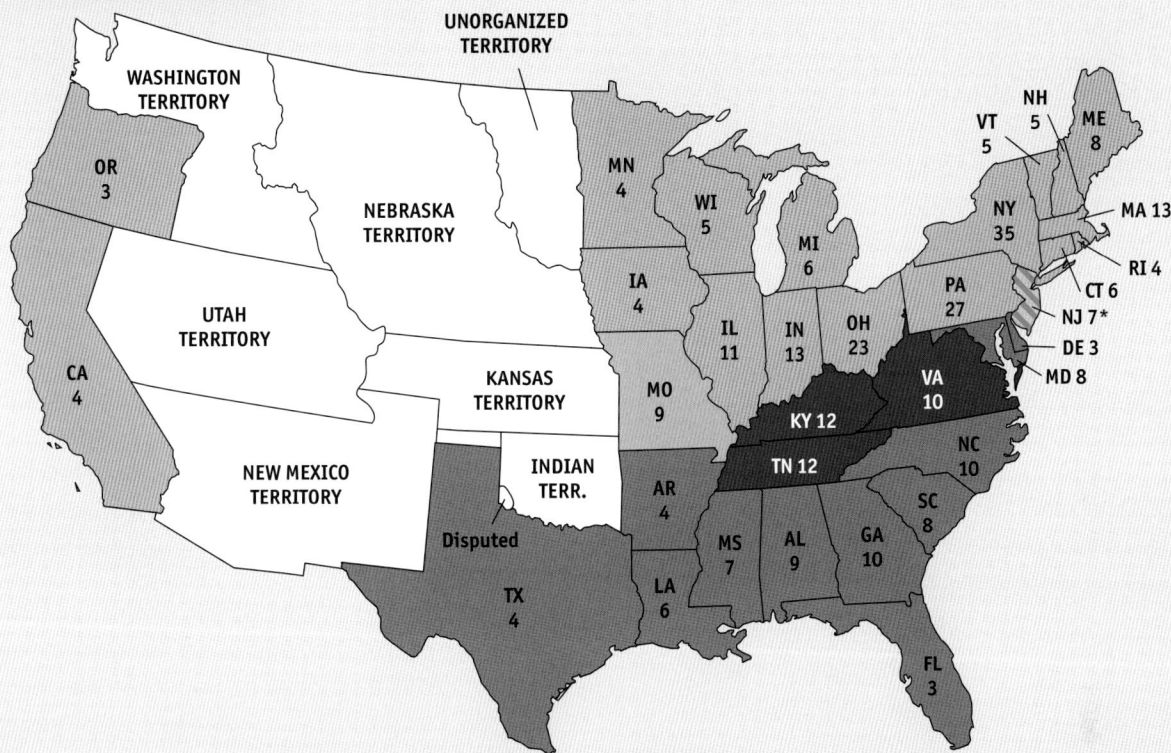

Candidate	Party	Electoral Vote	Popular Vote	Percentage of Popular Vote
Lincoln	Republican	180	1,865,593	39.8
Douglas	Northern Democrat	12	1,382,713	29.5
Breckinridge	Southern Democrat	72	848,356	18.1
Bell	Constitutional Union	39	592,906	12.6

*New Jersey cast four electoral votes for Lincoln and three for Douglas.

Figure 1.12: A map showing the states' votes in the 1860 presidential election

Consider the map in Figure 1.12. Which parts of the USA were represented by each of the candidates? Identify the five slave states immediately adjoining free states to the North. These were known as the border states. What do you notice about how they voted in 1860?

Secession of the seven Deep South states

A declaration issued by South Carolina, made in December 1860, shows how quickly the most militant of Southern states, decided its response: 'A geographical line has been drawn across the union and all the states north of that line have united in the election of a man to the high office of President of the United States whose opinions and purposes are hostile to slavery.' (The full declaration, can be seen on Yale Law School's Avalon Project site, https://web.archive.org.)

There was only the briefest of attempts to negotiate with the new president; no willingness to wait and see. Southern firebrands had no faith in a Northern president who said that 'a house divided against itself cannot stand'. They saw Lincoln as an abolitionist. South Carolina was joined by six other slave states in early 1861, as shown in Figure 1.13 and Table 1.5. This group then quickly formed themselves into the Confederate States of America (CSA). They chose as their leader Jefferson Davis.

There were 15 slave states. On becoming president, Lincoln was faced with a rebellion by seven of them, with eight still to make up their minds.

- Figure 1.13 shows that the further south the state was, the sooner it seceded, while the further north it was, the less likely it was to secede at all.
- Table 1.5 shows that the higher percentage of slaves in the population, the more likely it was to secede, while a lower percentage of slaves meant it was less likely to secede.

From December 1861, federal politicians in Washington DC faced a regional rebellion. Southern representatives supported this rebellion and withdrew from Congress. This handed control of the federal legislature to the Republican Party. The most practical problem for Washington was what would happen to federal property, personnel and funds in these states, which now no longer saw themselves as bound by the US Constitution, and which quickly devised their own. The issue focused on control of the federal forts built to protect the USA against attack from the sea. Two of these were now in rebel states. One was Fort Pickens in Florida. The USA kept control of this fort, in part because it was out of range of rebel guns. The more important, more symbolic, was Fort Sumter located in the harbour of Charleston, South Carolina, the most rebellious of the seven states and the first to secede. The fate of this fort would prove a decisive

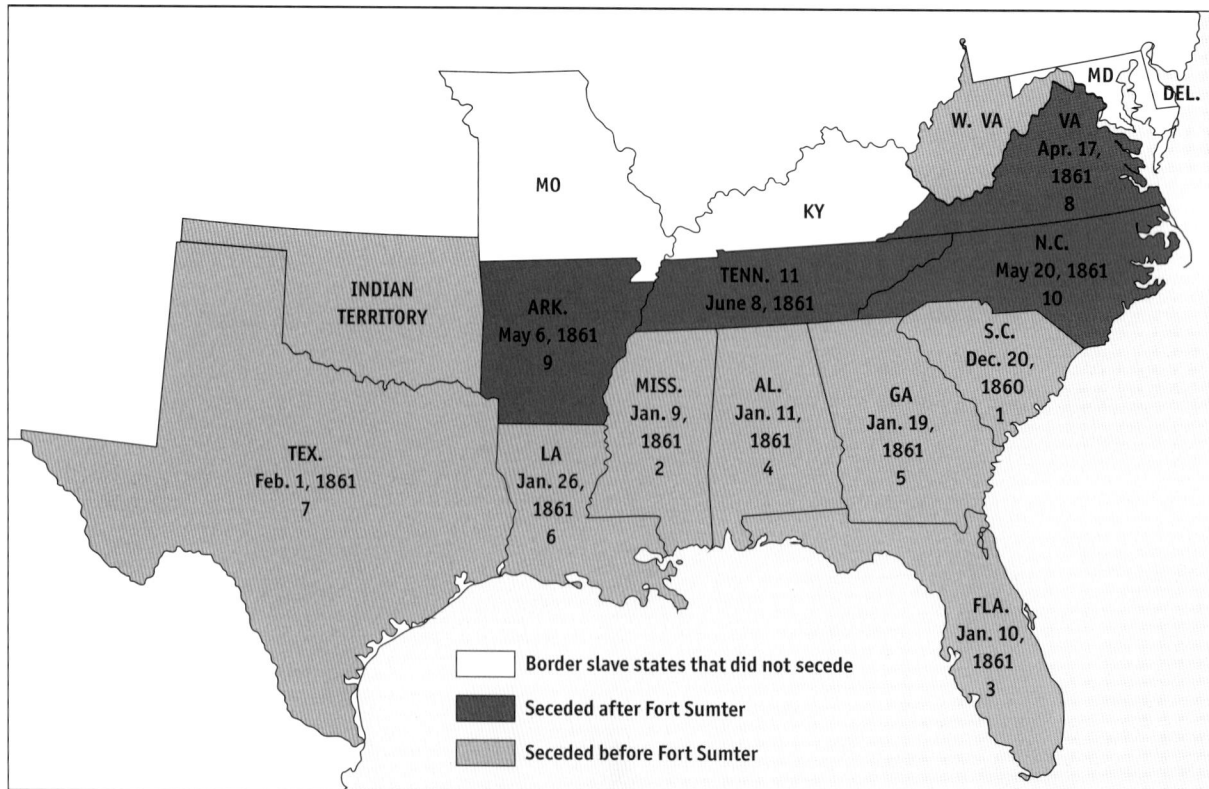

Figure 1.13: A map showing the order of secession of slave states

Seceding slave states				
Order	State	Date	slaves as percentage of population	Region
1	South Carolina	December 1860	57	**Lower South:** Average slave population percentage: 47
2	Mississippi	January 1861	55	
3	Florida	January 1861	44	
4	Alabama	January 1861	45	
5	Georgia	January 1861	44	
6	Louisiana	January 1861	47	
7	Texas	February 1861	44	
8	Virginia	April 1861	31	**Upper South** Average slave population percentage: 32
9	Arkansas	May 1861	26	
10	North Carolina	May 1861	33	
11	Tennessee	June 1861	25	
Non-seceding slave states				
	Delaware		2	**Border States** Average slave population percentage: 14
	Maryland		13	
	Kentucky		20	
	Missouri		10	

Table 1.5: The secession of slave states, and their slave populations as reported in the 1860 census

From Marc Egnal, *Clash of Extremes, The Economic Origins of the Civil War* (New York, Hill & Wang, 2009), p.272

flash point (see 'Fort Sumter and its impacts', below). The crisis of secession became ever more severe and so many politicians became more desperate in their attempts to contain the firebrands' efforts to end the Union.

The Crittenden Compromise, 1860–61

In Washington, Republicans were involved in frantic attempts to defuse the secession time-bomb. The best known attempt was the Crittenden Compromise. Senator Crittenden, an old-school Whig and by 1861 a member of the minority Constitutional Union Party, proposed six amendments to the Constitution. The most important would restore the Missouri Compromise dividing line between free and slave states, extending it westwards to the Pacific Ocean (see Figure 1.14). Another would protect slavery in existing slave states. The Compromise attracted considerable popular support, both North and South. It attracted much attention from the eight non-seceding Southern states. It was endorsed by former

Southern Democratic presidential candidate, Kentuckian John Breckinridge. As the Senate's presiding officer, he supported the Compromise in committee and in the Senate itself. If the Compromise was approved, the state would be much less likely to secede.

However, the Republicans in Congress ensured its rejection. A letter from Lincoln explains why. From his home in Illinois a month after being elected president, Lincoln wrote to a colleague: 'Let there be no compromise on the question of extending slavery. If there be, all our labour is lost, and, ere long, must be done again.'

The Compromise was judged as giving too much to the South, enabling the expansion of slavery into the territories of the West. Its failure showed that politicians could not agree on a compromise of sectional interests, as their predecessors had done in 1820 and 1850. By 1860, mutual fears and suspicions were too great. As Congressional politicians had failed to resolve the crisis,

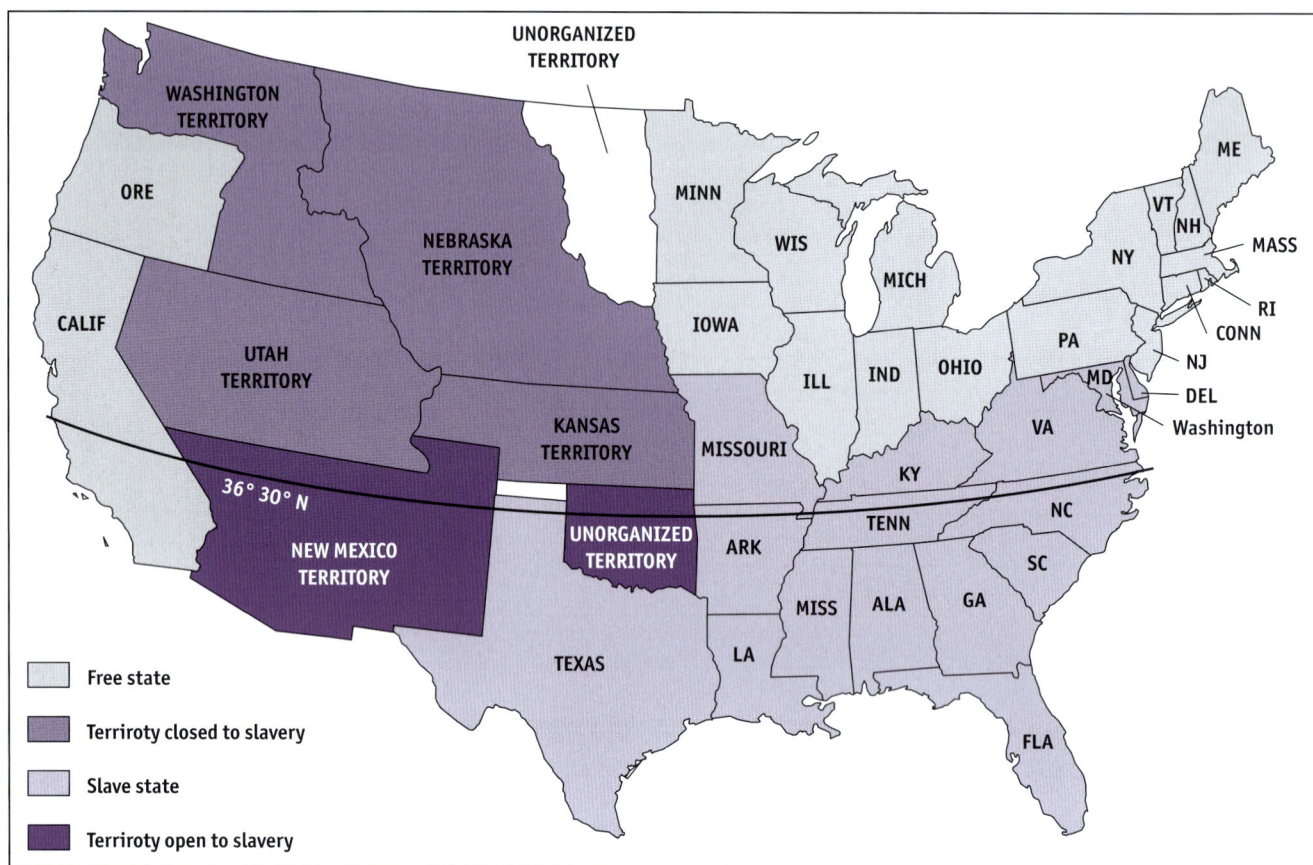

Figure 1.14: Map outlining proposed demarcations under the Crittenden Compromise, 1860–61

Map legend:
- Free state
- Terriroty closed to slavery
- Slave state
- Terriroty open to slavery

attention turned to the present-elect, who, in February 1861, made his way to Washington.

The Corwin Amendment and the Peace Conference, 1861

The Crittenden Compromise was not the only attempt to square the constitutional circle and dissuade the slave states from seceding. The Corwin Amendment was proposed to ensure that institutions established in individual states (such as slavery) were protected from abolition by Congress. Congress passed the Corwin Amendment, which was put forward by Seward in the Senate and Ohio's Thomas Corwin, a Whig turned Republican in the House of Representatives, a month after the CSA was formed. However the amendment was not ratified by the individual states, so never came into law and thus had no effect on the situation.

A 'Peace Conference' was held in February 1861, attended by leading politicians. It was a kind of reply to the several

meetings being held in Southern states to decide their future, and an effort to keep them in the Union. The confederacy of seven states were already holding meetings to form a CSA government.

These efforts did not end the process of secession. On March 4, Lincoln made an inauguration speech which attempted to conciliate the South while not upsetting his Northern supporters. He was keen to avoid any more states breaking away. His words seemed to work in the South, at least for the time being. However, he still had to decide what to do about Fort Sumter. His actions were to have a greater effect than his words.

ACTIVITY 1.22

Which had the greatest chance of success: the Crittenden Compromise or the Corwin Amendment or the Peace Conference? What do you think was the key reason why they didn't work?

Fort Sumter and its impacts

In his inaugural speech, Lincoln spoke with care about the federal forts in rebel territory but under federal control: 'The power confided in me will be used to hold, occupy and possess the property and places belonging to the government.' The most important of these places was Fort Sumter.

Around Fort Sumter in Charleston, South Carolina, a struggle for control had grown up between the state governor, and, later, the Confederacy, on one side and the US president and the commander of the fort on the other. Sumter was part of a series of fortifications designed to protect the port of Charleston from attack from the sea. It was the newest and strongest of the fortifications, although not quite complete.

Once South Carolina had decided to secede, the question of who controlled its forts became an issue of great importance to both sides. Thus both presidents, Buchanan and Lincoln, were involved in a complex series of talks and actions concerning the forts in the first four months of 1861. By the start of the year, the federal forces – fewer than 100 men – had withdrawn to Fort Sumter, the only fort in the middle of Charlestown harbour and thus much less vulnerable to overland attack. However, South Carolina quickly built up its forces around the shores of the harbour. The Union soldiers had to rely on their own resources and on being supplied from the sea as they were surrounded by hostile forces. As supplies on Fort Sumter ran low, relief supplies became essential.

The leaders of both sides faced some tough choices. Some were tactical: should the union reinforce Fort Sumter with men, weapons and supplies, or just supplies? Some were strategic: what would the effect be for each side of being first to fire? What effect would it have on the eight slave states yet to secede? Both sides looked carefully at which side Virginia would join. Of the eight slave states that had not seceded, Virginia was the most important. It contained key military assets: the federal armoury at Harpers Ferry and the federal naval base at Norfolk. Its capital, Richmond, was also the only industrial centre in the South.

At one stage, the Union government in Washington DC seemed close to surrendering Fort Sumter for greater strategic benefits in return – perhaps to keep Virginia on side or at least neutral. Lincoln, however, went against advice and decided to keep it supplied. His CSA counterpart, Jefferson Davis, decided to seize the initiative and ordered Fort Sumter to be bombarded if it refused to surrender. No surrender was given and the South opened fire. After 36 hours of bombardment, the surrender came. The Civil War had begun.

As the first clash of military forces in a long-lasting and bloody civil war, the attack on Fort Sumter has been the subject of much debate and disagreement ever since, over who was responsible. CSA troops fired the first shots, but those who see the North as responsible argue that Lincoln provoked the South into aggression, forcing them to decide that they had to prevent the North from keeping control of Fort Sumter. Such critics of Lincoln also believe that he double-crossed the South, saying initially that he would withdraw Northern troops from the fort, only to change his mind. Whoever was responsible, the consequences of the attack on Fort Sumter were great as it tipped the balance of states more towards the South.

For several months, Virginia remained divided about whether to support the South's rebellion. Even in early April, a month after Lincoln was installed as president, a state assembly decided it should remain part of the Union. Meanwhile, Lincoln raised a force of 75 000 men in an attempt to defeat the rebellion of the seven seceding states. In doing so, the federal government was taking on unprecedented power. The decision confirmed many Southerners' worst fears about the Republicans and the new president in Washington. Governor Lecher of Virginia was asked to provide 2340 volunteers from the state militia to serve for three months as part of this force. Virginians decided that raising a federal army against the CSA was undesirable and unconstitutional. On 16 April 1861, Lecher told Lincoln's secretary of war: 'Your object is to subjugate the Southern States and a requisition on me for such an object – an object, in my judgement, not within the scope of the Constitution or the [Militia] Act of 1795 – will not be complied with.' A state assembly quickly voted to leave the Union and Virginia became the eighth member of the CSA. Much of the Civil War on the eastern seaboard was fought over control of Virginia.

Figure 1.15: A 19th century illustration of the attack on Fort Sumter, April 12 and 13, 1861, the first battle in the US Civil War. How useful is this engraving in explaining the importance of the battle?

In the event, part of Virginia remained loyal to the Union. It formed itself into the state of West Virginia, which would join the USA in 1862 as the 35th state of the Union. To do so, it had to agree to the gradual abolition of slavery.

Three other states of the **Upper South** contained enough leaders who were equally appalled by being asked to provide troops to act against fellow slave states. Arkansas, North Carolina and Tennessee all broke away from the USA in April and May. Seven states became eleven. Lincoln's request for 75 000 soldiers had backfired. His first two decisions concerning the secession of the South meant that both Fort Sumter, most of Virginia and three other finely balanced states had been pushed into the arms of the CSA.

> **KEY TERM**
>
> **Upper South:** the most northerly Southern states, adjacent to the Mason–Dixon line, as opposed to the Lower or Deep South

The Aims of Abraham Lincoln and Jefferson Davis

On the outbreak of civil war in the spring of 1861, the main aim of the two leaders were quite simple, if completely opposite:

- Lincoln wanted to defeat what he labelled a rebellion, to win a 'Civil War'.
- Jefferson Davis wanted to turn a rebellion into a 'War of Southern Independence'.

In his inaugural address to the American people, Lincoln was careful to define the central issue of the conflict as secession rather than slavery. He even said he was agreeable to the constitutional amendment to protect states' rights, including, 'that of persons held to service … being made express and irrevocable'.

A year later, in August 1862, Lincoln wrote a public letter to an old friend from Whig days, former politician, newspaper man and co-founder of the Republican Party Horace Greeley, in which he explained that his main aim was to save the Union; and if it meant not freeing any slaves, he was prepared to do this.

By the time of his second inaugural address, in March 1865, Lincoln was prepared to say to the American people that although extending and continuing slavery was the cause of the war which broke the Union, the government had only wanted to restrict extending slavery to new states and claimed no right to abolish slavery.

President of the Confederacy, Jefferson Davis, in his own inaugural speech, supported his rival's analysis that the war was about the Union rather than slavery. Davis did not mention slavery once by name. His speech also focused on the decision to secede, its justification and its consequences.

By contrast, however, his vice president, Alexander Stephens, made the issue of slavery central in a speech which became known as the Cornerstone Speech. Speaking to an enthusiastic audience in Savannah, Georgia on 21 March 1861, he explained that the new Confederate constitution was based on the idea that black people were inferior to white people, meaning that slavery was justifiable.

Americans were faced with a crisis of disunity and division of their country. At the time, many thought that the crisis would be resolved only by the permanent division of the USA. As W.H. Russell, war correspondent of British newspaper the *Times*, found a few weeks after arriving in the USA in March 1861, most people in New York believed that the South would never rejoin the Union.

KEY CONCEPT

Causation

At what point did the Civil War become inevitable?

As you review your learning in reading this chapter, make a list of all the causes of the Civil War which you think are at all significant.

Arrange the causes in chronological order. At which point, if any, could war no longer be avoided?

You might, as some historians do, believe that nothing is ever inevitable until it happens. If not, how does your view of when the US Civil War became inevitable compare with your classmates' views?

ACTIVITY 1.23

Here are the opening lines of the Declaration of Independence, published in 1776 by the 13 British colonies in North America rebelling against British rule:

> We hold these truths to be self-evident, that all men are created equal, that they are endowed by their Creator with certain unalienable Rights, that among these are Life, Liberty and the pursuit of Happiness. That to secure these rights, Governments are instituted among Men, deriving their just powers from the consent of the governed.

Relate these sentences to the situation of the United States between 1846 and 1861. You should pay particular attention to the words 'liberty', 'we', 'men' and 'the governed'.

Reflection: How did you relate this source to the situation in the United States between 1846–1861? Join a study partner and discuss whether you reached different conclusions; did you use different information from the source, or did you interpret the same information differently?

Exam-style questions

Source analysis questions

Read all four sources and then answer both parts of question 1.

SOURCE A

A conversation between a fictional senator and his wife

'Well,' said his wife… 'What have they been doing in the Senate?'

Now, it was a very unusual thing for Mrs. Bird ever to trouble her head with what was going on, very wisely considering that she had enough to do to mind her own. Mr. Bird, therefore, opened his eyes in surprise, and said, 'Not very much of importance.'

'Well; but is it true that they have been passing a law forbidding people to give meat and drink to those poor colored folks that come along? I heard they were talking of some such law, but I didn't think any Christian legislature would pass it … I think this is something downright cruel and unchristian. I hope no such law has been passed.'

'There has been a law passed forbidding people to help the slaves that come over from Kentucky, my dear; so much has been done by these reckless Abolitionists, that our brethren in Kentucky are very strongly excited, and it seems necessary, and no more than Christian and kind, that something should be done by our state to quiet the excitement.'

'And what is the law? It don't forbid us to shelter those poor creatures a night, does it, and to give 'em something comfortable to eat, and a few old clothes, and send them quietly about their business?'

'Why, yes, my dear; that would be a crime.'

Adapted from Harriet Beecher Stowe,
Uncle Tom's Cabin, 1852

SOURCE B

That the Constitution, and all Laws of the United States which are not locally inapplicable, shall have the same force and effect within the said Territory of Nebraska as elsewhere within the United States, except the eighth section of the act preparatory to the admission of Missouri into the Union approved March 1820, which, being inconsistent with the principle of non-intervention by Congress with slaves in the States and Territories, as recognized by the legislation of 1850, commonly called the Compromise Measures, is hereby declared inoperative and void; it being the true intent and meaning of this act not to legislate slavery into any Territory or State, nor to exclude it therefrom, but to leave the people thereof perfectly free to form and regulate their domestic institutions in their own way, subject only to the Constitution of the United States: Provided, That nothing herein contained shall be construed to revive or put in force any law or regulation which may have existed prior to the act of sixth March, eighteen hundred and twenty, either protecting, establishing, prohibiting, or abolishing slavery.

From 'An Act to Organize the Territories of Nebraska and Kansas', 1854

SOURCE C

4. A free negro of the African race, whose ancestors were brought to this country and sold as slaves, is not a 'citizen' within the meaning of the Constitution of the United States.

5. When the Constitution was adopted, they were not regarded in any of the States as members of the community which constituted the State, and were not numbered among its 'people or citizens.' Consequently, the special rights and immunities guaranteed to citizens do not apply to them.

6. The only two clauses in the Constitution which point to this race, treat them as persons whom it was morally lawful to deal in as articles of property and to hold as slaves.

7. Since the adoption of the Constitution of the United States, no state can by any subsequent law make a foreigner or any other description of persons citizens of the United States, nor entitle them to the rights and privileges secured to citizens by that instrument.

8. A State, by its laws passed since the adoption of the Constitution, may put a foreigner or any other description of persons upon a footing with its own citizens, as to all the rights and privileges enjoyed by them within its dominion, and by its laws. But that will not make him a citizen of the United States, nor entitle him to sue in its courts, nor to any of the privileges and immunities of a citizen in another State.

From the ruling of the US Supreme Court in the case of Scott v. Sandford, 1857

SOURCE D

After John Brown's arrest following the raid on Harpers Ferry, Lydia Maria Child wrote to the governor of Virginia requesting to visit him in prison. Margaretta Mason of Virginia wrote critically to her and a correspondence followed.

You would sooth with sisterly and motherly care the hoary-headed murderer of Harpers Ferry! A man whose aim and intention was to incite the horrors of a civil war –to condemn women of your own race to see their husbands and fathers murdered and their children butchered. The antecedents of Brown's band prove them to have been the offspring of the earth; and what would have been our fate had they found as many sympathizers in Virginia as they seem to have in Massachusetts …

From the reply from Lydia Maria Child

The universal rule of the slave states is that 'the child follows the condition of its mother.' Marriages between white and colored people are forbidden by law; yet a very large number of the slaves are brown or yellow …

Throughout the slave states, the testimony of no colored person, slave or free, can be used against a white man. You have some laws which, on the face of them, would seem to restrain inhuman men from murdering or mutilating slaves; but they are rendered nearly null by the law I have cited. Any drunken master, overseer, or patrol, may go into the negro cabin and commit whatever outrage he pleases with perfect impunity, if no white person is present who chooses to be a witness against him …

From a letter from Margaretta Mason to Lydia Maria Child, 1860

1　**a**　Compare and contrast Sources A and D as evidence of the public debate regarding slavery.

　　b　'The division between North and South over slavery grew wider between 1840 and 1860.' How far do Sources A to D support this view?

Essay based questions

Answer both parts of the question below.

2　**a**　Explain why political violence broke out in Kansas, 1854–58.

　　b　To what extent was the Republican party's victory in the 1860 presidential election the cause of the outbreak of the American Civil War?

3　**a**　Explain why the Dred Scott decision was so important.

　　b　To what extent were divisions within the Democratic party responsible for the election of Lincoln in 1860?

Sample answer

Explain why political violence broke out in Kansas, 1854–58.

The political violence that broke out in Kansas 1854–58 was called Bleeding Kansas. This was because a lot of people travelled to Kansas to vote there. They did this because of the Kansas-Nebraska Act. The Kansas-Nebraska Act meant that there were two new US territories of Nebraska and Kansas. People who supported slavery wanted Kansas to vote for slavery. People who were against slavery wanted Kansas to vote against slavery. They were allowed to vote because Senator Stephens had passed an act allowing popular sovereignty. That is why a lot of people rushed to be there to vote.

> This is not a high-quality answer so far. The first paragraph does explain why many people went to Kansas and introduces the divisions there over slavery, but it does not explain why violence broke out.

The border ruffians were armed and came to attack slaves and their owners. They broke up printing presses and killed people. The fighting lasted in Kansas for two years. A lot of people were killed. That is why it is called Bleeding Kansas.

> The second paragraph mentions the border ruffians, but does not explain clearly what they were trying to achieve and what their role was in causing the violence. It focuses too much on why it was called 'Bleeding' Kansas.

Bleeding Kansas happened at the same time as the Fugitive Slave Act. It was about Manifest Destiny. There were a lot of immigrants coming into the United States from Ireland and Germany and other places and they wanted to be given farms. That's why the United States expanded westwards. Before a lot of this land had belonged to Mexico or Native Americans. Then the USA fought a war with Mexico and at the end of the war was given a big area of land called the Mexican Cession. Also Texas joined the United States. This land was disorganised which meant it did not have a governor. To give it a governor it was turned into a territory. But it might be a territory with slaves or a territory without slaves. If it had slaves the South would be stronger. If it didn't the North would be stronger.

> The third paragraph does not seem to be linked to the question at all. There is a lot of background material there, but does not refer to the causes of the violence.

At first Congress couldn't pass the Kansas–Nebraska Act. Then it did. This was because Stephen Douglas persuaded Congress. He did this with the principle of popular sovereignty, but also by separating Kansas from Nebraska and by telling them it would help build a railway to the Pacific. But although Congress passed the act a lot of people were very angry and that is why political violence broke out in Kansas 1854–58.

> The relevance of the fourth paragraph is not clear at all. It is only the last sentence that directly answers the question, but it does not seem to be linked in any way to the previous statements. There is really only very limited explanation in this response.

Summary

After working through this chapter, make sure you understand the following key points:

- the extent to which the Civil War was caused by arguments about slavery specifically, or how it was caused far more generally by sectional tension between North and South

- the attempts at compromise throughout the period leading up to the Civil War, why they worked initially and why they ultimately failed

- the significance of the changing ideas of Northern abolitionists in causing the Civil War

- the reasons for and consequences of the election of Abraham Lincoln as US president.

Further reading

Useful books on the Civil War and its causes include:

G. S. Boritt, *Why the Civil War Came,* Gettysburg, Civil War Institute Books, 2006.

A. Farmer, *The Origins of the American Civil War, 1846–61,* London, Hodder Murray, 2002.

J. M. McPherson, *Battle Cry of Freedom: The Civil War Era,* London, Penguin, 1990.

D. M. Potter, *The Impending Crisis, 1848–61,* New York, Torchbooks, 1976.

H. Tulloch, *The Debate on the American Civil War Era* Manchester University Press, 1999.

Sven Beckert *Empire of Cotton* London, Penguin, 2014 and P. Kolchin, *American Slavery: 1619–1877,* London, Penguin, 1995.

More general books on the USA that are also useful for this period include:

S. M. Grant, *A Concise History of the United States of America,* Cambridge University Press, 2012.

D. Murphy, K. Cooper and M. Waldron, *United States, 1776–1992,* Glasgow, Collins, 2001.

Sean Wilentz, *The Rise of American Democracy: Jefferson to Lincoln,* New York, Norton, 2005.

Online resources

An accessible summary of key statistics about African Americans in antebellum America can be found in *Slavery, by the Numbers* at www.theroot.com/slavery-by-the-numbers-1790874492

The Compromise of 1850 has its own dedicated website: www.compromise-of-1850.org

For a range of original documents, short commentaries and contextualising discussion, try www.archives.gov and www.americanyawp.com/reader.html.

Chapter 2
Civil War and Reconstruction, 1861–77

Learning objectives

In this chapter you will:

- learn why the Civil War lasted four years, including the military and political strategies, and the strengths and weaknesses of the two sides
- examine the immediate impact of the Civil War on American society, economy, politics and culture
- study both the intentions of Reconstruction and its actual outcomes
- consider how successful Reconstruction was, weighing up its achievements, comparing them with the initial aims and setting both in the context of time and place.

Timeline

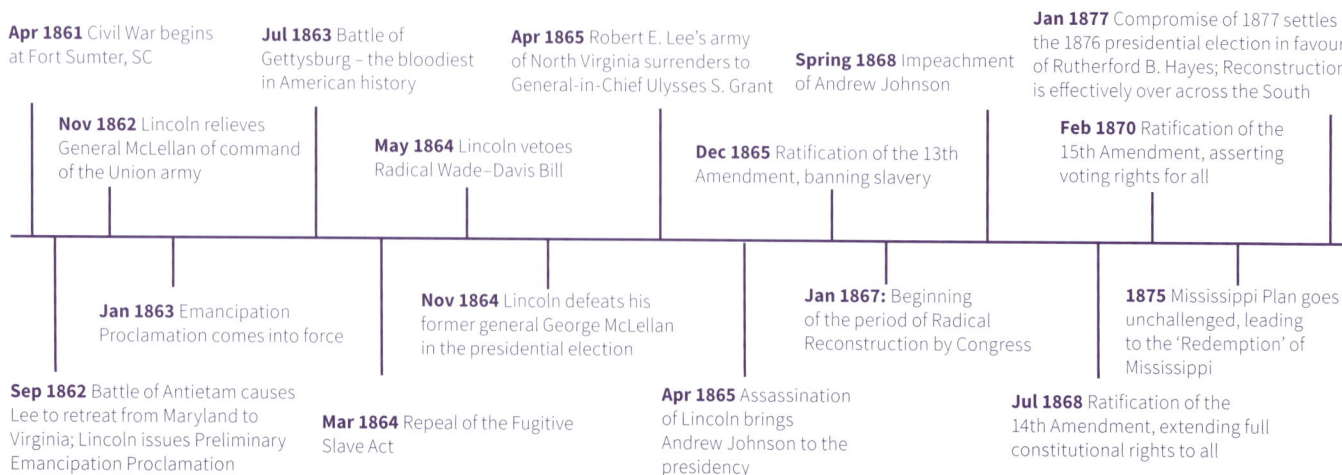

Apr 1861 Civil War begins at Fort Sumter, SC

Jul 1863 Battle of Gettysburg – the bloodiest in American history

Apr 1865 Robert E. Lee's army of North Virginia surrenders to General-in-Chief Ulysses S. Grant

Spring 1868 Impeachment of Andrew Johnson

Jan 1877 Compromise of 1877 settles the 1876 presidential election in favour of Rutherford B. Hayes; Reconstruction is effectively over across the South

Nov 1862 Lincoln relieves General McLellan of command of the Union army

May 1864 Lincoln vetoes Radical Wade–Davis Bill

Dec 1865 Ratification of the 13th Amendment, banning slavery

Feb 1870 Ratification of the 15th Amendment, asserting voting rights for all

Jan 1863 Emancipation Proclamation comes into force

Nov 1864 Lincoln defeats his former general George McLellan in the presidential election

Jan 1867: Beginning of the period of Radical Reconstruction by Congress

1875 Mississippi Plan goes unchallenged, leading to the 'Redemption' of Mississippi

Sep 1862 Battle of Antietam causes Lee to retreat from Maryland to Virginia; Lincoln issues Preliminary Emancipation Proclamation

Mar 1864 Repeal of the Fugitive Slave Act

Apr 1865 Assassination of Lincoln brings Andrew Johnson to the presidency

Jul 1868 Ratification of the 14th Amendment, extending full constitutional rights to all

Before you start

Understanding the events of the Civil War requires a grasp of its context. Consider these seven aspects:

1 Warfare: military training and strategies, the weaponry
2 Economics and finance: who was going to pay for the war and how it would be funded
3 Geography: the huge land area involved, plus the struggle to control the coast, the sea and trade
4 Politics: democratic processes including elections, freedom of speech and the press
5 Law: the power of the president, the balance between central and state government, the argument as to whether this was a rebellion or a war of independence
6 Slavery: whether Southern slaves would rise up, whether the North would declare a general emancipation, or even whether the Fugitive Slave Act still applied
7 Leadership: a lawyer with little experience of leadership and politics, and none of government or war, was facing a man with more experience of all four.

Introduction

Forty years of growing political conflict turned into four years of increasingly violent physical conflict, far worse than anyone had expected. In these four years more than 600 000 young American men were killed.

The subsequent 12 years is known as the era of Reconstruction. This neatly continues the housebuilding theme which formed the basis of Lincoln's pre-war 'house divided' speech: four years of demolition, 12 to rebuild – or to start to rebuild.

> **ACTIVITY 2.1**
>
> Research and write a short paragraph developing each of the seven points in *Before you start*. Which side seems to you to have a decisive advantage at the beginning of the war?
>
> The American Civil War and Reconstruction continue to affect economic, political, social and cultural events and debate. What knowledge, preconceptions or prejudices do you bring to the study of the war or of the way in which the USA was reconstructed after the Civil War?

2.1 Why did the Civil War last four years?

The process of secession ran from 1860 to 1861. Alabama's Montgomery was the first provisional seat of the Confederate government. It was centrally located in the Deep South, where secession came early. The convention met there to draft a constitution. Montgomery was not, however, large or well-served with amenities, and visitors, including the (London) *Times*' W. H. Russell and South Carolina's Mary Boykin Chesnut, a notable Confederate diarist, both recorded their dislike of staying there. Once Virginia had voted to secede, the decision was taken to move the seat of government to that state's capital, Richmond, a larger, better-served city, with an ironworks and railway connections. It was also, however, much closer to enemy lines. Each side now had a capital within striking distance of the other's army.

> **ACTIVITY 2.2**
>
> Our national troubles have been productive of at least one good result. The spirit of patriotism has been rekindled in the breasts of the people of the free state and their souls have been knit together as one man in defence of our flag, our government and constitution. Everywhere from Maine to California such a determination is manifested to sustain the authority of the government and maintain the integrity of the Union as must strike terror into the hearts of traitors … The call of the President for 75,000 volunteers has been responded to by

more than 250,000 men – and still they come! We do not believe that this confederate state … can resist the mighty torrent which is soon to pour down upon it from our northern hills. We have immense superiority in population, wealth, food, and manufacturing and naval power and, having bravery and endurance in equal quantities, can demonstrate success for our cause with mathematical precision.

From the Lansing State [Michigan] Republican, 24 April 1861

Was there ever in the history of an enlightened country, such a piteous spectacle seen as presented by Mr Lincoln and his swarm of demoralised subordinates? A President in antagonism with the captain of his armies – a **Cabinet** abused by its own party supporters – troops disorganised, unpaid, unofficered, with nothing but their valour to rely on – and, more disgusting than all, a horde of Abolition scribblers … prevaricating, exaggerating, moaning over disaster, or inventing ridiculous theories to prove defeat a victory – agreeing upon no one point except that all-absorbing one, the slavery question. Out of this conglomerated mass of discordant elements Mr Lincoln would reconstruct the Union. With such materials he would subjugate six million Americans – determined, well organised, confident, placing implicit reliance upon themselves and their commanders. He will sooner accomplish the ruin of his country and his own disgrace.

From the Richmond [Virginia] Daily Dispatch, 7 August 1861

Compare and contrast the accounts given by the *Lansing Republican* and the *Richmond Daily Dispatch*. Consider content, style and arguments. What is the 'president's call' which the Michigan newspaper refers to? (Look back into Chapter 1 if you need to.)

Research the figure the Virginian newspaper gives for the population of the South, the Confederate states. What do the statistics and choice of words tell you about the beliefs of the journalist writing the article?

The border states: Maryland, Delaware, Kentucky and Missouri

Both sides wanted to win the support of the four slave states which had not yet declared their intentions and which all had divided loyalties.

Maryland's decision was finely balanced as shown by geography and demographics. Half of Maryland's African American population were free and half were slaves. Also, Maryland surrounded the federal capital on three sides, while being itself largely surrounded by Northern states or the sea.

Four soldiers and 12 civilians were killed in the Baltimore Riot of April 1861, when a pro-secessionist mob attacked Northern troops on their way through the state's largest city to defend Washington DC. Lincoln made another controversial decision in his first few weeks in office, to keep control of such an important strategic route. (He had already chosen to resupply Fort Sumter and called for 75 000 volunteers.) This time, he used his power as commander-in-chief to suspend **habeas corpus** along key routes in Maryland. This enabled the North to imprison key politicians and newspaper editors.

Maryland's choice of side was made not by Marylanders, but by the federal government. In practical terms, the South could do little to help secessionists in Maryland.

KEY TERMS

Cabinet: The group of senior government ministers, all appointed by the president.

Habeas corpus: A legal provision which limits the time someone can be held by the authorities without being charged. It is a key judicial defence against arbitrary arrest.

Delaware, which was a state to the east of Maryland, was smaller and coastal, and lacked Maryland's strategic significance. It had not abolished slavery, but about 90% of the black population of the state were free. As it was divided in its support, it narrowly voted to stay in the Union in January 1861.

Davis was chosen as the Confederacy's first and only president. He was a Democratic party congressman and senator for Mississippi who served as secretary for war in the 1850s under Franklin Pierce, His family was wealthy from farming and owned a large cotton plantation with a slave workforce. He was a graduate of West Point military academy, he fought in the war with Mexico in the 1840s. He argued against secession but supported the states' right to leave the Union. Davis was disappointed to be offered the political leadership of the newly formed Confederacy as he had hoped for a military command. Historians have tended to judge him a poor war leader and sympathisers with the South tend to favour General Lee over Davis.

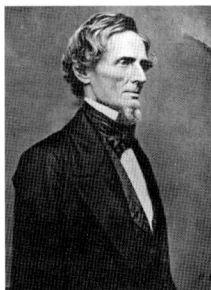

Further west, Kentucky, where both Lincoln and **Jefferson Davis** had been born, tried to declare neutrality. In September 1861, writing from Washington DC, Lincoln explained: 'I think to lose Kentucky is nearly the same as to lose the whole game. Kentucky gone, we cannot hold Missouri, nor I think Maryland. These all against us, and the job on our hands [becomes] too big for us. We would as well consent to separation at once, including the surrender of this capitol.'

There was an attempt to set up a Confederate government of Kentucky. Despite this, the unionist government in the capital Frankfort regained control of the state.

West of Kentucky lay Illinois' neighbour Missouri, the subject of so much political strife earlier in the century. Its state legislature voted decisely to stay in the USA.

A key reason for these four slave states of the border not joining the Confederacy was the presence there of US armed forces. Also, Lincoln had moved more quickly and decisively than Davis did.

ACTIVITY 2.3

Consider the approach Lincoln took to the border states. Do you think some of his measures might have been unconstitutional? How would you justify them?

Changing military strategies

The civil war was fought in three different **theatres**:

- east of the Appalachian mountains
- west of the Appalachian mountains
- at sea.

KEY TERM

Theatre: A general military term for the different areas in which a war might be fought.

The best-known battles of the civil war were fought in the eastern theatre, where the capital cities of the two sides were only 160 km apart. Each side tried to take the other's capital, knowing it would be a huge political as well as military victory.

The campaign at sea: the blockade, trade and foreign powers

Lincoln needed to stop the Confederate States of America's international trade, especially with Britain, the main market for Southern cotton; the question was how. Closing CSA ports would be effective but provocative; it would be an action under US, not international, law. **Blockading** CSA ports would be less effective but less provocative, and acceptable under international law.

However, could the North adopt a blockade without seeming to recognise the CSA as a sovereign state?

KEY TERM

Blockade: A concentrated effort to cut off trade and supplies from a particular state or, in this case, area, in order to damage its economy and perhaps deplete its resources so much that it is forced into submission.

Lincoln decided that the situation was both a rebellion and a war. Therefore he decided he could choose the rules and processes that best suited Northern interests from national or international law. In this case, it was better to blockade.

Jefferson Davis's officials failed to persuade Britain to recognise the CSA as a sovereign state and provide financial and diplomatic support. Britain:

- recognised CSA as belligerent under international law, giving the South some rights, but not as a state; it wouldn't sign any treaties with the CSA, and wouldn't send or accept ambassadors
- accepted the US blockade
- remained neutral throughout the war: UK citizens could not join the fight and UK companies would not provide ships.

This was a Northern success, as the South lost more than the North from Britain's neutrality. With the blockade in place, 90% of the CSA's trade with Britain stopped. A significant economic defeat. (See 'Impact of foreign influences', below, for more detail.)

Lincoln's interpretation of domestic and international law had helped the North's case. So, in relations with the border states and in negotiations with other countries, Lincoln had outmanoeuvred Davis.

Earlier strategies and campaigns, 1861–63

The CSA adopted a 'perimeter' or 'cordon' strategy, to defend its boundaries. As its own resources were insufficient to maintain this, it was soon abandoned for what was later called the 'offensive–defensive' strategy. This meant defending against US attacks and taking the offensive wherever possible.

The USA's original strategy was named the Anaconda Plan. It was devised by the USA's general-in-chief, Winfield Scott who was 74 years old, ill and too overweight to ride a horse. It included:

- A naval blockade was to be set up to damage the South's economy and prevent it resupplying. In fact, it proved impossible to prevent some ships getting through.
- Limited military action was to be taken to gain control of the Mississippi river, the key north–south route, cutting the South in two. This eventually worked.

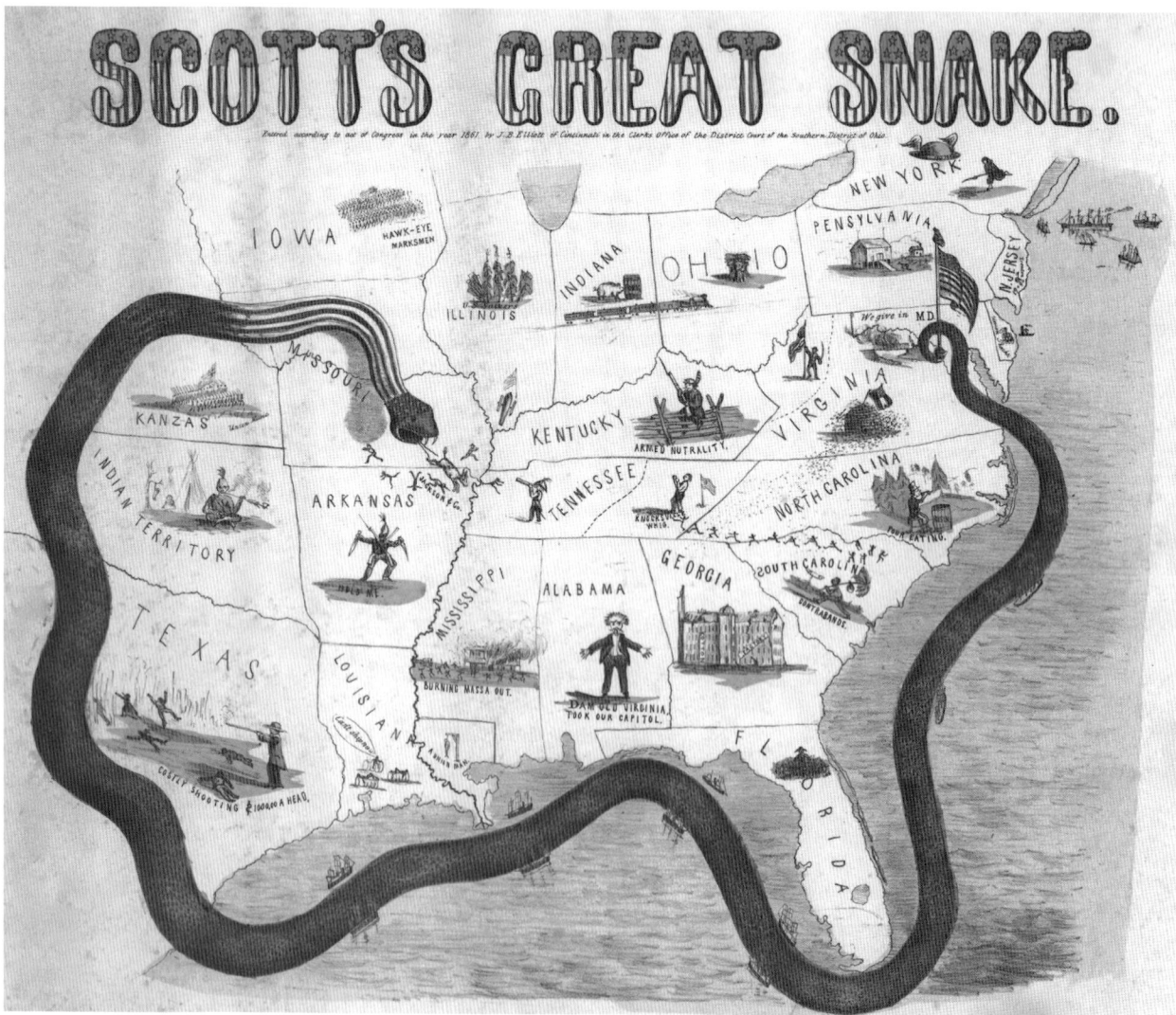

Figure 2.1: A contemporary cartoon of the Union's Anaconda Plan, created by J.B. Elliott, Cincinnati, 1861.
What does the use of a snake suggest about the cartoonist's attitude towards the plan?

The background idea was that, with casualties minimised, post-war reconciliation would be easier.

In the eastern theatre, the Northern strategy in 1861–62 was similar to the South's: defend when necessary, attack when possible. However, the leader of Northern forces in Virginia, George McClellan, became notorious for rarely thinking attack was possible.

ROBERT EDWARD LEE (1807–70)

General Lee was one of Winfield Scott's chief aides in the Mexican War 1846–48, working alongside future president Ulysses S. Grant. He was loyal to the USA in countering the Raid on Harpers Ferry and the secession of Texas. At the outbreak of war, Lee was offered commands by both sides. His views are the object of considerable dispute, but he seems to have been unenthusiastic about slavery. However, when Virginia seceded he accepted the command of the CSA's army of Northern Virginia from 1862 to 1865. At the end of the war he was the South's supreme military commander. He had a good record of winning battles against superior forces, but neither of his offences into Union territory was a success.

Northern newspapers such as the abolitionist *New York Herald Tribune* demanded immediate attack and rapid victory. In the 1862 Peninsular Campaign, McClellan cautiously advanced into Virginia. Union forces reached the outskirts of Richmond in June and were opposed by an equally cautious Joseph Johnson. When Johnson was injured, command passed to **Robert E. Lee**, who won the Seven Days Battles and led his men into Maryland only to be stopped at Antietam. This September day was the bloodiest of the whole war, with a total of over 20 000 casualties. Lacking the resources to continue to fight at Antietam, Lee retreated to Virginia. McClellan failed to follow up this success by advancing and then, a frustrated Lincoln replaced him as field commander in November.

The following year, US forces again advanced on Richmond. However, in April and May they were defeated at Chancellorsville, though the South lost one of its key commanders with the death of 'Stonewall' Jackson. The CSA army under Lee then seized the offensive, moving northwards through Maryland into Pennsylvania. After suffering a clear defeat at Gettysburg, the Confederate army retreated. Gettysburg was the war's bloodiest battle, with about 50 000 casualties over three days.

The eastern theatre 1861–63 saw a great deal of fighting in a small area, but the war was deadlocked. Attempts to seize the opponent's capital was defeated.

In the western theatre, the Anaconda Plan worked better. The North gained control of the Tennessee River following victory at Fort Henry in February 1862, and then the Cumberland river following victory at Fort Donelson. New Orleans fell to US forces in April 1862. These successes took them towards the goal of controlling the Mississippee and Ohio rivers.

While the North's commander in the east was the cautious McClellan, in the west it was the aggressive, decisive and successful **Ulysses S. Grant**. At the start of 1862, the battle of Shiloh was going the South's way before Grant succeeded in achieving victory in a two-day battle with heavy casualties. Grant later wrote in his memoirs that he had believed winning one battle would cause the CSA to collapse. However the battle of Shiloh convinced him that the only way to win the war was through 'complete conquest'.

Such a 'complete conquest' of the South implied a different style of warfare, with consequences for Southern civilians.

ULYSSES SIMPSON GRANT (1822–85)

Grant was a US general and later president (1869–77). When the Civil War broke out, he had retired from the army but rejoined and experienced rapid promotion and battlefield success. Lincoln gave Grant overall command of the Union armies, despite the fact that his victories came at the price of heavy casualties. In the end, he defeated Lee's remaining Southern forces and accepted his surrender at Appomattox in April 1865.

55

Later strategies

In the western theatre, by 1864, US forces had pushed deep into the South. Lee's forces were defending Petersburg, Virginia. In July, Lee sent a force across the Potomac into Maryland and Pennsylvania again, but this time just 9 000 men had the job of drawing Union troops away to defend Washington. The small force won the battle of Monocacy and pressed to attack the capital at the battle of Fort Stevens. During this, Lincoln came under direct enemy fire, and was forced to retreat South.

In the western theatre, Northern forces fought from December 1862 to July 1863 to capture the CSA fortress at Vicksburg on the Mississippee. A CSA victory at Chickamauga on the Georgia–Tennessee border was a setback. Union victory at Chattanooga in November 1863 gave the North control of Tennessee. The offensive moved to Georgia in May 1864.

In August 1864, Grant ordered his commander in the Shenandoah Valley, Virginia, Phillip Sheridan: 'Give the enemy no rest. Do all the damage to railroads and crops you can. Carry off stock of all descriptions, and negroes, so as to prevent further planting. If the war is to last another year, we want the Shenandoah valley to remain a barren waste' (H. W. Brands, *The Man Who Saved the Union*).

Sheridan's troops adopted the tactic of **scorched earth**, destroying farm buildings, equipment, crops and animals in what became known as 'The Burning'. Supplies to the CSA armies dwindled.

> ### KEY TERM
>
> **Scorched earth:** A military policy of destroying, often by fire, all resources that could be used by an opposing force, including food and shelter, in order to undermine their ability to fight. It can have devastating consequences for the civilian population in the area.

William Tecumseh Sherman, Grant's commander in Georgia and South Carolina, also pursued the idea of total war.

Halleck led an army from the Tennessee border through Georgia to Atlanta, burning much of the state capital, and then went on to coastal Savannah. The rapid advance depended on seizing supplies from enemy territory and avoiding pitched battles, while practising a policy of scorched earth.

After a few week's rest and recuperation, Sherman's army headed north-east through South and North Carolina, continuing the scorched earth tactics.

When Grant went to Washington DC to become general-in-chief in March 1864, Sherman became commander in the western theatre.

The speed of Sherman's advance contrasted markedly with the static trench warfare in Virginia. In April 1865, Petersburg fell, decisively, and the war quickly ended.

The conflict had lasted longer and cost more lives than almost anyone had expected. The South had made maximum use of its more limited resources and in Lee had a skilful military leader in the eastern theatre. The North had been poorly served initially by Scott and McClellan, and was slow to:

- mobilise its resources
- find its best military leaders
- appreciate the potential contribution of slaves (or former slaves) to the war effort as labourers and soldiers.

> ### ACTIVITY 2.4
>
> Where do you think the war was won: the western theatre, the eastern theatre or the sea? Explain your conclusion, setting out why one was more significant, but also why the other two were less significant.

Changing approaches of political and military leadership

In the North, Lincoln was formally commander-in-chief of the federal army as well as head of government. Although he was a lawyer, with no formal military experience, he began to study the history of war whenever he could. After Southern forces shelled Fort Sumter, Lincoln immediately called for a blockade of the coastline of the seceded states and requested 75 000 volunteer soldiers to enlist for three months. He was only partially successful in this recruitment (see Chapter 1.4), but the naval blockade continued for the duration of the war.

Initially, Lincoln appointed Winfield Scott, hero of the War of 1812 and the US–Mexican War, as his general-in-chief. Scott was one of the few who did expect a long conflict. He started to create a formidable Union army and designed the long-term plan that would ultimately win the war for the North. In 1861, however, Scott was 74 years old and he retired, handing over command to General George McClellan.

In the South, Davis was also both president and commander-in-chief. As he had led forces in battle, he could justify his role as a military leader more easily than Lincoln. Several hundred officers of the US army joined the CSA forces, which helped strengthen their military leadership. In March 1861, the Confederates' Congress initially approved an army of 100 000. This rose to over 350 000 by January 1862 and reached a peak of just over 480 000 in January 1864, before dropping to 445 000 in January 1865. Northern army figures for January 1862 were 575 000 and in January 1865 were 959 000. All the generals on the two sides had been educated at the same military college, West Point, where they had learned the same – now outdated – principles and strategies of warfare. However, the two sides' military tactics did begin to vary as their respective leaders faced different situations.

The South

The master of these strategies was Robert E. Lee, the greatest of the Southern generals. He believed that the only way to achieve victory was to defeat the enemy in direct battle. Therefore in both 1862 and 1863, therefore, he concentrated Southern forces on the eastern front and marched them into Northern territory. There was also an important logistical benefit as the troops lived off Northern farms and therefore used up Northern resources. Southern farmers were able to harvest the crops, leaving more food for the Southern people. The 1862 attack into the North led to the Battle of Antietam, the first Northern victory on the eastern front and the bloodiest battle of the war. The 1863 incursion ended in the Northern victory at Gettysburg in Pennsylvania. This was the furthest the South advanced into the North. There were terrible causalities: over 20 000 on each side at the Battle of Gettysburg. The North, however, with its larger population, could absorb these losses more easily.

After Gettysburg, despite Lee's best efforts, the South was forced onto the defensive. The Confederates rarely risked large-scale battles, mainly because they lacked the necessary resources. At this stage of the Civil War, the North also tended to avoid direct conflict, but this was for completely different reasons.

The North

When the North won battles and its armies advanced, it had to maintain lengthening lines of communication through hostile Southern territory. The high number of casualties resulting from the battles also created tension among the anti-war sections of the North, as people were greatly angered by any Northern loss of life. Lincoln had to be wary of public opinion as he needed public support for continuing the war and for winning re-election.

This is why the initial Northern strategy, devised by Scott with the support of Lincoln, aimed to strangle the South by surrounding it on all sides: the Anaconda Plan. Scott believed that the South might win if the North directly invaded the South. This was another reason for the North to take an indirect approach to victory by using the Anaconda Plan.

A year of conventional, limited war had brought little success. By the summer of 1862, the South was dominant on the eastern front and providing determined opposition on the western front.

Thus, the North decided it would go to war with the Southern people rather than their armies. It would wear down resistance by occupying more and more Southern land, controlling the CSA's economy and undermining its resistance. The North believed that this would win the war without the risk of fighting too many major battles.

Therefore, after the summer of 1862, the North began fighting a different type of war. It refined its military strategy by prioritising its main campaigns. Resources went to the campaign to gain control of the Mississippi River. The troops on the Virginian front to the east were instructed only to hold their position rather than advancing any further. The North's main priority was the western front. This was a reflection of two factors: Lee's dominance of the eastern front, and the relative success achieved by Northern forces west of the Appalachian Mountains under the leadership of Ulysses S. Grant and William T. Sherman in 1862–63.

Lincoln appointed Grant as the commander of the federal forces in March 1864. Grant made sure that the Northern military effort was unrelenting, keeping Southern forces fully stretched. Sherman, a close colleague of Grant, took his place as leader on the western front and also proved an effective military leader. Together, Grant and Sherman developed a new type of warfare that many saw as unconventional, and much more ruthless. Sherman's advance towards Atlanta in the spring of 1864 was coordinated with Grant's offensive on the eastern front. Here, Grant decided on continuous warfare against Lee's army. For 44 days in the summer of 1864, the armies of Grant and Lee engaged in a series of non-stop battles. After this both sides settled for trench warfare around Petersburg, south of Richmond. The constant fighting resulted in many casualties. In less than seven weeks, the North's army of the Potomac (the major Union force in the east) suffered 65 000 casualties, which roughly equalled the size of Lee's army. Such figures caused Grant to be seen as a callous leader, indifferent to the wellbeing of his men.

Throughout the autumn of 1864, the South experienced a rapid decline. Food was running short. By December, Sherman had taken both Savannah and Atlanta and cut the Confederacy in two. On Sherman's infamous 'March through Georgia' his men destroyed buildings and crops, and the terror they inspired demoralised the South. A few months later, after some final attempts to break the Northern stranglehold, Lee surrendered to Grant at Appomattox. His capital, Richmond, had been abandoned – and torched – a few days before. The war was over.

The contrast between Northern and Southern approaches to the war

Charles W. Ramsdell, in a classic analysis of the Civil War from 1944 (*Behind the Lines in the Southern Confederacy*), pointed to the Southern political leaders' failure to understand the centrality of economy and finance to success in war. The CSA suffered shortages of supplies, inflation, transport breakdowns and corruption – the latter always seeming to grow up in situations where the economic infrastructure does not deliver.

These deficiencies undermined the armies, but they also lowered morale on the home front, something which is essential to maintaining support for a conflict and also has a material effect on the fighting spirit of the armies in the field.

William Freehling, in *The South Vs. the South* suggests that a key weakness was that, whatever their views on slavery, states' rights and so on, half of all Southerners nevertheless opposed secession and the creation of the Confederacy. He argues that these anti-Confederate Southerners fatally undermined the Confederacy. White men in border states such as Missouri, Kentucky, and Maryland (which remained outside the CSA), had divided loyalties: fewer joined the Confederate army than joined Union forces or stayed home. If these Upper South men had enlisted in the way that Deep South white men did there would have been a smaller number of Confederate casualties, with a significant effect on fighting ability and morale.

The border states remaining in the Union also meant that much of the South's urban population and industrial capacity also remained there. In addition, escaping or liberated Southern blacks meant additional labour and troops for the North.

We should also remember that North and South were strongly contrasted societies. The Confederacy was more troubled by internal division than the North. Most obviously, there was a systemic conflict between state and Confederate governments. An aspect of this was that the South had state loyalty but no patriotism around CSA as such, unlike the concept of USA which had been allowed to develop for over a century. This created the military hindrance that the Southern forces were state armies, not CSA armies, so their primary aim was defending the home state, as can be seen in Lee's motivation for accepting the CSA commission over a Union one.

There were disruptive personal differences between members of Davis's cabinet, as well as between President Davis and almost everyone else – including generals, senators and his own vice president. Afterwards, unsurprisingly, beaten generals Lee and P.G.T. Beauregard both blamed Davis for defeat. (Beauregard later became an advocate of black voting rights.) Some historians agree that these divisions existed, but note that the North too faced internal conflicts and that, at points, Southern military policy came close to winning.

We should remember too that the two sides had very different aims for the war, and this difference affected their attitudes to its conduct:

- The USA was committed to the maintenance of the Union. This meant an aggressive course of action to retake the South and crush its forces.
- The CSA was committed to secession, so really only wanted to prevent invasion. Its forces crossed into the North only to knock out the USA. Therefore, occupying enemy territory was not as significant a success to the South as it was for the North.

Several historians contrast the personalities of Davis and Lincoln. Lincoln was skilled in both defining policy and coping with defeats and criticism, and Davis was less able to do this.

Leadership, economics, strategy, contrasting aims, morale, social and political division and, failed diplomacy were all significant.

Resources available

The USA had a great advantage in resources over the CSA from the start. As the *Lansing Republican* from the state of Michigan put it in April 1861: 'We have immense superiority in population, wealth, food, and manufacturing and naval power and, having bravery and endurance in equal quantities, can demonstrate success for our cause with mathematical precision.'

Superiority in population

The North had a huge advantage in population, as Table 2.1 shows.

US population 1860 (millions)					
States (number)	Whites	Blacks			Total
		Free	Slave	
Free	19	18.1	0.2	–	18.3
Slave	15	8.0	0.2	4	12.2

Table 2.1: Population breakdown of free and slave states in 1860

This advantage was also increasing with time. The total population of the USA was growing rapidly, by around one-third every ten years. In 1850 the population was 22.3 million. As the 1860 census explained, this growth was helped by 'a large immigration from Europe with an influx of considerable magnitude from Asia to California'. The Census later went on to explain that 'for each white immigrant located in the slaveholding states, eight have settled in the free states'.

So, the population of the free states was growing at around 40% per decade, while the slave states were growing at some 25%. Demographic changes had great consequences for the sectional balance of US government and therefore the composition of the US House of Representatives. In the Civil War, the imbalance was even greater as the four border (slave) states decided not to leave the USA: their combined population was around 2 million.

Superiority of wealth

Cotton grown in the South was extremely important because it generated significant wealth for the US economy as well as for slave-owners themselves. The growing industrial economy of the North appeared to be more prosperous than the seemingly static society of the South. However, but the evidence does not always support the assertion. The pioneering work of Robert Fogel and Stanley Engerman in *Time on the Cross: The Economics of American Negro Slavery,* published to great controversy in 1974, provides much data to show that the Southern economy was much more productive and dynamic than previously thought. In addition, the South argued there was little difference between the living standards of their slaves and those of the North's working class, who lived in slums and suffered harsh working conditions.

Superiority of manufacturing and naval power

The slave states produced just 5% of American iron according to the 1860 Census. All 470 locomotive engines produced in 1859–60 were manufactured in free or border states. The 1860 Census identified 239 establishments which made the firearms needed to fight the war. Nearly half were produced by just nine factories in the state of Connecticut. No Southern states were listed as producing a significant number of firearms. So, the industrial sector of the US economy was based in the towns and cities of the North. As for naval power, the US navy was an almost entirely Northern institution. At the start of the war, all 42 ships of the US navy stayed in the Union, as did most of its officers. The Confederacy had to rely on its own ingenuity or look to other countries to supply ships to challenge the US navy and its tightening blockade.

Superiority of railways

By 1860, the USA had 48 000 km of rail track. 34 000 km of this were in the North. These new tracks and trains had many limitations. The most obvious one was the different width of the rail racks of different railway companies (there were said to be 11 different gauges in the North). Nevertheless, the railways revolutionised warfare because they enabled large numbers of infantry and large amounts of supplies to travel quickly.

In January 1862, the North formed the United States Military Rail Road (USMRR) to coordinate the organisation of railways in the interests of Northern campaigns. Southern efforts to do something similar ran up against the reluctance of individual states to concede power over their railways to the CSA. States' rights here worked against the Confederacy which had been formed to protect the idea. The USMRR organised the best example of the strategic benefits of the railways. In September 1863, after the setback of losing at Chickamauga, the North used the USMRR to move 25 000 troops 1900 kilometres from Virginia to northern Alabama in just 11 days. This helped to ensure that the North kept hold of Chattanooga, 'the gateway to the South'. The military value of railways is further indicated by the fact that armies put time and effort into destroying their opponents' rail lines. During Sherman's march through Georgia, his troops tore up several hundred kilometres of Southern railway track.

59

Superiority of war finance

The American Civil War was extremely expensive. The war is estimated to have cost 1.5 times the country's Gross National Product in 1860.

Direct costs of the US Civil War, 1860 ($ millions)			
	North	**South**	**Total**
Government expenditure	2302	1032	3334
Physical destruction	–	1487	1487
Loss of human capital	1064	767	1831
Total cost	3366	3286	6652
Cost per head of population ($)	148	376	212

Table 2.2: The financial costs of the Civil War in 1860. (The monetary value placed on those soldiers who died or were injured during the war – human capital – is based on loss of subsequent earnings.)

The figures in Table 2.2 must be treated with great caution, especially those for the South, as their record-keeping during the war was often minimal. The most reliable figure is government expenditure, which reveals a significant difference between North and South.

In the 19th century, Americans were lightly taxed by both state and federal governments. During the war the rival governments took three steps, all with potential problems or disadvantages. They:

1 imposed new taxes; but taxes could not be raised too high or people would protest and/or avoid paying
2 sold bonds on which interest was paid' but the debt might get so great that the government spent too much of its current income on debt interest and lenders might believe the government was unable to fund new debts
3 circulated paper money which was not backed by gold or silver coins; but the more notes a government prints, the more the value falls, creating inflation.

Both sides tried all three methods of funding, but in different proportions at different times and with varying effects.

At the start of the war, while facing exceptional costs, neither side had much money.

The North first introduced **income tax** in 1861, but this was only done effectively with the 1862 Revenue Act. This was because the act created a federal Bureau of Internal

Revenue to collect all domestic taxes, direct and indirect. Soon some 4000 federal taxmen were assessing incomes. This development was only acceptable because of the needs of war. The South introduced an income tax only in April 1863 as the tradition of states' rights was so strong that there was no CSA equivalent of the Internal Revenue Bureau. As a result, the North raised much more in taxes than the South. One estimate says that direct taxes provided just 8% of CSA income compared with 24% of Union income. So, in 1863 the CSA introduced a tax-in-kind on farm produce in an unorthodox attempt to feed its armies, but this created its own problems. Collection from resentful producers (often women whose husbands were in uniform) was challenging and sometimes left farming families a step closer to starvation themselves. Storage and distribution turned out to be too complex for the state's infrastructure. The Confederacy became the owner of warehouses full of perishable supplies which it was often unable to transport before they rotted.

KEY TERM

Income tax: Tax taken as a particular percentage of the income of workers. In the modern world it is the most important source of governmental revenue, but, in the 19th century, it was a controversial addition to the more normal property taxes. In the USA and CSA alike, there were serious legal questions as to whether the central government, rather than the states, could collect it.

Both sides borrowed more. Here again the North was much more successful. The purchase of US bonds was much greater than investment in CSA bonds. In 1862, the North employed a banker, Jay Cooke, to sell its bonds. As part of his sales strategy, Cooke appealed to popular patriotic support for the war. The sales of bonds was so significant that, at the end of the war, in July 1865, the Philadelphia *Press* commented: 'This nation owes a debt to Jay Cooke that it cannot soon discharge … No one who appreciates the genius and patriotism which led us through the fiery ordeal would hesitiate to place the great financier of war alongside its greatest generals.'

Northern bonds could be bought with bank notes and redeemed in gold or silver. The North's credit was better than the South's, which lacked the tax base and resources needed to support its borrowing.

Both sides printed money. The South was first to do so, at the start of the war, mainly because it had less tax revenue. But using the Southern 'greybacks' was not made compulsory as that was thought too controversial. This was a major difference from the North, whose 'greenbacks' became the legal tender. Many Southerners chose not to pay their bills with greybacks. At the same time, individual states printed their own paper currency (and indeed within them some counties and banks). While there was some inflation in the North, in the South, inflation was soon out of control.

KEY CONCEPT

Causation

This section has been about the many advantages which the USA had over the CSA, which might make it seem that the CSA never had a chance, and that the USA's victory was inevitable. How far do you accept that this is so? Do you agree that these advantages were significant? If so, were economic reasons the key factor underlying the USA's victory?

Impact of foreign influences (Britain and France)

Given the immigrant nature of US society, European countries and their governments were closely involved in the American Civil War. Both North and South hoped for support from other states, particularly Britain.

Britain was important because it was:

- the leading industrial power of the time
- the main market for America's most valuable product, raw cotton
- home of many emigrants to America (at this time the UK included Ireland).
- the world's leading naval power
- the only great power with a land border with the USA – Canada, a destination for many fugitive slaves.

As such, its response to the outbreak of war could greatly affect the outcome.

At the start of the war, Britain saw the conflict as being about tariffs. Lincoln's inauguration speech showed his main concern was to preserve the Union, not abolish slavery.

The North wanted to protect their infant manufacturing industries against British competititon by raising tariffs. The South wanted to encourage trade and commerce, especially in their staple product, cotton, by keeping tariffs low. The British misread the passage of the Morrill Tariff Act in March 1862, which increased tariffs on all imports from around 14% to around 26%, as a cause of the conflict rather than a consequence.

The trade in raw cotton between the South and the UK was of great importance to both economies. 'King Cotton' was so important to the British economy that the South misjudged its position and power.

> The British journalist W. H. Russell reported in his published diary for 18 April 1861 a meeting with Southern businessmen:
>
> > These worthy gentlemen regarded her [England] as a sort of appanage [dependency] of their cotton kingdom. 'Why, sir, we have only to shut off your supply of cotton for a few weeks and we can create revolution in Great Britain. There are four millions of your people depending on us for their bread, not to speak of many millions of dollars. No, sir, we know that England must recognise us.'
>
> *From* **My Diary North and South,** W.H Russell, 1862

In May 1861, cotton producers in the South burned bales of raw cotton as part of an embargo on its export. This 'cotton diplomacy' was an attempt to influence Britain to support the CSA in order to regain cotton supplies. Britain simply looked elsewhere for replacement supplies and so the tactic was abandoned.

The South had expected Britain to recognise the CSA and even go to war on its behalf. Britain did neither. Supporting the South, particularly as an ally, could drive the North to attack British Canada. In the same month as Southerners began burning cotton, Britain announced its neutrality 'during the existing hostilities between between the United States of America and the states calling themselves the Confederate States of America', recognising the CSA as a belligerent but not as a state. The South's only comfort was that this awarded it belligerent rights to stop and search neutral shipping.

Such was British power at the time that all other major powers followed suit in not recognising the CSA as a state. A continuing issue for almost the rest of the war was whether Britain would abandon neutrality in favour of recognising the CSA and so tip the balance in favour of the South.

Neutrality also limited the scope for British shipyards to build warships for belligerents. Again, other powers followed suit. British shipbuilders and CSA diplomats did find ways around some of the laws of neutrality. Some ships were built without armaments, which were then added once the ship had left the UK. This was the case with perhaps the best-known example, the

CSS Alabama, which left Liverpool in the summer of 1862 under the name *Enrica* before being armed. As a commerce raider, it went on to inflict great damage on US commercial shipping. At the outbreak of war, only two state-owned shipyards (in Florida and Virginia) lay in CSA territory. There were already some privately owned ones but there was a shortage of expertise. From an unpromising start, the CSA navy expanded to over 100 ships. Nine of these were built in Europe. Many others were vessels that had joined as, for example, blockade runners or privateers. The war saw the first-ever battle of iron ships, at Hampton Roads, Virginia, over two days in March 1862.

The Northern *USS Monitor,* built in a New York shipyard, fought the Southern *CSS Virginia,* which had been rebuilt from a US warship skuttled a few weeks previously. The Battle of Hampton Roads was caused by the CSA's need to break the US blockade. Though it failed to do so, it showed the potential of iron-clad ships.

The CSA commissioned British shipbuilders to build two iron-clad hybrid steam and sailing ships called 'rams'. At their bow was a seven-foot iron spike which would ensure the destruction of any wooden ships which got in the way. The ships were designed to perform in coastal waters as well as the ocean in order to disrupt Northern trade and to challenge its blockade. Both were seized by the British authorities in October 1863.

Neutrality was also the cause of the most serious dispute between Britain and the North – the so-called Trent Affair of late 1861. US naval forces seized two Confederate diplomats sailing on a British ship, the *RMS Trent,* and took them to the USA. The Northern press was delighted, the British press outraged and the legal situation was disputed. An intense, if short-lived diplomatic and financial crisis followed. Britain sent 10 000 troops to stand by in Canada. Lincoln released the diplomats.

Southern **blockade runners** did their best to break the evermore effective blockade with ships such as the *CSS Alabama.* Measuring the effectiveness of the US blockade of CSA ports is hard to do, if only because the criteria for doing so can vary greatly. We know that some blockade runners got through, but, as the war progressed, the number of safe Confedrate ports became fewer and the ships' work became harder.

As the war dragged on into 1862, the impact on British cotton workers became greater, so Britain and France considered politicial intervention in the war by offering to mediate between the two sides. The closest they came to doing this was in the autumn of 1862. France's Emperor Napoleon supported the idea and suggested drawing in Russia. Russia had fought the Crimean War of 1854–56 against Britain and France and was not friendly with either country, and so refused to intervene. Britain and France could not agree. Britain stuck to its policy of neutrality.

KEY TERM

Blockade runner: A fast sea-worthy steamship used to evade the naval blockade undetected, usually by sailing at night. They would bring in vital imports, including munitions. They tended to be privately owned vessels, many built in Britain. If spotted, a blockade runner would attempt to outrun and outmanoeuvre the blockade patrol ships, often successfully.

ACTIVITY 2.5

Do you think mediation by Britain and France was ever a realistic option? Would Lincoln have accepted any intervention which implied international recognition of the CSA?

In 1863, Napoleon proposed Anglo-French intervention in the war on the side of the South, but could not persuade Britain to abandon neutrality. Then, in the autumn of 1863, Russia unexpectedly sent its Baltic Sea fleet to New York and its Pacific fleet to San Francisco. Both stayed for several months. The North welcomed the Russians as an implied warning to France and Britain not to intervene.

The war ends

While all this diplomacy was being worked out, the fighting continued. Eventually, Robert E. Lee's army of North Virginia surrendered to General-in-Chief Ulysses Grant at Appomattox Court House on 9 April 1865. The war was effectively over, though it took another month for all CSA armies to follow Lee's action, and sporadic guerrilla action continued for months and even years.

Figure 2.2: Robert E. Lee makes the official surrender to Ulysses S. Grant to end the Civil War, 9 April 1865

This painting is one of many made to commemorate the surrender at Appomattox, in what was apparently a meeting between an embarrassed Grant and an ashamed Lee. In what ways is this painting interesting as a historical interpretation?

Just five days after Lee's surrender, President Lincoln was assassinated by a CSA supporter. He was replaced by his vice president, Andrew Johnson, whose leadership was so controversial that, in 1868, he was impeached.

Jefferson Davis lived for another 24 years. He was captured and imprisoned for two years and then he was pardoned by Johnson in 1868. Davis eventually wrote his memoirs while becoming a focus for what became known as the Lost Cause. This was an umbrella term for all those who believed that the South was not as wicked and ineffective as it was portrayed, the North not so worthy and successful, and that the main cause of the great conflict was states' rights, not slavery. Nonetheless, after a war lasting longer than expected, battles causing more casualties, the South proving more resilient and the North acting more slowly, legal slavery had gone.

Re-read your response to Activity 2.1, regarding the advantages at the beginning of the war. Comment on how you think those advantages turned out and how they were used in the war itself.

Reflection: Would you change your original response to Activity 2.1? What has confirmed your opinion or changed your mind?

2.2 How great was the immediate impact of the Civil War (1861–65)?

Both sides in the American Civil War believed themselves to be democratic. Women could not yet vote, but nor could they in many other 19th-century democracies. Slaves could not either, but that was typical too, nor could the native populations in the developing European empires. The North was, initially, as committed as the South to maintaining slavery in the USA.

Both sides had codified constitutions which were hard to change and hard to ignore. Both constitutions limited the power of government and defined the rights of the individual. The founders of the Confederacy used the US Constitution wherever they could, amending it only where necessary. The US Constitution did not mention slavery, but it specified limits on the powers of its federal government, strengthening the rights of states.

Both the CSA and the USA held elections during the war. The 1864 presidential election in the North is remembered for the re-election of Lincoln. In the 1861 presidential election in the South, Jefferson Davis was the only candidate.

Limitations on civil liberties during the war

As the North treated secession as a rebellion, not a war, individuals fighting for the South were rebels, not soldiers. If captured, they were traitors, not prisoners of war, and thus subject to the laws of the Constitution. Civilians were divided in their attitudes to the war. A minority of Northerners, mostly Democrats (named Copperheads after a North American snake), opposed the war. A minority of Southerners supported the Union, opposing secession and the war: the creation of West Virginia stemmed from just such a division of opinion. Many Southern men joined Union forces.

What freedoms did these groups have? In a time of war, how far could they criticise their section's policies?

The Confederacy introduces conscription

In the first year of the Civil War, both sides had more than enough volunteers; more indeed than the armies could cope with. However, as the war went on, both sides needed to conscript. This had rarely occurred in the USA's history. The Constitution gave the federal government no explicit power for this.

The Confederacy was the first to introduce conscription. This was due to its much smaller population and so more urgent demand to maximise recruitment. In April 1862, the Confederate Congress passed a Conscription Act. Further laws, and modifications, followed between 1862 and 1865. The acts attracted considerable opposition. In the summer of 1862, Georgia's governor Joseph Brown said he considered the 1862 Conscription Act to be 'a bold and dangerous usurpation [taken illegally] by Congress of the reserved rights of the States and a rapid stride towards military despotism'.

Conscription was not universal. Only white men aged 18 to 35 were included, and even in this age group certain occupations, such as teaching, gave exemption. In addition, if drafted, men could nominate a substitute to join in their place or pay $300 not to join.

In October 1862, the Confederate Congress introduced another exemption. The 'twenty slave' law excused the owner or overseer of any plantation with 20 or more slaves. This was said to be in response to Lincoln's Provisional Emancipation Proclamation and the fear that it would encourage slave rebellions. Others believed the law simply preserved the interests of slave owners.

However, historians estimate that only 20% of Confederate soldiers were conscripts.

The Union introduces conscription

The Union passed the Enrolment Act in March 1863. Similar to the Confederates' 1862 Act, it too included exemptions and substitution. The law quickly provoked intense opposition: New York saw five days of rioting in June. These Draft Riots initially focused on the introduction of conscription, but then became an expression of white workers' fears about emancipated slaves taking their jobs. An estimated 120 deaths occurred, and Lincoln sent army units to restore order. However, opposition to the draft was less widespread than in the South. For one thing, the pressure on the Union forces was reduced by its willingness to recruit freed slaves, formalised in the Militia Act of 1862 and Emancipation Proclamation of 1863.

Like the South, the North introduced conscription using Congress. Historians estimate that only 2% in the Northern army were conscripts.

Steps to limit liberty in the Union

American authorities were unable to detain a citizen without following legal processes. If they did not follow legal processes the individual could ask a judge to issue a writ of 'habeas corpus'. If the writ was granted, the authorities had to release the prisoner. Section 9 of Article 1 of the US Constitution, referring to Congress, furthermore states: 'The privilege of the writ of Habeas Corpus shall not be suspended unless when in cases of rebellion or invasion public safety may require it.'

Faced with rebellion, and following the Baltimore Riots of April 1861, Lincoln suspended habeas corpus in some parts of four strategically important states.

Lincoln was worried about losing Maryland, thereby permanently isolating Washington DC. Marylanders had attacked US troops, and destroyed railroad tracks and telegraph wires in an attempt to defend their rights against the federal government.

Under Lincoln's latest orders, in the spring of 1861, a number of leading Marylanders seen as supporters of the Confederate cause were imprisoned. In Maryland, or Baltimore at least, habeas corpus was suspended and the town was under martial law.

One man challenged this. John Merryman, a Maryland farmer and militia officer was arrested for training militia men who went on to destroy railroad tracks. He applied to a US court for a writ of habeas corpus. The judge was Chief Justice Taney, who had led the Dred Scott judgement four years before, here sitting as a District judge. Taney duly issued a writ of habeas corpus, forcing the army either to release Merryman or bring him to court. The army refused, saying that it had suspended habeas corpus on the president's orders. Taney ruled that, under the Constitution, suspending habeas corpus was Congress's right, but not the president's. Lincoln disagreed, arguing that the Constitution did not specify who was responsible for any suspension. He ignored Taney's court order. Merryman stayed in jail for several months before being released without trial. In the summer and autumn, further Maryland politicians and newspaper editors were imprisoned. Lincoln asked Congress to approve his suspension of habeas corpus, but they didn't do this until March 1863. Until then, Lincoln continued to act against prisoners' rights.

In September 1862, he extended his suspensory action across the whole of the USA.

The reason he gave was: 'Disloyal persons are not adequately restrained by the ordinary processes of law from hindering this measure [the draft].'

Expanding the suspension of habeas corpus to cover all Northern areas, whether a theatre of war or not, created the military commission. These military courts tried soldiers and civilians for supporting the Confederacy, without the constitutional protections of the Bill of Rights. An estimated 4000 military commissions were held during the war. These were mainly in border states and mainly to hear charges such as being a Confederate spy.

By 1863, more people in the North were critical of Lincoln's war policies. Some said he had changed the aim of the war from maintaining the Union to abolishing slavery. Some opposed the introduction of conscription and the suspension of habeas corpus. The Peace Democrats, or Copperheads, wanted an early end to the war and some kind of settlement with the South.

'Copperhead' Clement Vallandigham's experiences of 1863–64 illustrate the complex issues raised by having to fight a prolonged civil war while also continuing with democratic politics under the US Constitution.

Vallandigham led the Peace Democrats in the House of Representatives. He became increasingly critical of Lincoln's strategies. He did not advocate the use of force to stop the war effort, but urged people to use their political powers at the ballot box. However, his language became heated and inflammatory. In one speech at a political rally of about 10 000 people, he was alleged to have urged the crowd to 'hurl King Lincoln from his throne'. In May 1863, he was arrested in the middle of the night by a troop of 100 US soldiers who broke into his house. Their authority came not from a judge but from General Burnside, the military commander for the region. Vallandigham was charged with breaching General Order 38, which Burnside had issued a few weeks earlier with the aim of subduing local opposition to the war. Vallandigham was accused of expressing 'disloyal sentiments and opinions'.

Vallandigham didn't face a court but instead faced the eight army officers of a military commission. He refused to recognise it because it was not properly constituted under US law and because civil courts were still sitting in Ohio. After a two-day trial, the commission found him guilty and sentenced him to imprisonment for the rest of the war. An application was made to a civil court for a writ of habeas corpus, but the judge ruled that in times of war military authority was needed to ensure victory. The US Supreme Court subsequently refused to consider Vallandigham's case because it had no authority to consider cases decided in military courts.

In the North, Burnside's actions against Vallandigham became perhaps the biggest political issue of the war. Rallies were held to protest. The first that Lincoln knew of it all, however, was when he read newspaper reports. Republicans as well as Democrats opposed Burnside's actions, including all of Lincoln's cabinet. Burnside offered his resignation. Lincoln refused to accept it: he had to publicly support his military leaders. Instead, he ordered that Vallandigham be exiled to the Confederacy, thus removing him from being the focus of protests in the North. The story did not end there for Vallandigham and Burnside. Vallandigham boarded a blockade runner to Bermuda, reached Canada and re-entered the North, where he drafted the Democrats' 1864 party election platform. The authorities ignored him. Burnside sent troops to close down the pro-peace *Chicago Times* in June 1863. This time, Lincoln ordered the decision be reversed.

When Lincoln received details of a New York state meeting criticising the government's record on civil liberties, he skilfully used it to write a detailed reply justifying the government's actions, which he then published. The best-known extract from this vigorous, carefully argued reply is his rhetorical question: 'Must I shoot a simple-minded soldier boy who deserts while I must not touch a hair of a wiley agitator who induces him to desert?'

Steps to limit liberty in the Confederacy

In 1861, the South was not as vulnerable as the North was with regard to Maryland, so there was not another Merriman. In 1863, there were no Southern Unionists arguing that Jefferson Davis had changed the goal and methods of war, so there was no Vallandigham.

Nevertheless, like Lincoln, Davis argued that the special needs of war meant limiting civil liberties. The South had its critics. Many people were subject to martial law, which was first passed in February 1862, then extended in various parts of the South thereafter, with growing opposition as the war progressed. There were no Southern military commissions, but there were Habeas Corpus Commissioners employed to decide whether civilian prisoners in military prisons should be freed, sent for civilian trial or detained indefinitely. However, Confederacy court and prison records were often incomplete, however, and the topic of civil liberties in the South has, until recently, been relatively neglected. As a result, it is more difficult to get a clear and accurate picture of the imposition of military rule in the South.

If there were similarities of process between North and South, there were also some distinctions. In part, this was because of a big difference between Northern and Southern attitudes towards each other:

- The North saw the South as part of the United States, thus all Southerners remained US citizens.
- The South, claiming independence, saw the North as a separate state and its citizens as foreigners.

In this context the CSA took two notable steps:

- The Alien Enemies Act of 1861 required all Southerners to declare themselves to be Confederacy citizens or leave or face arrest.
- The Sequestration Act of 1861 allowed the seizure of the property of absentee Unionists, or property which might be transferred to absentee Unionists, such as via the wills of the deceased. The implementation of this act led to considerable resentment across the South, even though there was little obvious opposition.

Like the North, the South issued internal passports – travel passes – to those travelling between the two. Unlike the North, it also introduced documents for travelling within its own territory. Issued by an army officer, each pass validated a particular journey. Few requests for a travel pass appear to have been rejected. If introducing the pass was intended to limit the movement of enemies of the Confederacy, its implementation seems to have had little effect, apart from inconveniencing people who had to apply for one or whose journey was interrupted because they didn't have one.

The 1863 Impressment Act gave Confederate armies the power to seize what they needed in terms of supplies, whether of food, fuel or slaves. Local Impressment Boards fixed the prices of supplies for people to buy, almost always at levels lower than the market prices.

In addition, the 1863 Tax-In-Kind Act enabled state officials to collect 10% of certain crops, such as corn and wheat, to help the war effort. Tax-in-Kind Assessors – soon dubbed TIK men – visited family properties, deciding what they would take as their one-tenth tax. The two acts caused much resentment. A state-regulated economy was the last thing expected of a Confederacy based on the rights of states and individuals. This legislation helped to provoke the Richmond Bread Riot of April 1863, even if the main causes were economic rather than political. The headline in the *New York Daily Tribune* outlined the essential features of the riot:

BREAD RIOT IN RICHMOND

THREE THOUSAND WOMEN IN REVOLT

They are Armed with Guns, Clubs and Stones

GOVERNMENT AND PRVATE STORES BROKEN OPEN

The Militia Fail to Check the Rioters

Jeff Davis Makes an Address and Restores Order

Headlines from The New York Daily Tribune, April 1863

This was one of a series of bread riots across the South. Its size suggests it had been planned. Its leader was Mary Jackson, a meat seller. She organised the march through the capital, a woman taking a lead in political protest at a time when men dominated public life. The *Tribune*'s report omits to mention the arrest of some of the rioters.

Reasons for and responses to the Emancipation Proclamation, 1863

Reasons behind the proclamation

Since the beginning of the war, the institution of slavery had started to crumble. Northern armies were advancing into slave territory. Slavery was abolished in Washington DC. Fugitive slaves headed for the capital and for Northern army camps, where they often worked for the army.

By the summer of 1863, Lincoln had argued publicly for the offer of freedom to slaves in slave states controlled by the rebels. No offer of freedom was made to slaves in the four border slave states which had joined the North in 1861. Like the blockade, the proclamation was an attack on the South's economy: if they knew they would be freed, more slaves would run away and the CSA's war effort would be undermined.

Lincoln's colleagues persuaded him to delay announcing such a radical change of policy until there was some good news for the North. On 22 September 1862, a week after the relatively successful battle of Antietam, Lincoln issued the Preliminary Emancipation Proclamation: slaves in rebel states would be set free on 1 January 1863. The delay gave slave states the chance to end their rebellion and commit themselves to emancipation. None did so.

Like Davis, Lincoln had declared the war to be about the union. The Emancipation Proclamation meant Northern war aims were no longer to return to the position of 1861. Abolition was now the central issue of the fighting. The USA recognised the freedom of slaves in the Southern states which were still in rebellion and slaves 'of suitable condition' would be accepted to serve in the US armed forces.

The proclamation excluded the border states and West Virginia, which had stayed in the Union, and Tennessee and parts of Louisiana which Union troops had occupied. These limits to emancipation reflected Lincoln's fear that the Supreme Court would overturn the proclamation, deeming it unconstitutional.

Lincoln justified the change of policy by stressing that the Proclamation was 'a fit and necessary war measure' to suppress the rebellion in the specified states. He justified its constitutionality by arguing that it was an order of the president in his role as commander-in-chief of the armed forces. However, Lincoln did take care to discourage any slave uprising, urging slaves 'to abstain from violence, unless in necessary self-defence'.

The Emancipation Proclamation

Now seen as a key civil rights document, Lincoln's proclamation can also be seen in a different light.

I, Abraham Lincoln, President of the United States of America, and Commander-in-Chief of the Army and Navy thereof, do hereby proclaim and declare that hereafter, as heretofore, the war will be prosecuted for the object of practically restoring the constitutional relation between the United States, and each of the States, and the people thereof, in which States that relation is, or may be, suspended or disturbed.

That it is my purpose, upon the next meeting of Congress to again recommend the adoption of a practical measure tendering pecuniary aid to the free acceptance or rejection of all slave States, so called, the people whereof may not then be in rebellion against the United States and which States may then have voluntarily adopted, or thereafter may voluntarily adopt, immediate or gradual abolishment of slavery within their respective limits; and that the effort to colonize persons of African descent, with their consent, upon this continent, or elsewhere, with the previously obtained consent of the Governments existing there, will be continued.

From the Emancipation Proclamation,
1 January 1863

ACTIVITY 2.8

Read the beginning of the Preliminary Emancipation Proclamation below. Construct an argument that Lincoln's wish was to free slaves. Now think about the situation from the Confederate states' points of view. Other than winning the war, what might they have done to keep control of their slaves?

That on the first day of January in the year of our Lord, one thousand eight hundred and sixty-three, all persons held as slaves within any State, or designated part of a State, the people whereof shall then be in rebellion against the United States shall be then, thenceforward, and forever free; and the executive government of the United States, including the military and naval authority thereof, will recognize and maintain the freedom of such persons, and will do no act or acts to repress such persons, or any of them, in any efforts they may make for their actual freedom …

From the Preliminarily Emancipation
Proclamation, 22 September 1862

Responses to the Emancipation Proclamation

For the North, the proclamation meant that a war for unity was now also a war for emancipation. The mixed feelings about this may have been indicated in the 1862 mid-term elections (see 'The nature of democracy in the North and the South', below). For the South, a war for independence was now a war in defence of slavery. As the Union armies advanced, the freeing of slaves meant their owners' were deprived of a substantial part of their property. In addition, as news spread, the number of escaping slaves increased, making the already acute labour problem even worse.

A few leaders in the South argued that, to counter Lincoln's proclamation, the CSA armies should start recruiting black soldiers. The proposal never gained support and only tiny numbers were ever put in uniform in the South.

At first, the proclamation could change nothing for most southern slaves. A large minority, however – an estimated 500 000 to 700 000 – headed for Northern camps and freedom.

Northern forces moving into Southern territory in 1863 freed further slaves as they went. Some 10 000 black men served in the US navy, and 180 000 in the US army, most famously the 54th Massachusetts Regiment. Their contribution to the Northern war effort stimulated discussion of their future. Thus, in the later 1860s, they were granted US citizenship and the right to vote. Meanwhile, as Northern armies advanced, the issue of the post-war position of slavery became an urgent issue.

The Emancipation Proclamation was issued as a war measure and its legality under the Constitution was unsettled at first. The 1850 Fugitive Slave Act was repealed in March 1864, but until the Constitution was changed, slavery was still legal. Finally, in 1864–65, the Republican-controlled Congress passed the 13th **Amendment**, which abolished slavery in all states: 'Neither slavery nor involuntary servitude, except as a punishment for crime whereof the party shall have been duly convicted, shall exist in the United States, or any place subject to its jurisdiction … Congress shall have the power to enforce this article by appropriate legislation.'

Passed by Congress in early 1865, three-quarters of the states approved the change, as the Constitution required, and, in December 1865, the 13th Amendment became law. The USA, at least on the subject of slavery, was no longer a house divided.

> ### 🔑 KEY TERM
>
> **Amendment:** The US Constitution is the supreme law of the land. It can only be permanently changed by a process known as amendment. In the case of the Reconstruction amendments this required two-thirds of the House of Representatives and two-thirds of the Senate to propose the amendment, and three-quarters of the state legislatures to ratify them.

Life in the Confederate States

Labelling the 11 rebel states and their 11 million inhabitants as 'the South' or 'the Confederacy' suggests a unity which did not exist in practice. In addition, by 1864, the enthusiasm with which most white Southerners had welcomed the war was long gone. Life in the South had become hard for many, especially for those who sat directly in the path of Union armies. Even for those communities not directly involved in the fighting, the Civil War affected every aspect of life in the South.

Social divisions, including slavery

The biggest, most obvious division was a social one – the fact that 3.5 million people in the South, one in every three, were slaves. According to the 1860 Census, there were also some 130 000 free blacks in the Confederacy. Once the Civil War began, many whites expected slave rebellions. At the same time, many slaves began to hope that the war might lead to their freedom, even though in the first 18 months of the war the North's declared aim was to restore the Union and not to end slavery. The slaves began to act in a variety of ways against slavery, from resisting their owners' actions on the plantations to walking to enemy lines and seeking military protection.

Jefferson Davis's 1000-acre, 200-slave plantation, close to his brother's, was located in an important theatre of war, the Mississippi Valley. In May 1862, New Orleans, 390 km down-river from Davis, fell to the Unionists. Their forces could then be expected to advance northwards to gain control of the strategically important Mississippi River. Davis ordered his brother to move important possessions, including some slaves, away from the river and into the interior of the state. Slave overseers remained, but their authority was overthrown by the slaves who had remained. The remaining slaves took control of both estates. They destroyed the brother's home and his crops and refused to work. They looked for help from Unionist forces to the north, who were involved in trying to capture Vicksburg, but initially received little, while Davis brought in Confederate soldiers. In the continuing struggle, there were losses on both sides, before Union troops were sent to liberate the remaining slaves.

ACTIVITY 2.9

Do the events on Jefferson Davis's plantation deserve to be described as a rebellion? What justifies defining it that way and what suggests a different interpretation?

The slaves' actions on the Davis plantations highlight the extremely deep divisions between slaves and their masters. Divisions also existed within in the white majority, for example between the plantation owners of the Deep South and the more independent farmers of the Upper South. At the start of the Civil War, most white Southerners supported the move to independence. The plantation owners were the focus of the North's opposition to slave power, and were probably keenest to break away in order to maintain the slavery which their wealth was based on. They tended to dominate Confederate politics, even though they formed a relatively small proportion of the total population. Most whites were not plantation owners. Some had only one or two slaves, many had no slaves and were farming alone or in small rural communities. Hence the phrase now used to illustrate this socio-economic division during the civil war: 'a rich man's war but a poor man's fight'.

ACTIVITY 2.10

Do you think that the phrase 'A rich man's war but a poor man's fight' applies more to the South or to the North? What evidence would you regard as decisive for answering this question?

The 1862 Conscription Act added to the resentment felt by the poorer majority of people towards the richer minority. The act gave an owner of at least 20 slaves exemption from military service, and, until 1864, substitutes for the draft were allowed for those who could afford to pay for them. Though the motive for this was security against slave unrest on the planations – itself an important indication of Southern fears – some criticised it as simply the rich looking after their own. In late 1863, the exemption was withdrawn, so great was the shortage of military manpower.

Political divisions

The people of the Confederacy were also divided in their loyalty to the Confederacy, as a new, slave-based social, political and economic system. There were many Southern Unionists, and every Southern state except South Carolina raised at least one unit in the Northern army. Most just kept quiet for the duration of the war. However, some did act against the Confederacy. Sometimes this was secretly, which makes providing reliable evidence of their activities difficult. Sometimes, Southern blacks fighting for freedom and Southern whites, wanting to maintain the Union, worked together to weaken the CSA's war effort. This seems to have been the case with what became known as the Richmond Underground. With echoes of the Underground Railroad, this was a small group of blacks and whites who used their positions in Confederate government departments to provide information to Unionist armies. Two of the group were women. The white woman was Elizabeth Van Lew and the black woman was one of her slaves, to whom Van Lew gave her freedom, Mary Bowser.

Another division emerged during the course of the war between those parts of the Confederacy occupied by Northern forces and those which escaped military occupation. This became especially clear once Unionist forces moved deep into the South in 1864–65, and aimed their 'scorched earth' policy as much against the people as against Confederate forces. States hardest hit included Virginia, a major theatre of war from start to finish, and, in the latter stages, Georgia and South Carolina.

The Confederate economy

In 1861, the Southern economy was based almost exclusively on agriculture. Plantations typically produced sugar, tobacco and cotton for sale in the North and Europe. At this time, the South produced two thirds of the world's cotton. So, plantations were the main source of wealth in the South. However, the majority of the white population lived in small rural communities, farming cattle, pigs and crops which were traded locally.

Although a similar percentage of the population lived on farms in the North as in the South, there were few factories in the South compared with the North. In 1861, there were approximately 110 000 factories in the North, compared with 20 000 in the South. Before the war, most of the South's manufactured goods, including munitions and clothing, were imported from the North and from Europe.

Following the outbreak of war, the people of the South soon experienced economic hardship. The naval blockade by the North quickly had a devastating effect, as the South's cash crop of raw cotton could not be exported to Britain and manufactured goods could not be imported. Basic foodstuffs such as salt, essential as a preservative, were soon in short supply. By December 1861, a few months into the war, the price of salt in one city in Georgia had risen from 50 cents per sack to $10, a 20-fold increase.

The naval blockade caused exports of cotton to almost completely stop. Only small amounts carried by blockade runners could be exported. The CSA had planned to finance the war through tariffs on imports and taxes on exports, but it was unable to do this because of the naval blockade. Instead of raising taxes, the CSA government printed money and issued bonds. This led to rapid inflation and price rises for basic goods such as flour, shoes and cotton yarn. By 1863, 10 Confederate dollars had the same value as 1 Confederate dollar had in 1861.

Before the outbreak of war, the South relied on a large network of rivers and coastal ports to transport food and crops. The railway had developed as an addition to the river network, with many railroads connecting ports with inland plantations and cities, or connecting two towns which were not connected by river. Many of the railroads were short and did not connect key areas. In 1862, the Union navy gained control of the rivers in the South and blockaded the major coastal ports. The rail network struggled to transport food and goods without access to rivers and ports, which caused food shortages in many areas in the South. In 1863, the Confederate government took control of the railroads for military activity, which caused further food shortages.

The lack of transport and rapid inflation affected the urban population as food prices increased. In 1863, riots broke out in towns across the South, led by women in particular protesting against high food prices and a lack of basic goods. In April 1863, in Richmond (the Confederate capital), over 5000 people looted shops in the city for food, causing President Davis to stand on a cart and personally plead with the women to stop.

Despite widespread inflation and food shortages, people could sometimes find the resources to defy their difficulties and celebrate a special occasion, as a diary entry for Christmas Day 1863 in Richmond shows: 'We had for dinner oyster soup besides roast mutton, ham, boned turkey, wild partridge, plum pudding, sauterne, burgundy, sherry and Madeira. There is life in the old land yet!' However, the entry makes it clear that this meal was exceptional. The meal and the diary entry itself were both calculated acts of defiance and shows a refusal to be intimidated.

The introduction of a 10% tax on all farm products in 1863 did not seem to greatly affect the lifestyles of the wealthy. Conversely, poor farmers struggled as they found themselves being forced to hand over 10% of their produce.

However, by the end of the Civil War even the rich Southerners were feeling the negative effects. The diary entry of Mary Boykin Chesnut, on 23 April 1865, gives an example of this. Her family lost its 1000 slaves. 'My silver wedding day and I am sure the unhappiest day of my life. One year ago we left Richmond. The Confederacy has double-quicked downhill since then. Now we have burned towns, deserted plantations, deserted villages … poverty with no future and no hope.'

Everyone in the South suffered, if in varying degrees, from the effects of inflation, dislocation of trade and the destruction brought about by the war. White families lost sons, brothers and fathers in the continuing death toll of the battlefield, not to mention the sickness that followed every army at this time. In general, slaves benefited from moves towards emancipation, especially after 1863. However, except for those who escaped, the period of wartime itself did nothing to improve their situation in the short term. The Unionist victory provided a few years of freedom and advance, but even that ended as Unionist soldiers and politicians left the South to government by its white majority.

ACTIVITY 2.11

How far do social divisions prevent us from generalising about life in the South during the Civil War? What key differences do we need to draw attention to in order to develop a more precise understanding?

Reflection: What evidence did you use in answer to these two questions? How dependable do you think that kind of evidence is? Did other students reach the same conclusions as you?

The nature of democracy in the North and the South

One important feature of the American Civil War was that it was fought between two democracies. Both had constitutions to limit their government; the Confederate Constitution closely followed the Union one, but with several small but significant changes. The first ten Amendments of the US Constitution, more usually called the Bill of Rights, were incorporated into the CSA Constitution. Both sides allowed open elections during the war. The contest was more vigorous in the North. Lincoln faced a challenge that meant that until a few weeks before the election, he thought he would be defeated. The CSA held just one presidential election, in November 1861, but, as Davis was unopposed, he inevitably won.

However, politics involves more than just elections. By the summer of 1863, people on both sides were prepared to challenge government policies, using violence to get their message across if necessary. In Richmond, women rioted for bread. In New York, men rioted against conscription. In both cases, the governments were compelled to respond. Davis even took himself away from leading the war effort in order to address the demonstrators in Richmond.

Peaceful political debate, however, needed political parties for effective expression. The difference between North and South in this respect was significant, and this difference was a result of the different origins of the two sections. The North was the older of the two, with well-established institutions attempting to defeat a breakaway by a minority of its people. The South was brand-new, self-proclaimed but unrecognised by any other nation-state and was fighting for its freedom.

Southern politics

As a new political structure, the South was still developing its institutions. There were no Confederacy-wide political parties. For the 1861 presidential elections, there were no party conventions. The first Congress, separately elected in 1861, was broadly supportive of Davis's government, at least at first. The second Congress, in 1863, contained more who were critical of Confederate policies, but they did not group themselves into a political party.

Northern politics

In the North, candidates fought as Republicans, Democrats and smaller parties. In 1861–62, after Southern Democrats had left Washington DC, Republicans quickly passed three acts which strengthened their interests in the North and the West:

- The Morrill Tariff, 1861
- The Homestead Act, 1862
- The Transcontinental Railroad Act, 1862.

However, in the 1862 mid-term elections, when the war was not going well for the North, the Democrats gained some 25 seats in the House of Representatives, while the Republicans lost the same number.

The Republicans only kept control of the House because they allied with a smaller party composed mainly of 'War Democrats' who supported the war but disliked Republican economic policies and Lincoln's wartime violations of civil rights.

In 1864, Lincoln faced a challenge from the Democratic candidate George McLellan. Mindful of this, General Lee maintained continual fighting on the eastern front in the spring of 1864, hoping that heavy casualties would harm Lincoln's chances of getting re-elected. In July, CSA troops were within 8 km of Washington. Events such as the New York riots were a further cause of concern. Meanwhile, relations between Lincoln and the Republican Congress were strained, especially when the president vetoed a bill that would have imposed harsher terms on the CSA at the end of the war.

The Republican Party needed to respond to increasing unpopularity and war-weariness, and to avoid party loyalties by distinguishing Lincoln from the party in the 1864 presidential election. Lincoln thus stood for re-election as the '**National Union Party**' candidate to allow the War Democrats and supporters of smaller parties to vote for him, as the calculation was that they would not vote Republican.

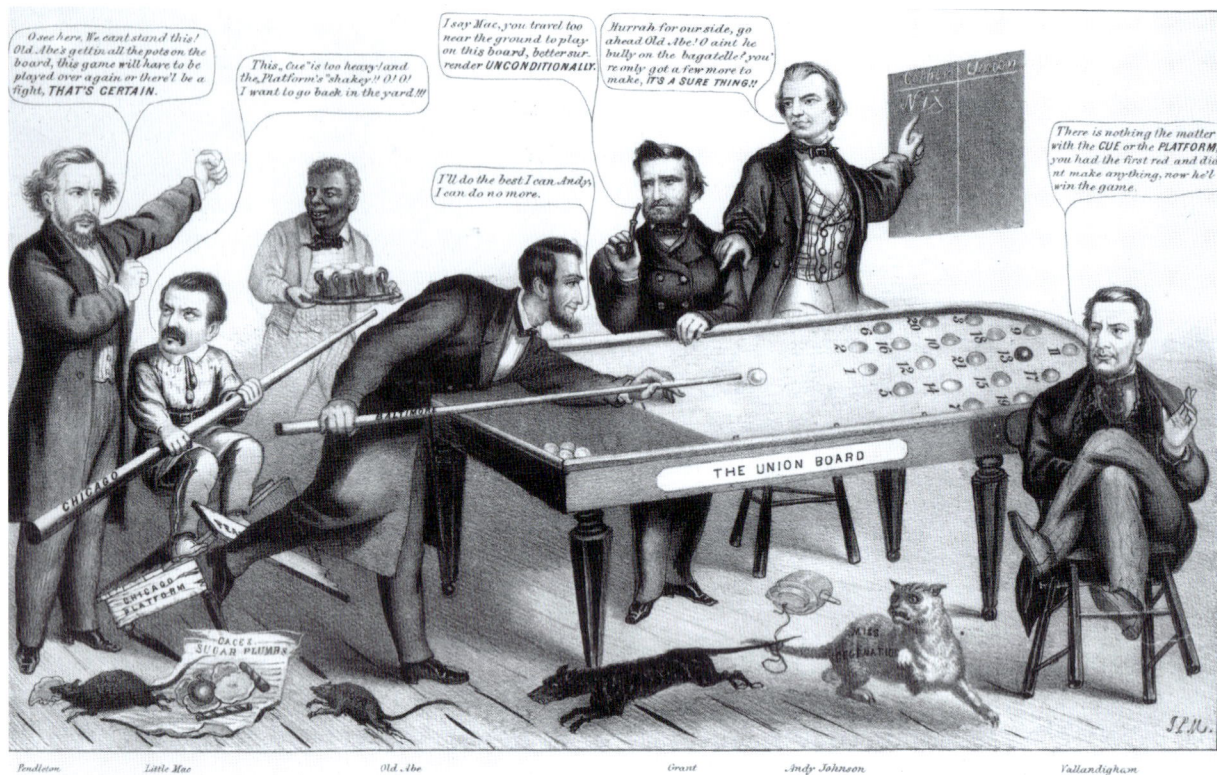

A LITTLE GAME OF BAGATELLE, BETWEEN OLD ABE THE RAIL SPLITTER & LITTLE MAC THE GUNBOAT GENERAL.

Published by J.L.Magee, South East cor. Third & Dock Sts. Philad.ª

Figure 2.3: An 1864 cartoon by John L. Magee, showing the major candidates in the presidential election, watched over by Clement Vallandigham (see 'Limitations on civil liberties during the war', earlier in this chapter). How does this source reflect the opinion of the cartoonist?

KEY TERM

National Union Party: A party created by non-radical Republicans at their party convention in 1864. They did this in order to ensure that Lincoln could stand for re-election on a moderate conservative platform, and to enable War Democrats, such as Lincoln's vice-presidential candidate Andrew Johnson, to vote for Lincoln without having to vote Republican.

Then things began to change with the fall of Atlanta on 3 September, just two months before the election. In the campaign, McLellan made problems for himself by disassociating himself with the Democrats' policy of a negotiated settlement with the South.

Lincoln won in the popular vote (55% on a 74% turnout) and in states won by 22 to 12, giving him a massive victory in the electoral college (94%).

Just as significant for the future was the Republican triumph in the congressional elections of 1864, where 136 of the 193 congressmen were now Republicans (and a 137th was an Independent Republican from Missouri). These representatives were to play a great part in addressing the problems of the country's transition to peace.

Re-elected and successfully inaugurated, in April 1865 Lincoln heard the news that Lee, with his capital taken and his army surrounded, had surrendered to General Grant. However, Lincoln had little time to enjoy the victory and plan for peace as, within days, he had been assassinated.

2.3 What were the aims and outcomes of Reconstruction?

The period from the end of the Civil War in 1865 to the inauguration of Rutherford Hayes as president in the spring of 1877 is usually referred to as the period of **Reconstruction**. In reality, Reconstruction began before the end of the Civil War and had effectively ended before Hayes took office.

KEY TERM

Reconstruction: The contemporary name, and the one generally used by historians, for the process by which the Southern states were readmitted into the Union and slavery was prohibited, in the aftermath of the US Civil War.

The stakes were high after the devastation of the war. Of the states which seceded, only Texas was relatively unscathed by the fighting. Virginia had been almost entirely destroyed. Major cities such as Atlanta, Georgia and Charleston lay in ruins. The South had a debt of $250 000, few businesses, little infrastructure (in terms of railways, for example) and an ill-educated workforce. Southerners who had invested in CSA war bonds faced financial ruin, as the bonds became worthless once the CSA ceased to exist. The abolition of slavery wiped out most of the assets of the South. The North, meanwhile, had used the Civil War to industrialise and become nearly self-sufficient in agriculture. Any reconstruction process could not be carried out on equal terms.

The reintegration of the defeated southern states into the Union was a contentious process for a number of reasons.

First, what had actually happened legally during the Civil War? Had the rebellious states left the Union? In this case, they might be readmitted as they were. Or they might be deemed to have committed what Charles Sumner dubbed 'state suicide' in leaving the Union, returning to the status of territories which could be reorganised into different states at the will of Congress. (See 'Radical Reconstruction from Congress' for more on Sumner's interpretation.) Alternatively, had secession been so deeply unconstitutional that it could not be seen as having legally happened? In this case, the question was simply one of re-establishing southern state governments which would not attempt to act illegally.

The second point was a causal question, which seemed economic. What had caused the states to secede, and how could further problems be prevented? It seemed clear that slavery had been the issue, but would simply banning slavery be enough to ensure that no further conflict could occur? Would the South need to have its economic system reshaped, and if so, who would do this? What about its social system? What was, or should be, the social status of the freed slaves?

Third came practical politics. Who had actually led in this war? Who had won and who had lost? Had the whole South lost, or just the rich planter (and slaveholding) aristocracy, dragging the silent majority of poor white conservatives along with them? Would the North be entitled to claim the 'spoils of war'? If elements from the South resisted Reconstruction, how much force might the Union (the North) use in imposing its will?

Who would lead Reconstruction?

There was a final question, one almost hardwired into the American system of government. Who would lead the Reconstruction? Northerners or Southerners? The federal government or the individual states? If it was the federal government, would the president, the courts or Congress be in charge?

During the Civil War, the president was in charge of the army, and the war effort, using his power as commander-in-chief. Congress, though, remained in charge of the country. Congressmen and senators were also becoming concerned about the expansion in presidential powers which war had prompted. Congress tried to make their own opinions heard to help to gain victory in the peace.

However, Lincoln's initial efforts at Reconstruction were part of the war, and it was winning the war which remained his priority. He wanted to encourage his opponents to surrender, meaning that the South would have to be treated favourably. He also wished to promote the electoral chances of his particular wing of the Republican Party, ensuring that the war was won in the correct way.

Lincoln's difficulty was that he preferred the middle of three options which seemed to be available, and was therefore at risk of criticism and electoral challenge from both sides.

Political view	Radical	Conservative	Copperhead
Party affiliation	Republican	Republican/National Unity	Northern 'Peace' Democrats
Essential position	• The war should be won by the Union (North). • Slavery should be ended and civil rights sought for black people. • The South should be altered so it does not rebel again.	• The war should be won by the Union (North). • Slavery should be ended. • The South should be re-integrated and normality restored.	• The war should be ended immediately. • Slavery should continue. • The war is a conspiracy by northerners to enslave poor southern whites, and is damaging the cotton trade.

Table 2.3: Northern views of the war and Reconstruction in the early to mid 1860s

Reconstruction began in 1862–63 with the appointment by Lincoln of provisional governors in newly defeated states such as Tennessee. Here, the first governor was Andrew Johnson, a politician who immediately became a general, for this was a military governorship under Lincoln's control.

During 1863, Lincoln let it be known that he intended mercy in victory. Southern states should, in his view, be readmitted to the union when 10% of their citizens had sworn loyalty, and when they had an education system which would be able to cope with the new freed slaves and constitutions which banned slavery. Beyond that, the states would retain their old powers and status. Lincoln did not wish to appear spiteful in the victory which, by the middle of 1863, seemed to be sure to come. Congressional Radicals, meanwhile, refused to seat the House and Senate delegations from newly defeated Tennessee, Louisiana and Arkansas, thus denying them parity with the northern states.

In 1863, to Lincoln's great relief, Conservative Republicans, and the now-allied War Democrats, saw off a series of challenges from Copperheads in congressional and state governer elections. They did this without giving any ground to the Radicals. In 1864, Lincoln won the nomination for the presidential election of this year, but not for the Republican Party; for the National Union Party, with Andrew Johnson, a War Democrat, as his running mate. Lincoln made sure that the Radical platform was heard at the nominating convention. He ran for re-election (the first president in 30 years to do so) on the grounds that it was 'best not to swap horses when crossing streams'.

Presidential Reconstruction: Abraham Lincoln and Andrew Johnson

With his renomination for president assured in early June 1864, Lincoln felt able to take two actions against the Radicals of his own party. He dismissed Treasury Secretary Salmon P. Chase, who was clearly surprised to have been fired despite having spent a year causing trouble trying to replace Lincoln as president. Chase objected to Lincoln's decision to offer not to emancipate slaves from states which surrendered. Later in the year, Lincoln made Chase chief justice, partly to keep the Radicals onside.

THE COPPERHEAD PARTY.——IN FAVOR OF *A VIGOROUS PROSECUTION OF PEACE!*

Figure 2.4: Named by their enemies after a species of venomous snake, Copperheads adopted the appellation themselves and used it with pride. This cartoon appeared in *Harper's weekly*, February 28th, 1863. Can this image be considered a useful historical source?

In 1864, Lincoln was faced by the Wade–Davis Bill. This was the first Reconstruction Act written by Congress. It provided for the readmission of states only when 50% of their citizens had sworn an oath to the Union (rather than Lincoln's preference of 10%), and would have forced Southerners to prove that they did not fight willingly against the North (both sides were using conscription to fill their armies). In July, Lincoln was keen to lay the ground for post-war reconciliation. He agreed to an analysis that the CSA states had never legally left the Union and opposed the bill. When both Houses passed it, he simply took no action, a tactic known as a 'pocket veto': without his signature, the bill could not become law.

Once inaugurated for his second term in 1865, Lincoln began to promote the Radical policy of amending the Constitution to abolish slavery. He made it clear that he saw this as the extent of the compulsion which would be necessary for the moment. States might choose their own means of assuring their citizens' loyalty: the federal government would only intervene if something was going wrong. The Radical objection to Lincoln, as expressed by Chase – that Lincoln had not thought things through – began to look hollow. Perhaps he had, and was simply playing politics – and was playing well.

In March 1865, Lincoln and Congress jointly established the **Freedmen's Bureau** to provide for the immediate needs of those who had been freed from slavery, or would be, upon the surrender of their states. In the short term, this meant providing food and shelter. In the medium term, it meant negotiating jobs for the freedmen. Because of the situation, these jobs were not very different from the agricultural labour they had performed as slaves.

KEY TERM

The Freedmen's Bureau: The Bureau of Refugees, Freedmen and Abandoned Lands was established in March 1865 as part of the Department of War to care for freedmen in the immediate aftermath of their emancipation. Initially established for one year, the bureau's continued operation was then vetoed by Andrew Johnson on the grounds that it was an agency of war and therefore inappropriate for peacetime. With Congressonal support, the bureau continued its work until 1869.

One of the great 'what if' questions of history is: What if Lincoln had completed Reconstruction? Would he have done it well? Historians usually conclude that he could, at least, hardly have been worse than his successor. On

14 April 1865, he was shot by a Confederate sympathiser while attending the theatre. He died the next day, and Vice President Andrew Johnson became president.

Reconstruction under President Johnson

Johnson was a War Democrat who became Lincoln's running mate on the National Unity ticket for the presidency in 1864. A Tennessean, and the only Southern senator not to follow his state in seceding in 1861, he then became the first military governor appointed under Reconstruction. When he suddenly became president, many Republican Congressmen put aside their doubts about his background as a Southern Democrat, and about his apparent alcoholism and consequently bad behaviour, to look forward to working with someone who would continue Lincoln's work. After all, in the presidential election campaign, he had declared that 'traitors should be punished'.

For Johnson, it was the South's defeat in the Civil War which showed that, constitutionally, it had been wrong to secede. The poor quality of the democratic process in the South showed that it now needed attention. This would mean completing the work of emancipation and re-equipping southern governments to engage in the politics of the USA. For Johnson the problem was that the Southern planter aristocracy had effectively taken control of Southern governance. They ran the South to the detriment of the majority of the white men there, who were yeomen smallholders. Johnson himself came from such stock. All that was required, then, was to bring the states of the South back into the Union, with the power of the planters diminished. Congress was not in session and was not due to be until December 1865, but that was not a problem as Johnson did not need their assistance. The two stories of his attempts at presidential Reconstruction are the way his relationship with Congress became hostile, and the way he changed his mind about whom he should support in the South.

In May 1865, Johnson:

- pardoned ex-Confederate soldiers and civilians, with exceptions such as major political and military office-holders and those with property, which now meant land rather than slaves, worth over $20 000
- did not change voting rights, instead suggesting that Southern states enfranchise their freedmen (but without him enforcing it as that would be an unconstitutional abuse of his power)
- where possible, returned land to its pardoned owners.

In a general atmosphere of reconciliation, only one Confederate was executed – the brutal Henry Wirz, the commander of a prison camp. The former Confederate president Jefferson Davis was imprisoned for two years, without much judicial process. This was only after Johnson considered having him executed but was told that he could not. There were no treason trials. To prove that the rebels were traitors would have been to define the legal status of the war as a defeated rebellion, rather than as a war of reconquest of the part of the USA. Johnson responded by issuing as many pardons as he could. The Southern states then accepted that they, rather than the country as whole (the economy and tax base of which was dominated by the North) would have to pay the Confederacy's war debt. They also accepted the 13th Amendment and banned slavery.

In the elections of November 1865, it became clear that the old Southern planter aristocracy remained. The former Confederate vice-president Alexander Stephens was released from prison and only a month later was nominated for the US Senate by the new legislature in Georgia (senators were not then directly elected). A series of similar results suggested that the South was unrepentant and the planters were still in control. Johnson seems not to have been entirely happy with this: he had hoped that poorer whites might take control in the South, but it is difficult to trace Johnson's views, as, by the middle of 1866, he was firmly on the side of the Southern aristocracy.

This was because of his rift with Congress. Until December 1865, Congress could do nothing official unless Johnson recalled them. The Northern Republicans who dominated Congress increasingly regarded Johnson as just a Southern Democrat who had only become president by accident. Congress had expressed its views in the Wade–Davis Bill. Johnson enacted various measures against their intentions, acting without the political skills that had allowed Lincoln to survive vetoing Wade–Davis. While waiting to be recalled, Congressmen considered what to do when they reassembled.

Congressional Republicans immediately refused to acknowledge the newly-elected senators and representatives from the South. This was a surprise to the Southern politicians as they had believed Johnson's assurances that they would be accepted as part of what he termed 'restoration' rather than Reconstruction. Over the next few months, Congress prepared legislation to extend the mandate of the Freedmen's Bureau. This was passed in February 1866, but Johnson vetoed it. This was on the grounds that the bureau was a military institution and, that the military should not be able to overrule the (state run) civil courts, as would have been necessary to enable the bureau to function despite Southern opposition. In March, Johnson vetoed Congress's Civil Rights Bill, which aimed to protect and enfranchise freedmen, this time on the grounds that it could not be constitutional to change the law so fundamentally when the South, the target of the legislation, had not even been allowed to sit in the Congress which had passed it.

> **KEY TERM**
>
> **Overriding a veto:** This describes the situation when a bill becomes law even when the president has vetoed it, because two-thirds of each house of Congress has voted to pass it despite his objections. The Civil Rights Act of 1866 represents the first time that this had happened on an important bill.

This time, Congress was able to **override the veto** and, in April 1866, the bill became law. Johnson, however, still controlled the federal government and the army, and was able to frustrate any attempt to enforce the new act. When the leaders of Congress attempted instead to have the Constitution amended, Johnson embarked on a speaking tour of the country, called the 'Swing around the circle', in which he forcefully and sometimes incoherently (some suspected drunkenly) campaigned against the ratification of the amendment, and against the re-election in November 1866 of his congressional enemies in the Republican Party he supposedly led.

What did Johnson seek to achieve? Some historians have judged that he simply did not want to lose. Others believe that when he failed to advance the cause of poor white Southerners against the rich Southern planters, he took the part of the rich Southerners instead, perhaps because they alone could control the demands of black Southerners. Others have judged that he did not wish to give congressional leaders the satisfaction of victory. Whatever the truth, presidential Reconstruction had seriously stalled by the middle of 1866, and was in ruins by the end of it. The 14th Amendment was adopted in July, and the Congress which emerged from the mid-term elections was radically opposed to the president.

ACTIVITY 2.12

Using the information in this chapter, make some notes about the aims of Reconstruction. Construct a case for the argument that Johnson performed well and was unfairly blocked by Congress.

Reflection: How easy did you find it to make a case for Johnson's success? Would you have found making a case for his failure easier? Why?

Radical Reconstruction from Congress

Even in Lincoln's time, Charles Sumner, the Massachusetts senator who had survived a famous 'caning' (see 1.2–'The caning of Senator Sumner, 1856'), suggested that in leaving the Union the Southern states had lost their identities. He called this 'state suicide'. They should be treated as not-yet-organised territories, and be readmitted to the Union with different boundaries and under different names. He argued that the South needed to be radically changed in order to prevent it from rebelling again. Arguably, this attitude began life as a negotiating point, rather than a genuine analysis intended to be final.

In the House, the leading voice for radical change was the Pennsylvanian Thaddeus Stevens. His politics were similar to Sumner's, although Stevens concentrated more on the issue of slavery and seemed to his contemporaries to be more vindictive than Sumner. Stevens was unusual as a Radical as he had a genuine belief in equal rights for African Americans. Under Lincoln, Sumner and Stevens had viewed their politics as radical in opposition to Lincoln's conservatism, and they wanted to use the outcome of the war as a way of driving deep-seated change; a **Radical Reconstruction**. Under Johnson, it became clear that their views were so different from the president's that they were not really in the same party.

KEY TERM

Radical Reconstruction: The name given to the form of Reconstruction which broadly aimed to change the South fundamentally after the Civil War, without seeking consensus from former Confederates. It was led mainly by Republican Radicals in Congress, notably Representative Stevens, Senator Sumner and later Senator Wade, although others, such as Lincoln's treasury secretary and then chief justice Salmon Chase were also Radicals. In the sense of Radical Reconstruction from Congress, the term refers to the actions of the 40th Congress in 1867 and 1868.

Congressmen had been attempting to lead Reconstruction for some time. The Congress which first met in 1867 was different from earlier ones for four reasons:

- It had a clear Radical majority, sufficient to override presidential vetoes. It could therefore pass whatever laws it liked, whether Johnson approved or not.
- Benjamin Wade who was the Senate's new leader gained his position largely because he was seen as a champion of the 14th Amendment, and therefore as a Radical. Thaddeus Stevens, was the powerful chairman of the Ways and Means Committee and effectively led the House. This meant that both chambers of Congress had Radical leadership.
- Johnson's campaign tour prior to the 1866 elections, and the thumping defeat of his candidates and positions, made it clear that the new Congress had a mandate to oppose him.
- Johnson was now firmly identified with the Southern aristocracy and the former Confederate leaders.

The Military Reconstruction Act of March 1867 divided the South into five districts. Each had a military governor, in which Radical Reconstruction could be carried out. This meant that the terms of the Wade–Davis Bill were effectively implemented. It meant too that there was real pressure for full civil rights, including the right to vote, for African Americans. When Southern states appealed to the United States Supreme Court for relief from the rule of the military governors, Radicals raised doubts about whether states which had 'suicided' had access to the Supreme Court. The Supreme Court (now led by Salmon Chase, himself a Radical) insisted that

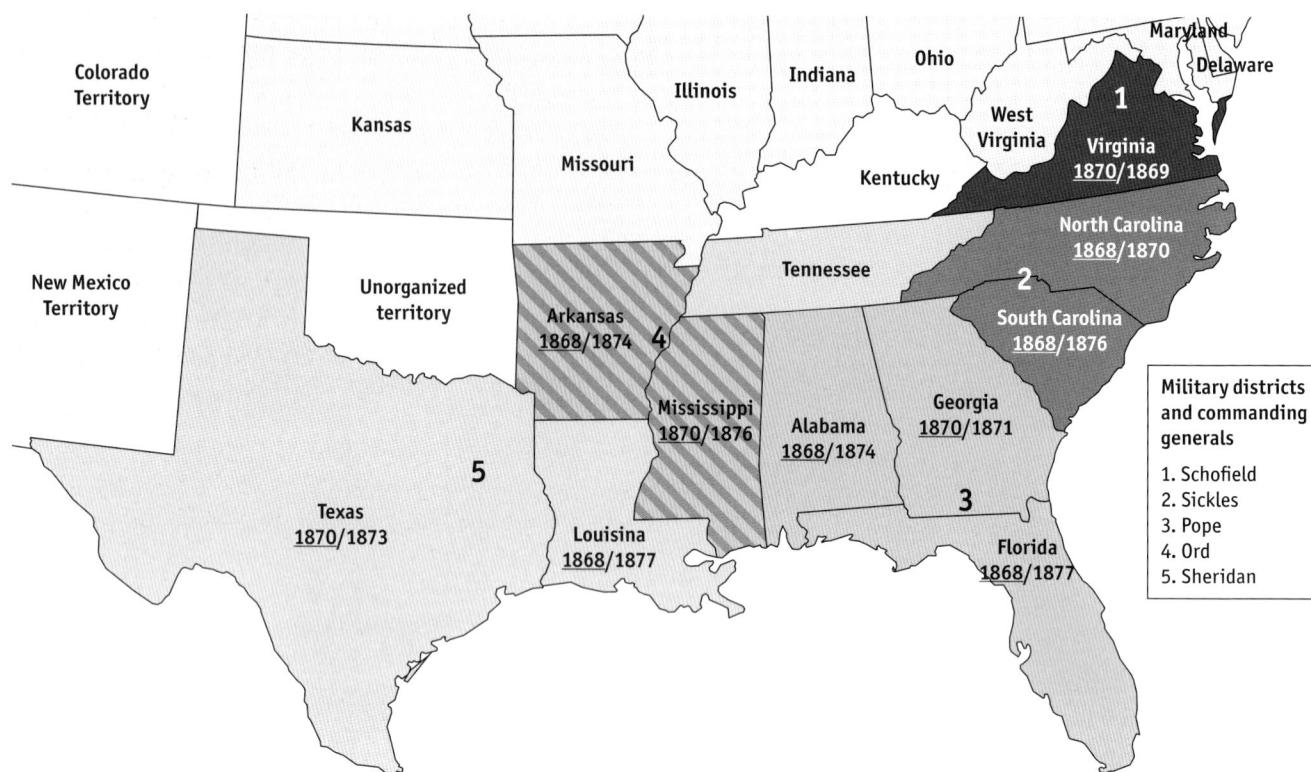

Figure 2.5: The military districts of the South, 1867

they did. Congressmen then openly began to wonder whether they might have the votes for a constitutional amendment to abolish the Supreme Court. Johnson, meanwhile, was expected to use his power as commander-in-chief of the army to order the military governors to back down.

Congress was ready for this. Two other laws were passed at the same time. All three were vetoed, and then the vetoes were overridden. The most directly relevant was the Command of the Army Act. This aimed to limit Johnson's power as Commander-in-Chief by allowing him to issue military orders only through the leading general, Ulysses S. Grant. Grant was not allowed to leave Washington except with the express permission of the Senate. The military governors – congressional appointees – could not therefore be commanded by anyone. They had licence to ignore Johnson's orders.

Finally, Congress passed the Tenure of Office Act. Cabinet members appointed by the president already had to be approved by the Senate. This new act meant that they could also be removed by the Senate. Edwin Stanton, the secretary of war, was the target of this Act, and he was immediately fired. Grant was sent to ensure that he complied. There were problems with the plan: it was probably unconstitutional and it was so badly worded that it misfired. It applied to those appointed to the cabinet by the sitting president. Stanton was Lincoln's appointee, not Johnson's. Grant therefore refused to follow the instructions of Congress, and allowed Stanton to barricade himself into his office.

ACTIVITY 2.13

Look at the three acts passed in early March 1867. Make a list of what Congressmen wanted to achieve by them. Share your ideas with others so that you have as many ideas written down as possible, and then try to arrange them all in a mind map showing the relationship between Congressmen's aims, and their relative significance.

So, what was Congress trying to do? Historians' opinions vary. Some argue that Congress was trying to secure Reconstruction, with the 13th and 14th Amendments being implemented in the South, and with no further aims to return to the previous situation from the defeated Southern aristocrats. Others claim that Congressmen were seeking personal revenge upon Johnson, who they wanted to humiliate. The fact that the Tenure of Office Act could not apply to Stanton suggests one of two situations: either the drafters of the act were unbelievably careless or, that they did not care about legal details. The second situation is more likely as they had plenty of time to plan what they would do. Another interpretation is that Congressmen intended in this act to reassert the superiority of the legislature (Congress) over the executive (the president). This had been the pre-war norm, and also restricted the president's military role.

In terms of Reconstruction itself, it is worth noting that this is the period during which the legal systems of the Southern states were reshaped to reflect the priorities of Northern-style economics. So, it became easier for companies, including railroad corporations, to do business in the South. Industrial capital took precedence over agricultural capital (or human capital), and property taxes were raised in order to pay for infrastructure and education. These were both priorities for an industrial, rather than agricultural, economy.

The Radical Republicans had a majority in Congress, but their unity was by no means guaranteed. In the House, some thought that Representative Stevens was going too far, both in his general behaviour and in his pushing of rights for African Americans. Many Republicans were uncomfortable with this. Lincoln himself, they remembered, considered the idea of sending as many African Americans as possible back to Africa. Meanwhile, in the Senate, Wade seemed overbearing, and, while the Radicals clearly had no love for Johnson, some did not much like Wade either.

The impeachment of President Johnson

As 1867 came to a close, three things were clear. Firstly, Johnson, who Sumner called a tyrant and a representative of the slavers, was not going to give in and would frustrate the Radicals whenever he could. Secondly, the Radicals were getting their way in the South. It was true that Congress had needed to frame legislation to do this, but

it was working, and states were even being readmitted to the Union at a reasonable pace, and with solidly Radical governments in place. Thirdly, Stanton remained: both literally and metaphorically barricaded into his office.

Johnson's term as president was due to expire in March 1869. In February and March 1868, a committee of the House led by Stevens voted to impeach him. In the Senate, Chief Justice Chase presided over the trial. A two-thirds vote against Johnson (36 senators) would be enough to remove him from office. But what was the point of trying to remove him? Why not simply wait?

- A show of Radical strength might have had an effect on the 1868 elections, ensuring that a Radical received the Republican nomination and also that Radical candidates were elected to Congress.
- Johnson would be humiliated.
- Congress could devote its time to finishing the job in the South, with a cooperative president not disrupting the role of the military governors.
- In the absence of a vice president, Senator Wade would assume the presidency.

The trial cited 11 articles of impeachment, most about the Tenure of Office Act, but also including disgracing the presidency and ridiculing Congress. Legally, Johnson could be dismissed for 'high crimes and misdemeanours' (even if, for example, the Tenure of Office Act had actually applied to Stanton, most American legal experts thought it unconstitutional). In reality, he would be dismissed if, and only if, 36 senators decided both that they wished to be rid of him and, crucially perhaps, that the overbearing Wade would be a better choice of president. He would almost certainly be nominated by the Republicans to run in the 1868 election, and would almost certainly win. Perhaps he was thinking about the Constitution, and perhaps he was thinking about his own ambition to be nominated for the presidency. Moderate Republican senators decided that the status quo was preferable to President Wade. Johnson was acquitted by one vote (with 35 against him) and the trial was abandoned in May.

All this happened with great press and public excitement. After his trial, Johnson realised he would not be nominated as presidential candidate by the Republicans. He was not able to convince the Democrats, including his new allies in the South, to nominate him either. He served out his term without providing much further resistance. The death of Thaddeus Stevens in August 1868 served further to calm

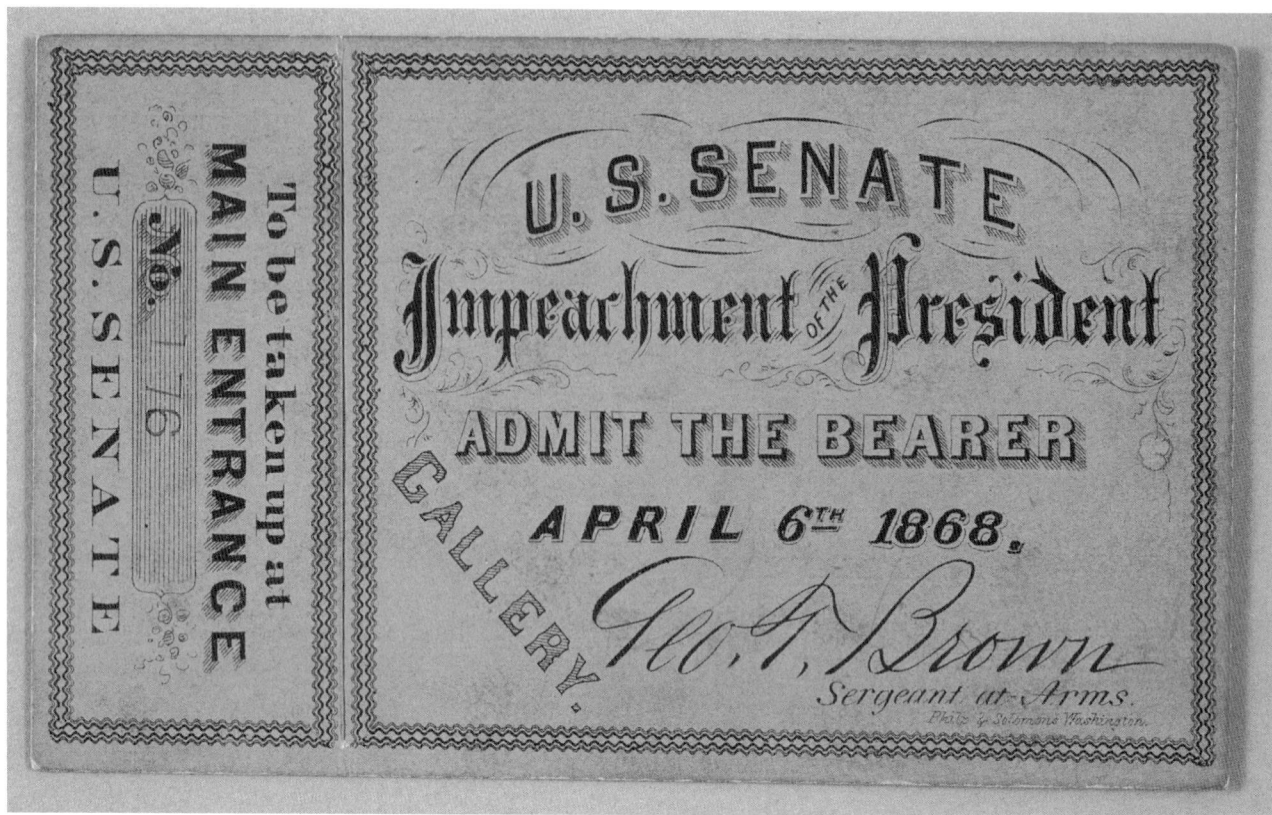

Figure 2.6: A ticket for the gallery of the Senate, a week into Johnson's trial. What does this suggest about Johnson's trial and how it was viewed?

things down. General Grant became a popular Republican president. The Radicals won reasonably well in Congress. And Senator Wade lost his seat.

THINK LIKE A HISTORIAN

Many historians think that the impeachment of President Johnson was more about personal politics than the Constitution, or his 'high crimes and misdemeanours'.

What examples of recent leaders can you find who have been, or are being, investigated for political reasons which are presented legally or constitutionally?

Reasons for and passage of Constitutional Amendments 13, 14 and 15

The second half of the 1860s is particularly notable for the adoption of three changes to the US Constitution. These were the first three amendments which were not either part of a political deal (the first ten) or the recognition of a system which had not worked as intended. Collectively known as the Reconstruction Amendments, the 13th, 14th and 15th made fundamental changes to the way in which the United States was governed. All three Reconstruction amendments are still part of the Constitution, and therefore are principal to the law of the USA.

The 13th Amendment

The three Reconstruction Amendments were, and are, significant for different reasons. The 13th, which banned slavery throughout the United States, was proposed in Congress in 1864. Although Lincoln had published the Emancipation Proclamation, its legal status was uncertain because it was felt that he had possibly exceded his powers. A change to the Constitution was essential to prevent individual states passing their own laws. Following his re-election, President Lincoln was able to persuade those House Democrats who had held up its passage to vote for it on the grounds that it was going to happen eventually – and so the sooner the better. There is strong evidence that representatives were promised the best jobs and, indeed, money, in return for their overcoming their states' rights objections to the amendment. There is less strong evidence that Lincoln was personally directing the operation, although some of his contemporaries certainly thought he was. In the early months of 1865 he was certainly responsible for securing the final few votes.

At the time of his death, Lincoln was beginning to worry about whether the three-quarters of the states required to ratify the amendment should, or should not, include those currently suspended from the Union. The issue was ultimately resolved under Andrew Johnson, who accepted congressional demands that ratification of the 13th Amendment needed to be a part of the deal for states wishing to return to the Union. By the end of 1865, the amendment had become law.

The 14th Amendment

The lengthy 14th Amendment was intended to give black people equality under the law with white people. It goes beyond anything envisaged in the 13th Amendment and came from the frustration of congressional Radicals at President Johnson's support for the Southern courts. These courts allowed discriminatory laws – the Black Codes – to be enforced in the South. This amendment would destroy the possibility of the entire Civil Rights Act of 1866 being found unconstitutional and therefore thrown out. More basically, there were Republican concerns about the new status of African Americans in the South.

With emancipation, the number of citizens (as opposed to people) in the Southern states rose, meaning that, under the Constitution, they needed additional representatives in Congress. Now that they were no longer slaves, they counted as whole persons: with 4 million freed slaves, the population of the South, and therefore its right to representation in Congress, went up by 1.6 million. This meant that Southern voters would gain 15 seats in Congress at the expense of Northern voters. Part of the point of the 14th Amendment was to ensure that those Southern voters included the (presumably sufficiently grateful) freedmen.

The 14th Amendment addressed the short-term problems faced by African Americans in the South and radical congressmen in Washington. It is therefore good evidence of the nature of those problems: if it was in the 14th Amendment, it must have seemed to matter.

There were, and are, unintended consequences of Section 1 of the 14th Amendment. Citizenship rights for African Americans, for example, was extended to Chinese Americans and Native Americans. More controversially, the 'equal protection' clause was extended in the 1880s to corporations – which are therefore legally classed as 'people' in the United States.

ACTIVITY 2.14

The 14th Amendment

Section 1 All persons born or naturalized in the United States, and subject to the jurisdiction thereof, are citizens of the United States and of the State wherein they reside. No State shall make or enforce any law which shall abridge the privileges or immunities of citizens of the United States; nor shall any State deprive any person of life, liberty, or property, without due process of law; nor deny to any person within its jurisdiction the equal protection of the laws.

Section 2 gives the vote to all citizens of the United States except those who have rebelled against the United States, or committed a crime.

Section 3 bans senior ex-Confederates from being elected to the US Congress.

Section 4 makes clear that the South must pay Confederate war debts, and that there must be no compensation paid for the loss of a former slave.

From the Fourteenth Amendment to the United States Constitution, adopted on 9 July 1868

List the issues which the 14th Amendment appears to address. (You could look up the full text to see how carefully language was chosen.) How do the elements of the 14th Amendment fit into the overall story of Reconstruction? Do they tell us more about the conflict between the North and the South, or about that between the different branches of the federal government? Do you agree with others in your class?

Reflection: Review your list. What evidence in the source was important in leading you to list the issues? What additional evidence might you need to further support the issues you have listed?

The 15th Amendment

The purpose of the 15th Amendment is short and simple: race, colour, or having been a slave are not adequate

81

grounds on which to stop someone voting. Of course, strictly speaking this was already covered in the 14th Amendment: only a crime could stop someone from voting. Although the Southern governments were in the hands of Radicals, there was still plenty of local opposition to African Americans voting. For example by introducing a law that only those people whose grandfathers had been voters could vote.

In the elections of 1868 the Radical majorities in Congress fell back and Ulysses Grant won the presidency for the Republicans. This sent a clear message. First, any further Radical action would have to be taken promptly, before the new Congress met. Second, Grant won a huge majority among African American voters. While their disenfranchisement would not have led to his losing, the election would have been close. The 15th Amendment was seen as a way to consolidate the gains of the 14th, and to prevent Radical worries about what might happen with a Congress less willing to enforce the 14th.

The 15th Amendment was watered down in Congress, to ensure that it would pass. Nevertheless, Sumner voted against it because it did not prevent states from imposing literacy tests or poll taxes. In fact, these two techniques

were used to prevent African Americans from voting. As it was, even with the strong support of the new president, and even in a weaker state, the amendment was only just passed by three-quarters of the states, a year after it had passed Congress. It became law in February 1870. By 1876, it had been seriously attacked. By 1896, it had become almost useless in the South. In its first 100 years, the main effect of the 15th Amendment was in finally guaranteeing African Americans the vote – in the North.

ACTIVITY 2.15

Revisit your answer to Activity 2.1, on the legal, economic and political issues facing the United States. How would you rewrite your answer now? Do you think that Reconstruction was successful?

2.4 How successful was Reconstruction?

We have seen that different politicians involved in Reconstruction had different aims, and the term 'Reconstruction' emerged among other terms such as

ACTIVITY 2.16

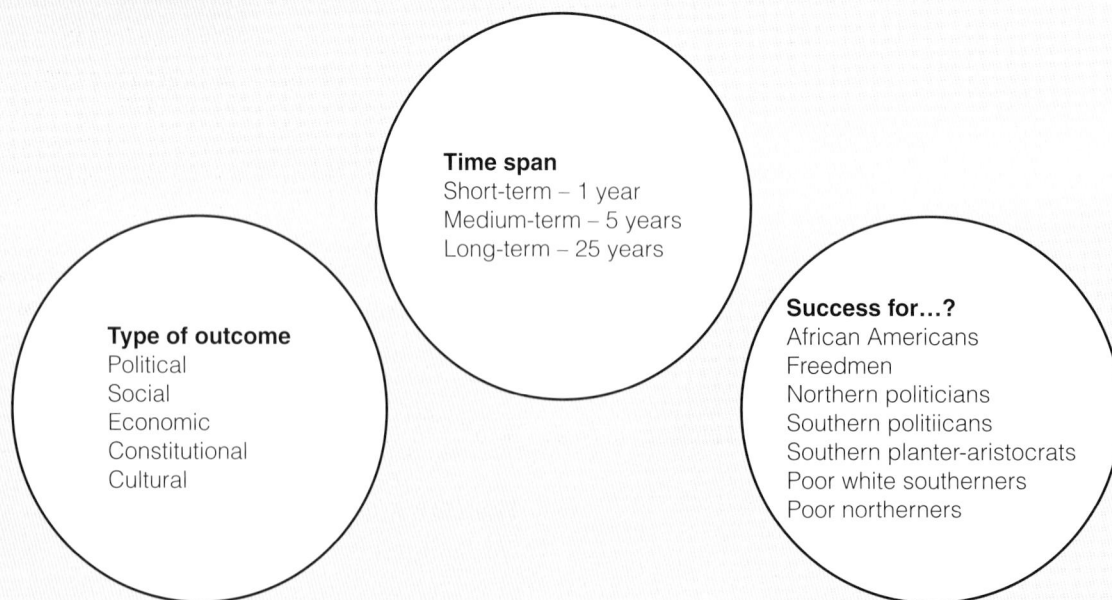

Time span
Short-term – 1 year
Medium-term – 5 years
Long-term – 25 years

Type of outcome
Political
Social
Economic
Constitutional
Cultural

Success for...?
African Americans
Freedmen
Northern politicians
Southern politiicans
Southern planter-aristocrats
Poor white southerners
Poor northerners

Figure 2.7: Factors to consider when measuring the success of Reconstruction

Look at the various factors which have an impact on how the success of Reconstruction is measured. Put together some sentences based on what you already know, linking time-span, type of outcome, and people involved. For example: 'In the short-term, I expect political success for northern politicians ...'

'restructuring' and 'repair'. The differences between them mattered: the term which won through suggests that something fundamental had changed.

It had. Black people in the South had civil rights, access to education and legal protection. The planter aristocracy would no longer be able to govern the South for its own purposes. Meanwhile, the Union would remain unchallenged, and unchallengeable, with no further threats of secession or civil war. The last few pages of this chapter have been about what politicians were trying to achieve. Now let's consider if it was successful.

Success is not an easy term to define. There are a number of factors to consider. Success for whom? Success in which area of human activity? How long does the success need to last? When should a measurement be taken and a judgement be made?

The changing position of ex-slaves

The first problem faced by former slaves was immediate, and economic. Newly emancipated, they were certainly legally free; they were also potentially unemployed and homeless. The reality of the situation was that many slaves had little practical choice but to live on the same plantations as they had before and work for the same masters. In these cases, the most visible change was in the distribution of freedmen's houses and working areas, as African Americans chose where and with whom they lived and worked, as far as they could. The other change was less immediately visible. It was that freedmen worked considerably shorter hours than they had when they were slaves, leading to a drop in productivity on the land.

The actual manner of slaves being freed varied. Legally, emancipation occurred at the moment of a state's surrender or defeat in the Civil War. Practically, plantation owners were not enthusiastic about sharing the news of freedom with their slaves. This was sometimes left to Union soldiers in the months following the conclusion of the war. In Texas, this occurred on 19 June 1865, a date still celebrated as 'Juneteenth' in many parts of the USA. Typically, Union soldiers would pass the word around that everyone was free – but there was little more immediate information or support.

Some slaves were freed earlier, and some left the South entirely. This was easier for those in the Upper, rather than Deep, South. Jourdan Anderson was one slave who did this. He was freed in Tennessee in 1864 and by the end of the summer of 1865 lived in Ohio. He sent a letter to his former master, apparently in response to a request from that master asking him to return to his old job. (Anderson's sardonic letter, which can be easily found online, is worth reading in full.)

a) What inferences can you draw from Anderson's letter about the situation for ex-slaves in 1865?

Letter of Jourdon Anderson printed in the *New York Daily Tribune*, 22 August 1865

The introduction reads: 'The following is a genuine document. It was *dictated* by the old servant, and contains his ideas and forms of expression.'

Dayton, Ohio, August 7, 1865
To my Old Master, Col. P.H. Anderson, Big Spring, Tennessee

Sir: I got your letter and was glad to find that you had not forgotten Jordan, and that you wanted me to come back and live with you again, promising to do better for me than anybody else can …

I want to know particularly what the good chance is you propose to give me. I am doing tolerably well here: I get $25 a month, with victuals and clothing; have a comfortable house for Mandy (the folks here call her Mrs. Anderson), and the children, Milly Jane and Grundy, go to school and are learning well; the teacher says Grundy has a head for a preacher. They go to Sunday-School, and Mandy and me attend church regularly. We are kindly treated …

Now if you will write and say what wages you will give me, I will be better able to decide whether it would be to my advantage to move back again.

As to my freedom, which you say I can have, there is nothing to be gained on that score, as I got my free-papers in 1864 … we have concluded to test your sincerity by asking you to send us our wages for the time we served you. I served you faithfully for thirty-two years, and Mandy twenty years, at $25 a month for me, and $2 a week for Mandy. Our earnings would amount to $11,690 …

We trust the good Maker has opened your eyes to the wrongs which you and your fathers have done to me and my fathers, in making us toil for you for generations without recompense.

From the New York Daily Tribune, 22 August 1865

b) There are indications in this letter which have led some historians to believe that it was not entirely written by Anderson, but by Northern anti-southern campaigners. Make a list of three examples which you believe make this likely. Even if this is the case, what useful inferences can still be drawn?

The new Southern economic model

The economy of the South had been shattered, not just by war, but also by emancipation. Before emancipation, the value of the South had not been in the land, but in the workforce. Cotton requires land in warm areas (the reason why slavery was prevalent in the warmer South) and a plentiful supply of labour: looking after and harvesting cotton plants is time-consuming and fiddly. Value was held in the slaves themselves and mortgages were secured against them. So the banking system of the South was ruined by the sudden declaration that the banks no longer had collateral. They did not even really have enough cash to deal with an economy in which labourers would expect to be paid, rather than just be given food and lodgings. Meanwhile, the market for cotton was no longer cornered by the South. The Civil War disrupted cotton production, distribution and export to Liverpool and Manchester, and Indian cotton took its place.

It was in the immediate economic interests of those freedmen who did not or could not leave the South, and of the owners of the plantations, to cooperate to produce something worth selling in the immediate aftermath of emancipation. The solution adopted by around a third of the South by 1868 was the practice of **sharecropping**.

KEY TERM

Sharecropping: An economic model in which most, if not all, of the rent that a tenant-farmer pays for land is paid in crops rather than money. In the South this could also include payments made for seed purchase and tool hire in shops, which were also owned by the landlord.

Sharecropping was the only solution to the immediate economic problem. It also appeared to limit any economic progress made by ex-slaves in the South. Former slaves had no land, tools, seeds or seed capital. Without cash in hand or crops to sell, what could they do except agree to pay part of their future crop in return for the means to create it? They lacked the education needed to read or understand the contracts they were signing and were exploited. This left them with little real hope of saving enough to escape the system, especially in a failing cotton market. There was also widespread destruction of crops from the spread of the boll weevil which made things even worse for newly freed families.

An alternative model was suggested by the Southern Homestead Act of 1866 which was passed eventually over Johnson's veto. Available land in the South would be redistributed to those who needed it – mostly freedmen, although some white farmers benefitted too. General Sherman, the Union general in charge in the South, promised '40 acres and a mule' to emancipated slaves. He made this promise in January 1865, with the support of Representative Stevens and Secretary Stanton who were at that stage on broadly the same side. It had no legal force, but was something which many freedmen expected and it became the first great disappointment of freedom. Nobody received 40 acres or even a mule. Around 1000 freed farmers received some land, but in some cases this was rapidly extorted away by white southerners who still owned tools and seed.

Achievements of the Freedmen's Bureau

The Freedmen's Bureau had positive short-term achievements in respect to some freedmen, but was not really able to secure positive long-term improvements for former slaves as a whole.

Most clearly, the bureau dealt with the basic needs of newly freed slaves. It provided clothing and food relief for those who owned nothing, as well as advice about what to do next and reassurance that news of freedom was true. For example, when freedmen asked if they could now get married or move around, the bureau helped them to do so. Marriages occurred in large numbers, and around 10 000 families relocated. The bureau also provided some medical relief, and played a humanitarian role for all the poor people of the heavily damaged South.

To address the twin problems of economic mobility and access to civil rights, the Freedmen's Bureau, along with the American Missionary Association, promoted education for freedmen. Some poor Southern whites took advantage of this too, although the classic picture is of multiple generations of the same freed family learning to read together. Perhaps 200 000 people learned to read in the years immediately following the Civil War.

This had an effect on African American religious worship, which was able to formalise its distinctive style now that pastors could read the Bible. Both the Bureau and the American Missionary Association set up universities and schools, including the prestigious Howard University in Washington DC and the Hampton Institute in Virginia. The positive effects were only temporary for the vast majority of those people educated by these institutions. Initial enthusiasm for education was generated by the sense that it had been forbidden under slavery, and that it might lead to something better. However, the Southern economy had nothing much better to offer, and even the best education did not provide jobs on its own.

Another important goal of the Freedmen's Bureau was to enable freedmen to help themselves, especially politically. 'Black' Reconstruction, as it came to be known – the label is a hostile one – was ultimately a failure in political terms. No black governors were elected. Only two black US senators and 15 black House representatives took office. There was only ever a black majority in the legislature in South Carolina and that was a narrow majority. Despite all the efforts of the Freedmen's Bureau and others involved in Reconstruction, African American progress was repeatedly knocked back by the white response which followed.

> **KEY CONCEPT**
>
> ### Change and continuity
>
> How much changed in the lives of black people in the South in the second half of the 1860s, and how much stayed the same? Work in a small group to look at the various different ways in which life changed (or failed to). Share your ideas and prioritise them in two ways:
>
> - Where were the biggest changes found? What were the biggest differences?
> - Where were the most significant changes or continuities found? What mattered most?

Responses of the white South

The label 'white South' implies a degree of unity among white Southerners which might be misleading. We have previously seen that class, just as much as race, divided the South. Southerners who couldn't afford to own slaves, often smallholding farmers, were at a competitive disadvantage relative to the plantation-owning aristocracy. Poor black and poor white southerners shared goals, but, by the end of Reconstruction, it was race, rather than class, which became the more important factor. It should not be assumed that responses to Reconstruction were common to all white Southerners. Many responded by helping Reconstruction along, for reasons ranging from securing their own economic advantage to righting the moral wrongs of the era of slavery. However, by 1877 the white South was broadly united.

Political and legal responses

In 1867, Radical Republicans were mostly successful in excluding the planter aristocracy from control of Southern governments. Active politicians therefore comprised poor Southerners (white and black) and Northerners coming into the South either to provide governmental assistance or for their own profit. These Northerners were known, insultingly, as **carpetbaggers**. Some came because the South represented a land of opportunity. It had been so dependent on plantation agriculture that little other work had been done there, and the Southern wilderness contained untapped minerals which could be exploited.

85

Figure 2.8: This 1872 depiction of Carl Schurz as a carpetbagger, from *Harper's Weekly*, provides an interesting comment on Schurz's career. Schurz was a general in the Civil War, then a newspaper editor, then (carpetbagger Republican) senator for Missouri. In 1872, he helped to form the Liberal Republican Party, which opposed the Radicals on the grounds that the job of Reconstruction was now done. The politics of the Reconstruction-era South were not straightforward. Do you think this is a reliable depiction of Carl Schurz? What other information would you need to assess the source's reliability?

Similarly disliked by aristocratic Southerners, by now almost entirely identified as Democrats, were the **scalawags**. They aimed to express their opposition to slavery, and to the planter aristocracy, by joining local Republican parties. James Alcorn who was firstly a governor of, and then senator, from Mississippi, became simply a conservative (that is, non-Radical) Republican by 1873. Like many 'scalawags', he was unprepared to carry on the work of Radical Reconstruction past the 15th Amendment. This was because he thought the work was done.

86

KEY TERMS

Carpetbaggers: Northern Republican politicians who moved South in the immediate aftermath of the Civil War, intending to participate in Southern governments. The name refers to the cases they were thought to use to transport their belongings. The term is more generally used for anyone who seeks political office in an area in which they have no connections.

Scalawag: A derogatory term for Southerners who supported Reconstruction. Often former opponents of slavery, secession and the war, they joined the Republican Party in order to serve in Southern governments after the war. However, as Southerners, some were not allowed to serve in any official capacity at first.

The Southern governments of 1865 and 1866, before Radical Republicans took hold of Congress, consisted of carpetbaggers, scalawags and African Americans, and also of Democrats who were opposed to the work of Reconstruction. This produced political and legal compromise. As a whole, laws passed in the South to regulate Reconstruction (actually, to regulate African Americans) are known as the Black Codes. This is a set of legislation which balanced concessions to black Southerners with restrictions and limitations. At the time they seemed like a reasonable (sometimes) and politically convenient compromise. Now it is clear that they were the forerunners of 'Jim Crow' legislation to come. Mississippi's law – the first – was called an 'Act to confer Civil Rights on freedmen'. Although it did allow marriage and property ownership, overall it gave very few rights to freedmen.

The Black Codes

These were a set of laws from various Southern states, adopted gradually by those states rather than in an official, organised way. Example legislation includes:

- Vagrancy laws. In most Southern states, anyone unable to prove that they were employed was liable to be arrested. These laws were enforced mostly against black people. In Mississippi, anyone in a mixed-race relationship was considered a vagrant.
- Disproportionate punishment. In South Carolina, the death penalty could be enforced for stealing cotton.
- In Florida, it was illegal to disrespect a white employer.
- Servitude, including for the children of offenders, was a common punishment.

The name Black Codes was an unapologetic reference to previous 'Slave Codes'.

During the period of radical ascendancy legislative attacks on African Americans were more limited by the presidency of Ulysses S. Grant. However, the Radical project was losing its way. Southern legislatures tried a variety of ways to deny black people the rights promised in the 14th and 15th amendments. A series of US Supreme Court decisions of 1873 regarding cases relating to the Chicago slaughterhouses, found that it was legal for states to set their own criteria for voting rights. It was typical to impose a poll tax, or a literacy test or an impossible registration process, and enforce this only against black people. 'Grandfather' laws were common: a man could only vote if his grandfather had been a voter, which of course excluded slaves.

The Peculiar Institution and the Ku Klux Klan

There are isolated stories of Northern visitors to the South, whether carpetbaggers or soldiers, expressing surprise at the reaction of Southerners, particularly women, to their presence. The people who had been known for being very welcoming were often the exact opposite. Immediately the cultural response to Southern defeat in the Civil War was to express ideas which carry on to this day including in the writing of history:

- the romanticised ideal of the 'Lost Cause' of the South – a pastoral idyll which glossed over or ignored the fact of slavery
- slavery as an essentially benevolent 'Peculiar Institution', restating an idea from before the war implying that Southern slaveholders had *helped* their slaves to organise their affairs and looked after them in happy families
- the Civil War as a revolution, carried on to the detriment of the South (the behaviour of Radical Republicans did nothing to take away from this).

If these things were true, it meant that Reconstruction was at best unnecessary and at worst a punishment. The presence of this cultural interpretation of the war which had just occurred helped to demonstrate that white Southerners would not simply divide along class lines, as many, including President Johnson, had expected. Instead, some white Southerners found a sectional identity in opposition to African Americans and those who helped them, including the 'Union leagues' of Northern whites.

In 1866 there were race riots in Memphis and New Orleans. The first of these saw the birth in Tennessee of the Ku Klux Klan (KKK). Originally an economic organisation devoted to furthering the white cause, it rapidly became a viciously racist secret society which used violence and intimidation to restrict the progress made by African Americans. It was one of nearly 500 such groups – another was the 'Mississippi Plan' of 1874, which involved white rifle-club rallies being set up in ways designed to intimidate black voters. By 1867, with Radical governments refusing to enforce the Black Codes, the KKK and groups like it enforced the Codes instead through campaigns of violence. Typically, they might threaten African Americans, demanding that they produce papers and punishing them when they could not. By 1869, the KKK was a fully fledged criminal organisation headed by Nathan Bedford Forrest, former Confederate general and first KKK 'grand wizard'. There were operations ranging from racketeering to lynching – the heinous practice of extra-judicial killing, typically by hanging. In this respect, life became extremely dangerous for African Americans. Previously, no one would have injured or killed another man's slave: that was his property. However, at this time the violent impulses of a significant section of white society were unleashed.

The activities of the Klan and similar groups were serious enough that President Grant's administration used legislation to attempt to stamp them out. The 1870 Force Act was general, and partially successful, and the 1871 Ku Klux Klan Act effectively eradicated the Klan until it was re-presented to the country in the movie *The Birth of a Nation* in 1915.

ACTIVITY 2.18

Consider the various ways in which white Southerners' responses to Reconstruction made African Americans' lives worse. Make a mind-map showing how these responses made the lives of African Americans worse. Work with another student to identify what, in particular, was effective in the responses of white Southerners. Did any of these white responses help to end the process of Reconstruction?

" Hang, curs, hang! * * * * * * * *Their* complexion is perfect gallows. Stand fast, good
fate, to *their* hanging ! * * * * * If they be not born to be hanged, our case is miserable.''
The above cut represents the fate in store for those great pests of Southern society—
the carpet-bagger and scalawag—if found in Dixie's land after the break of day on the
4th of March next.

Figure 2.9: A 1868 cartoon published by the *Independent Monitor*, Tuscaloosa, Alabama, expressing the opposition of the KKK to carpetbaggers and scalawags. How useful is the image for understanding the opposition of the KKK to carpetbaggers and scalawags?

Ulysses S. Grant's Reconstruction policies

The presidency of Ulysses S. Grant (1869–77) was in many ways unremarkable by comparison with that of his predecessors. There were no attempts on his life or on his tenure as president. He didn't achieve, or even attempt, all that much in terms of Reconstruction. While this might seem strange to modern ears nowadays, it did not seem at all strange to his contemporaries. Until Lincoln's time, nobody had expected an active presidency.

Grant was the candidate of the Radical Republicans. However, his conduct during the crisis over Stanton's (non-) dismissal showed that he was no extremist. Grant came to power in a political climate in which the Radical senator Benjamin Wade had lost office. So, he had no particular mandate to do anything other than carry on the work of Reconstruction much as it was. The death of Thaddeus Stevens in 1868 had also robbed Radical Republicanism of many of its ideas and much of its momentum.

Grant's first task was to promote the passage and implementation of the 15th Amendment, an act which the Radicals recognised as necessary because of their expected future weakness: their majorities and mandates were declining, and this consolidated the gains of the

other Reconstruction amendments. From early in Grant's presidency, there were therefore clear signs that the job was almost done.

However, it was only clear in Washington. In the South itself, it was becoming clear that things were going wrong for Reconstruction, and that what had been done by any progress the Freedmen's Bureau and others had achieved was already being undone. The Black Codes were still in force. Southern governments were becoming more Democratic. Grant's administration had to use military and legislative power to crack down on violent groups such as the KKK. This approach was generally successful in shutting down existing groups, though not at preventing new ones from springing up to take their place. It was not guaranteed that Grant's administration would take action against all the groups; the KKK was a particularly high-profile target. Grant used the military as well as legislation to enforce elements of Reconstruction until the election of 1872. In the end bills such as the Force Bill of 1874, which was designed to attack the Mississippi Plan, failed in the Senate (in 1875). Why attempt to pass a Force Bill when there was no possibility of force being used? (Grant did not wish to send Northern white troops to support black people trying to vote.) The template of the Mississippi Plan was copied elsewhere in the Deep South the following year. However, in Grant's first term, **Force Acts** were passed to enforce portions of the 14th and 15th Amendments.

KEY TERM

Force Act: A piece of legislation designed to help Congress and the president to enforce another act, typically part of a constitutional amendment. The Force Act of 1870, for example, (also known as the Ku Klux Klan Act) was designed to enforce the 15th Amendment's section about suffrage. There were successful Force Acts in 1870 and 1871, and an unsuccessful Force Bill in 1874–75.

The following extract is from the autobiography of Benjamin Butler. He was the general who, by 1869 had become the member of the House responsible for preparing the first Force Bill in 1870. He describes the congressional reaction to news of the Klan.

Meanwhile some States were admitted, and the ballot having been by constitutional amendment granted to the colored men, the white citizens of those States undertook to control the negro in the use of that ballot by a series of outrages and murders never equalled in a civilized country. There were numerous large bands of organized marauders called the Ku Klux, who were dressed in fantastic uniforms, and who rode at night and inflicted unnumbered and horrible outrages upon the negro so that he should not dare to come to the polls. Indeed, the men of the South seemed to think themselves excused in those outrages because they wanted to insure a white man's government in their States.

I desired that Congress should pass laws which, with their punishments and modes of execution, would be sufficiently severe under the circumstances to prevent these outrages entirely. What those laws should be was the subject of most bitter controversy. Many of the Republicans in the House were more bitter in their opposition to stringent laws than were gentlemen on the other side who had served in the Confederate armies.

From Butler's Book, *by Benjamin F. Butler, published in 1892*

Two points are of particular note. The first is that the problem either was, or seemed to Congress to be, mainly focused on violence connected with preventing African Americans from voting. The second is that the Republicans were not united in their attitude to the Klan, even early in Grant's presidency.

Electoral politics formed part of Grant's problem. He was elected amid declining enthusiasm for Reconstruction. In 1874 – six years and therefore one complete electoral cycle later – the Democrats won control of the Senate. This ended any earlier arguments about who should control the Senate Republicans. Charles Sumner, the man who had not quite controlled but had at least directed the Radicals had died earlier in the year. Grant had been re-elected in 1872 against a challenge only from other Republicans. These were moderate Republicans such as Carl Schurz and Horace Greeley. They used their media output to argue that the job of Reconstruction was complete because the Union was secure, slavery was finished and there were rules in place to ensure that African Americans had rights – even if those rules were not really observed. Also in 1872, the Amnesty Act ensured that all former Confederates now had the right to stand for election again. This was another part of the general mood of reconciliation between whites that was evident in the elections that year.

The Reconstruction policies of Ulysses S. Grant might be summarised as:

- Enforcement Acts (Force Acts) of 1870–71 to encode and enforce equal protection for African Americans, including those standing for political office.
- Opposition to high-profile violent anti-black groups such as the KKK. This included military action until 1872.
- Freedmen's Bureau was allowed to lapse in 1872.
- Amnesty Act, 1872.
- Intervention to support Republican candidates in corrupt elections, for example in supporting William Pitt Kellogg for governor of Louisiana in 1872: troops were sent in to ensure that the electoral board was not unduly influenced in favour of Kellogg's ex-Confederate opponent.
- In 1873 this intervention led to the Colfax Massacre in Louisiana, the biggest single incident of violence in the Reconstruction period. It is estimated that nearly 300 African Americans were killed in a struggle between black Republicans and white former Confederates who were trying to regain control of local politics. Grant's federal prosecutors brought charges against the white perpetrators, but their convictions were overturned by the Supreme Court as being unconstitutional in *United States v. Cruickshank* (one of the accused) in 1876.
- 1875 Civil Rights Act, which Grant did not enforce.
- Refusal to send troops to prevent the Red Shirts (another violent white supremacist group) from barring African American participation in elections in Mississippi in 1875, following the failure of a Force Bill.

The Civil Rights Act of 1875

The most significant piece of legislation passed during Grant's time might have been the Civil Rights Act of 1875, if things had been different Grant wanted an act which enabled him to prevent violent suppression of the black vote in states such as Mississippi. Instead the bill originally drafted a year earlier by Sumner was passed in tribute to him. This Civil Rights Act was intended to outlaw segregation, which was beginning to appear in the South. Grant might have doubted its constitutionality (ultimately the act was struck down as unconstitutional in 1883); he certainly doubted his ability to enforce it. He did not think that it was a priority as there was the more urgent issue of racial violence which was continuing in the South.

Grant did not attempt to enforce it at all. He was aware that the Civil Rights Act was unpopular, and was perhaps thinking about his chances of re-election for a third term in 1876, on a platform which seemed to reflect his policy. This was that: violence and violent interference with voting rights were unacceptable – anything less than that was beyond the scope of the federal government. This was not just a legal issue. Grant viewed his role as moving the country on from the horror of the Civil War and its aftermath.

This time, re-election would not come. In 1872 Grant had been lucky in that there was no coherent opposition outside his own party. The Whigs had disappeared and the Democrats were still too disorganised. Grant ran against a Republican who didn't have enough Democratic support to unseat the president. Grant was lucky because the story of the rest of his presidency was chaotic. Although he had personal integrity, he totally lacked judgment in the choice of his advisers and associates. In 1869, his own brother-in-law was involved in attempts to control the market in gold. This cost the country, and its businessmen, money, and left the president looking foolish. There was then a long argument over the precise status of treasury bonds. Meanwhile, Grant's administration appeared to consist of his friends rather than anyone of any particular political talent. Worse, they were corrupt. Grant's personal secretary was allowed to escape punishment for his part in the 'Whiskey Ring' fraud. Separately, the secretary of war was forced to resign after taking bribes. Meanwhile, Vice President Colfax, the only senior Radical in the administration, declined to run again after being implicated in several scandals at the same time.

Much of this had occurred before Grant was re-elected for his second term. He would not be that lucky twice. A financial panic – not his fault, but he did not deal with it well – hit early in his second term, and without the full support of his party he would not stand a chance against a properly organised Democrat in 1876.

ACTIVITY 2.19

Working with another student, prepare a pair of briefing papers for President Grant (imagine, perhaps, that you are Hamilton Fish, Secretary of State, widely regarded as the only highly competent member of the cabinet). One briefing paper should emphasise the reasons for Grant to intervene more vigorously in promoting Radical-style Reconstruction policies. The other should urge caution. Which seems the more convincing, and why?

Reflection: Compare your briefing papers with another pair. How easy did you each find it to complete each one? What made the process easy or difficult?

The Compromise of 1877 and the end of Reconstruction

With the benefit of hindsight, the failure of Reconstruction seems inevitable. It probably did at the time, too. As ever, the language used tells a story. The Southerners battling against the Radical Reconstruction governments called themselves **Redeemers**. The name had strong religious associations and showed that they wished to be seen as putting right the wrong which had been done to the South. Somehow, just ten years after the end of slavery, the insults against the good reputation of the South and the attack on its character and institutions, could be portrayed as worse than slavery. In trying to assess the causes of any change, there are two questions to consider why did one side want change, and why did (or could) nobody else stop them?

KEY TERM

Redeemers: Southern Democrats who worked to overthrow Radical Republican governments in the South. This was mainly during Grant's second presidential term. Redeemers aligned politically with 'Bourbon' Democrats, a more conservative and pro-business wing of the party.

The election of 1872 showed that the Republican Party was no longer united. The mid-term elections of 1874 showed that the Democrats, essentially under Bourbon control, were now able to challenge on a national level. This further prompted the Republicans to consider precisely how radical they wished to be. In fact, there was little choice for the Republicans with Grant's support for moving the country forward. They had lost all their leaders through death or scandal. Radicalism had lost its attraction, and there was no desire in the North to start it up again. The North developed a desire to put the years of conflict behind it. It was distracted by westward expansion and arguments over tariffs, the financial panic of 1873 – and even by the emergence of Major League Baseball.

Meanwhile, in the South sharecropping appeared to be sustainable as long as the North bought the cotton. Cotton prices were rising and food prices were falling. In an economy which was short of cash and depressed, the status quo appeared to be as good as it was going to get. Violence had clearly shown that the 15th Amendment was ineffective. The North did little to tackle this violence. *United States v. Cruickshank* seemed to confirm this. On the other hand, slavery had been banned. In theory, African Americans were free to take their labour wherever they liked, to worship and to marry in freedom, and were US citizens, although disenfranchised. There was no more desire to send white soldiers to enforce black rights, which was the growing story of the Civil War.

So, in the South by 1876 there were Redeemer governments in all states, with the exception of Florida, South Carolina and Louisiana. In South Carolina, two different electoral commissions certified two different sets of results, and two legislatures claimed control. This was the background of the presidential election of 1876.

The election compromise of 1877

In the USA, presidential elections are won not by the number of individual votes but by the number of Electoral College votes won. This effectively means that winning states is what matters because each state has a different weighting according to its population. In 1876, there were 369 Electoral College votes available. This meant that a candidate needed 185 (half plus one) to win. The split was:

	Rutherford B. Hayes, Republican	Samuel J. Tilden, Democrat	Undetermined
Electoral College votes won	165	184	20
States won	18	17	3 (Florida, Louisiana, South Carolina) plus one disputed vote in Oregon

Table 2.4: Results of the 1876 presidential election

The Democrats were helped by winning the Northern state of New York, which was the biggest state with 35 College votes (and the home of an impressive Democratic organisation as well as their candidate Samuel Tilden). They appeared to be ahead with three states left to declare. Those three states were the 'unredeemed' Southern states still with functioning Radical governments (although barely functioning in the case of South Carolina, whose own legislature was disputed). In each case, Tilden appeared to have won. He only needed to win one more vote, and therefore one state, to win the election. However, in each case there were allegations of violence directed at black, and therefore Republican, voters and fraud. This was notable in South Carolina, where more ballots were cast than there were eligible voters. The elections weren't free, and the count was not fair.

In each of the three states, the Republican electoral commissions awarded the votes to Hayes. This meant that the election was a tie and depended on the disputed vote in Oregon. This should clearly go to Hayes, who would therefore win the election. The vote would then go to Congress to be certified. As the Democrats were in a majority there, Congress was expected to refuse certification.

A commission was therefore formed from Congress and the Supreme Court. It consisted of seven Republicans, seven Democrats and a neutral, Supreme Court Justice David Davis. He was nominated to the Senate by Illinois, presumably in return for a vote for Tilden. Davis wanted to be seen as neutral and so he withdrew from the commission. He was replaced by a Republican Supreme

Court Justice, as there were only Republicans left to replace him. The Commission then voted entirely upon party lines on all 20 disputed votes.

The Democrats accepted that their candidate could not win the election when they realised that they had been outmanoeuvred by Justice – now Senator – Davis's insistence on remaining neutral. Grant's term as president expired on 4 March, whether a successor was declared or not. He had made the precaution of strengthening the military presence around Washington, but no one wanted conflict, nor a presidential vacancy.

A compromise was therefore found. Hayes promised to withdraw federal troops from the South and to appoint a Southerner to the cabinet, and to move funds to improve the railroads in the South. The country waited for the outcome and then Hayes was inaugurated. Immediately, he kept his promises. The troops withdrew, taking the Radical governments in Florida and Louisiana with them: the South Carolinian Redeemers had already won. A Tennessean Democrat became postmaster general. This was a key cabinet post with plenty of backing for Southerners to take advantage of. The man now nicknamed 'His Fraudulency Rutherfraud B. Hayes' served four mediocre years in the White House. The Democrats, with Grover Cleveland, eventually won a presidency in 1884. Under Hayes, Reconstruction was halted, and in fact began to be reversed. There were no more serious attempts to enforce voting rights for black Southerners in the lifetime of anyone trying to vote in 1877.

Exam-style questions

Source analysis questions

Read the four sources and answer both parts of
question 1.

From The War-time Journal of a Georgia Girl

I almost feel as if I should like to hang a
Yankee myself. There was hardly a fence left
standing all the way from Sparta to Gordon
[about 40 miles]. The fields were trampled
down and the road was lined with carcasses
of horses, hogs and cattle that the invaders,
unable to consume or carry away with them,
had wantonly shot down to starve the people
and prevent them from making their crops.
The stench in some places was unbearable;
every few hundred yards we had to hold our
noses or stop them with … cologne.

Frances Andrews, The War-time Journal of
a Georgia Girl *(New York, D. Appleton and
Company, 1908)*

*From a Civil War ballad, 'Marching Through
Georgia'*
Chorus:

Hurrah! Hurrah! we bring the jubilee!
Hurrah! Hurrah! the flag that makes you free!
So we sang the chorus from Atlanta to the sea
While we were marching through Georgia.

(Chorus)

How the darkeys shouted when they heard the
joyful sound
How the turkeys gobbled which our commissary
found
How the sweet potatoes even started from the
ground
While we were marching through Georgia.

(Chorus)

Yes and there were Union men who wept with
joyful tears,
When they saw the honored flag they had not
seen for years;
Hardly could they be restrained from breaking
forth in cheers,
While we were marching through Georgia.

(Chorus)

'Sherman's dashing Yankee boys will never reach
the coast!'
So the saucy rebels said and 'twas a handsome
boast
Had they not forgot, alas! to reckon with the Host
While we were marching through Georgia.

(Chorus)

So we made a thoroughfare for freedom and her
train,
Sixty miles in latitude, three hundred to the main;
Treason fled before us, for resistance was in vain
While we were marching through Georgia.

SOURCE C

Figure 2.10: The ruins of Richmond, Virginia at the end of the Civil War, 1865

SOURCE D

Letter of William T. Sherman to James M. Calhoun, E.E. Rawson, and S.C. Wells (representing the City Council of Atlanta), September 12, 1864

The use of Atlanta for warlike purposes is inconsistent with its character as a home for families. There will be no manufactures, commerce, or agriculture here, for the maintenance of families, and sooner or later want will compel the inhabitants to go ... those who brought war into our Country deserve all the curses and maledictions a people can pour out ... Once admit the Union, once more acknowledge the Authority of the National Government, and, instead of devoting your houses and streets and roads to the dread uses of war, I and this army become at once your protectors and supporters ... I myself have seen in Missouri, Kentucky, Tennessee, and Mississippi, hundreds of thousands of women and children fleeing from your armies and desperadoes, hungry and with bleeding feet. In Memphis, Vicksburg, and Mississippi, we fed thousands upon thousands of families of rebel soldiers left in our hands, and whom we could not see starve. Now that war comes home to you, you feel very different. You depreciate its horrors, but did not feel them when you sent car-loads of soldiers and ammunition, and moulded shells and shot, to carry war into Kentucky and Tennessee, to desolate the homes of hundreds of thousands of good people who only asked to live in peace at their old homes, and under the Government of their inheritance.

From William T. Sherman, Sherman's Civil War: Selected Correspondence of William T. Sherman, 1860–1865 *eds. Jean V. Berlin and Brooks D. Simpson (Chapel Hill, NC, University of North Carolina Press, 1999)*

1 a Compare and contrast the attitudes towards wartime destruction in Sources A and D.

b 'The intention of the North was not merely to win the American Civil War, but to crush the South so comprehensively that the Union government would be free to carry out its programme without fear of opposition.' How far do Sources A to D support this view?

Essay based questions

Answer both parts of the question below.

2 a Explain why the American Civil War broke out in 1861.

b 'Union strength lay not in its armies but in manufacturing industry, railways and ships.' How far do you agree?

3 a Explain why Johnson and Congress were unable to agree a plan for Reconstruction.

b Was Radical Reconstruction a failure?

Sample answer

Was Radical Reconstruction a failure?

In some respects the policies towards the South which were put forward by Congress in the late 1860s and early 1870s could be seen to have failed, but in other ways they could be seen to be successful. Radical Reconstruction was the set of policies put forward by Congress during the presidency of Grant after the attempted impeachment of President Johnson. It was felt that Johnson's opposition to giving more rights to African Americans had been wrong and that there needed to be more equality between the two races in the South.

> This is a good start, but, to be even better, it might have reflected briefly on what the criteria for 'failure' are in this context. It could be argued that Congress and the president faced a huge challenge, and what they achieved was a great success in the circumstances. There should also be a firmer answer in the opening paragraph. A possible response might be: 'In the short term Reconstruction could be seen as a success, but in the longer term it was a clear failure.'

President Grant certainly hoped that his policies would achieve much of what the Civil War had been trying to achieve. He was prepared to use federal troops in states where black rights were threatened by groups like the Ku Klux Klan in states like Georgia. Grant also helped carry out the Force Acts against the Klan. He was a keen supporter of the 15th Amendment which gave the right to vote to all men regardless of race and he was a strong supporter of the Civil Rights Acts of 1875 which tried to stop discrimination against black people in any public place. He was hoping to help repair the damage done in the South during the war and help in the South at the same time. In the states in the South their constitutions were changed to make sure that black people got political rights and some were elected to hold office in some of the southern states. The Freedmen's Bureau was set up which did give some help to black people, especially in building schools for them. By 1870 all southern states had been allowed back into Congress and then Enforcement Acts were passed to give the federal government the power to try and end the Ku Klux Klan and discrimination. So in these areas Reconstruction could be seen to be a success.

> This paragraph shows good focus on short-term successes.

However, in some ways Radical Reconstruction could be seen to have failed. Having a lot of troops in the South did not help to persuade southern politicians to support reconstruction and giving support to black people. The Freedmen's Bureau lacked much support from the president after it was set up and the panic of 1873 meant that more attention was now being paid to the economic problems of the North. The biggest sign of failure was the growing number of Democrats, who were often racist, being elected in both state and federal elections, and therefore in a position to stop the progress of reconstruction. There was also a growing reluctance by Congress to keep paying for a lot of troops in the South to try and force policies on the South when the majority of the population there did not want them. Therefore Reconstruction could be seen to have failed.

> This final paragraph puts a good case for the longer-term failings.
>
> Overall, this is a competent response which, with care, could easily become an excellent one. There is a good focus on Reconstruction, and on the correct part of it. There is little irrelevance and only a brief and necessary mention of the Johnson era. There is, however, evidence of balance. Both the cases for and against Radical Reconstruction being seen as a failure are examined. There is a good coverage of the topic and the detail given is quite ranging and accurate. Points are made quite clearly and are backed up with relevant and accurate detail. The style and level of communication are good.
>
> Make it absolutely clear what the objective of each paragraph is, and link it back to the initial answer in the opening paragraph. Try to avoid a very brief conclusion which doesn't seem to agree with the weight of evidence.

95

Summary

After working through this chapter, make sure you understand the following key points:

- the causes of what might appear to be an inevitable Northern victory in the US Civil War

- the ways in which political culture and daily life changed in the United States during the Civil War

- the changes and continuities in the lives of black and white Southerners in the Reconstruction period

- the causes of the rise and fall of the Radical Reconstructionist wing of the Republican Party.

Further reading

The Era of Reconstruction (New York, Vintage, 1967). Kenneth Stampp makes the case in favour of the Radical Republicans for their noble aims and the real achievement of the 14th Amendment in.

Eric Foner's seminal *Reconstruction: America's Unfinished Revolution* (New York, Harper & Row, 1988) has dominated recent historiography. He tells the story of Reconstruction as a tragedy of missed opportunity. Foner has recently concentrated on Lincoln's attitude to slavery, and telling the story of Reconstruction from the point of view of black Southerners.

Race and Reunion: The Civil War in American Memory (Harvard University Press, 2002). David Blight paints a picture of Reconstruction as a cultural meeting of minds, undermined when white Northerners and white Southerners each conceded that the other had a point.

Chapter 3
The Gilded Age and the Progressive Era, 1870s–1920

Learning objectives

In this chapter you will:

- find out what specific factors led to unprecedented economic growth in the United States in this period
- understand the political, social and economic impact of this growth on the American people
- learn how and why movements to reform much of American life started in this period
- understand the nature and extent of the success of these reform movements.

Timeline

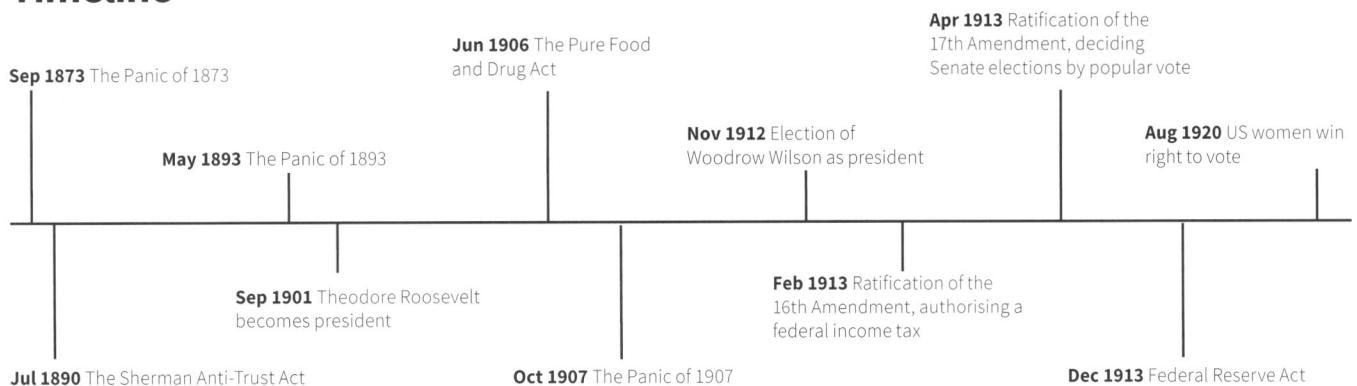

Sep 1873 The Panic of 1873

May 1893 The Panic of 1893

Jun 1906 The Pure Food and Drug Act

Nov 1912 Election of Woodrow Wilson as president

Apr 1913 Ratification of the 17th Amendment, deciding Senate elections by popular vote

Aug 1920 US women win right to vote

Jul 1890 The Sherman Anti-Trust Act

Sep 1901 Theodore Roosevelt becomes president

Oct 1907 The Panic of 1907

Feb 1913 Ratification of the 16th Amendment, authorising a federal income tax

Dec 1913 Federal Reserve Act

Before you start

Examine the Constitution of the United States from the 1870s to identify the powers given to:

- the president to manage the economy
- Congress to manage the economy
- individual states to manage the economy
- the Supreme Court to limit the states, Congress and the presidency.

How much territorial expansion took place within the United States in the period between the end of the Civil War (1865) and 1914? Did it acquire any colonies overseas?

Introduction

The period between 1870 and 1920 was a remarkable one for the United States. The country recovered rapidly from a devastating civil war in the 1860s and expanded and developed economically at a breathtaking pace. Few countries have seen such rapid economic development.

By the end of the 19th century, the United States was the world's greatest economic power and was producing more than other industrial nations, such as Germany and Britain. Capitalism was stronger than ever before and some people made millions of dollars. However, while there was great wealth and luxury for some there was a downside to the way in which capitalism developed in America. Mass urbanisation resulted in terrible living and working conditions for millions

of people. There were debates across the country about whether men and their businesses should be free from government regulation and allowed to make their millions of dollars without thinking about the consequences for others. A reform campaign, known as the Progressive Movement was born. It challenged this unregulated capitalism and demand many changes in society, government and the way the economy was managed.

This was a period of great social and economic change, and there were also major political and constitutional changes.

The **federal** system of government created by the men who drafted the US Constitution had given power primarily to the country's individual states. The American president was given very limited powers over domestic and economic issues. Congress had some authority to

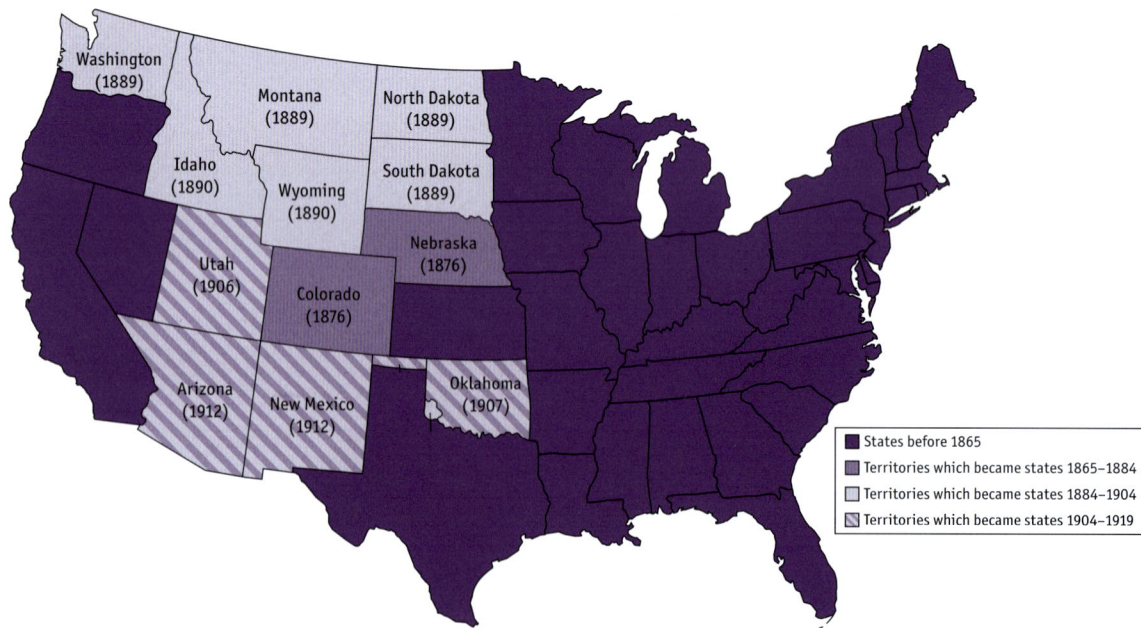

Figure 3.1: A map of the USA showing new states admitted to the Union after 1865

provide national leadership in economic matters, but was not able to deal with major challenges. The Civil War showed that unless it was persuaded to act in an emergency by the president, Congress did very little. In the period after the Civil War the United States struggled to adapt to the demands of a modern industrial economy. It was also an important period in the development of the office of president. Two presidents, Theodore Roosevelt (1901–09) and Woodrow Wilson (1913–21), rose to the challenges of the time and provided remarkable leadership as well as solutions to many of the problems which rapid industrialisation produced.

KEY TERM

Federal: A federal system of government divides power between different parts of government. Under the US Constitution quite limited powers were given to the national, or federal, government in Washington DC and most powers, such as economic regulation, were left to the individual states.

ACTIVITY 3.1

Working with another student, and using the map in Figure 3.1, consider the impact of the great expansion of territory that the United States underwent in the period between 1860 and 1914. What benefits might this expansion have brought to the country? What geographical factors do you think limited further expansion?

3.1 Why was the late 19th century an age of rapid industrialisation?

There is no single reason why the United States underwent such a remarkable transformation in the period after 1870. Many related factors played a part. These ranged the availability of raw materials such as coal and iron ore, to the attitude of the government. There was no point in businessmen building factories to make clothes, for example, if there was no transport system to bring in the necessary raw materials and take away the finished products. There had to be a supply of energy to drive the looms to make the cotton and plenty of labour to work them. There had to be capital available to enable the factory owners to borrow the money needed for their new machines at a reasonable rate of interest. There also had to be a demand for the clothing and consumers needed to be able to afford to buy it. All of these requirements

were available in America in this period. There was also a political system which put no obstacles in the way of this growth, and did all it could to encourage it.

Many factors came together to make this period one of great economic development, such as:

- the effects of the Civil War
- rapid population growth and the availability of food to feed a growing population
- the availability of land for factories, housing, transport and food production
- a rapidly expanding transport system
- access to raw materials such as coal, iron ore and cotton
- supportive federal and **state legislatures** and the absence of regulation
- great technological and business innovation and active support for both
- the availability of capital, a developed banking system and a good supply of money
- unrestricted growth of large businesses
- protective **tariffs** and growing export markets
- strong social attitudes which were sympathetic to capitalism and commercial and industrial growth.

99

KEY TERMS

State legislature: Every state in the USA has its own legislative body, democratically elected, which has the power to pass laws on every subject except those which are specifically given to Congress by the Constitution.

Tariffs: Taxes imposed on goods imported from other countries. If, for example, Britain made cheaper railway lines than was possible in the USA, the US government could impose a tax on imported British rails to ensure that it was cheaper to buy American rails. Tariffs were also a major source of the federal government's income.

The impact of the Civil War

In spite of the death and destruction it brings, conflict can often provide a great motivation to an economy. The US Civil War encouraged economic growth in a variety of ways. The victorious North created a very large army. That army needed guns, ammunition, clothing and transportation on a scale unknown in America before. The economy had to adapt to this sudden increase in demand and produce the vast amount of goods required. Goods were produced in large quantities. Mass production could deliver the materials that large armies needed and new methods of distribution were developed. Meanwhile, the government had to raise money to pay for the war. This led to a very sophisticated capital-raising system centred on Wall Street in New York. It also developed a new (and very expandable) paper currency known as the United States Note or 'greenback'. The country's banking system had to evolve to cope with the increasing amount of money in circulation and the government's growing need to borrow money. This banking system was vital in ensuring that industrial expansion could be financed. Tariffs were raised. This was partly to gain income for the government, but also to protect American goods, such as railway engines and wheat, from cheaper imports.

The Civil War was the start of a great expansion of industry in the United States. A lot of men made a lot of money out of the war by adapting and innovating in response to the demands of war. Many others wanted to do the same.

ACTIVITY 3.2

Work with another student to examine why the Civil War helped future economic growth. Which was the most important reason? Why? In what ways do you think the benefits to the economy outweighed the harm done to the country? Make a mind map or spider diagram of the reasons which identifies the links between them.

Population growth

The large growth in the population of the United States in this period was very important for industrial expansion. This population provided the workforce needed for industrial expansion. It also meant that there was an agricultural workforce which could feed this growing population. These people then became the consumers for the products that were produced.

There were two factors in this remarkable population growth. One was the growth of the existing population and the other was immigration.

The principal reason why the existing population grew so rapidly was the decline in the death rate, especially among

children. Improved living standards led to a substantial reduction in the death rate of children under the age of five. The infant mortality rate was approximately 181 per 1000 births in 1860. This dropped to 151 by 1890 and 96 by 1910 (although it is worth noting that it rose to 215 in 1880 before the cities were cleaned up). Healthier diet, greater medical knowledge and, above all, improved living standards in the cities were vital here. Better housing, cleaner water supplies and sewage disposal gradually made a difference too. Life expectancy for men also rose steadily in the period, from 44 years in 1860 to 57 years in 1920 (again with a drop in 1880). Life expectancy for African Americans, usually about 10 years less than for whites, also rose, and by the same proportion.

This rapid growth in population was a major factor in leading to an annual growth rate of the American economy by between 3.5% and 4% a year in this period. There are usually three major factors which lead to industrial growth: labour supply, availability of natural resources such as coal and availability of capital. In this case it is thought that the supply of a large amount of labour was the most important. In the USA, the workforce grew from 11.2 million in 1860 to 24 million in 1890 and to 29 million by 1900. It was that number of men and women capable of work that was so important to American economic growth.

The proportion of the workforce employed by agriculture declined from about 50% to about 35% in this period. However, the percentage of the workforce employed in manufacturing, mining, transport, construction, retail and business services such as marketing and advertising all grew considerably. **Real wages** rose by about 1% a year for non-farm workers in the period. There were more and more people in work earning more and more money to buy products with.

KEY TERM

Real wages: Income expressed in terms of purchasing power, as opposed to the actual income earned. If prices go up by 5% in a year, and your income only goes up by 1%, your real wages have declined.

ACTIVITY 3.3

Average population by decade

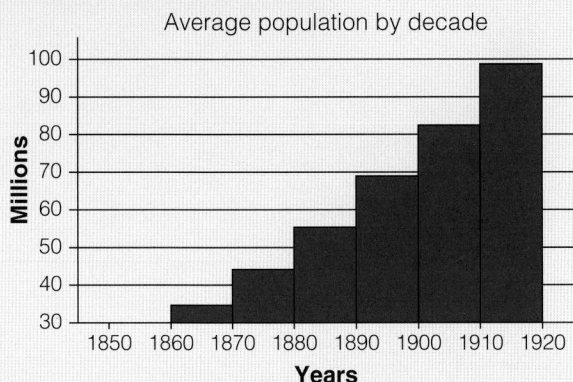

Figure 3.2: Average US population by decade, 1860–1920

Using the information in the graph above, why do you think this rapid population growth was so important to the industrialisation process in the USA? Place your reasons in order of importance and give reasons for your choices.

Land availability

One vital component in America's industrialisation was the availability of large amounts of land. The USA is a big country. Between 1800 and 1860, with acquisitions and gains such as the Louisiana Purchase (see 'Attempts at compromise' in Chapter 1.1) and lands taken from Mexico, the area of the United States went from approximately 2 million km² to over 7 million km². The **Homestead Act** of 1862 allowed farmers to settle huge areas in the West. But there were still large areas of land available for ownership by the states as well as for business and transport. Although many farmers did not prosper in this period, it did mean that there was always food available for the growing urban population. Farm productivity grew because of increasing mechanisation and the spread of greater knowledge about farming techniques. The creation of the Department of Agriculture in 1862 did much to circulate knowledge about more productive methods.

KEY TERM

The Homestead Act: This opened up millions of acres in the western United States to settlement. Any US citizen who paid a small fee would receive 160 acres of land in the West. Over 1.6 million did.

The growth of the railroads

Manufacturers needed a way to bring in the right raw materials and the coal needed to power the engines. This needed to be done efficiently and cheaply. In addition, manufacturers could do little without being able to then distribute the goods they produced. Initially, the United States developed along the eastern coast with its ports and up the major rivers such as the Mississippi. Therefore, most of the large cities were on the coast or on navigable rivers. The railroads transformed the USA by opening up the West and making rapid industrialisation possible. By 1900, every major city and its surrounding region, and all the states, were linked by one of the most comprehensive railway networks in the world. Cattle could now be easily transported from Texas to the Chicago meat-packing plants and coal from the West Virginia coalfields to the factories of New England.

What happened to the cost of freight was also critical to industrialisation. If the cost of transporting a finished product, bringing in raw materials or the wheat grown is too high, then the railroad is no use. Transport prices dropped from 2 cents per mile per ton in 1865 to 0.75 cents per mile per ton in 1900. Such low transport costs were vital for both producer and consumer. By 1890, American railroads were carrying about 79 billion tons per mile of rail each year. It was a huge achievement.

By 1900, the railways employed nearly 1 million workers, and their construction had employed many thousands more. They provided an excellent example of how a large organisation could work efficiently. They required a sophisticated capitalisation process. This stimulated the money and capital markets even more. They also revealed

101

1860

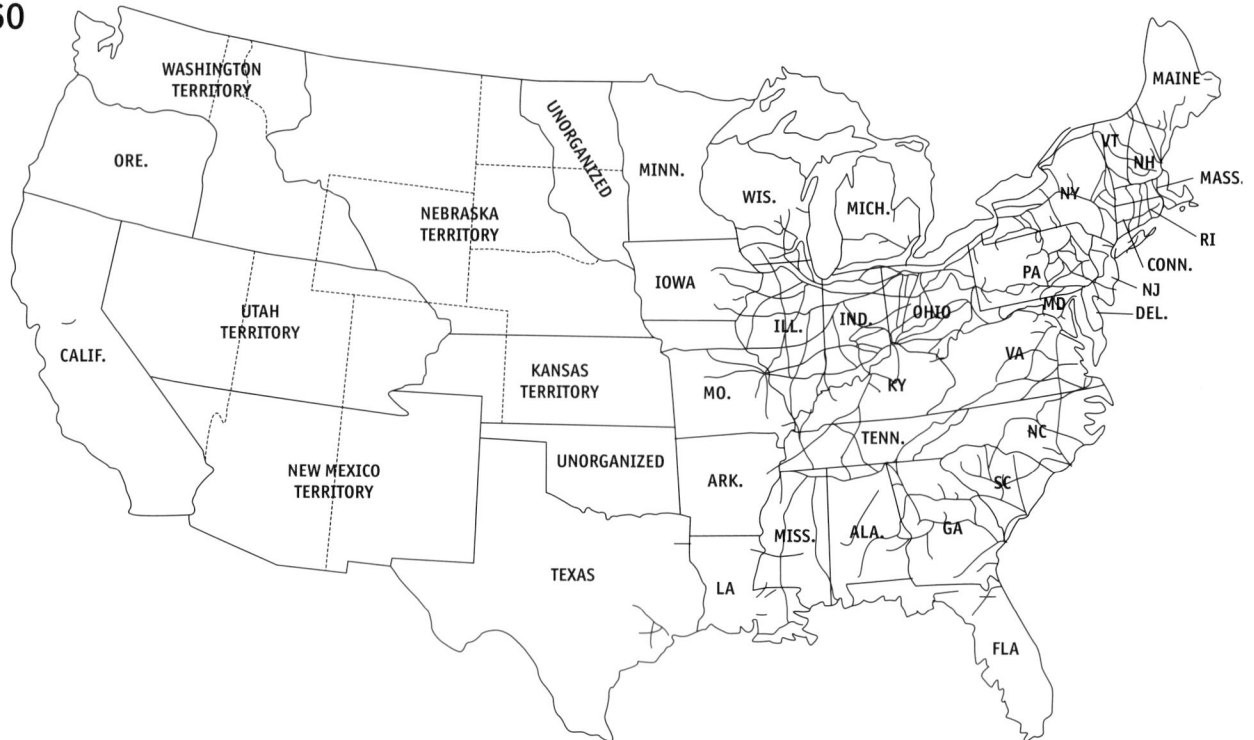

1900

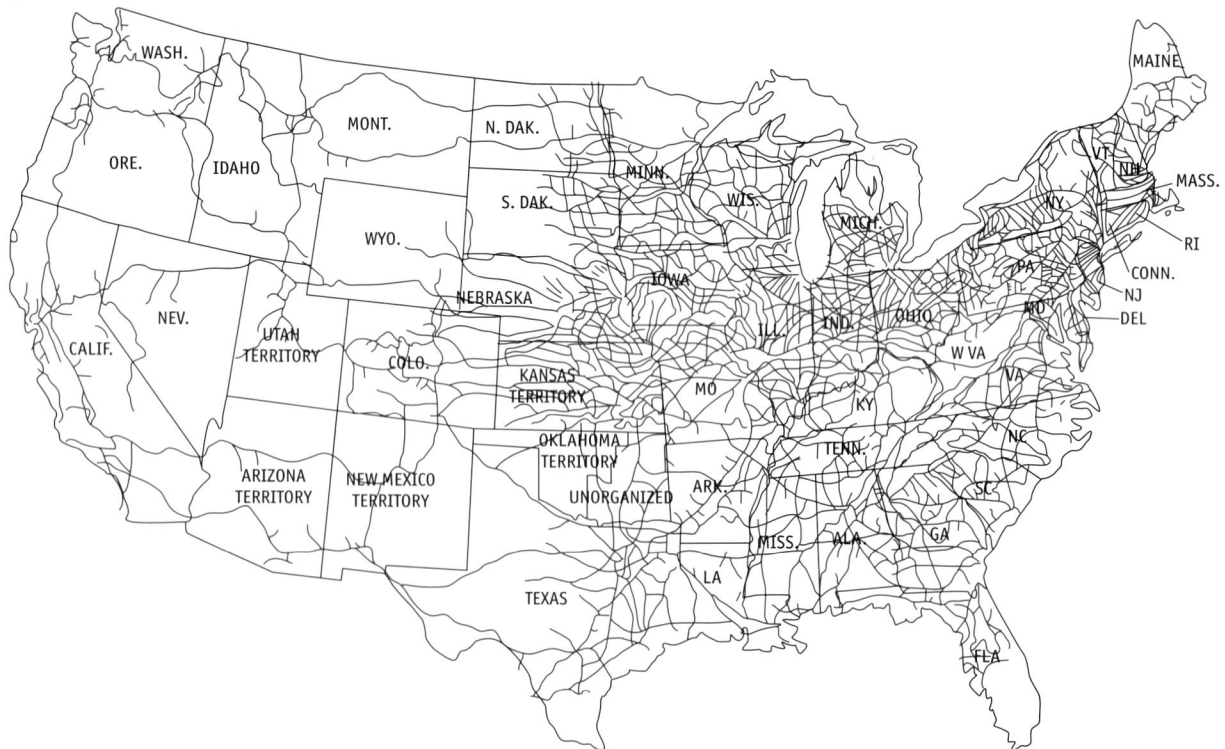

Figure 3.3: Maps showing how the US railroad network intensified with the growing population between 1860 and 1900 and contributed to the settling of territories west of the Mississippi River.

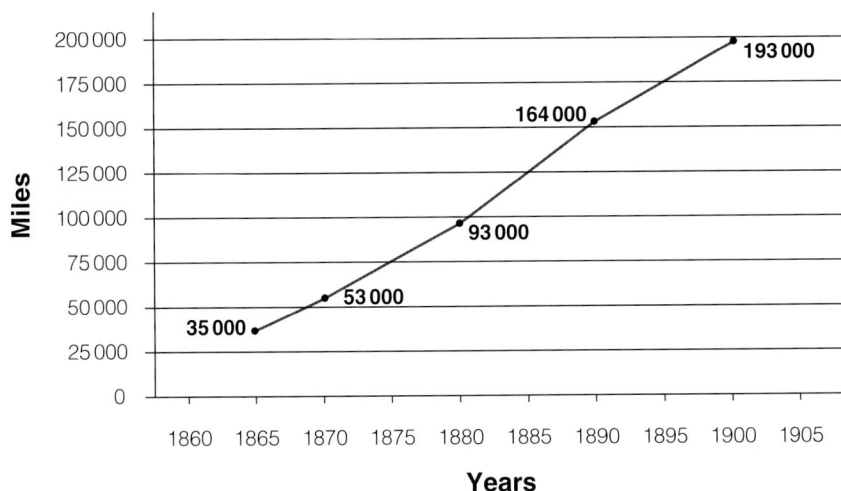

Figure 3.4: The increase in miles of railroad track in the United States. The vast majority of the US population lived near a railroad by the end of the period.

some of the risks of capitalism when the banking and financial panic of 1873 happened. Above all, the railway stimulated demand. The 311 000 km of track needed a lot of steel, and that steel needed a lot of coal to make it. New engines and rolling stock for carrying people and goods seemed to pour out of the factories. Tough competition between railroad companies kept prices down at first. The safety and efficiency requirements generated an urgent demand for technological innovation in areas such as braking and signalling. The engineer George Pullman developed special new train carriages so that passengers could travel in luxury. Retailers could send their goods to remote corners of the country. New stations were built, as well as bridges and tunnels. Engineers and architects and builders gained contracts and made profits. Even farming was boosted as American corn could now be easily exported.

There was active support from government for railroad expansion. There were few obstacles – other than natural ones such as the Rocky Mountains. Over 170 million acres of public land was given to the railroads by a sympathetic government. Much of the land which in fact wasn't needed by the railroads was sold on. The money from these sales was never returned to the government. There was no regulation or control in this vital development stage and without the railroads, there would have been limited industrialisation.

ACTIVITY 3.4

Why were railroads so important to American industrialisation?

Work with a partner to identify as many reasons as you can. Put the reasons you have identified in order of importance. Be prepared to defend your choices by making notes to show the significance of each one.

The availability of raw materials

America was fortunate in having the crucial raw materials needed for its industrialisation. Nearly 20 states had substantial deposits of coal, essential for powering textile factories, steel mills and railways engines. Coal could also provide the warmth needed by the growing city populations. America had more coal deposits than it needed and the surplus was exported using the new railroads and the new merchant ships made out of iron. There were also good supplies of iron ore, which again the railroads could transport cheaply to the steel mills. The South could produce the cotton for the textile mills of New England. The forests of the West and North could provide the timber for housing and railway sleepers. So, the raw materials essential for rapid industrialisation were already there.

103

●●● THINK LIKE A HISTORIAN

Consider the role of the state in society. Questions were being asked by some in the USA whether the state should or should not intervene in the management of the economy. Develop cases both for and against this. Then identify a current issue where you feel that the state should intervene, and explain why, but also consider what objections there might be to an intervention.

Technological innovations, such as electrical power and the telephone

There were many great success stories of businessmen and innovators in this period, and there would not have been the rapid industrialisation without them. These were men who either saw the opportunities to develop new techniques, or came up with inventions themselves. For example, engineers saw the need to develop a good braking system for railway engines, so they invented and **patented** these new pieces of equipment and made great profits. George Pullman did not invent the railway carriage, but he developed luxury carriages for the wealthy, and made a fortune that way. Two of the best-known examples of innovators like this are Andrew Carnegie and Thomas Edison.

KEY TERM

Patent: The right given by the law for an inventor to be the only person allowed to make, and profit from, an invention, usually for a fixed period of years.

Carnegie and United States Steel

Andrew Carnegie (1835–1919) was a Scottish immigrant who came to the United States as a child. He started working as a messenger boy and ended up dominating the production of steel in the country. He died a multimillionaire. Carnegie realised that the demand for steel after the Civil War was going to grow, but it was expensive to produce. He saw a new way of making steel called the Bessemer process when he visited Britain in the 1860s. This cut the price of steel by nearly 80%. It improved its quality and the speed of production and lowered labour costs at the same time. He also knew that this steel was much better for railway track as it was stronger and more hard-wearing. Working closely with Henry Frick, who controlled much of the energy supply needed for the steel mills, Carnegie built up a steel company – United States Steel. On its own, it was

producing more steel than Britain by 1900. That year, his company made a profit of $42 million.

In addition to developing the technology, Carnegie's companies invested heavily in new manufacturing plants and equipment. So, Carnegie controlled the whole steel process, from sourcing the raw materials needed, such as coal and iron ore, through the manufacturing process to distribution. He innovated, invested and kept prices as low as possible. In good times, he banked profits to keep his plants operational in bad times. However, he ruthlessly opposed any attempts to form **Labor unions** in his plants. When his workers went on strike for better pay and working conditions, Carnegie was prepared to bring in his own armed guards and to use violence to stamp out the strike. Several workers were killed and wounded in the struggle and no judicial action was taken against their employer.

KEY TERM

Labor union: An organisation of employed people, who earn their living in the same type of work as one another, such as coalminers. The union campaigns for higher wages and better working conditions for its members, and defends them against unfair dismissal or mistreatment by their employer. It might also pursue a political agenda. These organizations were also known as trade unions.

Edison and electrical power

With the Bessemer process, Carnegie showed that inventions were important, but that the ability to spot the commercial possibilities of an invention were vital. In Britain Michael Faraday made the key scientific discoveries about electricity. However, it was Thomas Edison (1847–1931) in the United States who made electricity 'commercial'. Edison was almost totally self-educated, but he was one of the greatness inventors of all time and had a great understanding of the commercial possibilities of electricity.

There are three particular reasons why Edison is such a good example of the entrepreneurship of this period:

- He was responsible for a large number of inventions, such as the light bulb.
- He had the skill to industrialise inventions, make them commercially viable, and produce and sell them on a very large scale.
- He developed the first great industrial research laboratory, with chemists, engineers and mechanics, to work on inventions.

Edison was helped considerably by the Patent Acts passed by Congress, which stopped other manufacturers from copying his ideas.

Bell and the telephone

Alexander Graham Bell (1847–1922) and the telephone was another great example of entrepreneurship in the period of industrialisation. Bell was born in Edinburgh, Scotland, but went to Canada where he became a teacher for deaf people. He moved to Boston in the USA, and was always interested in acoustics as well as electricity. Bell experimented with to produce what became the telephone. Finally he developed and patented it. (Whether he actually invented it is open to debate.) Bell had strong technical skills but also quickly saw vast commercial potential of such an invention. The Bell Telephone Company (later AT&T), more or less had a **monopoly** by 1880. This was achieved by buying up patents in the technology necessary to expand the telephone system on a national scale and by making use of the **holding company** system. The first telephone exchanges were being built by 1878. This meant that there could be communication within towns and cities, and then intercity communication became possible by 1890. This was very important to the development of business across America. By 1900, there were 600 000 telephones in the United States, and there were 5.8 million by 1910. Bell controlled the entire system, and was a multimillionaire.

> **KEY TERMS**
>
> **Holding company:** A company that does not actually make anything or provide a service. All it does is own assets, such as shares, in other companies.
>
> **Monopoly:** A commercial situation in which one individual or company owns the whole supply of a particular commodity or service.

Capital availability

While labour and resources were vital for industrialisation, so was the availability of capital. Railroads and steel mills, factories and city electrification projects needed substantial amounts of initial investment. The long-term returns on that investment were large. However, building generators to provide electricity for a city, and laying miles of cables, was an expensive process.

By 1870, a highly sophisticated capital-raising system, the stock market, had developed in New York. This was mostly due to the stimulus provided by the Civil War, when government needed money to pay for the war and arms manufacturers needed capital to build or expand their factories.

The huge profits generated by the war were invested in this stock market. It was here that the capital needed to build new steel mills or build a railway across the United States could be raised. People could invest their savings and manufacturers could invest their profits in the stock market. Both hoped for great returns on their investments. Banks invested their deposits, and insurance companies their invested clients' premiums. Institutions sprang up which specialised solely in investment. By 1865, the annual turnover on the New York Stock exchange was over $6 billion and, by 1880, it was the second largest money market in the world. The funds for industrialisation could be raised here, and investors could make money (as well as lose it) by buying shares in new companies. They hoped that they would get good **dividends** on those shares and that, if the company did well then the value of their shares would rise. However, there was no regulation of the stock market or the banking system at this time. Three serious crises, in 1873, 1893 and 1907, showed the potential weakness of the system.

> **KEY TERM**
>
> **Dividend:** When an individual invests in a company, known as buying a share, they expect to get a financial return on that investment. Companies pay this out every year in what is called an annual dividend. So, if a dividend is 10%, and you have invested $100 in a company, you will get $10.

The growth of trusts and corporations including robber barons

The effects of minimal legislation

The Constitution of the United States gave the federal government virtually no role in managing the economy. There was no desire from presidents or Congress to intervene in economic matters, except in emergencies.

There were no laws restricting the hours of labour. There were no taxes on profits. There were no rules about how business had to be conducted. State legislatures and judiciaries were in a position to bring in rules and regulations in their own states. However, they were usually dominated by local business or agricultural interests. Businessmen soon learned how to use money and pressure to ensure that the limited state control there was did not harm their interests. The law provided few, if any, obstacles to entrepreneurship. The one attempt to impose regulation, the **Sherman Anti-Trust Act** of 1890 passed by Congress, was not enforced effectively for much of the period.

KEY TERMS

Sherman Anti-Trust Act: This was designed to restrict concentration of economic power in too few hands, which could interfere with trade or reduce economic competition. Some states had already passed such measures, but without coverage of all states they were ineffective.

Corporation: A legally recognised firm. It is quite separate from its owners. It is owned by its shareholders who share in the profits and losses the corporation makes.

Trust: A simple, but legal, device to avoid some state laws which prevented companies established in one state from owning property in another state or shares in other companies. Trusts were vital for the creation of monopolies.

The United States had no tradition of labor unions in the 19th century. The few unions there were usually divided between those of the skilled workers and the unskilled, who tended to have very different interests. Some unions were prepared to use peaceful methods to achieve better pay and conditions and others were not. When industrial disputes rose, both state and federal authorities used troops to assist owners in defeating worker protests for improved pay and conditions. State assemblies, local judiciaries and police forces, largely dominated by business interests, showed little tolerance for those who went on strike during an industrial dispute. An employer could manage his workforce in any way he wanted as there were no laws or other sanctions protect his workers.

The complete absence of any formal rules and regulations until the Sherman Anti-Trust Act meant that businessmen were free to create organisations that could manage national expansion. With this, the **corporation** emerged.

For example, a corporation could own a large number of railways. It could hire the management it wanted to run them. It could sue (and be sued). It could buy, sell and own property in many states. It could merge with other railways and take over companies which made railway

engines. It could become big enough to undercut the prices of rivals and force them out of business before raising their own prices. There were many examples where corporations eliminated competition and gained the advantages of a monopoly. It could attract investors and speculators and its managers could own shares in their own companies and run it for their own benefit. There were no rules about keeping accounts or reporting to anyone such as their investors. Corporations were the perfect way for giant industries to grow.

Trusts also helped this massive expansion. Some states had existing laws that prevented a company set up in that state from owning property in another state or from owning shares in other companies. Henry Flager found a way to avoid these laws by creating a trust. This was a simple legal strategy. Flager, the secretary of Standard Oil, a vast corporation, appointed himself as a 'trustee' for the stocks and property that the company was not allowed to own. Three employees of the Standard Oil Company of Ohio, including Flager, were trustees of all the properties and assets of Standard Oil outside Ohio. Flager had created a simple and perfectly legal device to allow his company to dominate oil supply, refining and distribution in America. This company ended up controlling almost the entire US oil industry. The same thing happened in other vital areas such as steel production and railway ownership.

It was quite common by the 1870s for competing businessmen involved in a single industry, for example sugar refining or steel making, to make informal agreements together to divide up the trade and share the profits. This allowed them to avoid business threats, such as sudden recession and excess capacity and overproduction. It lowered their risks and meant they could survive the hard times. It also enabled them to control or collectively negotiate the prices of things like coal and freight. Combined size meant greater strength and increased profits.

ACTIVITY 3.5

Analyse the cartoon in Figure 3.5. What impression is the cartoonist giving of :

a   the figures leaning over the Senators at the back?

b   of the Senators themselves?

c   what is the overall point the cartoonist is trying to make?

d   how valid is his point?

e   does this cartoon show bias? If so, how?

Figure 3.5: *The Bosses of the Senate*, by Joseph Keppler. First published in Puck, 1889, this cartoon shows the major trusts in the United States leaning over senators as they debate the Sherman Anti-Trust Bill.

Industries under one-man control

With the growth of trusts a significant number of major industries gradually came under the control of one man. These trusts were usually controlled by a single individual. Oil was the first industry to be controlled by one man. Standard Oil of Ohio became a trust in 1882 with John D. Rockefeller in charge. Other major industries followed, with Andrew Carnegie controlling steel, Gustavus Swift controlling meat packing and J.P. Morgan controlling much of America's banking and railroad systems. In most cases, they had monopoly control of their industries, and competition was eliminated. They nearly always became multimillionaires. They were well known for their efficient management methods but usually treated their workforce badly. Their focus was on profit and dominance. As a result they became known as the '**robber barons**'.

KEY TERM

Robber barons: A phrase used first of all at this time by journalists, and later by historians. It was originally used in the Middle Ages to describe how a noble and his followers were able to force money from local people and travellers in a system that varied between taxation and a protection racket.

Figure 3.6: A German cartoon from 1903 of Carnegie, Morgan and William Rockefeller portrayed as kings of the areas of the economy they dominated. William Rockefeller co-founded Standard Oil with his older brother John D.

JOHN D. ROCKEFELLER (1839–1937)

Rockefeller created the Standard Oil Company through very aggressive business methods and came to dominate the oil industry in the United States. He was the first American billionaire. When he retired, he devoted his life to charitable works.

John D. Rockefeller and Standard Oil

He started as a bookkeeper in 1862 and made a $4000 investment in oil, seen as an exceptionally risky business then. By 1870 he had built up a thriving, if small,

business in oil refining through hard work, incredible personal economy and tough management. However, his aim was to dominate the entire oil business. As he started with about 3% of the refining capacity of the USA, he was aiming high. He gave rail owners shares in his company in order to get cheaper freight rates than his rivals. This meant he could undersell his rivals, then force them out of business and thus gain monopoly control. By 1880, his company produced only 2% of the nation's oil, but he controlled 90% of the refining capacity. As a result of this, he controlled the price of oil in the USA.

Backed by his enormous profits, John D. Rockefeller and his younger brother and partner William Rockefeller were able to gain more control of oil production, much of the transport system and also significant parts of the national banking system. Competition was reduced or eliminated. He controlled everything from New York, brilliantly managing and manipulating the trust system.

He took great care to gain great influence in any state legislatures which had the ability to restrict his business.

His methods did attract criticism. In 1886, an investigating committee of the US Senate reported:

> It is well understood in commercial circles that the Standard Oil Company tolerates no competition. Its settled policy and firm determination is to crush out all who may be rash enough to enter the field against it; that it hesitates at nothing in the accomplishment of this purpose, in which it had been remarkably successful, and that it represents the acme [high point] and perfection of corporate greed in its fullest development.
>
> *From Ida Tarbell,* The History of the Standard Oil Company (1904) (available, for example, at www. pagetutor.com/standard/)

However, Rockefeller didn't stop. Legislation was passed against trusts to prevent the commercial methods of men like Rockefeller but his large team of lawyers came up with a new legal device to get around this law. In 1889, the holding company (a business formed to sell and buy shares of other companies which it then controls) was formed, allowing Rockefeller to maintain control over the oil industry. Enormous profits poured into his bank accounts. He seemed above the law.

By 1900, he controlled the domestic and foreign oil market and the whole industry from the oil wells to the automobile's lubricating oil and petrol tank. His organisation also made the asphalt which made the roads which the automobiles drove on. His company was making nearly $20 million dollars a year profits for him by 1890 and paying out dividends of over $11 million to his delighted shareholders.

J. P. Morgan and investment banking

Like several of the other robber barons, J. P. Morgan (1837–1913) did not come from a poor background. His father was a wealthy and successful investment banker and Morgan followed in his footsteps. In the 1860s he saw opportunities in the growing railway industry and he joined the group of robber barons. Some railway companies were having financial difficulties. This was due to a mixture of overbuilding of tracks in some areas, falling prices and national recession. Morgan invested in many of these companies and took control of them. Many of these companies were in the heavily populated north-east of the country, and gradually he gained control of passenger

and freight prices. This enabled his companies to build up substantial profits.

These large profits were usually gained by a degree of monopoly control. He invested in, or just bought out, a large number of banks in New York, insurance companies and investment trusts. By 1900, he had enormous influence on railroads as well as the capital market in the United States. Major corporations such as Edison Electric (the new electrical industry) and International Harvester (farm machinery) got their start-up funding from Morgan. Morgan played a substantial role in the resolution of the two financial crises in 1893 and 1907. He became enormously influential as he preferred cooperation to open rivalry. In 1901, he took over Carnegie's steel empire and created the United States Steel Corporation. This was the world's first billion-dollar corporation. So, he controlled most of the steel industry and capital in America. In 1901, he created his Northern Securities Corporation which controlled much of the rail network in the north-east as well. He also bought out the struggling *New York Times* to ensure that he got a favourable reports in the newspapers.

Trade policies and protectionism

Congress in this period was largely influenced by business interests as presidents and their cabinets were highly responsive to the needs of US industry and overseas trade. The economic policies of government helped commercial expansion. Congress was happy to impose protective tariffs and the government enforced them. The intention of the tariffs was to ensure that foreign-made goods were always more expensive than home-produced ones, therefore protecting US producers. These duties could be as much as 50% of the cost of imported goods and effectively forced people to buy American goods. Tariffs could be unpopular with many consumers as they also pushed up prices of the imported items that they needed to buy, like sugar. Tariffs were the principal source of the federal government's income which was another complication. (A federal income tax or tax on business profits was not introduced until the next century.) There was little chance of significant change while business interests controlled Congress and the government needed income to pay for the civil service and the military.

Tariffs remained controversial, especially in the 1880s and 1890s. Manufacturers liked them, as they reduced competition from aboard, but the farmers of the South and West did not as they increased their operating costs. Other countries responded by imposing similar tariffs on American goods which therefore damaged exports. The Republican Party supported tariffs and the Democrats opposed them. However, they remained as the Republicans were dominant in both the presidency and Congress in the latter part of the 19th century. There were two changes in the 1890s, but they were relatively minor. The first, known as the McKinley Tariff raised the rates imposed on imported goods, which hit consumers very hard. When the rate on imported sugar was later cut, the Sugar Trust, which controlled the whole market, kept the prices artificially high and made even greater profits. This really angered many voters. The only real change from the 1890 Act was the decision to lower tariffs on goods coming in from the foreign nations who would also agree to lower their tariffs on goods they imported from America.

Tariffs became a major issue in the elections of 1890 as a result of the McKinley Act. The Republicans, the party of business, supported them, while the Democrats strongly opposed them. The Democrats did well in elections to the House of Representatives in particular. They ran a campaign arguing that high food prices were caused by the Republicans and their tariffs and that 'two thousand millionaires were running the country in their own interests'. In 1894, the Democrats put a bill through Congress, known as the Wilson–Gorman Bill, which tried to cut many tariffs. However, Republicans in the Senate were able to add so many amendments that there were hardly any reductions in the end. This led to a growing demand to change the way Senators were elected. At that time, they were chosen by the State Legislatures. These were often business-controlled, and Senators and were not directly elected by the people of the state like members of the House of Representatives were. Protective tariffs remained a major issue between the two parties throughout the period.

The government also provided assistance to the industrial process with its foreign policy. Great care was taken to ensure that much of the Caribbean and Central America was open to US business. The same happened in the Philippines, China and Japan. A growing US navy (another boost for American industry) ensured that American trade was protected overseas. The State Department did all it could to support US commerce, especially in the potentially vast markets of China and Japan.

There was rapid industrialisation in the US in the final three decades of the 19th century. This was due to a combination of human dynamism, unlimited resources, bold entrepreneurship, plenty of labour and great demand, as well as a lack of serious obstacles or regulation.

ACTIVITY 3.6

Working in a group, allocate each member one of the principal causes of American industrialisation in this period. Each member should research their cause in depth and bring back to the group four key points why their cause was critical, with supporting detail. Reach a conclusion about which cause should be seen as the most important, and why.

Reflection: Consider why industrialisation was so rapid in this period. Discuss with your group how you would define 'rapid', and agree on a definition.

3.2 How great were the consequences of rapid economic growth in the late 19th century?

The American economy grew at an exceptionally fast rate and the statistics look impressive but there were inevitable human consequences. Unregulated capitalism had its failings. The principal criticisms that could be made of this rapid growth were:

- The accumulation of political power, and the abuse of that power, by powerful men in the rapidly growing cities who became known as the 'bosses'
- The concentration of wealth and political power held by the robber barons
- The impact that economic recession had on industrial workers and their families
- The impact of urbanisation on living conditions, housing, health and safety.

New immigration from southern and eastern Europe

There was an extensive supply of immigrant labour, desperate for employment and prepared to work long hours. This was very important to the industrialisation process.

Few of the second-generation Americans were willing to tolerate the conditions in most factories in the cities so this immigrant workforce, which was largely unskilled, provided one of the most important elements in any industry, the labour. In the early part of the industrialisation process, most of the migrants, like Andrew Carnegie, came from northern and western Europe, mainly England, Scotland, Ireland and Germany. However, by the end of the 19th century the majority were coming from countries like Italy, Greece, the Balkans, Russia and the Austro-Hungarian Empire in southern, eastern and central Europe. These people were encouraged to leave their homes because of religious persecution, poverty, unemployment and a desire for political freedom and economic opportunity. A demand for cheap labour led to the United States welcoming them. It was one of the most remarkable migrations in modern history as millions of Americans moved west, and millions more new 'Americans' arrived. The fact that these different people could come together so peacefully, and could then play such an important role in making the United States into a great economic and world power, is a tribute to the wisdom of the men who drafted the American Constitution.

Industrial growth and periods of economic recession

The period between 1860 and 1914 was overall one of economic growth but there were three major setbacks which demonstrated how fragile the American economic system was. There were three major 'panics' when growth stopped and unemployment rose rapidly. They came in 1873, 1893 and 1907. These were mostly due to failings in the country's largely unregulated banking and stock market system. One result was to increase the demand for regulation in those areas. They also had a major impact on the lives of millions of working-class Americans who suddenly lost their jobs. A growing proportion of the population was dependent on a regular wage from a factory or railroad company to feed and house themselves and their families. There was no welfare system so unemployment led to hunger and destitution on a large scale. This also led to a demand for economic change.

ACTIVITY 3.7

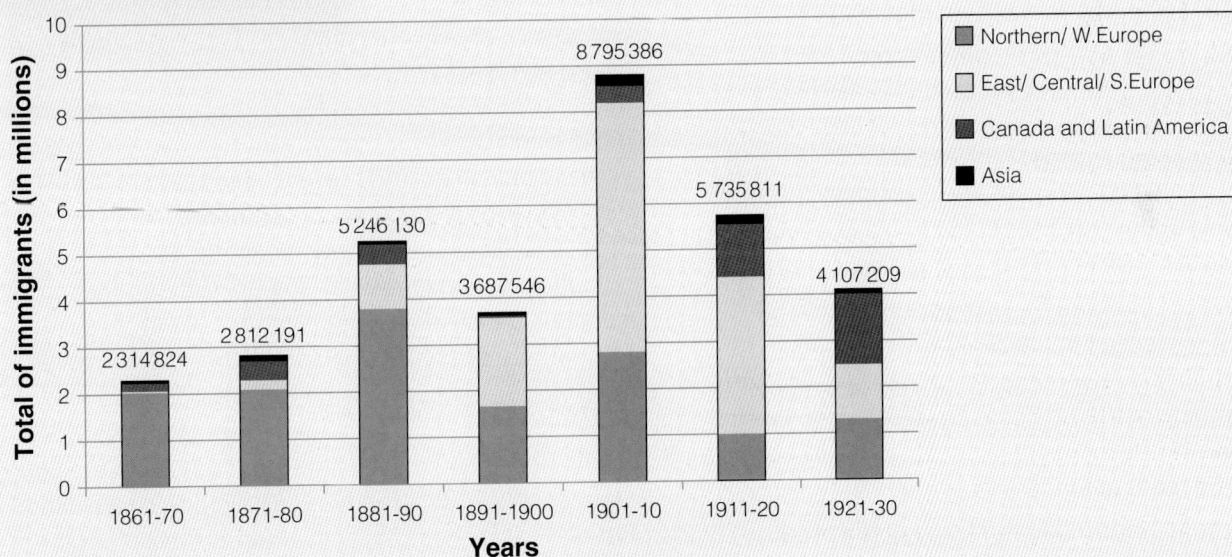

Figure 3.7: Number and origin of immigrants into the USA, 1861–1930

Analyse the graph above showing immigration data. What do you think is the link between this data and industrial growth? What do you think explains the highest and the lowest figures?

The Panic of 1873

The first major recession to hit the United States came in 1873. The principal cause was speculative railroad expansion. Too many rail companies were building tracks to nowhere in the hope that a major city would grow as a result. These railroad builders and their investors were often disappointed as this did not happen. The other problem was the lack of a regulated national banking system. Unlike in Britain, for example, where there was a central bank (the Bank of England), which had some control over both the supply of money and the conduct of individual banks, there was nothing similar in the USA until 1913. The many small local banks tended to keep just small reserves of cash, and placed most of the money deposited with them in the big New York banks. These deposits counted as their reserves. If a large number of local bank depositors wanted their cash, the local bank could get it back quickly from New York. Of course the New York banks loaned out their huge deposits. This was often to railroad companies for their projects which were often risky.

The weakness in this system became clear when the activities of the companies that received the large loan by the New York banks, failed. When this happened, and railroad companies went bankrupt and were unable to repay loans, panic spread. Local depositors demanded their money back, in cash. However, the New York banks were unable to return cash to the local banks. The stock market shut down for a period and even banks had to close down. People who had their money deposited in those banks lost it. Meanwhile, developing industries could not raise loans and any money they had borrowed was demanded back. There were a great many bankruptcies of large and small businesses.

Although accurate statistics are hard to find for this period, it is estimated that unemployment among industrial workers rose to 14% in 1873–74 and many businesses cut their employees' wages by up to 25%. This reduced buying power and made the recession worse. It also hit farming very hard. This was partly as prices for farm produce dropped, and partly because many farmers had borrowed against crops in the ground. These loans were recalled by local banks before the crops could be harvested. Farmers could not repay their loans at short notice, so they too went bankrupt. This increased the movement of people from rural areas to the cities. Together with mass immigration, this made the employment situation even worse. Unemployment didn't drop substantially and real wages didn't rise until the end of the 1870s.

The Panic of 1893

There was a much more serious crisis in 1893. It was known as the 'Great Depression' until an even worse one hit in the 1930s. It caused greater distress and lasted longer than the crisis of 1873, but had basically similar causes. These included an overexpansion in industry and railroad development, along with speculation in the stock market and a weak banking system. The central bank was not strong enough to slow down the economy when it was needed. The fact that the federal government didn't have a coherent monetary policy didn't help the situation.

Severe drought in farming regions made the situation even worse, reducing spending power, and again speeding up the move from countryside to the city by the poor. There was also a considerable fall in exports because of political and economic problems in Europe, and the prices farmers could get abroad for wheat and cotton dropped drastically.

Statistics are not very accurate in this period, but unemployment rose from around 3 million in 1892 to around 10 million in 1893 and around 13 million by 1894, and did not fall significantly until at least 1899. There was a large reduction in the consumption of all goods. Large scale strikes in both the coal and rail industries worsened the situation, many workers were already facing severe wage reductions. There was much less demand for steel and coal as railroad expansion slowed down significantly and this meant that many workers in those industries and those related to them lost their jobs. The export market was declining at the same time, so selling goods unwanted in the USA was not an option. Urban industrial workers suffered the most from this. Stock market speculators (who received little sympathy) and bankers had difficulties too. Levels of poverty rose as there was no welfare system to provide benefits such as unemployment insurance. Nearly 500 banks closed and many failed for good. Almost 15 000 separate business closed in 1893–94. The construction industry, a large employer in better times, suffered particularly badly.

The government provided no support for the unemployed. In addition, it made little attempt to analyse what had happened and why perhaps to ensure it did not happen again. While individual states did take some actions to remedy what they saw as local issues, the federal government in Washington simply did not see it as its problem and did not feel that it was its responsibility to act. In addition, business interests were so strong in both Houses of Congress that any action which might be seen to harm them was very likely to fail. However, it was remarkable how J.P. Morgan played a crucial role in ending the currency and stock market crisis. His power was worrying as he was able to help to prevent the flight of gold abroad as he bought shares to restore business confidence. It highlighted how much influence one extremely wealthy individual who was unelected into any office had. He was representing only himself and his own interests, but he played such a decisive role in managing the whole American economy.

The Panic of 1907

This crisis was known as the 'rich man's panic'. The focus of both its causes and results was primarily the New York stock exchange, Wall Street. As in 1893, there were influential factors beyond the US, with banking crises in several European countries. However, the crisis in the USA started in the New York stock market. Again, speculation was the cause of the problem. Banks usually had to keep about 25% of their depositors' money in cash or gold reserves. This was so that if some customers needed their money back in a hurry, there was cash available to give to them.

However, there had been a large growth of investment trusts where individuals could leave their money for the trust to invest on their behalf. These tended to have much more limited reserves of cash. In 1907, a major investment trust called the 'Knickerbocker Trust' collapsed as a result of poor investments. This meant that its customers lost their money and many depositors in other trusts feared the same would happen to them. Therefore they demanded their money back. Some trusts did not have the money available and became bankrupt themselves. So fear spread and share prices dropped and so did much investment.

This series of bankruptcies had a wide-ranging effect on US industry. Industrial production dropped by 11% nationally in a single year. Demand for goods fell and many workers lost their jobs and others faced wage reductions. Unemployment, which was mostly in industrial cities, rose from 3% to 11% and there was a substantial increase in poverty. The depression remained until 1914 when war in Europe led to a major increase in demand for products that the USA could make. The same thing happened in the 1930s, when war played a major role in American recovery from its next major depression.

J.P. Morgan was to play a major role in alleviating this crisis too but overall this crisis was different from previous ones. While it also highlighted the failings of the banking system and the stock market, this time government was prepared to act in attempting to prevent it from happening again. The need for a strong central bank, similar to the Bank of England was made very clear. The Federal Reserve Bank was created in 1913 as part of a wider reform and regulatory process (see page 136). However, no action was taken to deal with the problems facing unemployed industrial workers or those whose wages were so reduced they were unable to feed their families.

ACTIVITY 3.8

COPPER BREAKS HEINZE WATERLOO COMES TO YOUNG NAPOLEON AND BANKS TOTTER

"Sensations followed each other in rapid succession in the financial district today as the result of the collapse of the projected corner in United Copper and the suspension of a prominent brokerage firm yesterday, As a result of these sensations the stock market was halting and irregular, but there was an apparent feeling that the break of the attempted corner in United Copper had cleared the atmosphere somewhat, and the market rallied before the close."

October 18, 1907 Boston Post *headline and newspaper article extract*

Analyse the source above. What does the article suggest are the main reasons for the collapse of the company? To what extent does this explain the causes of the Panic of 1907?

What other factors could be seen to cause the Panics? Weigh up the various factors and put them in order of importance. What are your reasons for placing them in this order?

The concentration of wealth and political power held by the robber barons

By 1900, the newly industrialised USA produced an unusual phenomenon. A small group of businessmen succeeded in dominating American business, and at the same time had a significant social impact as well. The barons had been criticised for how they had accumulated their money and often acquiring monopoly control over an industry, were also criticised for the ways in which they spent their money. They had huge amounts of money. The railway and shipping industrialis Cornelius Vanderbilt left $105 million when he died in 1877. Andrew Carnegie sold his businesses for $480 million in 1901 and Rockefeller was estimated to be worth $2 billion in 1916. They built themselves large mansions in New York, and additional summer and winter homes which used for only a few weeks in a year. Their agents toured Europe buying up thousands of works of art and library collections to decorate their mansions. They brought dress designers to America from Europe for their wives and daughters, French chefs for their kitchens and French wines for their cellars. They became the nearest the United States had to an aristocracy, and their daughters often married European aristocrats. The large gifts of cash that the daughters took with them when they married would help to restore, for example, an old aristocratic castle in Britain.

By the time of his death in 1913, J. P. Morgan's organisations controlled resources of over $22 billion. As one critic pointed out, this was more than the collective resources of the 22 states to the west of the Mississippi river. It was the first time that so much economic power was held by so few people.

Perhaps it was unusual that most of these tycoons gave away much of their fortunes. Men like Carnegie gave museums, libraries and universities large amounts of money. Hospitals and medical research benefitted as well. The United States had been seen as a cultural backwater, with many of its artists and writers moving to Europe, but this was reversed with the donations of the money of often poorly educated men. By the First World War, the USA was as strong intellectually and culturally as it was economically. This was largely due to the philanthropic work of these men.

Although some of the barons donated large amounts of their profits to good causes, such as education, museums and public libraries, the degree of power and influence, as well as the methods they used to accumulate and retain their wealth, was a problem in the industrialisation process. Alongside this, the way they showed their wealth in their huge mansions, estates and lifestyles was an obvious contrast with the appalling living and working conditions of so many of their employees. This would produce strong reactions.

ACTIVITY 3.9

Compare and contrast the different views on Trusts expressed in both the image, and in Carnegie's quote, taken from the image caption. Which makes its point most effectively?

This political cartoon appeared in Harper's Weekly (October 20, 1888). The artist was William A. Rogers. The image depicts Andrew Carnegie speaking with Uncle Sam while a 'beast' stands behind him. Below is the caption that accompanied the image:

A Trustworthy Beast.

'The public may regard Trusts or combinations with serene confidence.'

Andrew Carnegie, in an interview with the New York Times, *October 1900*

The impact of urbanisation on living conditions

One of the most obvious features of rapid industrialisation, apart from factories and steel mills, were the rapidly growing cities. The majority of Americans in 1860 lived in rural areas, on farms or in small towns. Half a century later, industrialisation led to a major change in where Americans lived. Small towns, particularly in the north-east, became great cities. Some of the new city-dwellers were native-born Americans moving from farms to factories; others were the new migrants coming from Europe.

Date	Urban dwellers (millions)	% of population living in cities
1860	6.2	20
1870	9.9	25
1880	14.1	28
1890	22	35
1900	30	40
1910	42	46

Table 3.1: The number of people living in urban areas of the USA and as a percentage of the whole population

The management of cities and the growth of the 'boss' system

US towns before this period had a system of local government which was adequate for small towns. As many hundreds of thousands of new citizens arrived into these towns, along with factories and railroads, there were problems. It placed enormous strains on how cities could be.

An alternative system developed in many cities to deal with this new range of issues. These included public health, housing, welfare, provision of services like clean water and sewage disposal, jobs, transport and law enforcement. A new, largely informal, arrangement emerged to deal with the needs and problems of:

- providing jobs and housing for immigrants and the poor coming in from rural areas
- legitimate businesses which needed factory sites, land for railroads, contracts for road making and facilities such as transport provision
- illegitimate businesses and criminals where some organisation would help to avoid a degree of conflict between rival gangs.

The new city leaders (the 'bosses') and their organisations – known as 'machines' – provided for these varied needs. In most cases this was very profitable for the `bosses'.

Perhaps the most successful and best-known example was **'Boss' Tweed** and his organisation in New York in the 1860s and early 1870s. Tweed was elected to a local government position in 1851, just as New York was starting its rapid expansion. With three colleagues, also local officials, he created an organisation which gave them power over the city and great personal wealth through corruption. In each local part of the city, known as a ward, the Tweed 'machine' had a paid agent. This was the man

who a new migrant to the city would go to for a job or housing or to get family member out of trouble with the police. This was the man who could sort out permission for a new factory site or persuade the police to ignore criminal activity.

New migrants were expected to repay these favours with their votes. Businessmen or criminals would pay in cash. Tweed gained enormous power and wealth as he took control of all the major services in a city, such as transport, and controlling all the jobs in the city, including policemen and tax collectors. He was associated with dishonest elections. There were several elections in New York where more people voted for the Tweed-approved local candidate than there were actual residents entitled to vote. The phrase 'vote early and vote often' was regularly heard in New York. Tweed raised money for city improvements but much of it ended up in his own pockets. He bribed legislators in both New York City and State, and judges and police chiefs too. It was said that 'It was better to know the judge than know the law.' However Tweed was careful to make it well known that he gave money to charity, schools and hospitals. He did this, but it was only a tiny fraction of what he kept for himself.

William M. 'Boss' Tweed rose through the New York political system and he and his associates dominated both the city and the state until his arrest for corruption. He was able to steal millions of dollars from both the city and the state through his control of the local Democratic Party, with its headquarters at Tammany Hall. He was finally exposed after a major campaign by the *New York Times*, and was arrested and died in jail.

His downfall came when he finally caused too much anger among the middle class of New York over the building of (or rather the failure to build) a new courthouse in New York. The *New York Times* ran a very effective campaign against him. It became known that Tweed and his colleagues had managed to raise over $13 million to build the new

Figure 3.8: A cartoon showing Tweed and his corrupt cronies welcoming death in the form of cholera and Asia (as written on Death's bag) into the slums of New York. They were the men who had the political power and could have improved the quality of life in the city, but actually made conditions worse. How reliable is this cartoon as evidence for how bossism was viewed in this period?

courthouse, which was never finished. Most of the money was kept by Tweed and his fellow criminals. It was estimated that over a 30-month period towards the end of the 1860s:

- the income of New York City and State was approximately $72 million
- the city, run by Tweed and his associates, paid out $139 million, but it was not clear where the money went
- Tweed and his associates stole about $45 million of public money.

Tweed and his associates were eventually driven out of office and jailed, but the public's money was lost for ever. The system of corruption and incompetence he created took years to overcome. The public did not get the services it had paid for, and hundreds of thousands of city dwellers continued to live in appalling conditions which could have been avoided. Similar 'machines' were found in other growing cities, such as

Chicago, Philadelphia and St Louis, and in many cases these 'machines' lasted well into the 20th century.

ACTIVITY 3.10

Why did 'bossism' emerge in the United States in this period? Identify at least three reasons which explain the rise, together with at least two factual examples to support each reason. Which do you think is the most important reason, and why?

Housing, health and safety

Industrialisation leads to urbanisation. As we have seen, after the Civil War, US cities grew in size and population For example, Chicago's population went from 300 000 in

Figure 3.9: A photograph revealing the poor living conditions in a New York City tenement for recent immigrants at the end of the 19th century. The photograph was taken by Jacob August Riis, a journalist and early photographer who used this medium to campaign for social reform.

1870 to over 1.5 million by 1900, which made it one of the fastest-growing cities in the world. It was a canal junction and a railhead, as well as a regional hub. It was a major centre for the cattle and grain industries. Meat-packing industries grew up there on a huge scale. It became a huge centre for manufacturing, transport and commerce.

The affluent middle class could take advantage of their horses and the new railroads to commute from the outer suburbs. However, most of the workers and their families lived in a comparatively small area, close to the factories and meat-packing plants where they worked. These areas had a very high population density. In the main working-class districts, as many as 340 people per acre were packed in. In 1890, it was estimated that 7300 children lived in just three city blocks. In New York in 1890, over 1 million people, about two-thirds of the city's population, were crammed into about 32 000 **'dumbbell' tenement buildings**. These were given names like 'Poverty Gap' and

'Misery Row' which provide a powerful picture of how their inhabitants viewed them.

> **KEY TERM**
>
> **Dumbbell tenement buildings:** Accommodation blocks, five to seven stories high, built with two air shafts on the inside, and designed to house as many people as possible in as little space as possible. They always lacked light, ventilation and proper sanitation.

Living conditions were dreadful in many of these tenements. The aim of the landlords was to squeeze as many people as possible into limited space so as to maximise their profits. No attention was paid to important factors such as safety, heat, ventilation, light, clean water or sewage disposal. The majority of tenements did not have access to clean water or effective sewage disposal until well into the 20th century. Sewage was dumped in the streets or open sewers. The large number of horses that used the streets added to the filth. Street cleaning was limited or non-existent. Unsurprisingly, cities became breeding grounds for ill-health.

Further problems were caused by a contaminated water supply. In Chicago, the drinking water for the inner-city population came from Lake Michigan, which the Chicago River flowed into. This river contained the untreated industrial waste from Chicago's factories and meat-packing plants, and also the raw sewage from the tenements.

Even though the link between contaminated water supplies and diseases such as cholera had been known since about 1860, that information was not considered:

In a dark cellar filled with smoke, there sleep, all in one room, with no kind of partition dividing them, two men and their wives, a girl of thirteen or fourteen, two men and a large boy of about 17, a mother with two more boys one about 10 years old, and one large boy of 15, another woman with two boys, nine and eleven years of age – in all fourteen persons.

From Charles Loring Brace, **The Dangerous Classes of New York and Twenty Years Work Among Them** *(New York, Wynkoop and Hallenbeck, 1872)*

Diseases such as cholera, smallpox (for which a vaccination had been available for decades), measles, diphtheria, tetanus, tuberculosis and, above all, cholera, were widespread and killed thousands housed in these appalling living conditions. The average life expectancy for a man living in Chicago or Philadelphia at this time was 44 years and was 48 years for a woman. In rural areas, the life expectancy was 54 for men and 55 for women. A child in a city was more than twice as likely to die as one in the countryside and about 25% of urban children died before the age of 5. While some cities did appoint public health officials, they often had limited powers and funds, and doctors often saw them as a professional threat. Too much of local government was controlled by men like Tweed whose main interests were power and wealth for themselves. It was not until after 1900 that a determined effort was made to end the appalling conditions that many lived in.

Working conditions

The first really accurate survey of working life in the USA came in 1900. In that year, over 35 000 men, women

and children were killed in industrial accidents and over 500 000 injured. In some industries, such as mining and meat-packing, you were more likely to be killed, seriously injured or contract a serious disease caused by your working conditions than to avoid these disasters. Almost no compensation schemes were available. Fewer than 5% of working men lived over the age of 60. It seemed that people worked in unsafe conditions until they died. At the same time, there were over 1.7 million children under the age of 15 working in factories.

ACTIVITY 3.11

Compare Fig 3.9 with the source below. In what ways does the photograph reinforce the points made in the Source?

Contrast the validity of the two sources. Which source is more reliable and why?

It is almost everywhere true that people die more rapidly in cities than in rural areas. There is no inherent or eternal reason why men should die faster in large communities than in small hamlets. Leaving aside accidental causes, it may be affirmed that this excessive urban mortality is due to a lack of pure air, water and sunlight, together with uncleanly habits of life induced thereby. Part cause, part effect, poverty and overcrowding, high rates of mortality are found together in the city tenements.

From Adna Weber, **The Growth of Cities in the Nineteenth Century** *(New York, 1899)*

Several factors contributed to these poor working conditions:

- an almost endless supply of cheap labour, as immigrants came in to the United States in large numbers and people looked for a way out of rural poverty
- weak labor unions which were unable to organise effectively
- limited or no regulation by the local or national governments
- businesses controlling of the local, state and federal legislatures which were in a position to change conditions
- a long tradition of letting things take their own course in the United States.

The standard working week for men was a minimum of 60 hours. They had few breaks and often no sanitation facilities. Management made sure the workers worked very fast and factory work was often both tedious and physically demanding. There was usually no sick pay or holidays, no unemployment insurance or job security. Employers could hire and fire when they wanted and a recession could leave an entire community out of work. Researchers in 1902 found women working over 70 hours a week in New York clothing factories in temperatures of over 100°F for $2.5 a week. They had fewer than 30 minutes break a day. There was no running water available or proper sanitation and there were serious fire risks but no fire escape.

KEY CONCEPT

Cause and consequence

Look at the information in this chapter on living conditions in many American cities in this period. Were poor living conditions solely the consequences of rapid population growth and immigration, or did other causes contribute? Make a list of as many causes as you can that explain why urban living conditions were so poor for so many of the working class. In what ways can you link these reasons together?

ACTIVITY 3.12

Study the Factory Inspector's comments below. Why do you think such working conditions were tolerated? Why do you think they had actually come into existence? What do you think is the link between these conditions and economic growth?

From 1902 to 1907, factory inspectors produced an unofficial journal, including the following three extracts:

> At a steel mill in Butler, Pennsylvania, a heavy pot of hot metal spilled molten steel onto wet sand, causing a huge explosion which destroyed part of the plant. Streams of hot metal poured down on the workmen, engulfing and literally cooking some of them. Four men died and 30 more were injured. The explosion shook buildings in the town and caused panic among the populace. Thousands turned out to watch the huge fire that ensued.
>
> Two employees at a steel plant in Youngstown, Ohio were sent to clean out the dust underneath the blast furnaces. Suddenly there was a slippage of tons of molten fuel and ore inside the furnace, causing large amounts of very hot dust to fall on them. One of the men was completely buried in it and died in great agony. The other escaped with severe burns.

> In plain sight of a hundred fellow-workmen, Martin Stoffel was cut into small pieces at the Philadelphia Caramel Works... He was dragged into the machinery and his head severed... A second later both legs were cut off. Then one arm after the other fell into the lesser wheels below, both being cut into many parts. Before the machinery could be stopped, Stoffel had been literally chopped to pieces.

It is estimated that in each year of the inspectors' journal, 1200 men were killed or injured from a workforce of about 10 000. In one horrific accident, a man was roasted alive by molten slag that spilled from a giant ladle when a hook from an overhead crane slipped. The ladle lacked proper fittings and the hook was attached dangerously under the rim. The company, U.S. Steel, could have stopped such accidents but didn't have a strong incentive to do this. When a man was killed on the job, there was only one chance in five that the company would ever have to pay compensation to his family.

The USA's economic `miracle' gave too much power and wealth to a small number of people, and meant that millions lived and worked in awful conditions. Inevitably, there would be demands for change. After 1900 the changes started to come.

119

> **Reflection:** What evidence was important in leading you to answer the questions? What additional evidence might you need to support your answers further?

The rise of organised labour in industry and agriculture

The labour unions

In this period, trade unions, where groups of workers join together to protect their employment interests, achieved little. The US Constitution gave people a right to associate and communicate freely, but there were many barriers which stopped the new industrial workforce from getting better pay and working conditions. Labor unions had existed before this rapid industrialisation, but they tended to be small groups of skilled craftsmen, such as watch-makers or hat-makers. They came together to preserve their status as skilled men and provide benefits such as pensions for their members. The arrival of the factory, which demanded fewer skills and greater discipline, changed this.

It was now much easier for the large numbers of men in factories to group together to press for better wages and conditions. However, there were many obstacles to labor unions achieving these objectives, including:

- a hostile environment in the United States towards anything that might limit the right of an individual employer making maximum profits for himself
- the tendency of government at all levels to support employers who were in dispute with their workforce. This meant that the courts and the police almost invariably sided with the employer
- Congress and state legislatures were still dominated by business interests and so they were reluctant to enact laws which might in any way damage employer interests
- a large supply of cheap labour coming in from Europe, and now the Far East, prepared to put up with low pay and bad working conditions
- the prevailing laissez-faire beliefs which considered that it was wrong for anyone or any organisation to interfere with an individual's right to make his own decisions about where he worked, who he worked for, and under what conditions.

There were also many divisions within the labor movement. Some were more concerned with looking after the interests of the better-paid and highly skilled men rather than the low-paid unskilled men. Some were racist and others wanted to ban immigration. Some were committed socialists aiming to end capitalism. Reaching agreement on objectives was difficult.

The first attempt to form a nationwide trade union in the United States came in 1866, with the National Labor Union. This developed into a larger organisation in 1869 known as the Knights of Labor. It recruited members from a wide range of industries and was open to both skilled and unskilled workers. The recession which developed in 1873 helped recruitment considerably and the union grew to over 700 000 members by the middle of the 1880s. While it could achieve little in some industries, such as mining and iron and steel, because of determined employer opposition, it had more success elsewhere. The strike was its major weapon. For example, in 1886 the Knights helped to organise over 1400 separate strikes involving over 600 000 men. It was calculated that, between 1886 and 1889, just under 50% of all strikes over pay and conditions were successful.

However, there were also significant defeats. In 1877, there was a major strike on the railroads when employers cut wages and increased hours. They could easily fill the places of workers who objected as they knew that there was high unemployment and plenty of workers due to a drift from countryside to town and immigration. The strikes led to violence across many parts of the United States, and state and federal troops were brought in to keep the railroads running. Over 100 people were killed. The strikers lost their jobs, wages were cut and working hours extended. While some employers might have become cautious about cutting pay, mostly workers suffered during this period.

Another major setback came when Carnegie decided to destroy unions in his steel mills. In 1888, he ended a strike organised by the Knights at one of his plants. He locked out the workers, employed the Pinkerton's Detective Agency to fortify the plant. He then took on new workers, requiring them to accept 12-hour days and lower wages than the former employees. He then did the same at his vast Homestead plant in 1892. He again cut wages and demanded longer hours and also insisted that wages in future be tied to the price of steel, not the company's profits. He used similar tactics as he locked out the workforce, fortified the plant, employed hundreds of Pinkerton's men to protect it and had the local militia break up demonstrations by strikers. The new workers who accepted his terms paid a high price. Between 1907 and 1910, a quarter of the 3723 recent migrants working in one of Carnegie's steel plants were killed or seriously injured. Men who hadn't eaten enough and were working 72 hours a week were likely to have accidents.

By the 1890s, it was clear that the Knights of Labor were unable to achieve much, and membership dropped. A new national labour organisation emerged in 1886, the American Federation of Labour (AFL), but it too was to have limited success. It was a loose federation of craft unions working towards improving pay, benefits, hours and working conditions, and it was sternly opposed to immigration. In 1894, the Pullman Company, which ran luxury passenger carriages on railroads across America, felt it had to reduce its operations after the Panic of 1893. It cut its workforce by 3000 and cut wages as well. Workers who lived in company-owned houses had to pay increased rents. The Pullman workers walked out on strike. The newly formed American Railway Union (ARU), linked to the AFL, was determined to support the Pullman men, and refused to work with any Pullman carriages. The railroad bosses were determined to resist at all costs. Troops were brought in to keep order, break the strike and the attempts by other railway workers to stop Pullman carriages being used. There were riots and men were killed. In the end, the ARU leaders were arrested and the Supreme Court backed the use of force against the strikers. It ruled that the actions of the ARU in supporting the Pullman workers was illegal. The strike was over and it had failed.

Labor union activity went on until the outbreak of the First World War, but there was little progress. Continued immigration and strong employer opposition prevented any progress. From 1913, President Woodrow Wilson's administration aimed to keep the peace. This government was reluctant to takes sides in industrial disputes, preferring a more neutral role. However, there would be no real advances in pay and conditions until there was much greater legal protection for unions and their members. More employers like Henry Ford were needed. He argued that there was no point in making lots of motor cars if you did not pay your workers enough to be able to buy them.

Farming organisations

Farmers were the biggest occupational group in the United States in this period. Farming was a diverse industry and included huge vast cattle ranches of the West, smaller single family units of the Midwest and tiny sharecropper units in the cotton-growing regions in the South. What was in the best interests of one group and region was often not in the interests of others, so there was limited scope for coordinated and strong action by the farming community.

For much of the period, farming throughout America was in depression. With the opening of the Midwest to farming after the Homestead Act, thousands settled there and created new farms. This led to over-productivity which led to falling prices. There was also growing competition from overseas and from Canada as the great wheat fields there were developed. There was also the problem that farmers depended on the new railroads to get their produce to market. With monopolies becoming established in railroad industries, railroad bosses were able to dictate freight prices and warehouse charges. They made great profits at the expense of farmers. Another issue facing farmers was debt. They usually had to borrow from the banks to fund the purchase of seed and other essentials and repay the loan when they managed to sell their crops. When banks failed and farmers' loans were called in at short notice, this was disastrous for farmers, particularly in the Panics of the 1870s and 1890s. Of course farmers were also dependent on the weather, of course, and, after the terrible harvests across America in 1886, there was an exceptionally hard winter in 1886/7. This caused great distress in all farming communities.

The Granger Movement

There were various attempts by farmers to organise themselves in the same way as trusts helped business organisations and labor unions aimed to assist industrial workers. Farmers felt they would get limited assistance from either of the two main political parties. The Republicans were felt to be the party of Northern business while the Democrats seemed to be interested only in preserving the interests of the racist landlords of the South.

The first major attempt by farmers to organise on a national scale came in 1867 when Oliver Kelley in Minnesota founded the Patrons of Husbandry, which became known also as the Grange. It was open to all farmers in the United States, including women, and, by 1875, had gained about 750 000 members. Its focus was cooperative action by all farmers to achieve certain objectives. If they grouped together, they could cut the prices of what they needed to buy, but also improve their ability to sell their produce. Above all, they wanted to unite against the railroads who had raised the prices of freight and warehousing to unrealistic levels.

With the Panic of 1873 hitting farmers hard, the Grange's aim to avoid getting directly involved in politics vanished. Cooperative action had done too little. In many states, the Grange either put forward 'Granger' candidates, or endorsed candidates from parties who promised to support their views. This was successful and several states passed 'Granger' laws where the states began to regulate what railroad companies could change for freight and warehousing. When the railroad bosses took the states to court the Grange fought back and the Supreme Court in 1877 upheld the new regulations. However, the Grangers failed in their attempt at currency reform. They were sure that the existing system was having a severe impact on the low prices they were getting for their produce.

By the late 1870s, the Grange was declining in numbers and was divided over both aims and tactics. The number of members had dropped to well under 100 000 by 1880, and the movement came to an end. It was replaced in the late 1870s by the Farmer's Alliance. This grouping showed more awareness of the different needs of farmers across America, as it was an association of groups from different regions. It demanded that the federal government take action to deal with the many problems which farmers faced. At first it had limited success. After the bad harvests and weather conditions of 1886-67 the Alliance asked for assistance from the federal government. President Cleveland vetoed a Congressional Bill which would have helped by arguing that 'People support the government, not government support the people.'

Figure 3.10: A postcard inspired by the Granger Movement. How does the postcard show the aims and concerns of the Granger Movement?

With such lack of support and continued falling prices for produce while farm costs rose, the Alliance decided on more open political action. They put forward or endorsed candidates in the congressional elections of 1890. Over 40 were elected. They promised much greater regulation of the railroads, and currency reform. They also insisted that when federal land was distributed, small farmers were given preference over corporations and speculators. The Alliance groups were encouraged by this and met in 1892 at the Omaha Convention. Together with the Knights of Labour and the currency-reforming Greenback Party, they decided to put forward their own candidate for the presidency against the Republican and Democratic nominees. As well as arguing for many of the traditional 'farming' policies on railroads, banks and currency reform, they also made many other demands, such as reform of elections to the Senate

and public ownership of the telegraph and telephone systems. The Alliance candidate did not win the election (the presidential electoral system does not favour small parties which try to challenge the two major parties). However, they did win some congressional elections, but they would do little to influence the dominance of the two major parties in the White House and Congress.

In the end the farming groups achieved little. Farming remained in depression until the First World War came. It was only when the Democrats under Wilson came into office in 1913 that some of the demands of the Grange and the Alliance were implemented, with greater regulation of the railroads and reform of the banking system. However, it was not until after the Great Depression of the 1930s that the deep-rooted problems facing US agriculture were really tackled.

ACTIVITY 3.13

What does the author of the source below see as the principal causes of the problems facing US farmers, which led to the Granger movement? What other factors might be seen as major causes ?

The Granger Movement In Illinois By A. E. PAINE, A. M.

THE GRANGER MOVEMENT IN ILLINOIS.

The new order came into being shortly after the Civil War.

It was a favorable time for such a movement. For two decades a feeling of dissatisfaction had been spreading among the farmers.

For a time it had found sufficient expression in the political agitation against slavery, but otherwise had played no important part in the economic growth of the nation. It was temporarily overshadowed by more vital questions, but gained new life in the west as railroad building progressed and increasing migration brought about more extensive competition among the farmers. This competition lowered the prices of their products, while at the same time their purchases had to be made at exorbitant prices. They were at the mercy of the middlemen, whom they were unable to oppose successfully owing to lack of organization, and because their own inertia had prevented them from undertaking to deal directly with the manufacturers.

The motives of the middlemen were not entirely selfish.

That their operations brought injury to the farmer was rather their misfortune than their fault. They found the farmers poorly supplied with cash and were forced to sell on credit.

The railroads, too, were a source of irritation. Discriminations, high rates with their accompanying phenomenon of stock watering, and the attitude which the railroad managers assumed toward the shippers, together with a succession of sharp practices, gradually aroused the public and led to organized opposition.

In other sections of the country there were additional causes. The farmers of the south had been left in an unfortunate condition as a result of the Civil War. If we add to these causes of discontent, the general feeling of unrest commonly prevalent among the tillers of the soil, we have a sufficient explanation of the causes of the widespread movement among the farming classes, which resulted in the organization of the Patrons of Husbandry.

Extract from the University of Illinois Bulletin: The University Studies vol.1, no. 8 September 1904.

3.3 What were the main aims and policies of the Progressive Movement and how popular were they?

Many Americans accepted the benefits of rapid industrialisation. However, by the 1890s there were many who were seriously concerned about its social, economic and political implications. They became known as the 'Progressives'. They disliked the behaviour of some individuals, such as the robber barons, and their clear consumption which contrasted so strongly with the poverty of millions. The Progressives were worried that this poverty might cause many to look to anti-capitalists or socialists for help. They were deeply concerned with the growing industrial unrest, with its strikes and violence. They worried that the obvious lack of opportunity for those living in the new cities would lead to popular unrest. They were not radicals wanting wide changes. They wanted to adapt the traditional American values of freedom, independence, equality and opportunity to the changed economic and social conditions of the late 19th century. The US Constitution had been written in very different conditions a century earlier. These men and women seeking change wanted to take the opportunities offered within that constitutional system and keep its core values but to adapt it to the needs of a society that had changed.

The Progressive Movement had a wide range of aims which were sometimes rather vague so it is difficult to assess the success of the movement. Some of those involved wanted a specific objective, such as making employers pay compensation to injured workers. Others had much broader objectives, such as regulating big business or creating a welfare state. Some were concerned with providing opportunity and reducing class divisions or extending educational provision. Some were quite radical and others very conservative. The white, middle-class elite who dominated much of the movement had their own priorities and often had little sympathy with trade unionists or small farmers. Broadly speaking, there were three categories of aim represented by the Progressive Movement: political, economic and social.

Limits on party machines and bosses
Radical reform of the management of the cities
Many cities were run by corrupt officials like Boss Tweed. Often, mayors, police, local judges and local officers, such as those responsible for providing water and public transport, lacked any sense of public duty.

They were appointed by the boss and were unqualified for the jobs they did. In many cities, local taxation increased but services got worse. Many local leaders were more interested in their own private gain rather than public service. The Progressives aimed for an open and democratic system of local government with full accountability and care taken to ensure that elections were free and fair. Many were shocked by evidence of the appalling housing conditions and high death rates in the slums of America's cities. They wanted the cities and states to take strong action to end these conditions.

Reform of political parties

US political parties were often controlled by tiny minorities or were wide open to business influence. One example was how Rockefeller's Standard Oil Company dominated the politics of states such as Ohio. The states, which did have the constitutional power to act, were dominated by businessmen whose interests would be damaged by regulation. This meant that there was little regulation of business by 1900. Candidate nomination in parties, whether for a local mayor of police chief, was often controlled by a small group of businessmen who mixed business and politics to their own advantage. There was a real desire to open up the whole political process to a wider electorate. One of the main demands was for **primary elections** for candidates for office. This was one of the many success stories of the Progressive Movement. The primary election is still the main method of choosing candidates for Congress and the presidency.

> **KEY TERM**
>
> **Primary election:** A system to enable all local party members to vote for party candidates. In the two major political parties, Democrat and Republican, candidates for election to any office had nearly always been chosen by leading figures in the party itself. Ordinary party members, or those who might vote for the party, had no chance to choose candidates. The primary election made the process much more democratic.

Changing the Constitution

Some argued that for the USA to adapt to the changed conditions of a much bigger and industrialised nation which was now also a major world power, the Constitution needed to be changed. For example, women should be able to vote and senators should be directly elected, rather than appointed by business-biased state legislatures, in order to make them more accountable to their states and voters. They wanted a federal income tax to replace tariffs as the main source of income for the government.

Most taxes that people paid at this time were collected by the states and local communities, and usually based on property. A federal income tax would be paid on personal income, and go directly to the federal government.

The regulation of private corporations

The Progressives wanted regulation of business by federal or state government and believed that government should play a different, and greater, role in the economy. It should not just encourage and assist, but should regulate too. Such a government should protect against business excess and exploitation. The Progressives also wanted businesses to benefit the community, not just the super-rich and so wanted a different relationship between capital and labour. The Progressives were not anti-capitalist, but they felt that government could and should act to protect its citizens from exploitation by their employers.

The movement wanted to see tougher enforcement of existing legislation such as the Sherman Anti-Trust Act and the Interstate Commerce Act, along with new rules, such as:

- recognition of labor unions by employers
- regulation of hours of work for all
- separate regulations for the employment of women and children
- compensation for injury at work
- insurance schemes for unemployment, sickness and old age
- regulation of banks, insurance companies, the stock market and business, especially the trusts
- measures to protect consumers against **food adulteration**, rigged prices, monopolies and dirty water supplies
- conservation legislation to protect the environment.

> **KEY TERM**
>
> **Food adulteration:** The addition of cheap and lesser quality ingredients to foodstuffs, such as flour or rice, in order to increase their bulk and boost sales profits. Around the turn of the 20th century in the USA, this unscrupulous practice resulted in frequent outbreaks of food poisoning.

In addition to this legislative approach, the Progressives wanted to alter the basis of the currency. As we have seen (see 'Industrial growth and periods of economic recession' earlier in this chapter), this was traditionally based on gold. Many, particularly the Democrats, wanted to introduce a silver-based coinage that they felt would raise prices for farmers and reduce the power of the trusts and big business. There was actually little economic sense in this objective, but it was very popular.

Female emancipation

Greater freedom for women was a key Progressive aim. In 1890, two major women's groups formed the National American Woman Suffrage Association to campaign for women to have the right to vote in local, state and national elections. Many of those who were strong supporters of female suffrage were equally strong supporters of other Progressive policies. The demand for votes for women went back to before the Civil War, and once the war was over, there was constant pressure on politicians at all levels to give women the vote. However, the moral position of most Progressives was weakened as although they were strong supporters of middle-class white American women getting the vote, they often did not want African Americans, Native Americans and recent immigrants of both sexes to get the vote at all. The women's movement itself was divided on the issue of race, which limited its effectiveness.

The route to female emancipation was a long one. The main method was quiet lobbying and maintaining pressure on decision makers. Public rallies were preferred to the more violent tactics used by a minority of suffrage campaigners in Britain, such as smashing politicians' windows and other acts of vandalism. The status of the movement was helped by the examples set by many of the leading female Progressives. These included **Jane Addams** and Ida Tarbell (see 'Who were the principal Progressives and what methods did they use?', on the next page). These women achieved a lot in what had been seen as traditional male occupations, such as journalism and factory inspection. Social attitudes were changing too, as a growing number of middle-class women gained university degrees and wanted to do a great deal more than just having children and running a home. Two of the most influential leaders of the movement were Susan B. Anthony (1820–1906) and Elizabeth Cady Stanton (1815–1902). Both had been involved in the Temperance Movement and anti-slavery campaigns early in the 19th century, and had then focused on equal rights, before spending the last part of their lives on female suffrage.

Women were first given the vote at local level. For example, in 1869 the territory of Wyoming allowed women to vote. In 1887, Kansas allowed women to vote in municipal elections and then states like Idaho (1896) and California (1911) gave women the right to vote in all state-wide elections including for that of state governor. In many other states, women could vote for local school managers and many became school managers themselves.

JANE ADDAMS (1860–1935)

Addams was a pioneering social worker in Chicago who founded an organisation called Hull House to fight against poverty amongst women and children. It proved to be an excellent example of welfare work in the USA that was followed in many other cities.

Female suffrage

Although it had the considerable successes, one of the weaknesses of the Progressive Movement was a degree of division within the movement itself. Initially, there were two rival movements – the National Women's Suffrage Association and the American Women's Suffrage Association. They had differing personalities in charge and disagreements about the methods that should be used to achieve the vote for women. However, they merged in 1890 to form the National American Women's Suffrage Association. They took key decisions such as to first focus on winning the vote for women in local and state elections before starting to campaign for the vote in congressional and presidential elections. This was a successful policy.

The suffrage campaign faced many obstacles, too, including male prejudice. Churches often disapproved, and used the bible as justification. Businesses, led by the brewing and saloon interests, strongly opposed, as they felt that the growing Temperance Movement, which was largely made up of women, would legislate against alcohol if it gained political power. Some women opposed the campaign too, arguing that the place for women was in the home, not out participating in politics. Conservatives felt that female suffrage would change both local and national constitutions for the worse. The Supreme Court –made up entirely of men – used their interpretations of the Constitution to disallow attempts to gain the vote for women. In 1887 it annulled a law and cancelled women's right to vote in Washington State. The principal obstacle was Congress and the state legislatures who had the constitutional right to amend the Constitution so that women could vote. With an all-male electorate which had an interest in maintaining the status quo, few politicians were prepared to do this. Many feared, especially

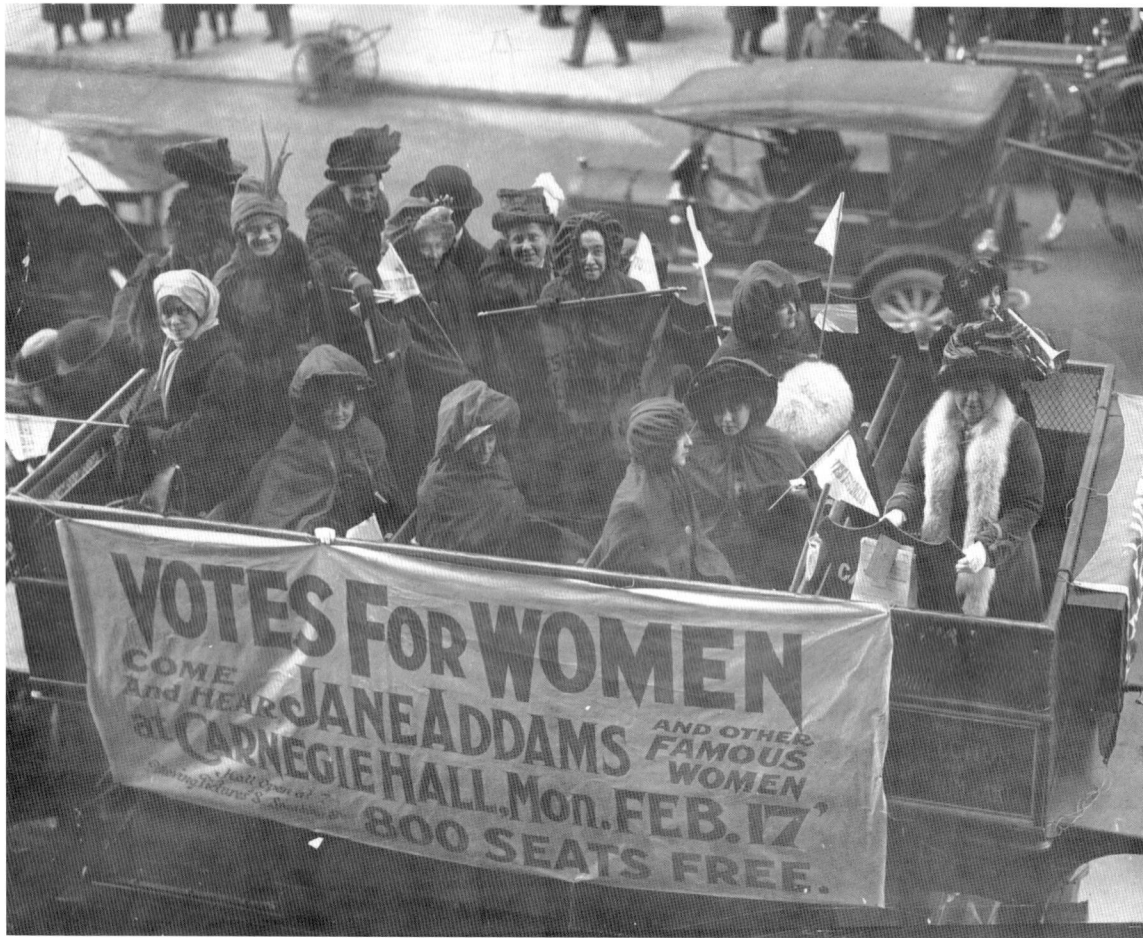

Figure 3.11: Expanding the suffrage to give women the vote was one aspect of the Progressive Movement. How useful is this photograph as evidence for support of women's suffrage?

Republicans, that the business domination of state legislatures and Congress would end and unwanted state regulation of business would follow. In 1912 a presidential candidate came out in open support for the vote for women for the first time. This was Theodore Roosevelt, former president and now leader of the new Progressive Party. Woodrow Wilson won the election and would be seen to be a highly Progressive president, but he was much more cautious on the subject of female franchise. He didn't want to upset his strongly conservative southern supporters.

War was the key factor in changing opinion. Even before 1917, there were many examples of women working at a high level in traditionally male areas. In states where women had the vote, the disasters imagined by the opponents of women's suffrage had not occurred. The decision to go to war in 1917 led to the mobilisation of millions of men. Women were needed to manage the farms and work in the expanding munitions industries. The demand for women in a large number of occupations, such as nursing, teaching and secretarial, grew and so did the need for them to take on manual work usually performed by men. The catastrophe predicted by the male opponents of women's emancipation did not come. The Constitution was duly amended in 1920 to give all women the vote. This was seen by many as a reward for the contribution made by women to the successful war effort.

Who were the principal Progressives and what methods did they use?

The Progressive Movement did not have one overall leader, although some individuals assumed leadership of separate parts of the movement. It was unusual in that so many women took leading roles and were also some of the most enthusiastic participants in the demand for change.

Denied the vote in federal elections and access to most public offices, women had to use other methods to attract the attention of those who could make decisions. Some petitioned, some demonstrated, others did their best.

Women had to use other methods to attract the attention of those who could make decisions as they couldn't vote in federal elections and didn't have access to most public offices. Some petitioned and some demonstrated. Others did their best to publicise and to make the public aware of what they felt the failings of industrial America and the way in which it was governed were. Some did things designed to improve the lives of others, and their example was followed. The role of the press and publishers was extremely important to the whole movement. Reporters and writers brilliantly highlighted many of failings that existed in late 19th-century America as they took advantage of the freedom of the press guaranteed in the First Amendment of the Constitution, and of the tradition of journalistic independence and diversity long present in America.

Jane Addams was inspired by what she saw on a visit to London's revolutionary Toynbee Hall settlement, and founded Hull House in Chicago in 1889. It was the most famous of all the **settlement houses** in America and influenced hundreds of others across America. Hull House was a training ground for social workers. It provided a wide range of social and educational services to the poor of Chicago, and especially its women and children. Addams's ability to research and to motivate others and to put pressure where it mattered was impressive. The work of Hull House led to the Illinois Factory Act of 1893, which started factory reform in Chicago. Addams battled to overcome basic hygiene problems, such as the provision of clean water and proper sewage disposal. In fact, she was appointed an inspector dealing with garbage disposal: not the most glamorous of occupations, but vital for public health. She never stopped fighting for better care for children and for the need for effective public health provision. She taught, lectured, wrote and publicised. Her settlement produced evidence on a range of social and healthcare issues, including the causes and spread of typhoid, the impact of overcrowding and juvenile crime. This led to reforms being passed by the city and state. Addams played a key role in setting up the National Child Labor Committee, which led to the creation of a Federal Child Bureau and finally to the Federal Child Labour Act of 1916. This was due to the combination of her hard work, setting a powerful example, inspiring others, good use of publicity and pressuring politicians.

Like so many of the other Progressives, Florence Kelley (1859–1932) was extremely well educated. She started work in Jane Addams's Hull House settlement in Chicago and was particularly horrified by the terrible working conditions which existed for many women and children.

She saw children as young as four at work in dangerous and unhealthy conditions. She organised a detailed survey of these conditions, which she presented to the Illinois state legislature. As a result of this pressure, the state banned labour for those under 14. The legislature was so impressed by Kelley that she was employed as the state's first female factory inspector to enforce this law.

KEY TERMS

Settlement houses: Usually large buildings in poor areas of a city where middle-class volunteers lived alongside working-class people. Their aim was to help with a range of social services such as childcare, education, advice on nutrition; anything, in fact, to improve the living conditions of those living in slums.

Boycott: Refusing to buy or use the goods or services of a company and persuading others to do the same.

Encouraged by this, Kelley moved to New York to continue her work in factory reform. She formed the National Consumer League (NCL) with other Progressives. This organisation decided to promote the products of manufacturers (especially clothing) who treated their employees well and to encourage a **boycott** of manufacturers who did not. The NCL also started a national campaign to end food adulteration and pushed Congress to pass the Pure Food and Drugs Act in 1906. National campaigns by the NCL led to 14 states passing minimum-wage laws which were well enforced. Kelley also played a key role in getting the Supreme Court to finally uphold the law restricting hours of work for women to 10 hours. She was also a founder member of the National Association for the Advancement of Colored People (NAACP) and a strong supporter of women's suffrage. Her careful research led to detailed evidence. She was very effective as she used this to campaign boldly and widely to gain publicity. She was also good at applying pressure on those with the power to act.

Ida Tarbell (1857–1944) was another remarkable woman. She could be seen as the founder of modern investigative journalism. She was initially a student of history and started her writing career (one of the few open to women in the 19th-century USA) working on biographies of Lincoln and Napoleon. She learned how to undertake detailed research doing this. Her father had been in the oil refining business in Ohio, but had been forced out by the aggressive and untrustworthy business practices of Rockefeller and Standard Oil who were determined to eliminate any competition. Tarbell's investigation into Standard Oil found many illegal practices, including their secret and corrupt deals with the railroads. In a series of highly critical and widely read magazine articles and a book, *The History of the Standard Oil Company*, Tarbell showed just how Rockefeller and Standard Oil achieved their near-monopoly status and vast wealth. The outcry and protests caused by these revelations led to the successful prosecution of Standard Oil for violating the Sherman Act (and the case was fought right up to the Supreme Court) and even the break-up of Standard Oil itself. The power of the pen in this journalism was very well demonstrated, and the freedom of the press was shown to be extremely important.

ACTIVITY 3.14

Many of the principal Progressives were women. However, for a long time they had no vote in most state elections and no vote in elections for Congress and the president. Make a list of the methods used by the principal female Progressives to successfully campaign for change. How are these different from the methods used by male Progressives? Why do you think these differences occurred?

Temperance and Prohibition

The Progressive Movement did not have a single overall aim, and those who saw themselves as Progressives did not always agree on their objectives. For example, some were in favour of racial integration, while others opposed it. Some suggested direct action and civil disobedience to achieve their aims; others wished to only use peaceful and legal methods. The Temperance Movement was one leading movement, and was sometimes seen as part of the Progressive Movement, but at other times was quite separate from it. There were two elements to this campaign. The first was to discourage the drinking of alcohol and closely regulate its manufacture and sale. The other element, known as the Prohibitionists, wanted to totally ban the manufacture or sale of any alcoholic drinks in the whole of the United States. The anti-alcohol campaign was strongest at the same time as the main Progressive actions, in the latter part of the 19th century and early 20th. In 1920, the movements achieved their objective in amending the Constitution to ban the sale and manufacture of alcohol and Congress passed an act enforcing it.

Not all Progressives supported this campaign. Some felt the ban would restrict individual liberty. Others felt that it would put many people off other Progressive reforms – votes for women in particular. Similarly, some

Prohibitionists did not support women's suffrage. Increasingly, historians see the Temperance Movement as quite separate from the Progressive Movement, but just happening at the same time. Perhaps the most remarkable factor about the anti-alcohol movement was the fact that it achieved total success in attaining its objectives. This was mostly by using peaceful and legal methods, at a time when most of its activists were women who did not have the vote. It was an excellent example of how a determined pressure group, probably supported by only a minority of the population, could succeed in imposing its wishes on the nation as a whole.

There had been temperance movements before the Civil War, particularly in some strongly Protestant communities. It developed into a mass movement after the war. In 1873, the Women's Christian Temperance Movement (WCTU) was founded. Its leading members tended to be deeply religious Protestants actively trying to improve society, while converting others to their way of religious thinking. They argued that many social evils were linked to alcohol consumption, ranging from domestic violence to illness, and that it caused the break-up of families and poverty. They had wider aims as well. The WCTU was active in working for educational reform, arguing against the publication of pornography, opposing divorce, while at the same time demanding a maximum eight-hour working day and other labour reforms. They did get support from some employers suffering from absenteeism and other disruptions because their workers drank too much. Progressives gave them some support too, as they were aware that alcohol did cause serious social problems and the saloons where alcohol was served were where the bosses ran their corrupt political organisations from.

The WCTU did make steady progress by determined pressure. This was in spite of opposition from the drinks companies (always a powerful lobby), the many males who liked a drink after work and politicians who had no wish to offend voters and were in some cases linked to the alcohol industry anyway. For example, in 1880 it succeeded in getting the city of Kansas to ban saloons. When this law was ignored because the local police and politicians were too close to the saloon owners, determined members of the WCTU entered them and smashed them up.

In 1893, another temperance organisation was founded in Ohio. The Anti-Saloon League (ASL) was more militant and had a more specific target. It became a national organisation in 1895. It wanted to amend the Constitution to end the sale and purchase of alcohol in the USA. It led a

FRANK LESLIE'S ILLUSTRATED NEWSPAPER.

IMPORTED WINES & LIQUORS

FRESH COOL LAGER BEER

THE OHIO WHISKY WAR.—THE LADIES OF LOGAN SINGING HYMNS IN FRONT OF BARROOMS IN AID OF THE TEMPERANCE MOVEMENT.—SKETCHED BY S. B. MORTON.—SEE PAGE 391.

Figure 3.12: This illustration titled 'The Ohio Whisky War' shows one method used by the Temperance Movement. The women are singing hymns (religious songs) outside a saloon, trying to shame the men. The illustration was published in Frank Leslie's Illustrated Newspaper in 1874, sketched by S.B Morton. What does this image tell us about the reaction to the methods used during the Temperance Movement? Do you think they were well received?

highly organised and well-funded campaign. It had a clear target and knew how to reach it. It employed experienced people to deal with the press and ran an effective public relations campaign. At first, the ASL placed its focus on the states. It gave considerable support and publicity to those seeking election who agreed to vote for the constitutional amendment. Those who would not support it received a very hostile press and publicity, suggesting that they were supporters of all the evils linked to alcohol. This method worked. In 1905, the Republican candidate for the governorship of Ohio, a strongly Republican state, lost his election after a very determined campaign by the ASL against him. By 1907, Georgia and Oklahoma had become '**dry states**'.

KEY TERM

Dry state: A state in which alcohol was banned. (A 'wet' state was one where it was still legal.)

Although politicians often tried to follow the advice of President Roosevelt when he wrote that 'my experience with the Prohibitionists is that the best way to deal with

them is to ignore them', the pressure was non-stop, and ignoring the Prohibitionists lost men elections. Increasingly the focus of the Prohibitionists was on Congress instead of the states because this would be essential when it came to amending the Constitution. In 1913, Congress passed a law stopping the shipment of alcohol into dry states from wet states. President Taft vetoed the Bill, but Congress then overturned his veto. The 'dries' were growing more powerful in Congress. Both presidential candidates in 1916, Woodrow Wilson and Charles Evan Hughes, ignored the issue, but the new Congress elected in 1917 had more dries than wets in both parties in both Houses. The pressure campaign had worked brilliantly.

War in 1917 gave the movement even more strength and it was seen as patriotic. The crops needed to make beer and whisky were needed elsewhere for people and animals. Members of the large German-American community, strong opponents of Prohibition, were seen as 'un-American' when war was declared on Germany. After the war, Congress passed the constitutional amendment and it was approved by all but two states. Congress then passed the Volstead Act giving the federal government the power to enforce the ban on the sale and manufacture of alcohol. The Temperance campaign had turned out to be very popular and a total success. It was a remarkable achievement and many saw it as the high point of the Progressive movement. However it would prove to have some devastating consequences.

Other Progressive aims

The Progressives also wanted to see:

- Welfare reforms. There was never the demand in the United States for the degree of state-funded welfare benefits, such as pensions and healthcare, that countries such as France and Germany were adopting. However there was growing pressure to provide at least a safety net for people facing desperate distress, as was seen in many cities after the recession of 1893. Many Progressives were shocked by the poverty and filthy working conditions the '**muckrakers**' had revealed and felt that action should be taken to end the worst failings of capitalism.

- Reform of the federal government. There were two broad areas suggested for change. The first was for the federal government to intervene more in the economy and society. The second was for it to use its powers more effectively, such as enforcing the Sherman Anti-Trust Act more aggressively and intervening to support workers during strikes.

- African American rights. Many African Americans had moved North in this period to escape the poverty and white hostility of the South. In some parts of the North, black and some white Progressives aimed to improve the situation of African Americans. This was sometimes a difficult issue within the Progressive movement, as some were in favour of racial segregation.

- Equality of opportunity. It was less easy to define the desire of many Progressives simply to end what they saw as a growing class divide between the rich and the poor. Some were committed to improving provision and access to education. Others were anxious to give more people more leisure and the opportunity to use that leisure to improve the quality of their life and their minds.

KEY TERM

Muckrakers: The name given to journalists such as Ida Tarbell who exposed bad living and working conditions in US cities and factories, and who also drew attention to the evils of 'bossism' and the robber barons.

ACTIVITY 3.15

Do you agree that The Progressives were often either progressive or liberal?

Work with another student to define the words 'progressive' and 'liberal' in the context of early-20th-century America. Don't judge them by 21st-century standards. Then assess how far the Progressives met those criteria. Treat the two words quite separately in your response. One possible view might be that you felt they were very 'progressive' but not very 'liberal'.

Reflection: What evidence was important in leading you to answer the questions? What additional evidence might you need to support your answers further?

The congressional elections of 1904 and 1906 began to show that the Progressives were having an effect. They managed to put reform very much on the nation's agenda, and promoters of Progressive ideas were winning elections at local and national level. The speeches given by the movement's leaders attracted thousands and the 'muckrakers' were read by millions. Determined pressure-group action, from preserving forests to removing the 'bosses', was achieving results. There was an opportunity for real change when a serious Progressive arrived in the White House: Theodore Roosevelt.

●●● THINK LIKE A HISTORIAN

Look at the methods pressure groups such as the Progressives used to achieve their ends. Could they have achieved more if they had used different methods? Consider the methods used by contemporary pressure groups. Are they more effective?

3.4 How successful was the Progressive Movement up to 1920?

Put simply, the Progressive Movement was very successful. By 1920, there had been substantial achievements, largely as a result of the pressure it had put on politicians. The principal gains were:

- Several amendments were added to the Constitution.
- Federal and state governments took on new powers of regulation.

- There was a greater expectation that the president and federal government would act to deal with national issues, not just wartime crises.
- Laws were passed concerning working hours and child labour.
- A serious attempt was made to create a national banking system which could regulate banking throughout the United States and prevent any more Panics.
- Administrative reform in many cities and states meant the 'boss' system declined.
- First moves were made towards a social security system
- Women won the right to vote.
- Alcohol was prohibited.
- Major steps were taken towards protecting the environment.
- The civil service was reformed at national and local level.

However, the 1920s showed that there were still problems in the United States. More banks collapsed and poverty remained in some areas. Farming was a disaster area again and African Americans did not have equality. It was not really until the 1960s that major changes were eventually made to the welfare system and the rights of African Americans really improved.

Achievements of the Progressive presidents
The presidency of Theodore Roosevelt, 1901–09

An event vital for the Progressive Movement's progress came in 1901. The conservative Republican president, William McKinley was assassinated. Under the terms of the Constitution, the vice-president takes over the office for the remainder of the four-year term. So, Theodore Roosevelt became President of the United States.

Born into a wealthy family in 1856, Roosevelt was well educated and widely travelled. He had experience in both national and local government. He had been Assistant Secretary to the Navy in 1898, Police Commissioner in New York City and Governor of New York State. In the latter two roles, Roosevelt had established himself as a reformer. He had tried to end corruption and introduce methods of selection for key official positions by merit and not by party bosses in return for bribes or favours. During the war with Spain over Cuba in 1898, he had become a national hero.

THE NATION'S HEAVY BATTER STEPS TO THE PLATE TO KNOCK OUT A HOME RUN.

Figure 3.13: This cartoon from Puck magazine in 1904 portrays Roosevelt as the 'national' figure stepping up to the presidency plate with his bat of 'honest and upright government', ready to strike at the many interests, such as the trusts, which were harming the United States.

He was chosen as the vice-presidential candidate in 1900, as the running mate to the very conservative, and comparatively dull, McKinley. Selecting Roosevelt as the vice-presidential candidate was intended by the party to keep him quiet, as vice presidents had no power. It was hoped he would attract voters because of his reform credentials and reputation as a war hero.

Roosevelt's record as a Progressive needs to be judged by what developed during his Presidency (1901–09). He had to be quite cautious in his first three years, as he aimed for re-election. The fact that he was re-elected in 1904, as a known supporter of change indicates that the Progressive Movement was making an impact. Roosevelt had stressed his role in attacking monopolies and his support for the right of labor unions in his campaign.

Despite some caution in his first term of office, there were real achievements. Roosevelt focussed the presidential office on social and economic reform. He had great respect for the democratic processes set out in the Constitution and never favoured radical change. However, he did strongly feel that a president should use his influence, authority and the publicity that came with the office to highlight important issues such as tariff reform. He placed many of the issues of real concern to the Progressives on the nation's agenda, and he kept them there. In his first **State of the Union Address** to Congress. He appeared a little bland and conservative to appeal to some of his own party but he indicated that he was thinking seriously about taking action on issues such as trusts, rail regulation, tariff reform and conservation issues. This delighted the Progressives.

> **KEY TERM**
>
> **State of the Union Address:** At the start of each annual session of Congress, the president is required to give a speech in which he outlines his policies and recommends measures and issues which he feels that Congress should act on.

In 1902, Roosevelt instructed his Attorney General (the top law officer in the US Government) to start proceedings under the Sherman Anti-Trust Act against the Northern Securities Company. This was a vast holding company that controlled a large amount of the railway network in the north-east of the country. Some of the robber barons, including Rockefeller and Morgan, were involved in it. There was real, and valid, concern that the company was using its monopoly position to generate excess profits at the expense of both freight and passenger customers. The courts declared the company illegal and ordered

its dissolution. Thus, the government had struck the first blow against the great trusts and their monopolies through the courts. In the remaining years of the Roosevelt presidency, a further 44 large organisations were successfully prosecuted for illegal business practices, including the great Standard Oil Company of Rockefeller.

Roosevelt was also unusual in believing that labor unions not only had a right to exist, but should receive the same treatment by the legal system as employers did. For example, in 1902, 50 000 miners went on strike for higher pay, union recognition and improved working conditions. The mine owners refused to consider any of the miners' demands at all and a serious national coal shortage seemed likely. This would have been very harmful to the economy. Roosevelt threatened at one stage to send in the army (the president is commander-in-chief of the armed services) to run the mines. This forced the owners to compromise. Roosevelt was the first president to take a firmly neutral position in such a strike, and called both the unions and the owners to the White House to try to settle the dispute. His predecessors as president had been firmly on the side of employers.

As Roosevelt's presidency continued, legislation encouraged by him began to be pushed through Congress:

- The Expedition Act of 1903 employed more lawyers to work for the government so that more legal action could be taken under the Sherman Anti-Trust Act.
- The Elkins Act of 1903 started the process of regulating the railways.
- The Pure Food and Drugs Act of 1906 (partly inspired by Upton Sinclair's novel *The Jungle* about the appalling working conditions in the American meat-packing industry) set off the process of ending food adulteration.
- The Department of Commerce and Labor Act of 1903 created a new Department of Commerce with a cabinet secretary reporting to the president and Congress.

The Department of Commerce had the power to collect data from any business that dealt in interstate commerce. That data could be vital in identifying the need to regulate businesses if there was evidence of monopoly or price-fixing. Roosevelt played a key role in getting the legislation required to create the department through Congress. He started a campaign for the public to put pressure on their senators and representatives to pass the Bill. The work done by the muckrakers was also a great help in making sure the public knew what had been happening. Similar pressure was put on Congress to pass the Newlands Reclamation Act to construct dams and start environmental conservation. Major measures were also put through to establish National Parks and preserve American forests.

Once safely re-elected in 1904, Roosevelt set out a much more ambitious programme. His State of the Union message, while promising to uphold the basic principles of the Constitution and American system of government, added his wish 'that these principles be kept substantially unchanged, although of course applied in a progressive spirit to meet changing conditions'. His speech contained many items clearly influenced by the Progressives:

- employers' liability proposals, where employers had to compensate employees injured at work
- limitation of working hours
- safety measures for the railways
- wider regulatory powers for the government in the economy
- regulation of the insurance industry
- child labour restrictions
- factory inspections
- slum clearance measures.

It was a clear Progressive message.

The final two years of Roosevelt's administration, from 1906 to 1908, showed even more radical Progressive tendencies. The Progressive Movement across America was applying pressure from below, and Roosevelt applied it from the top. He would continue to demand reform until he left office. In his final State of the Union Address of 1908, he laid down an agenda that his Democratic successors from 1913 onwards would put into practice. He attacked the ownership and influence of excessive wealth and he made a series of recommendations for further action, including:

- taxes on income and inheritance
- further regulation of all interstate business
- further regulation of railroads
- postal savings banks to ensure small savers would not suffer in crises such as the one of 1907
- a more effective system of dealing with labour disputes
- an eight-hour working day for all
- compensation for injuries at work
- regulation of stock market speculation (again with 1907 in mind).

Roosevelt showed what a determined president could do, using the relatively limited powers given to him under the Constitution. He could publicise and use the power of public interest. He could, and did, appeal to the people directly to put pressure on their elected lawmakers to act. He was helped to make the US a better place by the organisations run and supported by people such as Addams and Tarbell, and the disgust at the excesses of the robber barons and the incompetence of city managers.

ACTIVITY 3.16

Contrast Fig 3.15, the cartoon, with the source below. Does the image conveyed in the cartoon agree with the views expressed in the article in the Independent magazine? To what extent did Roosevelt fulfill the claims in the cartoon?

The notable thing about his two presidential terms is the multitude of things he has said and done from the initiative of his own brain … he dared tackle the combinations of wealth and compelled them to cease their unfair competition … he has demanded a square deal for all, and we have loved him for the enemies he has made. It would have been vastly easier for him to have kept quiet … but he wanted the just thing done… he has purified the civil service as well as business methods, protected our forests, ended conflict with miners and investigated agricultural conditions.

From the article "An Assessment of Theodore Roosevelt's Presidency", Independent magazine, 1909

The presidency of William Taft, 1909–13

Although Roosevelt had a legal right to stand again as Republican candidate for president in the 1908 election, he chose not to. His successor was the lawyer William Howard Taft. Taft was an able administrator, but also conservative and had a reputation for being hostile to labor unions and their demands. Most of his cabinet appointments were from the conservative wing of the Republican party. He had little sympathy with Roosevelt's

133

highly active and progressive style of government. Much of Taft's period in office was spent dealing with foreign policy and with changes in tariffs, which split his own party. He was disliked by many Progressives after he sacked Gifford Pinchot, one of Roosevelt's key appointments in the conservation movement. However Taft did introduce a federal corporation tax (a tax on business profits) and a federal income tax. Both of these later had huge significance in covering increased government spending. He also started many more prosecutions under the Sherman Anti-Trust Act against the trusts and corporations, so his presidency was not a complete failure from the point of view of the Progressives.

The presidency of Woodrow Wilson, 1913–21

The high point of the Progressive era came with the election of Woodrow Wilson in 1913. For the first time in decades, a Democrat took up residence in the White House.

Wilson's great achievement in this election was bringing together three very different elements into the Democratic party:

- the deeply conservative and strongly racist South, where African Americans were largely deprived of the vote
- the liberal elite, which included the majority of the Progressives
- the industrial working class.

All of these groups had good, if different, reasons to dislike and vote against the Republicans.

134

WOODROW WILSON (1856–1924)

Wilson started his career as an academic and was President of Princeton University, before he became Governor of the State of New Jersey. In 1912, he successfully ran for the presidency.. He was president from 1913 to 1921. His tenure of office led to much Progressive legislation being passed by Congress. In 1917, he took the United States to war against Germany, and the latter part of his presidency was dominated by the war and the subsequent peace.

Wilson gained a reputation as a progressive reformer when he was Governor of New Jersey. He had campaigned as a Progressive there, and had helped to put through a range of reforms in the state:

- ensuring fair and free elections
- ending corruption among public officials
- workmen's compensation for industrial injuries
- regulating utilities such as gas, electricity and water.

During the election campaign he had emphasised his independence from any of the 'bosses'. He also stressed the large number of his other reforms which had made a large impact on the lives of New Jersey citizens. They ranged from the training and availability of nurses through to regulation of working hours and prison reform. He obviously appealed to the Progressives and all those who wished to see greater regulation and improvement in the quality of their lives.

In one of his campaign speeches, Wilson argued that:

Business is in a situation in America which it was never in before. It is in a situation to which we have not adjusted our laws. Our laws are still meant for business done by individuals; that had not been satisfactorily adjusted to business done by great combinations, and we have got to adjust them. I do not say we may or may not; I say we must; there is no choice. If your laws do not fit your facts; the facts are not injured, the law is damaged; because the law, unless I have studied it amiss, is the expression of the facts in legal relationship … Politics in America is in a case which sadly requires attention. The system set up by our law and our usage does not work, or at least cannot be depended on. It is made to work only by a most unreasonable expenditure of labour and pains. The government, which was designed for the people, has got in to the hands of the bosses and their employers – the special interests. An invisible empire has been set up above the forms of democracy.

From a speech published in Woodrow Wilson Papers: Series 7: Speeches, Writings, and Academic Material, 1873 to 1923

Roosevelt had decided to stand in the election as an independent candidate and had taken many votes from Taft. This helped him to win. As president, Wilson dominated the government and he took great care to try to work well with Congress. Under the Constitution,

Congress had the ability to approve all key posts in the government and could block or change any law which the president wished to introduce. Wilson helped to pass a remarkable number of Acts of Congress as well as major changes to the Constitution, although he was distracted later by foreign policy and involvement in the First World War. Like Roosevelt, and with the same limited powers given to him under the Constitution, Wilson showed what a determined president, backed by public opinion, and with the cooperation of Congress, could achieve.

KEY CONCEPT

Significance

Historians are likely to regard something as 'significant' if it tells us a lot about what was happening in a country at a particular time. Discuss with a partner why the Presidency and domestic achievements of Woodrow Wilson could be seen as highly significant. What reasons do you think are the most important? What connections can you see between these reasons?

These are just some of the changes put through during Wilson's presidency:

- The Federal Reserve Act of 1913. This was an act typical of Wilson, as it maintained a balance between the interests of big business and the needs of the wider community. It set up a Federal Reserve Board to oversee the banking system, and aimed to ensure that there was sufficient money available when and where it was needed. Many saw this as one of Wilson's greatest achievements, as it brought an end to the 'Panics' and introduced some stability to banking. Later, the Great Crash of 1929 showed the weaknesses in the system created, but the act was a fundamentally important start to fiscal regulation.
- The Underwood Tariff of 1913. Tariffs had been an important political issue for decades, as some gained and some lost with high tariffs on imports. The Underwood legislation involved a serious reduction in many tariffs. It was seen as a positive move by small business owners and farmers, but it was disliked by the large corporations.
- The introduction of a federal income tax. Income tax was intended to replace the government income lost when tariffs were reduced or abolished. With both Roosevelt and Wilson expanding the role of government into areas such as agriculture and commerce, it needed more income to pay for civil servants. Initially, income tax was paid only by those earning over $4000 a year,

which was four times a good industrial wage. It meant that the Federal government had a good source of income and could manage the increased expectations placed on it by the public.

- The Clayton Act of 1914. This gave more power to the government to enforce the Sherman Anti-Trust Act in order to break up monopolies and trusts.
- The Federal Trade Commission Act of 1914. This created a regulatory body for business that covered every possible questionable business action. Many felt it was not strong enough, but it established an important principle of federal regulation in this area and was a start in eliminating corruption.
- The first Federal Child Labour Act in 1916. This act was later annulled and cancelled by the Supreme Court, but it made a start in dealing with the 2 million children under 16 who were known to be in work and often deprived of education.
- The Department of Labor. Although this had been created by Taft, Wilson appointed its first **secretary**, William Wilson, a former miner and union leader who played a larger part in resolving disputes between management and their workers. This helped to prevent the often long, violent and disruptive strikes which had occurred so often in the past.
- Reorganisation of the Department of Agriculture. The aim of this development was to assist all those involved in farming, ensuring better credit for farmers and more efficient distribution networks to enable their produce to reach markets at home and overseas.
- The development of federal intervention in industrial disputes. Traditionally, if the federal government intervened at all, it had intervened on the side of the employers. Increasingly, the federal government took a much more neutral approach and was willing to take action to end strikes so that the public did not lose out when the employees had some genuine grievances dealt with.
- The Revenue Act of 1916. This act continued the policy of taxing the rich more and redistributing wealth. It also expanded more into the taxation of business profits and, for the first time, imposed a tax on large estates left by those who had died.

KEY TERM

Secretary: Every department in the federal government is headed by its secretary. The president nominates each secretary, but the Senate has to approve each nomination.

- A large number of other acts, such as the Seaman's Act of 1915, which regulated the pay and working conditions in the merchant navy, and the Adamson Act of 1916, which imposed an eight-hour day for those working on the railways. The latter was the first time the federal government had intervened to regulate the working conditions of a private company. It would lead to a reduction in accidents caused by tired workers. The railroad companies refused to carry it out and challenged it in the courts. However in 1917, the Supreme Court agreed that the regulation did not violate the Constitution, so Congress would pass the act and the government would enforce it.

The list of changes is extensive, and is a tribute to Wilson's progressive reforming enthusiasm as well as his ability to persuade Congress to pass the acts and defend them in court if needed.

Report from the Pujo Committee of Congress, 1913 – an investigation by Congress which was to lead to growing public support for reform and regulation of the banking system.

> There has been a serious growth of money trusts. By money trusts we mean an established and well-defined identity and community of interest between a few leaders of finance which has been created and is held together through holdings of stocks and shares, interlocking directorship and other forms of domination over banks, trust companies, railroads, publics services and industrial corporations. This has resulted in a vast and growing concentration of control of money and credit in the hands of comparatively few men… while your Committee has been denied access to some of the data we required, sufficient has been learned to reveal that these trusts and the use that has been made over them in building such a power over our financial system that permits little real competition in various fields of enterprise.
>
> *Published in William Letwin (ed.),* **American Economic Policy Documents,** *(Edinburgh University Press, 1962), pp.259–60*

ACTIVITY 3.17

Should Roosevelt or Wilson be seen as the greater Progressive?

Working with another student, what do you think are the criteria for 'greatness' in this context? Which man overcame the biggest obstacles? Which made the biggest difference to the lives of most US citizens? Which do you feel was responsible for the most progress?

Constitutional reforms

Pressure from the Progressives led to a large number of changes in the laws passed by the states and Congress, and also to changes in the US Constitution itself. As Wilson said in his campaign speech (see 'The presidency of Woodrow Wilson, 1913–21', earlier in this chapter), there were fundamental problems in both business and politics, which only constitutional change could deal with. The Constitution had been drawn up in the very different era of the late 1780s and needed to be modernised to meet the changes in 'facts' which Wilson mentioned. The Founding Fathers who drafted the Constitution were wise enough to realise that what they wrote might need to be adapted, and built in to it an amendment process. The Constitution could thus be changed with the consent of both Congress and the states. However, making changes was, and still is, a long and complex process.

16th Amendment to the Constitution: the raising of an income tax, 1913

The Founding Fathers had not envisaged that the federal government would need a substantial income. With individual states responsible for issues such as law and order and provision of education and roads, they felt that tariffs on trade would provide sufficient federal funding. However by 1900 many politicians argued that tariffs were harmful to trade and the economy, and that the federal government also had a vested interest in taking care of them. So, the federal government was now expected to involve itself in a range of areas in addition to defence and foreign policy. These included the economy and welfare, and the federal government needed a source of income to deal with these new responsibilities. There was also great pressure on the government to expand the US Navy to protect and help to advance American business interests in Central and South America and the Asian Pacific region. The upkeep of a large navy was expensive. Many Progressives argued for an income tax to fund these demands, as it could be structured to fall most heavily on the rich – those most able to afford to pay it. The Supreme Court had earlier ruled that an income tax was unconstitutional; therefore a change in the Constitution was required.

17th Amendment: the direct election of senators, 1913

The original US Constitution required that two senators from each state were chosen by the states' own legislature. Often just a single party (and sometimes just one 'boss') controlled the legislature. In some states, the railway or oil trusts were very powerful and ensured that the state senators worked primarily in their interests, not in the interests of the people of the state. The Senate was made up of a small number of men, but had great power, and had proved to be a major obstacle to reform in the past. Reform meant that these politicians would be directly chosen by the people of that state. Many states even introduced primary elections, where voters had a chance to choose the candidates from the party who would stand in the election for senator, making the process even more democratic and open. This system survives to the present day, and has played an important part in making the Senate a more accountable and democratic body.

18th Amendment: the prohibition of alcoholic beverages, 1919

Some parts of the Progressive Movement had always been strong opponents of what was called the 'saloon' culture in many states. They linked alcohol consumption to several social problems. By 1914, many states had gone 'dry' and banned the consumption and sale of alcohol, and Congress had attempted legislation which outlawed the transport of alcohol from 'wet' states into dry ones. The anti-alcohol group was very powerful and effective and it kept the pressure on throughout Wilson's administration. In 1919, the Constitution was amended to prohibit entirely the sale and transport of alcohol throughout the USA. Arguably, this proved to be one of the least beneficial of the Progressive demands (and there were many Progressives who opposed it). A huge illegal industry grew up to provide alcohol for those Americans who wanted to drink it. Prohibition also encouraged the development of much organised crime. So many people broke a law that they hated and saw no value in, that it brought law itself into disrepute.

19th Amendment: votes for women, 1920

A serious campaign for female suffrage began before 1900. By 1920, several states had granted women the right to vote in state elections. Under the Constitution, individual states were allowed to make their own rules about who could, or could not, vote. At this time, a greater proportion of women in the USA went to college than anywhere else

137

Figure 3.14: A cartoon published in 1900 addressing the issue of women not having the vote. What features of this cartoon show that it was produced by a supporter of women's suffrage?

in the world. As well as a growth in female education, the demand for female suffrage was strengthened by the increased number of women working outside the home. This rose to 25% of women by 1914. The pressure for the vote for women was unstoppable as so many of the key Progressives were women and over 1.5 million women had worked in war industries during the First World War. President Wilson was sympathetic to rather than enthusiastic for female suffrage, but helped to get the necessary Amendment through Congress.

Given the tremendous effort that had to be put into amending the Constitution, the Progressives could look back on their achievements with great satisfaction. These constitutional changes would have a profound impact on US government and society, but not always in the way anticipated. The granting of the franchise for women did not lead to speedy progress towards equality. Prohibition, brought in with the intention of improving society, led to the rise of organised crime. The Senate largely remained a rich men's club, and wartime emergency showed that income tax could hit the lower paid as well as the rich.

ACTIVITY 3.18

Compare the constitutional amendments above with the many reforming laws passed in both the states and Congress in the Progressive Era. Should these amendments be seen as the principal achievements of the Progressives?

Article XVI February 3, 1913

The Congress shall have power to lay and collect taxes on incomes, from whatever source derived.

[Article XVII] April 8, 1913

1: The Senate of the United States shall be composed of two Senators from each State, elected by the people thereof, for six years.

Article [XVIII] January 16, 1919

1: After one year from the ratification of this article the manufacture, sale, or transportation of intoxicating liquors within, the importation thereof into, or the exportation thereof from the United States and all territory subject to the jurisdiction thereof for beverage purposes is hereby prohibited.

Article [XIX] August 18, 1920

The right of citizens of the United States to vote shall not be denied or abridged by the United States or by any State on account of sex.

State v. federal successes

Every state in the USA has its own governor and legislature. It is entitled under the Constitution to administer itself and pass its own laws in all areas not specifically granted to Congress and the federal government. As early as 1900, many states were strongly influenced by Progressive ideas and were passing laws concerning consumer protection and restriction of working hours. Many of these were later adopted by Congress and imposed on all states. Some states also brought in legislation in an effort to break the power of the party bosses and to give their state a much more democratic system of government.

An example of the impact of Progressive ideas on state administration came in Wisconsin when Robert La Folette (1855–1925) was elected governor in 1900 on a clear Progressive reform programme. His first major task was to challenge and overcome the highly conservative and business-orientated state legislature and impose radical reforms. He managed to do this by mostly using a 'name and shame' approach. Major reforms followed in the state:

- The railroads were regulated.
- The tax system was changed to make it fairer and more efficient.
- Lobbying, the way in which pressure was put on legislators by business interests, was regulated.
- Major conservation programmes were started to protect the environment and prevent over-exploitation of natural resources.
- Outside experts were brought in to assist in planning the reforms (this was widely copied elsewhere).
- The civil service in the state was reformed to eliminate partisanship and patronage (employing or allocating jobs to certain men simply because they were supporters of a political party, or related to a member of the legislature).

In six years, the state of Wisconsin was overhauled by the determined work of one man, and other states and cities followed this example. Among the many reforms that Progressives introduced to other states were the use of direct elections and direct primary elections. State officials, such as judges and police chiefs, had often been appointed by the state legislature; they now had to be elected by the people and, in many cases, had to go through the primary process as well. Other new processes included:

- The referendum, in which all the voters in a state were asked to decide on a specific issue, such as whether the state should become 'dry' or not. Their decision was made into law.

- The initiative. Once sufficient numbers requested it, citizens could themselves put through a new law, or have an existing one abolished, by holding a direct vote on the issue.
- The recall. Citizens in a city or state could demand the 'recall' or the dismissal from office of any elected official, such as the governor.
- The commissioner system in cities. A city manager with specific powers was appointed, who worked with police, fire, education, transport and sanitation officials to provide overall government for a city. This official was directly accountable to an elected body. It was a vital step in removing all essential local services from party politics and in breaking the power of the bosses.
- Votes for women. Many states allowed women to vote long before they could vote in national elections.

Many state and cities pioneered the reforms that the administrations of Roosevelt and Wilson followed. The example that one state set, such as La Folette's Wisconsin, showed what one individual could do. However it does need to be remembered that some states, particularly those in the South, used this independence to exclude African Americans from the franchise and to deprive them of many of the rights and liberties seen as part of a democracy.

There is inevitably a debate on how much the Progressives achieved. If they had been more united and clearer in their objectives, much more might have been achieved. Some argue that the movement did little more than highlight issues such as exploitation, corruption and monopoly, and relied on tough-minded politicians like La Folette, Roosevelt and Wilson to actually change things. However many of their broad objectives were achieved and before long another Roosevelt would take their ideas much further.

ACTIVITY 3.19

Identify what you feel should be considered as the greatest achievement of the Progressive Movement. Then, as a group, pool your conclusions. Consider if this was a remarkable success story, or whether it was a fairly straightforward process dealing with the problems which arose from rapid industrialisation.

Reflection: How varied were the views shared with the group? What did others notice that you had missed? Did other people's opinions change your opinions and if so, why?

Limits of the Progressive Movement

Congress, the Supreme Court, state legislatures and governors could, and did, prevent the Progressives from achieving all their aims. After 1920 there were Republican presidents, who had no wish to be as active domestically as Wilson and Roosevelt had been. This stopped Progressive initiatives coming down from the White House. The United States had seen an enormous amount of fundamental reform in a very short period of time, as well as participating in a world war, and many people had no wish to see further radical change. Economic prosperity for many, along with a consumer boom in the 1920s, also played a role in the movement losing impetus. Farming did very well in the war years of 1914–18 as food demand from Europe rose hugely and American farm prices went up. When peace came, farming returned to being a real weakness in the US economy. The Great Crash of 1929 showed that there were still major failings in the US banking and securities system. The Great Depression that followed in the 1930s revealed further weaknesses in the economy and its management, and poverty returned on a very large scale to the American people. The Progressive Movement had not solved all of the country's problems.

Exam-style questions

Source analysis questions

Read all four sources, then answer both parts of question 1.

SOURCE A

NO MOLLY-CODDLING HERE

(This is the prevailing Wall Street notion of President Roosevelt's attitude toward corporate interests.)

From the *Globe* (New York)

Figure 3.15: *A cartoon from the* Globe *magazine of New York, presenting the prevailing attitude on Wall Street of Roosevelt's attitude to big business*

SOURCE B

Adapted from a letter from President Roosevelt to author Upton Sinclair, March 1906

There are doubtless communities where such self-raising is very hard for the time being; there are unquestionably men who are crippled by accident (as by being old and having large families dependent on them); there are many, many men who lack any intelligence or character and who therefore cannot thus raise themselves. But while I agree with you that energetic, and, as I believe, in the long run radical, action must be taken to do away with the effects of arrogant and selfish greed on the part of the capitalist, yet I am more than ever convinced that the real factor in the elevation of any man or any mass of men must be the development within his or their hearts and heads of the qualities which alone can make either the individual, the class or the nation permanently useful to themselves and to others.

But all this has nothing to do with the fact that the specific evils you point out shall, if their existence be proved, and if I have power, be eradicated.

Source: http://teachingamericanhistory.org/library/ document/to-upton-sinclair/

SOURCE C

Adapted from President Roosevelt's message to Congress, January 31, 1908

The recent decision of the Supreme Court in regard to the employers' liability act, the experience of the Interstate Commerce Commission and of the Department of Justice in enforcing the interstate commerce and antitrust laws, and the gravely significant attitude toward the law and its administration recently adopted by certain heads of great corporations, render it desirable that there should be additional legislation as regards certain of the relations between labor and capital, and between the great corporations and the public.

The Supreme Court has decided the employers' liability law to be unconstitutional because its terms apply to employees engaged wholly in intrastate commerce as well as to employees engaged in interstate commerce. By a substantial majority the Court holds that the Congress has power to deal with the question in so far as interstate commerce is concerned.

As regards the employers' liability law, I advocate its immediate re-enactment, limiting its scope so that it shall apply only to the class of cases as to which the Court says it can constitutionally apply, but strengthening its provisions within this scope. Interstate employment being thus covered by an adequate national law, the field of intrastate employment will be left to the action of the several States. With this clear definition of responsibility the States will undoubtedly give to the performance of their duty within their field the consideration the importance of the subject demands.

Source: http://www.presidency.ucsb.edu/ws/?pid=69649

SOURCE D

Adapted from President Roosevelt's State of the Union Address, December 1905

I do not believe in the Government interfering with private business more than is necessary. I do not believe in Government undertaking any work which can if necessary be left in private hands. But neither do I believe in the Government flinching from overseeing any work when it becomes evident that abuses are sure to happen unless there is government supervision.

Source: http://teachingamericanhistory.org/library/document/state-of-the-union-address-part-i-10/

1 a Compare and contrast Roosevelt's attitude towards business in Sources A and D.

b 'Roosevelt was determined to expand the role of the Federal Government.' How far do Sources A to D support this view?

Essay based questions
Answer both parts of the questions below.

2 a Explain why the Progressive Movement proved to be so successful.

b To what extent did the Progressives have a common aim?

3 a Explain why President Wilson was able to achieve so many reforms.

b 'The constitutional amendments were the most important achievements of the Progressive movement.' How far do you agree?

Sample answer

Explain why President Wilson was able to achieve so many reforms.

There are several reasons why Wilson was able to ensure so much reform passed while he was President of the United States. He had managed to unite the Democratic Party and not only did he win the Presidential election in 1912, but many Democrats were elected to Congress, which had been a major obstacle to reform in the past. Many of the reforms had already been passed in individual states and they were now extended nationally. There had been considerable pressure from the Progressives and other groups for many of the reforms, such as for a federal income tax and the creation of the Federal Reserve Bank. The public and Congress knew that many of the necessary reforms such as the regulation of child labour could only work if they were enforced by the federal government. Wilson was also helped by the tremendous publicity given to so many of the failings of the robber barons by the muckrakers and other progressives that there was acceptance by both the public and politicians that there had to be great change and that it was the federal government that had to play an important part in it. With Congress supporting him and many reformers in important positions in the State legislatures, it was possible to get the Constitution amended as well.

This is a very competent, but not outstanding, response. It focuses well on the question and makes some clear points which are supported with detail. The level of understanding as well as depth of knowledge is high. Mentioning that there needs to be support within the states to get the Constitution amended is a good example of this. There are several key points made, such as: the way Wilson united the Democrats and helped with Democrats' elections to Congress; the pressure from below for reform and the awareness that the federal government's involvement was vital for reform; the publicity of the muckrakers; the awareness of the need to amend the Constitution. All of these factors would gain credit.

To improve the response further, there needs to be some comment on why there were 'so many' reforms. Was it due to the pressure building up for a long period of time? Was it due to the large number of Democrats elected to state legislatures as well as Congress? Which were the most important factors? Why? A stronger response would have more evidence that there has been serious thinking and reflection of 'how' and 'why' factors, not just recall of key issues.

Summary

After working through this chapter, make sure you understand the following key points:

- the causes of the USA's rapid industrialisation and the way in which the USA transformed from being a comparatively minor player on the world stage to being the leading economic power in the world

- the social and economic impact of industrialisation, and the consequences of millions of immigrants coming from Europe to the USA

- the growth of a reform campaign, known as the Progressive Movement, which pressed for improvement to the working and living conditions of millions of Americans and to the way in which the country was governed

- the nature and extent of the Progressive Movement and its successes and failures

- the way Congress and the federal government began to become increasingly involved in both social issues as well as the economy.

Further reading

Peter Clements, *Prosperity, Depression and the New Deal, 1890–1954* (Banbury, Hodder, 2008). The first two chapters are excellent on the development of the US economy and the Progressive era.

H. W. Brands, *American Colossus, The Triumph of Capitalism 1865–1900* (New York, Anchor, 2010). This is an excellent account of the whole Gilded Age, but Part Four is particularly useful on the role of government, and Part One provides insight into the robber barons.

John Steele Gordon, **An Empire of Wealth: The Epic History of American Economic Power (New York, Harper, 2004).** An excellent outline of the social and economic history of the USA. Part Three covers the whole period of this specification and takes a really analytical approach to all the topics.

Michael McGerr, *A Fierce Discontent: The Rise and Fall of the Progressive Movement in America* (Oxford University Press, 2003). Chapters 3 to 5 in Part Two are excellent on the aims and methods of the Progressives. Part Three gives a very good analytical overview of the successes and failings of the Movement as a whole.

142

For more detailed research, recommended books are:

Richard White, *The Republic for Which it Stands: The United States during Reconstruction and the Gilded Age, 1865–1896* (Oxford University Press, 2017).

Stanley L. Engerman and Robert E. Gallman (eds.), *The Cambridge Economic History of the United States, Volume II: the Long Nineteenth Century* (Cambridge University Press, 2000). A range of topics covered in depth, from the rise and impact of the railroads to the social consequences of industrialisation.

The *New York Times* website has user-friendly, organised archives dating back to 1851 which deal in depth with every part of this syllabus.

The US government's own archives are also very easy to use and exceptionally well organised.

Other useful online resources are:

- Lone Star College, Kingwood: http://kwlibguides.lonestar.edu/PrimarySources-History/gildedage
- image and files from Middle Tennessee State University: http://library.mtsu.edu/tps/sets/Primary_Source_Set-Progressive_Era.pdf

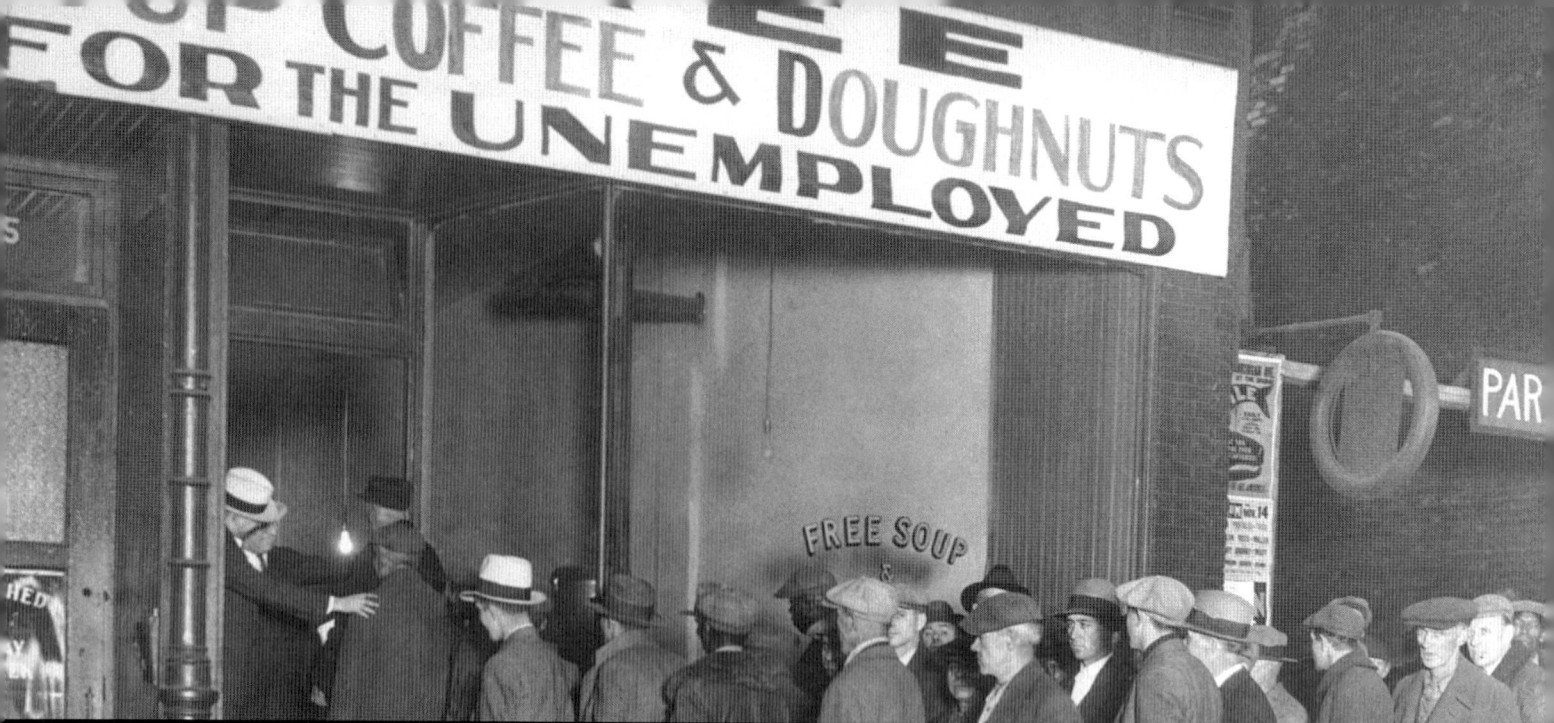

Chapter 4
The Great Crash, the Depression and the New Deal Policies, 1920–41

Learning objectives

In this chapter, you will:

- find out the causes of the greatest economic crisis to affect the United States in its history and how it affected the people and institutions of the country
- learn how and why United States governments between 1929 and 1941 reacted to, and tried to deal with, this terrible crisis.
- examine the effectiveness of the policies advocated by Presidents Hoover and Roosevelt to deal with the economic crisis
- consider why there was opposition, and the effectiveness of that opposition, to the attempts by governments to solve the crisis and help the millions that suffered as a result of it.

Timeline

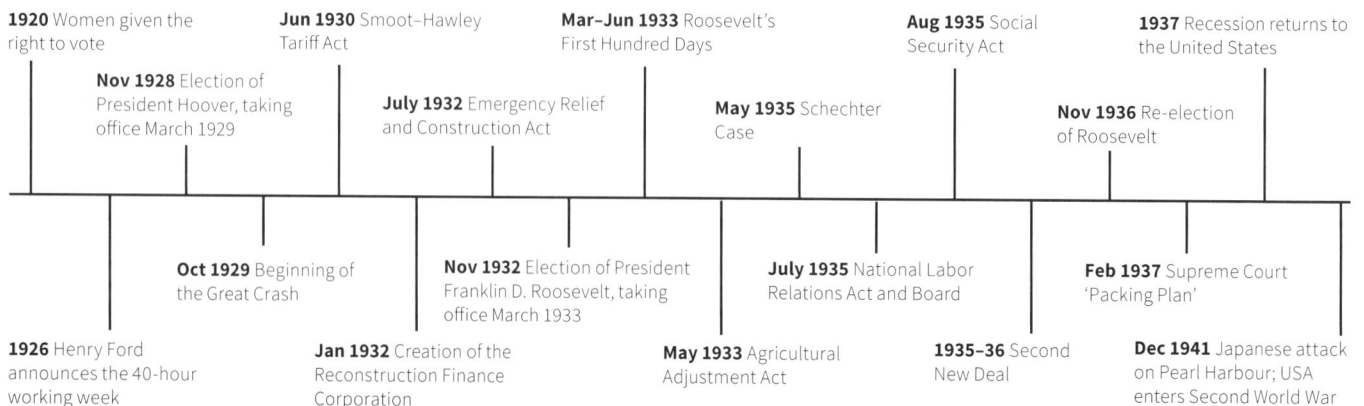

1920 Women given the right to vote

Jun 1930 Smoot–Hawley Tariff Act

Mar–Jun 1933 Roosevelt's First Hundred Days

Aug 1935 Social Security Act

1937 Recession returns to the United States

Nov 1928 Election of President Hoover, taking office March 1929

July 1932 Emergency Relief and Construction Act

May 1935 Schechter Case

Nov 1936 Re-election of Roosevelt

Oct 1929 Beginning of the Great Crash

Nov 1932 Election of President Franklin D. Roosevelt, taking office March 1933

July 1935 National Labor Relations Act and Board

Feb 1937 Supreme Court 'Packing Plan'

1926 Henry Ford announces the 40-hour working week

Jan 1932 Creation of the Reconstruction Finance Corporation

May 1933 Agricultural Adjustment Act

1935–36 Second New Deal

Dec 1941 Japanese attack on Pearl Harbour; USA enters Second World War

Before you start

To understand events in the USA in the 1920s and 1930s, you need to have a good grasp of what you have studied in the preceding chapters. Particularly important here are: population growth and immigration, the rapid growth of the US economy, the geographical size of the country and the structure of government. If you are at all unsure about these, reread and revise before starting this new topic.

Introduction

The period between 1919 and 1941 was traumatic and distressing for the USA and its people. The 1920s were a period of remarkable economic growth and social change. They were often known as the 'boom years', but prosperity came to a sudden end in 1929. The United States then entered an era of economic depression and high unemployment that lasted until war came in 1941. Two presidents, Warren Harding (1921–23) and Calvin Coolidge (1923–29) presided over the 'boom' years. Then Herbert Hoover (1929–33) and Franklin D. Roosevelt (1933–45) tried to solve the great economic and social problems which emerged after 1929, with varying degrees of success. In the process, the USA underwent enormous changes that last to this day. Perhaps the most important of these was in the role and responsibilities of the federal government, which went from playing a minor role in the economy to becoming a major force. It started to regulate business, direct farming, supervise banks and stock markets and create a **welfare state**.

ACTIVITY 4.1

Study Articles 1 and 2 to the United States Constitution. What specific powers are given to the President of the United States? In what ways is Congress able to limit those powers?

Work in two groups. One group should prepare and present an explanation of why presidents had sufficient power to deal with a major economic crisis facing the country. The other should explain why they did not.

🔑 KEY TERMS

Welfare state: A national system which is committed by law to provide financial support to any citizen during periods of poverty, such as when they fall ill, grow old, become unemployed or when their income falls below an agreed level.

GNP: Gross National Product, which is the total value of all goods and services produced by a country in one year.

4.1 What were the causes of the Great Crash?

Although the First World War of 1914 to 1918 was mostly fought in Europe and the Middle East, it played an important role in the economic history of the United States. The US economy appeared to be heading for recession in 1913–14, but the decision by the major European powers – Germany, Russia, France and Britain – to go to war in 1914 reversed that. The war made America the principal industrial nation in the world, and also the leading financial power.

War was a huge stimulus to the economy of the USA. With the other great industrial nations of the world fighting for survival, the USA profited. With Russia's grain-producing regions destroyed by war, it could no longer export any. There was increased demand for American grain and farm incomes rose rapidly as did farm prices. With American horses being sold at high prices to pull artillery guns in France, tractors came to replace them at home. This meant higher productivity and a great demand for those tractors.

Demand for manufactured products ranging from shells to ships to barbed wire increased rapidly. DuPont, a US company which specialised in chemicals, especially those involved in the manufacture of explosives, saw its revenues rise by 26% during the war years, while US **GNP** climbed by 21%. The stock market rose by 86% in 1915 alone and stayed very high. Britain and France had to sell off most of their great investments in the USA in order to fund their war effort. They also had to borrow huge sums from the USA to top up the war funds. These outstanding loans played an important part in international economic policy in the years to come. The war meant that the USA had gone from being a debtor nation to a creditor nation: several nations owed them a great deal of money. Income tax in the USA rose to pay for its own involvement in the war, much of the cost of sending troops to France in 1917 was funded by the Wilson government which borrowed increasingly large sums of money. While many Americans benefited substantially from the war, the **national debt** rose from $1.2 billion in 1915 to $25 billion in 1919. This figure worried government for much of the 1920s.

145

The boom years of 1915–18 came to rather a sudden end in 1919 with peace in Europe. A transition from a wartime economy to a peacetime one invariably causes dislocation:

- Returning soldiers wanted their jobs back.
- Factories making guns needed to return to making more peaceful products, which there might be less demand for.
- The huge orders from Britain and France stopped as their own industries slowly returned to peacetime production.
- European agriculture slowly recovered and then demand for American grain dropped sharply. Therefore farm incomes fell, as did investment in agriculture.
- Unemployment rose to 12%, causing real hardship.
- GNP dropped by 10% in 1919.

While there had been worries about rising prices – inflation – during the war, there was an even greater worry about falling prices after it. Prices overall fell by nearly 40% between 1920 and 1921, partly through overproduction and a lack of overseas orders, and partly as the **Federal Reserve Bank** pushed interest rates up to 7%. Borrowing by businessmen and farmers cost a lot more and they became reluctant to invest.

Government did little to manage the transition from war to peace. President Wilson was heavily involved in his struggle to 'win' the peace and to create the League of Nations. He was also seriously ill for much of the time until he left office in 1921. The new Republican President, Warren Harding, had little understanding of economics and even less desire to intervene in the economy.

> ### KEY TERMS
>
> **National debt:** The amount that the federal government owes the US public and other government agencies.
>
> **Federal Reserve Bank:** Created in 1913 to manage the currency, supervise banking, act as a lender of last resort in a crisis and to control interest rates for lenders.

Structural weaknesses in the American economy in the 1920s: the disparity between agriculture and traditional and new industries

Traditional and new industries

Before the First World War, much of the American economy was driven by the expansion and demands of what is known as 'heavy industry' – for example, steel, coal, rail and oil – and the system that financed it. These traditional industries remained important in the 1920s, but new businesses rose to rival them in importance to the economy. These new industries, such as electricity and automobile production, had a much greater focus on the individual consumer.

Automobile manufacture possibly did most to change the face of industry in the US. The internal combustion engine had been invented before 1900 in Europe, but it was in early 20th-century America that the automobile became a nation-changing innovation. **Henry Ford** revolutionised both the manufacture and price of the automobile.

HENRY FORD (1863–1947)

Ford was a pioneer of the motor industry who revolutionised car production by developing the assembly line. He had an enormous impact on technological development and the US economy as a whole.

By the late 1920s, Ford had been able to reduce the price of his car significantly, and was using assembly-line methods to produce millions of cars a year. His company led the way in creating possibly the largest new industry in the 20th century. He made the automobile affordable to the masses, including his employees, as he took care to pay them enough to ensure that they could afford to buy one of the cars.

The automobile industry was soon employing hundreds of thousands of men. Building cars required huge amounts of steel (and the coal to make it), glass and rubber. The industry also stimulated a vast road-building programme throughout the USA. Construction of new bridges was also required. Demand for oil and petrol increased and the petrol station and the accompanying motels arrived in large numbers. The automobile made commuting to work very much easier than the railway had done, and suburbs started to grow out from US towns and cities, creating a house-building boom. The Model T replaced the horse and cart in many rural areas, and the tractor replaced the plough horse. Farriers went out of business, but the demand for car mechanics soared.

Another major reason for the great success of US industry in the 1920s was the damage that the war had done to their great commercial rivals, Germany and Britain. The German economy had been destroyed by the war, and it had to pay huge sums in compensation to Britain and France. Britain had lost many of its overseas markets to the USA during the war. Britain's major industries – steel, textiles and shipbuilding – had all depended heavily on exports, but these markets were lost during the war. The USA was very fortunate because its traditional heavy industries included the rapidly growing automobile industry. This industry was very productive and provided a lot of jobs. US industry was also more efficient and productive and had benefitted from greater investment. Business interests also had much greater influence on government in the US than in Britain.

GNP increased by 59% between 1921 and 1929, and incomes across the US increased by 38%. The automobile industry contributed a lot to this but other industries were also important. For example, most of the key inventions in the electricity industry had been made in the previous century by men like Thomas Edison and Samuel Insull. However, in the 20th century, and in the US in particular, the electricity industry grew greatly. This helped many other industries to develop and enabled completely new industries to be created.

ACTIVITY 4.2

Year	Number sold	Price
1908	10 000	$850
1916	730 000	$360
1922	1.3 million	$319
1925	1.9 million	$260

Table 4.1: Sales of Model T Ford automobiles

Study the data in the table above. Investigate a) why prices were able to fall and b) why sales of cars rose so rapidly. How might these factors be linked to the causes of the Depression?

Agriculture

Agriculture did not share in the economic prosperity which old and new industries such as steel and automobiles saw in the 1920s. After suffering from depressions and mixed fortunes in the years before the First World War, agriculture had benefitted greatly from the war itself. Prices for all farm products rose rapidly during the war. Overall they went up by as much as 300% between 1913 and 1919. Marginal land was brought into use and the price of agricultural land rose. Mechanisation developed and productivity increased. Farmers could afford to borrow large sums of money to buy more land at high prices and could afford to buy new machinery and tractors. The amount of money that was owed to the banks by farmers increased rapidly.

The arrival of peace in 1919 had a drastic effect. Demand dropped as the USA no longer needed to feed Europe, and Europe was not really in a position to buy much imported food anyway. So, exports declined while production had been increasing. Prices dropped dramatically, but farmers could not sell much of what they produced. Domestic demand decreased as well as there was a fall in immigration after the war and a slowing of population growth. Farm incomes dropped and living standards declined among the 40% of the US population involved in agriculture. Many suffered severely as a result, especially African Americans in the South. African Americans were one of the most economically deprived groups. They moved North by the hundreds of thousands to find work in the cities. It was one of the greatest internal migrations in the country's history.

Although everyone in government and Congress knew that agriculture was a major area of concern throughout the 1920s, little was done to ease the difficulties of US farmers. There were three main reasons for this. The first was that US farming was very diverse. The needs and interests of the various sections, such as the cotton growers in the South, the cattlemen of Montana, the dairy farmers, the wheat growers and those concerned with fruit and vegetables, varied considerably. What might help one section might well harm another. Second, in 1889 a Department of Agriculture with a cabinet secretary was set up, but it had limited power to do anything. It mostly collected data, gave advice to farmers and helped to develop agricultural education. The secretary of agriculture at that time, Henry Wallace, was both an able administrator and an expert on agriculture, but there was little effective action he could take. Finally, the presidents of the 1920s had little interest in, or understanding of, agriculture. For ideological reasons, they were reluctant to intervene. Occasionally Congress was prepared to act, but the senators and representatives tended to focus on the specific interests of their own states, so it was difficult to agree any focussed action. For example, some regions might have wanted high tariffs, and others might have wanted much lower ones. Twice in the 1920s Congress passed bills which would have given the federal government the power, and the money, to buy up surplus agricultural produce at a reasonable price. It could then either be stored for future use, or sold at a much lower price abroad (known as 'dumping'). In both cases, President Coolidge vetoed the bills after taking advice from business interests who argue that farmers should not receive taxpayer support.

The only attempt to assist agriculture which was deep in poverty came in 1929. President Hoover put through the Agricultural Marketing Act, which created the Federal Farm Board. It followed the principles of the bills which Coolidge had vetoed, but it had two main failings.

- It did not deal with the key problem of overproduction. Farmers were still producing much more than was needed.
- The funds allocated to the board were far too low to really achieve much.

This combination of factors meant that agriculture, which still involved a substantial section of the population in the South and West, struggled throughout the 1920s and had no share of the 'boom' years. Therefore, when a national depression arrived, together with a severe drought and the creation of the **dust bowl**, this badly depressed industry was devastated. Many farmers were unable to repay their debts and lost their farms as a result, leading to destitution. Many families moving to cities in search of work.

KEY TERM

Dust bowl: The dust bowl was both a time and a place. In the 1930s, dry weather in the Southern US led to severe drought. Combined with the effects of mechanised farming practice. This left top soil vulnerable to being blown away from large areas of farmland. Soil erosion and the consequent piling up of soil 'dust' affected a vast area that comprised parts of Oklahoma, New Mexico, Colorado, Texas and Kansas. Huge numbers of agricultural workers migrated to towns and out to California in search of work.

ACTIVITY 4.3

Working in a small group, discuss the reasons why the problems facing agriculture in the 1920s proved so difficult to solve. Each member of the group should be allocated a reason, such as regional diversity or weak central government, and develop a case arguing that it is the primary reason. Then, still working together, put the reasons in order of importance by looking at the evidence supporting each reason.

Mass production and oversupply

As we saw in Chapter 3, the growth of a few huge corporations which dominated major industries such as steel, oil, transport and now automobiles, lowered competition in the markets and led to producer-dictated prices and production levels. These corporations ran very successful marketing campaigns, and developed manufacturing techniques that meant they could mass-produce, but had over-supplied their markets. They did seem to consider what might happen if large numbers of people stopped buying cars or other manufactured goods. What would happen to those who made, sold and serviced cars? For example by 1929, 4.5 million cars a year were being produced in the United States. When demand dropped, as it did by 1929, it of course affected not just the motor industry. But it also affected the industries which provided raw materials for the motor industry, such as steel, coal, glass and rubber.

In agriculture, post-war prices in the USA for products like wheat and meat dropped sharply. Approximately 30% of agricultural land which had been used to grow horse feed. This could now be used to grow human food crops. Farmers overproduced, even during a worldwide agricultural depression, and prices dropped accordingly, sometimes by as much as 60%. This hit farm incomes very hard. Despite this, attempts to help farmers were vetoed by President Coolidge. In the 1920s, about 25% of all US jobs were in agriculture. If that 25% was earning a lot less money, then they were not able to buy cars or radios or clothes, or even much food. Supply was plentiful, but demand was falling everywhere.

The impact of government policies

The Republican Party and its three presidents, Warren Harding, Calvin Coolidge and Herbert Hoover, dominated US politics in the period 1921–33. However,

Figure 4.1: The effects of the dust bowl on a farm in South Dakota, 1936. What do you think the purpose of the photograph may have been?

much of their understanding of the economy and America's role in world trade and economics, was based on the very different conditions which existed before the traumatic impact of the First World War. The war destroyed the great autocracies of Russia, Germany and Austria-Hungary and largely bankrupted countries like Britain and France. The USA became the biggest creditor nation in the world by 1919. By 1928, it was responsible for 42% of the world's manufacturing output. It was the largest exporter of goods and food in the world and the second largest importer of goods. It was the greatest supplier of capital in the world. However, the war's devastation of Europe and its economy meant that it also devastated the USA's biggest export market.

Europe also owed the United States enormous sums of money, and the US needed to ensure that the loan could be repaid. So, care needed to be taken. Imposing high tariffs on goods imported into the USA was perhaps not a good idea, as it restricted the ability to repay those loans.

Tariffs (see '3.1 Why was the late 19th century an age of rapid industrialisation?') were designed to 'protect' US industries from foreign competition, but inevitably other countries would respond by protecting their industries. High foreign tariffs on exported goods would be very damaging to the world's largest manufacturer and exporter.

High interest rates in Europe (and low interest rates in the USA) encouraged US banks to lend lots of money to Europe. These loans enabled Europe to pay for US imports, and, in the case of Germany, helped them to pay their **reparations** to Britain and France. Britain and France then put the reparations towards repayment of their loans to the USA. What would happen if either the money going out of the US stopped or the debtors were unable to pay?

US governments in the 1920s did not want to influence the direction of the US economy and in fact couldn't do this anyway. There were potential dangers, such as the badly depressed farming industry, high levels of consumer debt and the possibility of serious overproduction in the critical automobile industry. But government was content to let **market forces** rule.

KEY TERMS

Reparations: Payments which the victorious French and British insisted that the Germans pay them as compensation for the damage done in the First World War.

Market forces: Where prices and wages are left to producers and employers to decide, according to supply and demand, and there is no interference by government.

HERBERT HOOVER (1874–1964)

Hoover was considered by the Republican Party to be an excellent candidate. He was elected president in November 1928 and took office in March 1929. Hoover didn't come from a rich family background but he trained as an engineer and made a lot of money in the mining industry. He was appointed as an administrator by Woodrow Wilson, and played a great part in bringing relief to war-torn Europe in 1918–19. He was made secretary of commerce in Coolidge's cabinet in 1921 and stayed in this job for eight years. In this position, he was seen as partly responsible for the boom years. This image helped his victory in the presidential election of 1928.

150

The government was seen to be partly responsible for economic progress and prosperity because of this lack of involvement and its imposition of very low taxes. It was accepted that any attempt to control market forces or regulate business, would do more harm than good. There were three views, strongly held at the time by politicians and businessmen, considered to be vital to a healthy economy:

- Government might assist business and farming if there was a crisis, but never regulate or try to direct them.
- Privately-owned corporations and businesses were the key to wealth creation and the economic health of the nation.

- It was the individual citizen, not the federal or state governments, who was responsible for health, housing and, above all, employment.

The re-election of President Coolidge in 1924 and his succession by fellow-Republican **Herbert Hoover** in 1928 demonstrated the popularity of their laissez-faire policies.

Looking at this from one perspective, the US economy seemed to be very healthy when Hoover took office in 1929. However, there were structural failings which would bring that economy nearly to breaking point within three years.

ACTIVITY 4.4

From an economic point of view, the country is sound, because its prosperity is based, first on a boundless supply of natural produce, and second on an elaborate organization of industrial production, the perfection of which is nowhere approached in Europe...

From a moral point of view, it is obvious that Americans have come to consider their standard of living as a somewhat sacred acquisition, which they will defend at any price. This means that they would be ready to make many an intellectual or even moral concession in order to maintain that standard.

From a political point of view, it seems that the notion of efficiency in production is on its way to taking precedency of the very notion of liberty. In the name of efficiency one can obtain, from the American, all sorts of sacrifices in relation to his personal and even to certain of his political liberties...

Andre Siegfried, "The Gulf Between", Atlantic Monthly, Vol. 141 (March 1928), pp 289–96

a What points is the author making about the 'economic' and 'political' points of view?

b How accurate a picture is he giving of the US economy in the 1920s?

This transformation was not always smooth. Mistakes were made in what became a process of experimentation by **Franklin D. Roosevelt** and his government to help the unemployed, the destitute farmers and the bankrupt banks. Opposition to Roosevelt's policies was often lengthy and bitter, but he provided a democratic solution to a dreadful crisis. He found a path between the extremes of laissez-faire capitalism on the one side and the harsh state intervention practised by both socialist and fascist states on the other.

Growth of consumerism: hire purchase and buying on the margin

Borrowing for the consumer lifestyle

The introduction of electric light and heating in factories, along with the arrival of the small electric engine, played a major part in increasing industrial output. The availability of electricity in many US households also led to the creation of whole new industries to produce a whole new range of products. The electric refrigerator, iron, heater, vacuum cleaner and light changed the domestic lives of many. Incomes were rising for many Americans, and these products were in high demand by middle-income families as well as the rich. More and more people bought radios and phonographs, which led to new entertainment industries. With more leisure time and disposable income, there was a massive growth in cinema. Hollywood became a major employer, and every US town had its own picture house.

In the past, banks usually lent money to the rich, who could afford to repay it. Many Americans wished to purchase the new consumer goods like refrigerators and radios, but they did not always have enough money. However, with a regular income they could afford to take out a loan to buy them. The result was the rapid growth of consumer credit. Consumers bought the product with an initial smaller amount and paid the remainder in instalments over a period of time, in a system known as 'instalment plan' in the USA (or 'hire purchase' in the UK). The system made more products available to more people, so demand increased on a large scale. This led to increased profits which could mean a further reduction in prices. Of course it also meant that many people owed a lot of money to the lenders. This was fine when the borrowers were in work and able to pay, but any significant unemployment would cause considerable problems. The new industries suffered the drop in demand, and the institutions which had lent large sums of money suffered too.

FRANKLIN D. ROOSEVELT (1882–1945)

Roosevelt, a Democrat, had a privileged upbringing. In 1913, he was appointed as assistant secretary of the US Navy. He suffered waist-down paralysis after getting polio in 1921, but he went on to become governor of New York State in 1929, doing all he could to deal with the unemployment and poverty caused by the Depression. He defeated the Republican candidate, Herbert Hoover, in the 1932 presidential election. He spent four consecutive terms in office (until his death in 1945). His wife Eleanor redefined the role of 'First Lady' through her active involvement in social causes.

The stock market and 'buying on the margin'

The stock market crash and the wider Depression are sometimes seen as the same thing, but they need to be dealt with separately. The stock market crash was a catalyst. It made the crisis much worse and made it happen more quickly, but it was not the major cause of the Depression itself.

A traditional view is that the crash was caused when the United States stock market, based in New York's Wall Street, collapsed in the autumn of 1929 in what was called 'an orgy of speculation'. This dragged down the rest of the economy, leading to mass unemployment, bank failures and a collapse in investment. However, this is now seen as an incorrect interpretation of events. The current view is that the Wall Street Crash was caused by an economic depression that had already begun in the United States.

There was a brief recession in the early 1920s, caused by the adjustment from a wartime to a peacetime economy. Then the United States entered a period of growth, especially in manufacturing. The stock market boomed, with shares in major companies continuously rising. The **Dow Jones Index** went up by 400% between 1921 and 1929. By 1928, many shares were being bought and sold for a great deal more than they were worth. Companies and individuals bought the shares in the expectation that they would continue to rise in value and could then be sold at a profit. This practice was called speculation. Of course, if the share price went down, they would make a loss. However the upward trend across most of the 1920s gave people the confidence to keep on buying shares.

> **KEY TERM**
>
> **Dow Jones Index:** Created in 1896, this records and publishes share prices and activity on the New York stock exchange.

Much of the speculation was financed by borrowing. For example, a bank could buy a share for 10% of its value. The seller of the share would 'lend' the remaining 90%, using the share itself as security for the loan. The share then would rise in value (hopefully) and, by the time the outstanding 90% had to be paid back, the share had risen so much in value that the loan could be easily repaid. This all depended on the price of shares continually rising. Few speculators really understood that prices could go down as well as up. They didn't consider what might happen if too many shares were priced above their true value. The potential risk of prices dropping considerably did not seem to occur to many.

Most politicians and many in business assumed that the US economy was very healthy. However, a careful observer and analyst might have come to the different, and much more pessimistic, conclusion that all was not well with the economy. For example:

- Politicians and businesses apparently failed to understand the causes of the boom of the 1920s and see that there might be underlying problems. There was a degree of ignorance about how the post-war economy worked.

- Income and wealth were becoming increasingly unequally distributed. Wealth was becoming concentrated in fewer hands, making a small number of people very rich. Fewer and fewer people were able to buy goods. By 1929, less than 30% of all families in the USA had incomes of over $2500 a year. This was the figure seen as the amount required for a 'comfortable' family lifestyle in which people could afford to buy items like cars and other manufactured goods.

- Many of the major markets abroad, where the USA sold its manufactured products, cotton and wheat – such as Europe, China and South America – were facing political instability and simply did not have the money to continue buying American goods. When the US needed

to demand repayment of loans from the First World War, this situation got worse.

- High tariffs were also hitting US exports hard.

- New construction on facilities like roads and railways was declining by 1928, and car production was slowing.

- Areas of the USA faced serious poverty, especially rural areas and the South. In the North, where much of the manufacturing was concentrated, there were a large number of 'one industry' towns, where most employment was provided by one manufacturer. If it went out of business, the whole town would suffer.

- Wages were higher than they had been in the past but were still quite low as a result of immigration, mechanisation and weak labor unions. Low wages meant fewer people buying goods.

- There was an extremely inflexible monetary system which regulated how countries did business with each other, known as the **gold standard**. This system was probably out of date and was unable to deal with a world economic crisis.

> **KEY TERM**
>
> **Gold standard:** An international monetary system which provided a standard economic unit based on a fixed weight of gold. It placed a value on a currency and was also used to compare one currency with another for exchange rates.

With these factors in the background, the American economy was not really in any condition to withstand any shocks. After 1929 it suffered a series of major shocks which came close to causing total collapse.

> **ACTIVITY 4.5**
>
> Working in a small group, identify the principal weaknesses in the US economy by 1929. Were these a serious threat to the US economy as a whole? Why do you think there was so little awareness of the underlying economic problems which faced America in 1929?

> **Reflection:** Now look back through the preceding pages and note down weaknesses that you did not identify. Do these change your assessment in some way or confirm it?

4.2 What were the causes and impacts of the Depression?

There is inevitably a great debate over the principal causes of the Great Depression, and whether these causes originated in the USA or abroad. Many Americans, including President Hoover, tended to blame overseas factors. This was probably to move blame away from themselves or the USA. What the role of the government should be in such a crisis was also debated. Some people challenge whether the US government attempted to do enough to deal with the Depression or even took the wrong actions which did further harm.

Some historians and economists argue that the Great Depression should be blamed on long-term, deep-rooted factors over which there was no immediate control. These included the switch to new high-tech consumer-oriented industries that had different investment and labour needs from the USA's traditional areas of production. However, several factors undeniably played a large part in the developing crisis:

- the decline in agriculture
- overproduction in industry
- the US banking system
- growing tariff wars
- the failure of the market system. The mechanisms which connected investment with production and consumption just broke down
- lack of investment. Too much money had gone into speculation and not enough into the new plants, equipment, research and training necessary for industrial and business development.

In addition, there was serious **deflation**. Prices dropped, in manufacturing as well as agriculture, which discouraged investment and led to further contraction in the economy. It was this, combined with the huge fall in spending by the American people, that was really damaging the US economy by 1930. People were just not buying things, because many were struggling just to afford food to feed their families. Many retired people had lost all their savings in the crash when their banks failed.

> **KEY TERM**
>
> **Deflation:** A fall in retail prices. Like inflation, when prices rise, this can have very serious economic consequences.

The main features of the Great Crash of October 1929

In 1928–29, several factors occurred to bring about the eventual stock market crash. In 1928, the central Federal Reserve Bank increased interest rates on borrowed money and cut the money supply to the country as a whole. This meant that those who had borrowed money to buy shares had to pay more interest on those loans and therefore became reluctant to borrow and invest. Meanwhile, the head of the Federal Reserve Bank fell seriously ill, and the bank was therefore unable to provide strong leadership when a crisis struck. It would have been the only institution capable of managing this sort of crisis – but even then, it had limited powers.

There was also a growing awareness that depression was setting into the United States. This led to a loss of confidence in the markets and fewer people were prepared to invest their money in industry. Instead of investing wisely in potentially productive industry, large numbers of banks, insurance companies and businesses became heavily involved in speculating on the stock market. Their aim was to make a large amount of money in a short time for their managers and shareholders.

None of these institutions were effectively controlled, and the Federal Reserve Bank had only limited regulatory powers. There was nothing to stop a bank speculating on the stock market with money their customers had deposited as savings. Those savings might have been put away for their old age, for example. Most US banks were small and served only their local communities. They had few reserves and many were deeply involved in the speculation that led to the Great Crash when they collapsed. If the bank lost the money through unwise speculation, then it would simply go out of business and customers would lose all their money.

So, in October 1929, confidence collapsed on Wall Street and shares dropped in value by as much as 40% in a single day. No one is sure quite what started the crash itself. Perhaps a few individuals suddenly realised that there was a serious lack of financial common sense on Wall Street. In late September, there had been a sudden fall in stock prices, but the market recovered quickly. However, on 23 October over 6 million shares were traded and $4 billion was suddenly wiped off the value of stocks. Worse was to come the following day on 'Black Friday', when 13 million shares were sold and $9 billion lost. The final catastrophic collapse came on 29 October, when over 16 million shares were sold. Over one-third of the value of all shares had dropped in a month. Thousands of individuals were ruined, and many small banks and insurance companies went bankrupt. The customers who had trusted the banks with their savings just lost all their money.

The stock market recovered slowly over the next two years. Some argued that what happened was necessary to end unwise speculation by banks and businesses. However, it was a severe blow to confidence and didn't encourage new investment. Less than 3% of US citizens owned stocks and shares themselves, but many hundreds of thousands lost their life savings when the banks and insurance companies that had been speculating with their money collapsed.

As a result of the stock market collapse, what had been a slowly developing economic decline then accelerated into a major economic and social catastrophe.

154

ACTIVITY 4.6

Work in a small group, discuss who or what should be seen as responsible for the Great Crash of October 1929. Identify any individuals who you think could have been responsible. Then consider any institutions which could be blamed. Consider the source below and use the information to help you in your discussion:

> This panic was not "inevitable." It was the result of gross carelessness or wanton recklessness. The recording of its causes in frank language may help to prevent the recurrence of a similar situation at too early a date. . . . Yet within the past two years it has been indisputably true that this whole range of maxims [guidelines] has been abandoned by our banking community. Through their establishment of affiliated financing companies, they have put themselves into a position as issuers of stocks. Investment trusts, shares in affiliates or associates, and similar securities of all kinds, have poured forth from the banks, while many more have been issued by "groups," which were practically bankers and banking houses in another form. . . .
>
> The breakdown of 1929 was as nearly the result of wilful mismanagement and violation of every principle of sound finance as such an occurrence ever has been. It was the outcome of vulgar grasping for gain at the cost of the community. It has been a national disgrace and a source of untold national and individual loss. In paying the bill entailed by it,

> the American people should think seriously about how they can best avoid running up another.
>
> H. Parker Willis "Who Caused the Panic of 1929?"
> *The North American Review, vol. 229, no. 2; February 1930. Parker Willis was an economist who served as First Secretary of the Federal Reserve Board between 1914-1918*

The collapse of the financial system

In the months between Roosevelt being elected (November 1932) and taking office as president (March 1933), the economic crisis within the United States worsened dramatically. Hoover was still president until March 1933 and had ideas for dealing with the crisis. He wanted Roosevelt's cooperation to do this but Roosevelt refused to help. As a result, by the time Roosevelt was inaugurated as president, there was a major crisis in banking, and the banks in 32 states had closed. Banks which were still open were now limiting the amount of cash that could be taken out, as there had been a mass withdrawal of savings and funds by investors.

Meanwhile, investigations by the Senate revealed corruption and incompetence on Wall Street, and the New York stock exchange had closed. Such widespread closures were symptoms of a collapse which led to capital and gold flooding out of the USA. However, Hoover had refused to abandon the gold standard or declare the financial crisis a national emergency.

The whole country was affected by this crisis. The states' limited welfare funds ran out. National unemployment was over 13 million and was rising. The states were unable to provide any support for the unemployed. Violence was increasing in rural areas in protest against evictions for non-payment of **mortgages**. There were also a growing number of hunger marches in cities and other demonstrations.

KEY TERM

Mortgage: A very large loan made by a bank or other institutions to an individual so they can buy land or a house. Interest is paid on the loan by the borrower, who pays back the loan over an agreed period of time.

Those in power at both the national and local level feared that law and order might break down completely unless radical action was taken to deal with the financial crisis. There was a growing awareness that the federal government, led by the president, was the only institution capable of dealing with this situation.

Mass unemployment and its social impact: Hoovervilles and employment discrimination

The period between the end of 1929 and the summer of 1933 was one of continuous bad news for the American people. Millions suffered more than ever before in US history. Right across the country, many thousands of families were forced out of their homes because they could not pay their rent or mortgage and had to live on wasteland or in public parks in what became known as 'Hoovervilles'. In fact, these were shanty towns where homes were shacks made out of any waste material people could find, such as tar-paper or cardboard. There was no running water, sanitation, heating or electricity. These places were given the Hooverville nickname by Hoover's Democratic opponents, who also continually referred to the 'Hoover Depression', wanting to place the blame firmly on him. While most Hoovervilles disappeared when Roosevelt's **New Deal** was in force after 1933, some were still being lived in as late as 1941. There were endless shocking statistics about such deprivation, which reached their very worst in the hard winter of 1932–33:

- From a total population of around 126 million, it was estimated that 50 to 60 million were living in poverty. About 20 million Americans were at risk of starvation.
- In the cotton-growing regions of the South, cotton prices dropped from 18 cents per pound in 1929 (they had been 35 cents in 1918) to 5 cents per pound in 1933, there were known to be over 1 million people at the point of starvation.
- There were about 33 million people unemployed or seriously underemployed in 1933. Between 1928 and 1932, nearly 100 000 jobs were lost every week, with women and African Americans the first to be fired. In areas of the South where agriculture was the main industry, the unemployment rate for African American men was over 50% by 1932. In certain cities, such as Nashville and Memphis, the unemployment rate for black men was over 70% by 1934.
- Average family income dropped by 40% from 1929 to 1933.
- 250 000 families were evicted from their homes in 1932 alone for failing to pay their mortgage or rent. Many were forced to live in Hoovervilles, or live with relatives, which often led to serious overcrowding in cities.

- Over 5000 banks collapsed in this period, leaving those who had their savings invested in them without any cash. A further 6500 banks closed their doors in February – March 1933, including all banks in New York.
- Over 2 million men were known to be wandering the country in search of work.
- Many towns and cities went bankrupt as there was too little tax coming in, so they were forced cut the wages of their employees, such as teachers and police, or simply sack them. In the winter of 1932–33, over 1000 cities, towns and counties went bankrupt and were unable to provide any local government.
- In some areas, law and order broke down completely and food stores were looted by hungry people, while citizens grouped together to stop families being evicted from their homes and farms.

> **KEY TERM**
>
> **New Deal:** A series of schemes, public works projects, financial reforms and regulations introduced by President Roosevelt in response to the Great Depression (see 4.3 and 4.4).

The Great Depression devastated huge areas of the United States and directly affected the vast majority of its people. It was not just the factory workers or farmers who suffered, but also millions of middle-class citizens such as bankers, lawyers, factory managers and teachers. A working-class family evicted for not paying rent was perhaps not an unusual sight in some city districts, but large numbers of middle-class families being thrown out of their homes for failing to pay their mortgages, was.

There was also the possibility that if an investor had savings in a bank, and the bank went into bankruptcy, the saver lost everything. Bank and insurance company failures hit middle-class families particularly hard. Many of them had been saving for their retirement (the state did not provide pensions for the elderly) and company failures meant their income was lost.

Employment discrimination

The whole situation was very much worse as there was no welfare state. If a man was out of work, there was no system of unemployment benefit to enable him to feed his family and pay his rent or mortgage until he found another job. Circumstances for African Americans were desperate. Racial discrimination was not illegal, and where there were jobs available, black men and women were not employed. In the South, gangs of unemployed white workers harassed and threatened companies who employed

155

ACTIVITY 4.7

Study the photograph in Figure 4.2. Contextualise this image, drawing on your knowledge of the United States in the Depression, following the Great Crash.

Figure 4.2: A Hooverville near the waterfront in Seattle

black workers instead of out-of-work white men. Some companies recruited white migrants and women to fill jobs rather than employ local black workers. Even when African American men could find employment, it was in low-skilled jobs, and their wages were lower than those paid to white workers for the same jobs.

ACTIVITY 4.8

Prepare a presentation using a range of different data and sources. Illustrate visually the impact of the Depression on the American people. Remember that 'the American people' was a large, diverse group with different experiences. Study and make use of Fig 4.3 and the extract from the '**Report and Recommendations of the California State Unemployment Commission**' (below Fig 4.3) in your presentations.

What little welfare there was, was provided by either charities or, occasionally, local government. The federal government played no part at all. In the majority of cases, local government simply did not have the resources, or the will, to provide for millions of homeless and hungry families. Many states and cities had themselves suffered bankruptcy by the end of 1932. A small number of states, such as New York State under its governor Franklin Roosevelt, were able to borrow money to try to assist with feeding the very hungry. Even then, any support tended not to go to African Americans, Hispanic people and Native Americans, and their situation was often appalling.

By the spring of 1933, it was becoming clear that the USA was facing a serious catastrophe and there was little optimism for the future. The economy had clearly broken down.

Figure 4.3: Impoverished citizens of New York receiving food parcels, 1929. Do you think the photograph is recording an event, or showing an opinion?

Government seemed unable to deal with the problem and there were many cases of society and law and order breaking down as well:

Men, young and old, have taken to the road. Homes in which life savings were invested have been lost and never recovered. There is no security, no foothold, and no future to sustain them. Savings are gone and debts are mounting with no prospect of repayment. Women and child labour further undermine the stability of the home. Food rations are pared down, rents go unpaid and families are evicted. Idleness destroys not only purchasing power, lowering the standards of living, but it destroys efficiency and finally breaks the spirit.

Source: An extract from 'Report and Recommendations of the California State Unemployment Commission', Sacramento, 1932. Author: Edward Joseph Hanna; California State Unemployment Commission. Publisher: Sacramento California State Printing Office, H. Hammond, State Printer 1933.

What surprised many observers was how peacefully the vast majority of Americans reacted to the crisis. There were some outbreaks of violent protest and there was a growth in membership of communist, socialist and fascist parties, but not on a large scale, and those parties tended to be badly divided among themselves. In Germany, for example, citizens had looked to radical solutions such as those provided by Hitler. In the United States, there was some unrest, but overall people were generally willing to wait for the democratic process to find a solution.

Responses of the Hoover government and industry to the Great Crash

Hoover's economic and social policies

Within months of becoming president, Herbert Hoover was faced with a major economic crisis in the form of the Wall Street Crash of 1929. He later claimed, in his State of the Union Address in 1931, that: 'Our self-contained national economy with its matchless strength and resources would have enabled us to recover long since, but for the continued dislocation, shocks and setbacks from abroad.'

The traditional view of Herbert Hoover and his policies for dealing with the Great Depression was that he did too little to help and, in some cases, made the situation worse. To be fair to Hoover, there were limits to what a president could do under the Constitution at the time. All new laws had to pass through both Houses of Congress, and a president could do little to influence either House. The Senate was particularly conservative in economic matters. Hoover personally felt that it was not the job of the president to intervene extensively in the economy, as this might cause more harm than good. He also felt that much of the blame for the US crisis lay with other countries, which he had no control over. The worst of the crisis did not come until 1932 and early 1933, and before this time Congress and the public had tended to be reluctant for the government to intervene in economic matters.

The **Founding Fathers** had not anticipated how the US economy would develop, so economic matters had traditionally been firmly in the hands of either Congress or individual states. It was widely believed that the president should focus primarily on defence and foreign policy. However, the Great Depression presented a new challenge. Neither Congress nor the states had the ability to respond to a national crisis of this size. Therefore in the 1930s people increasingly looked to the president for action and solutions. Hoover did not feel that it was his role to actively manage the economy, and didn't feel that serious intervention by a president would actually help matters. However, he was determined to do what he could within those restrictions.

> **KEY TERMS**
>
> **Founding Fathers:** The men who wrote the Constitution at the end of the 18th century.
>
> **Pump priming:** A process of providing a stimulus to the economy. It includes lowering taxes, increasing government spending, reducing interest rates or printing more money. Any of these can put money into people's pockets and can increase spending and thus economic activity. However, they can also cause inflation, making them controversial steps.

Some historians argue that Hoover was right to be concerned that presidential influence would not help, as it appeared some of his actions made the situation worse.

He did not persuade the Federal Reserve Bank to increase the, supply of money in the economy. This might have reversed deflation and increased demand for manufactured goods. Increasing the money supply might also have helped employment and those who wished to borrow to invest in production.

Despite protests by many economists, Hoover signed the Smoot–Hawley Tariff Act in 1930. This introduced high tariffs on many imports. He had promised a tariff on agricultural imports to help farmers in his election campaign of 1928. However, when the bill for this went through Congress senators added tariffs on manufactured goods. This led to retaliation by other countries, such as Canada, Mexico, Australia and New Zealand. These countries normally bought goods from the United States and they put high tariffs on their imports of US goods. Of course, this reduced the sale of US goods abroad. This was catastrophic for the United States and its manufacturers and producers. These tariffs, and their retaliations, played a key part in the collapse of world trade. They are a good example of an action taken during the Depression which made it much worse. Many politicians did not understand the implications of these tariffs on either the US economy or the international trade which had been so beneficial to the USA. US exports were worth $5.2 billion in 1929 but had dropped to $1.1 billion by 1932.

In 1931, many European banks started to collapse and Britain came off the gold standard. Hoover and his treasury secretary insisted on 'defending', the dollar and staying on the gold standard. This limited investment and borrowing cut the supply of money in the USA, and led to further deflation. At the same time, there was concern about the federal budget being unbalanced, with more money going out on public spending than was coming in as taxes. Therefore, a recommendation was made to increase taxes to balance the budget. Congress agreed, and this cut the money supply even further.

The previous year, Hoover had opposed an attempt by the Senate to bring in unemployment insurance. He feared the creation of a welfare-dependent class of people who would not work. He also blocked a large public works programme which would have boosted jobs and businesses in construction. He believed that it would increase the federal budget deficit. Although this meant money would be borrowed by national and local government, it would be spent on increasing employment. Those who had jobs would then have more money to spend on food and manufactured goods which would further help US producers. It was known as **pump priming**.

Hoover did make several positive attempts to deal with the Great Depression, mostly with limited success.

In 1929, the Agricultural Marketing Act created the Federal Farm Board, which tried to stabilise demand for agricultural produce by setting up local cooperatives to deal with local issues. This achieved little as the problems in agriculture were too large for local management to affect.

Federal Land Banks were given $125 million to help small banks in rural areas which were failing. However, this was dealing with the effects of the crisis, not the cause. In addition, the sums allocated were too small to make a real difference. The Federal Home Loan Bank Act of 1932 was designed to prevent further foreclosures that were making millions homeless, but Congress reduced the act's provisions and it had limited effect.

Also in 1932, Hoover created the Reconstruction Finance Corporation (RFC). This did not provide what many wanted, which was direct relief to the unemployed. However, it did provide loans to banks, insurance companies and businesses such as railways which might have otherwise collapsed. Again, the sums involved were just too small to provide significant relief. This programme, like many of the others, was designed by conservative bankers and helped them most. The biggest loan the RFC made, of $90 million, went to support the Chicago Bank owned by the family of former Republican vice president, Charles G. Dawes. It did nothing to help the 750 000 jobless in the Chicago area or to pay the wages of teachers there who were collapsing from hunger in front of their classes as they could not afford food because they had not been paid.

Hoover also persuaded Congress to pass the Relief and Reconstruction Act in 1932. This allowed for $1.5 billion of federal spending on public works, such as roads, to create jobs. It also allocated $300 million to the states to help with welfare – basically feeding the hungry. He also had the Bank Credit Act passed through Congress in 1932, which provided some help to banks and stock markets. But it was all too little to have much impact on mass unemployment, wages or prices. Again, the focus was too heavily on the effects of the crisis and not on its causes.

ACTIVITY 4.9

Two schools of thought quickly developed in our administration discussions after 1929. First was the 'leave it alone liquidationists' headed by Secretary of

the Treasury Mellon who felt that government must keep its hands off and let the slump liquidate itself … it will purge the rottenness out of the system. People will work harder and live a more moral life … But other members of the administration believed with me that we should use the powers of the government to cushion the situation. To our minds the prime needs were to prevent bank panics. To mitigate the privation amongst the unemployed and the farmers …

Herbert Hoover, The Memoirs of Herbert Hoover, 1953

Analyse the comments from Hoover's memoirs above. Working in two groups, debate the following statements on Hoover:
- 'President Hoover failed the American people in their time of need.'
- 'President Hoover did the best job possible in the circumstances.'

159

Reflection: In what ways did you and your group agree or disagree when debating the sources? How far were you able to persuade one another? Were there points where you felt you needed to know more before forming an opinion?

The response of industry

In November 1929, Hoover summoned a group of prominent businessmen to the White House to urge them to take measures which would reduce unemployment and help to restore confidence in the American economy. He stressed the need for them to invest in new plants for factories and on all types of construction. They promised to do this but didn't. Investment of all types dropped and unemployment rose rapidly. Industry had little choice and laid off workers as demand for manufactured goods fell. While the Smoot–Hawley tariff was originally designed to help agriculture, manufacturers persuaded Congress to place high tariffs on any imports where this might protect their industries from foreign competition. As we have seen, this led to retaliation from foreign countries.

With many European banks failing in 1931, countries like Germany could no longer afford to purchase US goods, so US industry suffered further. Business confidence collapsed and the reluctance to invest worsened the crisis.

Hoover stood for re-election in 1932, but it was not forgotten that in 1930 he had cheerfully announced, 'The depression is over.' With unemployment of adult males at 25%, hunger and destitution spreading across the USA, wages falling and the majority of US banks suffering a total collapse, Hoover stood no chance of winning.

In addition, although Hoover was able and intelligent, he lacked charisma. He often seemed uncaring and cold. This was highlighted in 1932, in the middle of the election campaign, when 17 000 army veterans from the First World War marched to Washington DC, to claim payment of their **war bonuses**. The veterans were driven off their campsites in the capital and some of their housing-shacks were destroyed. They were treated very harshly by the US Army. While some believed these 'Bonus Marchers' were part of a revolutionary communist plot to seize power, most saw them as hungry men who had fought for their country and deserved decent treatment. This confirmed the impression of Hoover's lack of compassion, and led many to switch to voting for the Democrats. The Democratic candidate, Franklin D. Roosevelt, won the 1932 election easily.

KEY TERM

War bonus: A cash payment as a reward for their service to the country. The veterans had been promised that they would receive the bonuses in 1945, but they wanted the cash paid in 1932.

KEY CONCEPT

Change and continuity

Herbert Hoover and Franklin Roosevelt

Working in pairs identify the principal changes that Roosevelt brought to the United States through his domestic policies. Evaluate how fundamental they were. To what extent was the United States a very different country as a result of his administrations? How different were Roosevelt's administrations compared to that of Hoover? Assess the degree of continuity between his administrations and that of Hoover.

4.3 How effective were Roosevelt's strategies for dealing with the domestic problems facing the USA in the 1930s?

Franklin D. Roosevelt offered few policies to ease the crisis in the course of the election campaign of 1932. In some cases his policies were similar to those of Herbert Hoover, such as stressing the need for a balanced budget. However, while Hoover placed much of the blame for the economic crisis on the First World War and the situation in Europe, Roosevelt implied that it was more to do with structural and institutional failings within the United States. He had also gained a good reputation as governor of New York State when he set up a relief programme for the unemployed. His main slogan was to promise a 'New Deal' for the American people. He won the election by a massive majority. Some of the principal reasons for this great victory were as follows:

- Many Americans blamed Hoover and the Republican Party for the economic crisis, and wanted someone different in power.

- Roosevelt managed to produce optimism and hope despite offering few actual policies. He convinced people that he had solutions to the crisis, which had become so much worse in the months before the election in November 1932.

- Roosevelt had far more charisma than Hoover, and his effective use of the new medium of radio carried his message to a wide range of the public. He also had substantial support in the press.

- Roosevelt was an outstanding politician and was able to get the very different elements that made up the Democratic Party to work together and appear united.

- Roosevelt's record as governor of New York showed he cared about the troubles of the unemployed and was prepared to take action to help. However, he did not give any details of what a national recovery programme might consist of.

- Many traditional Republican voters simply stayed at home on election day, while many people who had not voted before chose Roosevelt.

Some signs of Roosevelt's principles had emerged by 1932, which also helped his election and indicated the sort of policies he might implement as president. He felt that the federal government had a larger role to play in controlling the economy, to ensure that the needs of the United States as a whole were not less important than the interests of the rich. As Hoover said in his campaign for re-election: 'This campaign is more than a contest between two men. It is more than a contest between two parties. It is a contest between two philosophies of government.'

ACTIVITY 4.10

I want to speak not of politics but of government. I want to speak not of parties, but of universal principles ... The issue of government has always been whether individual men and women will have to serve some system of government or economics, or whether a system of government and economics exists to serve individual men and women ... the task of government in relation to business is to assist the development of an economic declaration of rights, an economic constitutional order.

Franklin D. Roosevelt, in a campaign speech delivered in San Francisco, 1932

The Republicans won a series of presidential elections in the 1920s, only to lose badly in 1932. Do you think this was just because of the economy?

List the reasons – economic or otherwise – and say how they affected the 1932 election result. Given this context, how far do you agree with the view that the election was lost by Hoover rather than won by Roosevelt? Analyse the comments from Roosevelt's speech above, and Examine the factors that might persuade people to vote for or against both Hoover and Roosevelt, and then decide which the most important factors were, and why.

Roosevelt's First Hundred Days

Roosevelt was not lazy in the months between election and taking office. He built up a team of advisors and many of them were young academics. They were known as the 'Brains Trust'. Their analysis of the origins of the crisis was that internal factors were the main cause and that the focus of the solutions should be on, and within the United States. They felt that the federal government should play a much larger role in the regulation of the economic life of the country. The Brains Trust advisors firmly believed in both democracy and capitalism, but were also very progressive, adaptable and, above all, pragmatic. Men like Adolph Berle, Raymond

Moley, Rexford Tugwell and **Henry Wallace** came to Washington, often for little or no pay, to assist Roosevelt. They formed teams to look at specific areas of the economy, including farming, prices, jobs, welfare and banking. They prepared policies and possible new laws to deal with the problems they found. Many were very young, compared with most politicians at the time, and were willing to challenge what many saw were the right (and only) way of doing things. They were committed to bringing an end to the Depression and the devastating impact it was having on the American people.

It is open to debate whether they were right in their analysis of the causes and in their suggested solutions.

The Democrats had won the presidency, and also had a clear majority in both the Senate and the House of Representatives. However, there were large potential divisions within the Democratic Party. Democrats from the South tended to be both very conservative and racist. Those who came from states which depended very heavily on farming often had very different priorities from those who came from more urbanised states where there was a high level of manufacturing. However, Roosevelt appeared very confident that his party could deal with the crisis. He had great skill in getting people to work together and he managed both the press and the new mass media of the radio very effectively to get his messages across to the people. He was ready to take action with his New Deal by the time he moved into the White House in March 1933.

Wallace was from Iowa, a farming state, and he gained a degree in Animal Husbandry. He was a very successful farmer, businessman and newspaper editor.

He was a liberal Republican until 1936, and was a key member of the Brains Trust before Roosevelt took office. As secretary of state for agriculture from 1933 to 40, he was responsible for the New Deal policy towards agriculture.

HENRY WALLACE (1888–1965)

Figure 4.4: Future president Franklin D. Roosevelt campaigning in the presidential election in 1932. How useful is this photograph as evidence showing popular support for Roosevelt's election campaign?

The New Deal was an incident in American history which arose out of the great depression … most of its characteristics, however, developed from traditional progressivism and most of its devices were accepted items in the general armoury of government … it would be almost true to say that the New Deal of the thirties constituted of postponed items from Wilson's programme which had been abandoned in favour of preparation for war in 1916.

From an article by Rex Tugwell, 'The Experimental Roosevelt', Political Quarterly, 1950

As we have seen, under the US Constitution, the president does not have many powers when it comes to domestic policy:

- All Cabinet members have to be approved by the Senate.
- All new laws must pass through Congress, and both the House of Representatives and the Senate can reject a bill.
- If the president vetoes a bill, Congress can overturn his veto by a two-thirds majority.
- The president's budget has to be passed by Congress (and they would frequently make changes to it).
- If the president does get a law through Congress, the independent Supreme Court could declare that law unconstitutional and ban its implementation.

Roosevelt had to work within these limitations. However, initially he had a fairly easy task. The newly-elected Congress had a large Democratic majority, many from Northern cities where the effects of the Depression were severe. Congress wanted action. There was great public demand for change and solutions to deal with the crisis. Roosevelt appointed some moderate Republicans to his cabinet, including Harold Ickes as Secretary of the Interior and Henry Wallace as Secretary for Agriculture. These were both key appointments on the domestic front and helped to show a united approach to solving the serious problems facing the country. He also appointed the first female cabinet member as his Labour Secretary. **Frances Perkins** was a former social worker with an extensive knowledge of city poverty.

Once established, Roosevelt worked very hard to restore confidence in the US economic system, with his famous **fireside chats** on the radio and clever management of the press.

FRANCES PERKINS (1880–1965)

Perkins was the first woman in the US cabinet when Roosevelt appointed her as Secretary of Labour. She was a committed radical and humanitarian and was a great advocate for the Civilian Conservation Corps and supporter of issues such as minimum wages, restriction of child labour and maximum hours of work.

KEY TERM

Fireside chats: During the 1930s, Roosevelt gave regular national radio broadcasts in the evening to try to restore confidence in the government and to persuade people to support his policies. They were listened to by millions of US citizens.

THINK LIKE A HISTORIAN

In the 1932 presidential election, Roosevelt promised to 'balance the budget' (which he did not do), but had no clear plan of how he might bring about a 'New Deal'. Consider the methods used by politicians to win elections. How justified are they in focusing on the failings of their opponents? How justified are they in making promises they either cannot or will not carry out in order to protect a country from the damage their opponents might do? To what extent does the end justify the means?

Roosevelt was elected as president in November 1932 and had until March 1933 to prepare before his inauguration. His Brains Trust and new cabinet members had been busy. When they were in the White House, Roosevelt called Congress, which had a significant Democratic majority in both Houses, to an emergency session to pass new laws.

By the end of March 1933, he had ordered a bank holiday, which closed all the banks for four days and he pushed an Emergency Act through Congress which finally gave the federal government real powers to regulate the banking system. With an Economy Act, which promised to balance the budget and cut government spending (but carefully excluded any additional spending on recovery programmes) and a brilliant media campaign, he was able to restore confidence in the banking system. Within weeks, bank closures fell, deposits in banks increased, stock exchange prices started to rise and people started to spend again. The immediate crisis seemed over. This was to be only the start of Roosevelt's recovery programme.

By the end of June 1933, Roosevelt's government had managed to get a large number of acts through Congress and had taken on new powers which allowed it to regulate and control various aspects of the economy. No US government, before or since, has been able to take so much action in so little time. This period became known as the First Hundred Days.

Policies introduced during Roosevelt's First Hundred Days included:

- The Emergency Banking Act. This gave the government greater powers over banking. It also promised that money put into a bank by a saver would be secure. It was vital in restoring public confidence in banks. This passed through Congress in a single day.
- The Economy Act. This promised to balance the budget and control government spending, and calmed the fears of many conservatives and helped to restore confidence. However, it did not stop the federal government spending large sums of money on relief programmes.
- The Farm Relief Act (also known as the Agricultural Adjustment Act – AAA). This gave powers to the federal government to act in agricultural matters dealing with prices and production. This was revolutionary.
- The Civilian Conservation Corps (CCC). By the summer of 1933, over 300 000 unemployed men were put to work on conservation projects.

- The Emergency Relief Administration. This gave $3.1 billion to states and local governments to employ people in local projects. It was more expensive than giving cash relief, but it gave workers dignity and purpose and helped to put more money into the economy.
- The National Industrial Recovery Act. This enabled the government to regulate industry to ensure fair wages and prices. It included the creation of the Public Works Administration, which aimed to reduce unemployment and spent $3.3 billion in its first year on major projects like dams, roads, schools and hospitals.
- Regulation of securities in the stock market to prevent the sort of wild speculation which led to the Wall Street Crash.
- Farm mortgage assistance to help farmers in danger of being evicted.
- The Tennessee Valley Authority (TVA). This was a vast project designed to put public money into dam-building, help with the provision of cheap electricity, encourage industrial development and modernise agriculture in the region. It was the first time that the federal government had been involved in such a scheme.
- The Home Owners Loan Corporation. This helped many who were in danger of losing their homes through non-payment of mortgages, and also helped the institutions which had lent the money.
- A major financial bill, the Glass–Steagall Banking Act, which tightened regulation of banks and was designed to prevent speculation. It also insured money that savers had put into their banks.

Roosevelt also ended Prohibition, which banned the manufacture and sale of alcohol (see 'Temperance and Prohibition' in Chapter 3.3). It was intended as a measure to improve morality and health. However, it had actually led to criminal gangs competing violently to control the trade in illegal alcohol and to the bribing of officials not to investigate and prosecute them.

There was enormous public support for these measures because so many people were delighted that action was now be taken to deal with the crisis. The misery and fear during the hard winter of 1932–33 helped to persuade members of Congress to let through many major laws quickly and with little opposition.

These actions were seen by Roosevelt as essentially temporary measures to restore confidence and at least make a start on a programme of recovery. The real work would begin in 1934.

ACTIVITY 4.11

Working with another student, analyse the reasons why Roosevelt was able to achieve so much in his First Hundred Days. Make sure the focus of your work is firmly on providing explanations why, not just providing a list of facts. First of all, identify what you think the major reasons were. Then place them in order of importance and justify your order of priority. Then ensure there is a clear explanation, supported with evidence, of why Roosevelt's achievements were so extensive.

The development of the New Deal policies and the need for the Second New Deal

Between 1933 and his re-election as President in November 1936, Roosevelt continued to address the continuing recession in agriculture and industry as well as mass unemployment. Broadly, his aims were to save the democratic process in the United States, to promote recovery and to try to ensure that economic depression did not return to the country.

This Second New Deal in these years focused on:

- supporting agriculture
- overseeing industry
- reforming banking, finance and the stock markets
- providing relief for those out of work
- generating employment.

It was an enormous task as it tried to change many aspects of life and work in the United States.

Support for agriculture and farmers

The Farm Relief Act of 1933, which created the Agricultural Adjustment Administration, gave the federal government power over agriculture for the very first time. The government could control both production and prices of farm products. It also helped farmers who were struggling with huge debts. Prices were increased on some products which improved farm income, and farmers were compensated for producing less pork and cotton, for example, for which there was a lower demand. The government also bought products which nobody wanted to buy. As a result of these measures, conditions in agriculture where 25% of the population worked improved.

The policy was criticised by some for being too controlling and giving government too much power, while not doing enough for the poor and black people in the South (richer farmers tended to get most benefit). But there were real achievements:

- Rural unrest came to an end.
- Farm incomes rose.
- The huge numbers of bankrupt farmers and unemployed farm labourers leaving the land in search of work slowed to more manageable levels.
- Some stability was brought into farming practices.
- It started to deal with the issues of rural poverty, drought and the need for conservation.

As we shall see, much of the work done for agriculture would later be banned by the Supreme Court in 1936, but by then the worst of the crisis was over.

Industry and employment

There was great division among Roosevelt's advisers about the best way to help industrial recovery, and Roosevelt himself was uncertain. The US government had never been faced with such a crisis and had few formal constitutional powers to deal with it. Some argued that the way forward should be a partnership between government and business to manage the economy. Others suggested that raising prices and limiting competition might do more. Others felt that reducing the number of working hours and increasing the power of labor unions would achieve job creation and stability. The strongest suggestion was a huge public works programme which would spend large sums of money on construction and conservation projects. This would create millions of jobs. It would also put millions of dollars into workers' and managers' pockets to spend on food, housing and manufactured goods which would help farmers and manufacturers. The National Recovery Administration helped to rationalise competition and stabilise prices for industries like coal, oil, transport and communications. It brought in minimum wages and a 40-hour working week, which helped both employment and income for workers, and most importantly it spent a lot of money to create jobs.

Despite this, help for industry was felt to be the least successful part of the First New Deal. It did help raise prices and create jobs, but spent too little too slowly. It has been suggested that if the same money had been spent directly on investment in industry, it would have achieved much more.

Roosevelt said in a fireside chat in 1934: 'Private enterprise in times such as these cannot be left without assistance and without reasonable safeguards lest it destroys not only itself, but also our processes of civilization.' The assistance given to industry was part of the work done by Roosevelt and his government to save capitalism in the US. It was perhaps the least successful part of the New Deal. However, it developed stability for companies and gave more economic security to both businessmen and their employees.

ACTIVITY 4.12

Figure 4.5: 'What we need is another pump' 1933 cartoon by American School. A cartoon satirising Roosevelt pumping money into the economy

Study the cartoon above. What point do you think the cartoonist is making? What aspects could be seen as being critical of Roosevelt's policies? To what extent is this a biased view?

Banking, finance and the stock markets

Many people felt that as well as the Wall Street Crash of 1929, the whole Depression itself was caused by a weak banking system and irresponsible speculation in stocks and shares. Much of the work done by Roosevelt's government between 1933 and 1935 had a great impact on these sectors and has lasted to this day, in a series of acts such as:

- Glass Steagall Act of 1933
- Securities Act of 1933
- Securities Exchange Act of 1934
- Banking Act of 1935.

165

These major reforms brought order and stability to this vital area of US economic life. The powers of the Federal Reserve Bank were considerably increased and it was given much greater control over banks throughout the country. Banks were no longer allowed to speculate with their savers' money with so much freedom. The legislation helped to make private deposits secure so that people knew their savings were safe. Those who had borrowed money to buy houses were helped if they were unable to pay their mortgages. Increased government regulation was brought in to the process of buying and selling shares. There was also regulation of public utilities, such as gas and electricity suppliers, which was of real benefit to consumers. While many in business hated these regulations, they were passed by a Democrat-dominated Congress.

ACTIVITY 4.13

a   One of the many reasons why Roosevelt is praised is because he restored confidence in the US economy. Consider whether he achieved this simply because he took action, or whether it was the effect of these actions. If both, which was the most important?

b   Do you agree that the actions Roosevelt took in his First Hundred Days were of vital important in ending the Depression? Make notes explaining to what extent you agree or disagree. Remember to support your opinion with evidence.

Support for the unemployed

Roosevelt himself found unemployment and welfare difficult issues to deal with. Sometimes he wanted to balance the federal budget but also wanted to reduce the number of people out of work. By 1935, the Civilian Conservation Corps employed over 500 000 people in various projects funded by the federal government. The Federal Emergency Relief Administration had helped over 2 million people by 1934, and, by 1935, was pumping over $4 billion into the economy. Wherever possible, was on providing jobs rather than giving direct help in the form of unemployment pay. Although these programmes did not completely solve the unemployment problem, they gave some relief and showed that the government was determined to assist its citizens.

By 1936, however, when Roosevelt was elected for a second term as president with a large majority, opposition

to the New Deal was growing. He felt that his government needed to go in a different direction. The worst of the crisis was over, but Roosevelt felt there was scope for greater reform to help the public.

ACTIVITY 4.14

A national emergency productive of widespread unemployment and disorganisation of industry is hereby declared to exist. It is hereby declared to be the policy of Congress to remove obstructions to the free flow of commerce and to provide for the general welfare by promoting the organisation of industry for the purpose of cooperative action … to increase consumption by increasing purchasing power, to reduce and relieve unemployment …

United States Congress, Section 1 of the National Industrial Recovery Act, 16 June 1933

Analyse the source above. What measures were taken in the National Industrial Recovery Act to deal with the economic crisis? Discuss a) how effective they were and b) how successful they were. What might be the different criteria for 'success' and 'effective' in this context?

The end of the New Deal?

Roosevelt made remarkable achievements in a short space of time. The bank panic had ended and banks reopened. The principle of federal regulation in banking, industry and farming was established. The federal government had made a start on providing jobs and welfare, and some optimism and confidence was restored. Money started to move again and the stock market was rising by the autumn of 1933. It has been argued that this First New Deal was not a particularly coherent plan. It was just a series of experimental and innovative measures to deal with a crisis on a scale previously unknown in US history. Its critics stressed the lack of coherence and its comparatively limited impact in terms of jobs, production and investment. By the end of 1933, however, the situation Roosevelt had inherited from Hoover had at least stopped getting worse and there were genuine signs of improvement. Some confidence had returned. Unemployment had begun to drop and the economy had started to move again. By January

1934, the Civil Works Administration had 4.2 million men at work on projects such as road-building. These men were paid only a low wage, but it was enough to live on. Their work and their spending both contributed to the economy.

Some further reforms continued into 1934, such as the creation of the Securities and Exchange Commission (SEC), which regulated the US stock market and tried to prevent the sort of crisis on Wall Street that occurred in 1929. Arguably, the economic and political American system had been saved.

The Second New Deal

Despite the successes of Roosevelt's administration, the USA still faced major problems:

- Unemployment had fallen but remained high. It was still 20% in 1935.
- Agriculture had seen only limited improvement. There were still serious droughts in some regions, farmers were being evicted for debt in other areas, and there was still overproduction of certain crops. Some critics felt that the Agricultural Adjustment Act was more helpful to big commercial interests than to small farmers.
- Millions were still living in poverty.
- There was still a fear of radical action being taken in agricultural areas and possibly in the cities.
- Some aspects of the New Deal were clearly not working. The Public Works Administration and the National Industry Recovery Act were having limited effect: they had created lots of jobs for bureaucrats, but had done too little to reduce overall unemployment.
- The Supreme Court challenged the constitutionality of some of New Deal policies, such as the work of the National Recovery Administration.

Despite the continuation of the Depression and a growing hostility to the New Deal, the Democrats did well in the Congressional elections in November 1934. In January 1935, Roosevelt set out on his Second New Deal.

The focus of the First New Deal could be seen as survival, recovery and then growth. However, the Second New Deal focused on security, regulation and planned economic development. The major elements of this Second New Deal were:

- The Emergency Relief Appropriation Act. This was often known as the 'Big Bill'. It was designed to inject over $4 billion into the economy to spend on creating employment. This was the largest peacetime allocation of money by Congress to the federal government in US history to date. It gave work to 3.5 million jobless people, who would be employed on labour-intensive projects such as building roads, schools, hospitals, airports, electrification programmes and aircraft carriers. Eventually, 8.5 million people gained employment through this project.
- The Social Security Act. This was suggested by Frances Perkins, the Secretary for Labour. It brought in a system of unemployment insurance that would ensure some income when a worker became unemployed. The employee and the employer contributed to the scheme. The same system was applied to retirement pensions. The act was hated by many businessmen as it reduced their profits. Conservative opposition in Congress prevented it covering many agricultural and domestic workers, and black people in particular. However, it was the first step towards creating a welfare state.
- The 1935 Banking Act. This gave the Federal Reserve Bank, the nearest the USA has to a central controlling bank, a much greater role in regulating the money supply and the money markets.
- Wealth tax. This was designed to tax the highest earners. It did not bring in much income to the government, but it did appeal to Roosevelt's more left-wing critics. It made a start on wealth distribution, but opposition in Congress prevented it from achieving as much as Roosevelt hoped.
- Further moves were made to help areas like minimum wages, regulate hours, ending child labour and forcing employers to recognise labor unions.

Overall, this legislation – particularly the Social Security Act – was not as radical as first hoped. Health care was excluded from the act, and over 9 million citizens (many of them African Americans) were not covered. However, 26 million people were covered for the first time. The Social Security Act is considered the most important piece of social security legislation in the country's history, because of the principle established about the role of the federal government in social welfare. It brought some security into the lives of millions and relieved two of the greatest fears of many workers: how to deal with unemployment and with old age.

167

Figure 4.6: A work-creation programme during the time of the New Deal, 1933 How would you asses this photograph's usefulness as source providing evidence for success of the New Deal?

ACTIVITY 4.15

I knew Roosevelt long enough and under enough circumstances to be quite sure that he was no political or economic radical. I take it that the essences of economic radicalism are to believe that the best system is the one in which private ownership of the means of production is abolished in favor of public ownership. But Roosevelt took the status quo (the existing capitalist system) as much for granted as his family … He felt the system ought to be human, fair and honest and those adjustments ought to be made so that people would not suffer from poverty and neglect and so that all would share.

Frances Perkins, The Roosevelt I Knew (1947)

A comment on the Social Security Act

A number of individuals have been making cruel promises and raising useless hopes by noising about several impossible ideas. It is all right for little children to believe in Santa Claus but when these alleged leaders offer their fantastic schemes to adults under the guise of pension plans and prosperity restoratives it gets nauseating …

The President has presented to Congress a solid plan for economic security. There will be unemployment compensation. If a worker loses his job there would be a fund from which he would receive a benefit for a certain period of time … Now about old age. There must be security for those who are working and security for those who are already old … and help for widows and children in homes where this is no breadwinner.

Pamphlet by Harry L. Hopkins, Head of the Federal Emergency Relief Agency, 1935

Analyse the Source above written by Frances Perkins. What points is she making about Roosevelt's policies? Using your own knowledge, how valid do you think those points are?

Then look at the pamphlet written by Harry Hopkins. To what extent do you think that the Social Security Act was putting into practice the ideas suggested by Frances Perkins?

The effectiveness of the New Deal

In simple statistical terms, the New Deal had some success. Real earnings and GNP both radically improved between 1933 and 1937. Unemployment dropped from 25% to 14% in the same years and 8 million people found work. There were no more stock market crashes or major bank failures in the period, and there was steady growth in both farming and manufacturing. Only Japan and Germany had more growth and they both had totalitarian systems of government spending enormous sums on military rearmament. Confidence in the economic system of the United States was restored.

However, success was not total. Unemployment rose again to 19% in 1937 and did not really improve until war came in 1941. The government borrowed huge sums of money, and critics felt that this increased intervention by the government did not help investment, and in fact held recovery back. Prices of farm produce were still too high for many consumers, but too low for the producers.

Reflation and deficit spending policies had the most beneficial effect on the country's financial problems. Roosevelt's plans could be seen as a great achievement considering how little was really known and understood about how modern economies worked, and the limits imposed on him and his government by the Constitution.

ACTIVITY 4.16

Draw a mind map showing how the different elements in the economic crisis (unemployment and so on) were related to one another. Then write a paragraph describing the content of the mind map and explaining how the interconnections made intervention complicated.

Referring to that context, discuss which New Deal policy you think had the greatest impact in reducing unemployment.

Roosevelt's political strategies, such as the New Deal Coalition

It was not just popular demand for action and consequent public support that helped Roosevelt to bring about both New Deals. He also had great ability as a politician. As well as considerable charm, charisma and skill as a public speaker, he had a great understanding of what was possible within the highly complex structure of US politics. He had political experience at both national and local level, which was an enormous asset. He was also a skilled radio broadcaster and was the first major politician in the USA to use this medium effectively. Roosevelt's ability to manage the press was impressive too. He made himself available to journalists, both individually and in larger press conferences, to answer questions and to put forward arguments in favour of his policies. He was an excellent communicator who made good use of the mass media available at the time. He carefully managed powerful state governors and city mayors, and was very aware of the damage they could do to the New Deal.

Roosevelt also faced problems with his own political party, the Democrats. The previous Democratic president, Woodrow Wilson (1913–21), had done an impressive job in starting to bring together the very different, and often conflicting, elements that made up the Democratic Party. Roosevelt spent considerable time and effort continuing the process and formed a coalition of politicians that worked together in Congress. There were several different groups which Roosevelt worked with to make up this coalition.

The South

Democrats in states such as Mississippi were deeply conservative and very hostile to anything that might challenge white supremacy. Their senators and members of the House of Representatives often sat in Congress for decades. This made them a very powerful force and allowed them to block a president's legislation. Roosevelt had to be careful not to upset such men. Most African Americans in the South were excluded from voting in the Southern states. Therefore he could have lost white votes but not gain any votes from African Americans. This might have been a consideration. One reason why Roosevelt was so keen on the Tennessee Valley Authority was because it would bring aid in a variety of forms to the South. This would help the poor and the African Americans without offending Southern Democrats.

The Northern industrial cities

Immigrant and working-class voters tended to support the Democrats in the big industrial cities like Chicago. However, the management of these cities was often in the hands of mayors or 'bosses', who could be both very powerful and extremely corrupt. (See Chapter 3.3.) Their administrations, known in the USA as 'political machines' provided housing and jobs for workers, but the workers were expected to repay these favours with their votes. Many of these bosses played a major role in national politics, and Roosevelt knew he had to manage them carefully. Often, the interests of a Northern industrial worker and the mayor of a city conflicted with those of a deeply conservative cotton farmer from the South. Roosevelt had to use great skill to keep both these different supporters happy.

The educated and liberal elite from the north-east

Most of Roosevelt's Brains Trust and some of his other key advisors were well-educated professionals, often from the less conservative north-east of the country. Many of the ideas behind the New Deal came from these people. They tended to be much more liberal-minded than Southern Democrats on matters of race. They failed to comprehend why a policy which might help black people would be blocked by members of Congress from the South.

The labor unions

The various employment unions were not a united movement, and contained many different forces. Some union leaders were deeply conservative, particularly those who led the unions for skilled men. Those leading the unskilled workers were more radical; some were even socialist. Union leaders disagreed on whether the unions or the government should provide benefits, such as pensions. The unions contributed a considerable amount of money to help the Democratic party win elections.

Other potential voters

Roosevelt had to consider which different groups in society could be persuaded to vote Democrat in order to ensure Democrat success in the mid-term election of 1934, and his own re-election in the presidential election of 1936. A potential voter might be a migrant farm worker in California, a teacher from Oregon or a small farmer in Kansas. Roosevelt had to win over the undecided or reluctant voter as well.

ACTIVITY 4.17

I can get a job today even if we got a depression. I don't mean that I wasn't on relief when things got tough because there was a time when everything was shut down and I had to get on relief for a job. It isn't so long ago I was working on WPA. Believe me it was a big help. But it wasn't the kind of a job I should have had because this town is Republican and I am a Republican and I was a good worker for the party – making voters and helping a lot of people out – getting their taxes rebated [abated]. Getting jobs for them. When it came my turn that I needed help the politicians told me that I had to go on relief – well, when I did I was handed a shovel and pick …Roosevelt is a damn good man – you take all these young fellows and you can't talk to them like in the old days to swing them over. Today all these kids are satisfied on WPA and the NYA. My son works there and gets 44 cents an hour …

From American Life Histories: Manuscripts from the Federal Writers Project 1936–40

Analyse the excerpt above. What are the main points being made here? To what extent can the comments be seen as being critical of the New Deal? In what ways can they be seen as supportive? How useful are such sources to a historian?

Reflection: Do you think your presentation shows a balanced view? Have you just focused on where the New Deal brought benefits to the USA? Have you shown material where the New Deals could be seen to have failed? Is it possible to present a balanced view?

The mid-term elections of 1934

The success of the Democratic Party in the mid-term elections of 1934 was largely due to the New Deal policies. These had showed positive action by Roosevelt's government to address the problems of recession. The electorate was prepared to give the Democrats and their president more time to solve the problems facing the USA.

As always, Roosevelt went on the 'stump' – travelling around the country by railway, giving many speeches to gain support. The American voters liked to see the candidates. Roosevelt's fireside chats were very popular and were extremely helpful in maintaining confidence in the Democratic Party. Many of the Democratic Congressmen and governors who were elected or re-elected in 1934 and 1936 clearly owed their successes to Roosevelt and the New Deal. This helped to gain support from the states as well as easing the passage of legislation through Congress.

The presidential election of 1936

In the 1932 presidential election, Roosevelt had been cautious about committing himself to specific policies. When Roosevelt was chosen as the presidential candidate at the Democratic Party Convention in 1936, he was much more specific, and arguably made a significant move to the left in terms of policy. With the two New Deals on his record, a recent tax on undistributed corporate profits and payment of the War Bonus to veterans, he argued that he had already done much to help ease the Great Depression.

At the Democratic Convention, Roosevelt launched an attack on 'the economic tyranny of the few' and 'organised money', big business and Wall Street. Some felt that he was making unnecessary enemies. However, Roosevelt believed that with growing radicalism in the USA, he might lose working-class votes to more extreme candidates unless he made it clear which side he was on. There was still serious unemployment in the cities, and drought was affecting the farm states in the Midwest.

Roosevelt's main opponent was the Republican presidential candidate, Alf Landon. Landon offered little new in terms of domestic policy. The New Deal was clearly very popular and showed signs of working. Landon differed from Roosevelt on foreign policy, but what was happening outside the USA was of little interest to the vast majority of American people.

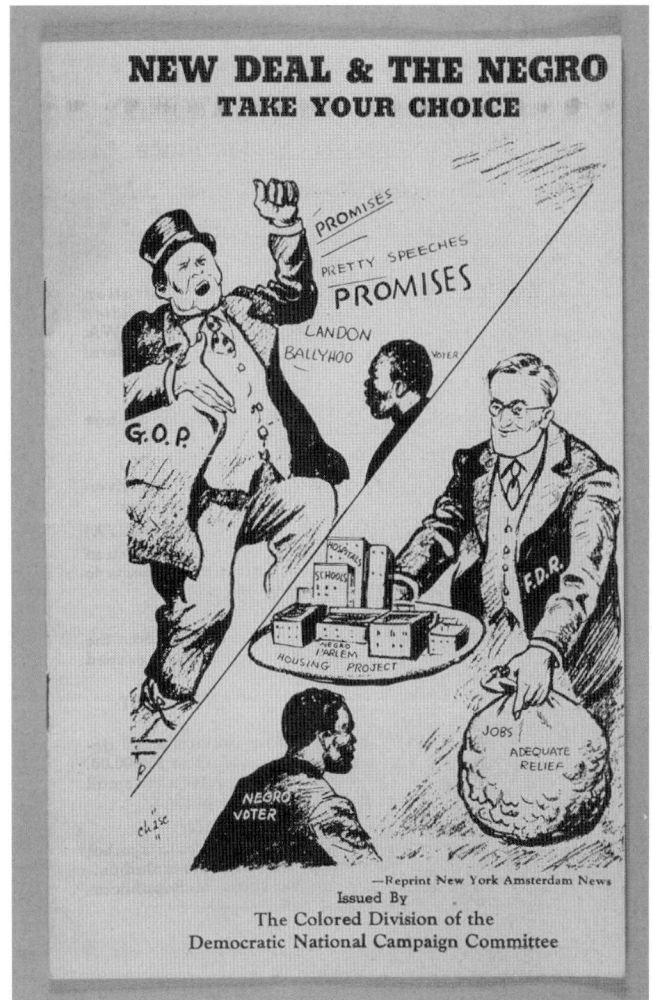

Figure 4.7: A pamphlet produced in support for Roosevelt in 1936. What features of the pamphlet show Roosevelt's attempts to appeal to non-traditional Democrat voters?

Roosevelt was comfortably re-elected for his second term and the Democrats were successful in elections for the Senate and the House of Representatives. The Democrats also did well in elections for many state assemblies and governorships. This tremendous endorsement from the American people was useful for Roosevelt when facing up to his many critics and opponents.

There were several reasons why Roosevelt won the election:

- The New Deal was immensely popular and a clear majority of Americans supported it.
- Roosevelt was a very capable politician and was extremely clever in his use of patronage, giving jobs in his government to important and potential supporters. This was not limited to major government appointments such as the Cabinet. The way the New

Deal ensured that Democrat administrators in cities and states were able to use these new jobs to support their own position and reward their supporters.

- His criticism of the Supreme Court and its role in blocking New Deal legislation was initially popular.
- He had tremendous support from the labor unions, the labour movement generally and from African Americans who had the vote, particularly those who had moved to the North and found it easier to register as voters.
- Those employed by the Public Works Administration were naturally enthusiastic supporters of a man whose opponent might well end the scheme.
- He had support from the 4 million homeowners whose homes were saved from foreclosure.
- The millions of people whose bank deposits and life savings had been saved in the dark days of 1933 were grateful to him. Gratitude is not always a strong factor in voting behaviour, but in this case it was.

Reasons for the Roosevelt Depression (1937–38)

While the results for himself and his party in 1936 might have made Roosevelt happy, he faced a series of problems after his inauguration in 1937. One of these was the return of recession to the US economy. The statistics which poured in throughout 1937 were terrible. The overall value of shares dropped by nearly 35% by the end of October. GNP dropped by over 6% in the year, corporate profits dropped by 40%, over 2 million workers were laid off and unemployment rose to 19%. It was a depression within a depression. Its impact was not as severe as the depression of the early 1930s, and this was largely as a result of the New Deal. However, it was a serious blow to hopes of recovery.

There are a number of reasons suggested for this economic downturn:

- It was part of a normal business cycle, which had come at a bad time. The hope was that things would improve in due course.
- The Federal Reserve Bank, making use of its new powers, made banks across the United States increase their reserves, which meant they lent less money to business.
- The federal government cut back on public spending in order to move towards balancing the budget.
- Many blamed the government for being 'anti-business'; that its policies were damaging business confidence and therefore business was reluctant to invest. One contemporary comment was that 'capital had gone into hibernation'.

- Roosevelt's opponents encouraged the idea that there was no point in investing for the future, as the president was failing to balance the budget, increasing taxes and imposing endless regulation on business to achieve state control over the economy.
- The problems which faced the American economy were so serious that even the steps that Roosevelt had taken in both New Deals were insufficient to help.

The administration was badly divided about how to solve the problem. Some wanted to move towards their Republican rivals, try to balance the federal budget, cut back on regulation and federal government involvement in the economy. They argued that this would restore business confidence and get investment moving again. Others, particularly the younger 'New Dealers', wanted a much more radical programme of spending. They thought the federal government should borrow even more money and increase spending on public works programmes. Roosevelt himself tended to see the return of depression as part of the political attack on him by business.

Ultimately, little further action was taken. Unemployment remained high and large-scale investment did not really start again until late 1938 and early 1939, and then it led to only a gradual improvement. It was not until 1941 that unemployment dropped substantially and the economy improved. As was the case from 1915 onwards, it was war in Europe, and then in Asia, which restored American economic fortunes.

4.4 Why was there opposition to the New Deal policies and what impact did it have?

Roosevelt was praised by many for his work on the New Deal and also for many other aspects of his work as president, such as his leadership of the United States in the Second World War. However, he was also criticised for his work between 1933 and 1941. Some see him as the man who saved American democracy and its people by leading the USA on a moderate path. His interventions brought the state into many aspects of the economy and society. Although highly controversial at the time, it might have been this movement away from unregulated capitalism that kept the USA from adopting the far more extreme measures of either fascism or communism. Others argue that his work had limited economic impact and that he did more harm than good to the economy. They argue that getting more power for the federal government to regulate the economy and the workplace was seen by some as destructive to American values of individualism, self-sufficiency and free enterprise.

The New Deal was not universally supported, and opposition came from a variety of sources. For example, Republicans could be expected to oppose as a matter of course. One major opponent was former-president Herbert Hoover, who was bitter about losing the election in 1932. There were also obstacles to the New Deal in the states (for example, resentment at national powers, and disapproval of black emancipation), the Supreme Court and Congress, based on the powers given to them under the Constitution. The US Constitution is very clear on what the federal government can and cannot do.

The individual states expected to play the major role in governing the lives of US citizens. Issues such as education, welfare and economic regulation had been the responsibility of a state. State assemblies and their governors disliked taking orders from Washington. It was felt that Washington was unaware of local feelings and issues.

Congress, consisting of the Senate and the House of Representatives, can impose legislation on an unwilling president, block any legislation he might want by a simple majority in either House, block or amend his budget and reject any of his appointments to the cabinet. However, for much of the New Deal period Congress was not a major barrier to Roosevelt's wishes, as the president's polices proved to be enormously popular.

Opposition from the Supreme Court

The Supreme Court has the ability to declare any act of Congress unconstitutional and to stop it operating. It can also declare any act passed by a state legislature unconstitutional, as well as any action by any member of the federal or a state government. If an individual or a business feels that an action of any member of any executive, or any law passed by any legislature, violates their rights under the Constitution, they can take their case to a federal court. If they don't accept the decision of a lower court, they can appeal to the Supreme Court of the United States.

It is not unusual for the Supreme Court to take decisions that have enormous impact. For example, in the 1857 *Dred Scott v. Sandford* case (see Chapter 1.2), the Supreme Court upheld the rights of slave-owners over their slaves. This played a part in causing the Civil War. In 1898, in the case of *Plessey v. Ferguson,* the Supreme Court allowed racial segregation to continue in Southern states.

The Supreme Court is made up of nine justices that are appointed for life, and it is virtually impossible to remove them. When there is a vacancy because a justice has either died or retired, the president can nominate a successor but the Senate has to approve the appointment. All of the nine justices when Roosevelt took office in 1933 had been appointed by preceding presidents, and he had no way to influence them.

The striking down of the New Deal acts

There is a tradition of litigation in the United States. As mentioned above, if someone does not like a decision taken by someone in authority, or an act of a legislature, they can take the issue to court to challenge it. If the result is unsatisfactory, they can take the case on to the Supreme Court. This is precisely what happened to aspects of the New Deal. Three cases illustrate this well.

In the 1935 Schechter *Poultry Corp v. United States* case, often known as the 'Sick Chicken Case', the owners of a company that slaughtered and processed chickens were fined and imprisoned for not following the regulations laid down by the National Industrial Recovery Act. They appealed, and the Supreme Court ruled that the federal government did not have the power under the Constitution to make such regulations. Effectively, the Supreme Court struck down the National Industrial Recovery Act and its administration (NRA). The Supreme Court said that the Schechter Company had the right to:

* break the NRA's wage code and underpay its employees
* break the NRA's code for the number of hours employees could work
* keep out government inspectors trying to prevent it selling diseased chicken to the public.

The Court ruled that the government had no right to delegate powers to the NRA to regulate business. It was, one of the Justices claimed, 'delegation run riot'.

The following year, the *United States v. Butler* case reversed much of the good work that the Agricultural Adjustment Administration was trying to do to help agriculture in the United States. The Court ruled that the federal government had no power in this area – this was for the individual states only. Also in 1936, the Court sat for the *Morehead v. New York* case. It ruled that the New York legislature's Minimum Wages Act was unconstitutional. It thus effectively destroyed all attempts by all states to regulate any aspect of the economy in their states.

These rulings were a major blow to the whole New Deal. Further Supreme Court decisions revoked 11 further New Deal acts.

By this time, public confidence had generally been restored in Roosevelt's administration and the Court's decisions were not too damaging. However, they did encourage others who opposed the New Deal by showing that some of the New Dealers' policies might be unconstitutional. In 1937, Roosevelt attempted to increase the number of Supreme Court judges in a controversial 'Court Packing' plan so he could appoint those who might be more favourable to New Deal legislation. The attempt was unsuccessful, and much disapproved of.

The upholding of the New Deal acts

Fortunately, the obstacles which the Supreme Court imposed on the New Deal did not last long. In 1937, two vital cases indicated that the Supreme Court was changing its approach.

In the Parrish case of 1937, a hotel chambermaid lost her job and asked for the $216 back pay she was entitled to under the Washington State minimum wages law. The company which owned the hotel offered her only $17, so she sued them. The company fought the case all the way to the Supreme Court, which cost them a great deal more than the $216 they owed. The Supreme Court, by a 5 to 4 majority, ruled that the Washington State law was constitutional and the state could regulate both wages and the local economy.

Meanwhile, Congress had given powers to the National Labor Relations Board (NLRB) to assist workers trying to join labor unions. A steel company had sacked employees for joining a union. In a long and complex ruling on the NLRB case of 1937, the Supreme Court upheld the rights of the workers, and also the role of the NLRB. In addition, it effectively upheld most of the vital New Deal legislation which gave the federal government the power to intervene in the economy, and also substantially increased Congress' power to act.

Roosevelt had made a mistake in trying to change the Supreme Court's numbers. It did nothing to help him reach his objectives, and only gave ammunition to his enemies. But the situation changed in his favour by 1937 anyway. Some justices retired and Roosevelt could appoint their replacements. Others moved to support the New Deal, and there were no further rulings from the Supreme Court which struck down New Deal legislation.

ACTIVITY 4.18

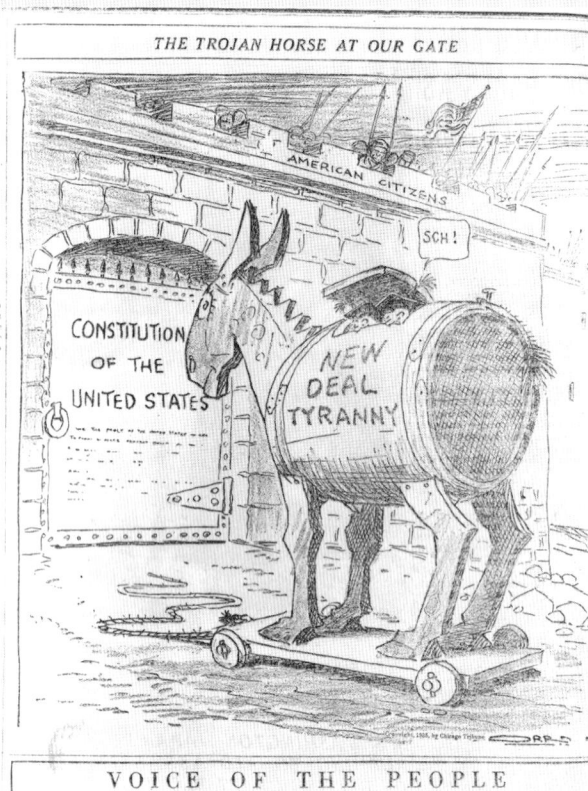

Figure 4.8: A cartoon presenting the New Deal as a Trojan horse 'gift' for the US Constitution. The 'horse' has been replaced by a donkey, the symbol of the Democratic party.

First analyse the cartoon (Figure 4.8), then discuss whether the Supreme Court was justified in blocking New Deal legislation. You need to ensure you reach a conclusion based on evidence. Start by identifying the cases for and against the actions of the Supreme Court justices. Now weigh up the two sides. Which side has the more convincing argument? Do different people in the debate hold different views?

Now write your conclusion in such a way that you show that different interpretations are possible, and explaining what your own view is and how you reached it.

Reflection: How did you reach your conclusion? Are you confident that it was genuinely balanced? If not, how could you make it more balanced?

Opposition from the liberal left

There was a broad range of opposition to Roosevelt and the New Deal. Opponents often had very different views from each other, so stood little chance of working together or affecting policy. However, in a variety of ways, they still had an influence on the president and the New Deal.

Liberal Republicans

The two main parties in the United States, the Republicans and the Democrats, both represented a wide range of views. Some Republicans were much less conservative than others, and the liberal Republicans did not like Roosevelt's very cautious monetary policy. They felt that he needed to spend much more money to stimulate the economy. Some were very hostile to 'big business' and Wall Street and wanted a great deal more government regulation of all types of business. Many other Republicans wanted the government to spend a lot less money and balance the budget. It was helpful to Roosevelt to have his main opposition party divided over this issue, but there were several liberal Republicans who held important positions in the Senate and Roosevelt had to consider this.

Intellectuals and academics

Many intellectual commentators wanted Roosevelt to expand the role of the government. They thought that government should regulate economic life far more, including areas such as utilities and banking. Roosevelt recruited many of the men who carried out the New Deal from the great universities such as Harvard and Yale and they had a major influence on his thinking and his government.

The Communist Party

Some countries that suffered mass unemployment in the Great Depression were drawn to communism, but in the USA, the Communist Party remained small and isolated. Bitter divisions between supporters of Stalin and Trotsky led to a split, with some leaving the party to form a different socialist party and others leaving altogether. The party had gone from being small in the 1920s to being even smaller and less influential in the 1930s. It offered a candidate for the presidential election of 1932, at the height of the Depression and its mass unemployment, and gained only 102 000 votes (compared with Roosevelt's 22.8 million). Communism was regarded by the vast majority of Americans as dangerous and 'un-American'. Although it shared some of the New Deal ideology in campaigning for workers' rights, the communist newspaper, the *Daily Worker*, called the NRA a 'fascist slave programme' and compared Roosevelt to Hitler. However, communist ideas of an economy and society entirely controlled by the state did not fit in with the American tradition of 'rugged individualism' and free enterprise. With fewer than 30 000 members nationally by 1934, the Communist Party was only a marginal opposition force.

Francis Townsend and the Old Age Pension Movement

The Old Age Pension Movement developed in traditionally radical and very depressed California. It was led by Dr Francis Townsend and proposed giving all those over 60 a pension of $150 (later $200) a month if they retired from work and agreed to spend the $200 in the month they received it. The pension would be funded by the federal government imposing a tax on the sale of all goods. This would stop those over 60 having to work, freeing up jobs for the young, and would also put a great deal more money into the economy. The organisation he set up to promote this idea quickly grew to 5 million members. It presented a petition of 25 million signatures to Roosevelt during the course of the Second New Deal.

The scheme was economically unsound, but had huge appeal. It was calculated that it would take up about 50% of national income and double the national tax burden. It would never be acceptable to Congress. One economist commented that the proposal was 'lunacy'. Despite this, the newly-elected Congressional delegation from California arrived in Washington DC in 1935 and demanded that the plan was implemented. With Roosevelt trying to bring in a very different (and considerable less expensive) Social Security Act which seemed likely to pass and there was a real risk of failure to achieve anything.

Townsend was a retired doctor and was appalled by how poverty affected the elderly. In 1936, he unsuccessfully ran for public office standing on this issue alone. However, his well-supported movement and its petition demonstrated popular demand for change.

Dr FRANCIS TOWNSEND (1867–1960)

Figure 4.9: Female Communist Party supporters demonstrate in Boston for better working conditions

Upton Sinclair and 'muckraking'

Dr Townsend was not the only Californian to cause problems for Roosevelt. In 1934, the novelist and 'muckraker' (see 'Temperance and Prohibition' in Chapter 3.3) Upton Sinclair, who had done much to expose the dreadful conditions in the meat-packing industry in Chicago, won the nomination as the Democratic candidate for governor of California. While Roosevelt felt that he should support another Democrat, he had a major concern about Sinclair's campaign. Sinclair had founded the EPIC (End Poverty in California) organisation. This wanted the State of California to take all unused land and factories and to give them to unemployed workers who would manage them 'cooperatively'. The aim appeared to be to drive out private industry. Naturally, this was very strongly opposed by the entire business community in California, particularly the vast Hollywood film industry. Millions of dollars were poured into a campaign to defeat Sinclair. A Republican opponent of Roosevelt was elected and Roosevelt suffered both by failing to support a fellow

Democrat and by being associated with Sinclair and his apparently socialist ideas.

Father Charles Coughlin and the National Union for Social Justice

Charles Coughlin was a Canadian-born Roman Catholic priest who had been appointed to a church in a largely working-class Catholic area of Chicago in the American Midwest. Most of the men who came to his church with their families were involved in the automobile industry. They had been quite well off in the 1920s but they suffered badly in the depression of the early 1930s, and felt that the Protestant elite from the East was neglecting them. Coughlin was a brilliant radio speaker and by 1932 he had a nationwide audience of millions and wide influence. Initially, he only spoke on purely religious and moral issues, such as birth control, but soon moved into political and economic issues. Roosevelt made sure of Coughlin's support for his election in 1932. In one of his broadcasts, Coughlin said that the 'New Deal was Christ's deal'. His anti-Hoover, 'big banker' message was influential in helping Roosevelt to get elected.

However, Coughlin soon felt that Roosevelt was not being nearly radical enough and he became a strong critic. He founded the National Union for Social Justice in 1934, which allegedly had over 8 million members. The government could not ignore Coughlin because he had a huge following in the Northern industrial cities and the Midwest. These were vital areas for Roosevelt's re-election. Coughlin was a brilliant organiser, journalist and speaker on the radio. By 1936, his radio programme had an estimated weekly audience of over 30 million, and he was getting up to 80 000 letters of support every week – more than Roosevelt himself. There was little religious content in his broadcasts now, which mainly advocated a vast programme of nationalisation of major industries, wider state control of economic life and more rights for workers. He became a bitter critic of Roosevelt, saying he should follow a programme similar to that adopted by Mussolini in Italy and Hitler in Germany. Coughlin also became very anti-Semitic.

Coughlin showed his influence in 1935. Roosevelt was becoming increasingly worried by the growth of potentially dangerous regimes in Japan, Germany and Italy, and considered joining the World Court in the Hague. Roosevelt ensured that he had sufficient support in the Senate, which had to approve such a measure, before he started. However, Coughlin decided that the Court – designed to promote peace, prevent war and end disputes between nations – was 'evil' and part of a conspiracy by international bankers to take over the world.

He started a massive campaign to put pressure on the Senate to reject Roosevelt's plan, and was successful. This did great harm to Roosevelt's reputation in Congress and the country (and to the cause of world peace). Coughlin became less influential as he grew more anti-Semitic and pro-fascist. He continued to criticise the New Deals for being ineffective. It was only the outbreak of the Second World War that allowed Roosevelt to stop Coughlin broadcasting his hostile messages, as he was seen to be supporting America's enemies.

Huey Long and radical Democrats

Of all his opponents on the left, Huey Long was perhaps the cleverest and the most dangerous to Roosevelt and the New Deal. Long was able, rich, ambitious, a brilliant politician, utterly ruthless, an effective writer and an exceptional speaker both on the radio and to large audiences. He was elected governor of the state of Louisiana, campaigning for equality for all (but not African Americans). He attacked the business oligarchy which dominated the state. Once elected, he substantially increased local taxes on the rich and on businesses, and spent the money on roads, schools and hospitals. He dominated the state like an old-fashioned 'boss' with ruthless and corrupt methods. He dealt brutally with opposition.

Like Coughlin, Long was an early supporter of the New Deal but soon turned against it for not being radical enough, particularly the NRA. He argued that the Economy Act was damaging and failing to bring about equality. He founded his 'Share our Wealth' Society in 1934, which proposed:

- heavy taxation of the rich
- confiscating large estates
- old-age pensions
- a grant of $5000 for each family, giving them enough for a home, car and radio
- large-scale public works to create employment
- greater spending on education and welfare.

HUEY LONG (1893–1935)

Long was governor and then senator for Louisiana. He was a powerful speaker who was feared for his forceful, populist tendencies. He could have been a serious threat to Roosevelt's re-election, but he was assassinated in 1935.

Economists thought the economic implications of Long's programme were even worse than Townsend's. Long tried with some success to build an alliance with Coughlin and his movement, as well as with the supporters of Townsend and Sinclair in California. This alliance threatened to drive most moderate supporters of Roosevelt and the New Deal towards the conservatives, who opposed the New Deal entirely. As Roosevelt said: 'I am fighting communism, Huey Longism, Coughlinism and Townsendism.'

By the middle of 1935, Long was considering running for president in the following year's election. Roosevelt and his supporters felt this plan would lead to a Republican victory and the end of the New Deal. 'Long plans to be a candidate of the Hitler type for President,' Roosevelt said. Long was assassinated in 1935 by the son-in-law of one of his political opponents who Long had driven out of office.

The death of Huey Long removed the most serious threat to Roosevelt and the New Deal from the left. These forces were certainly an influence in keeping Roosevelt's focus on the welfare aspect of the New Deal. Perhaps more importantly, they persuaded Congress to pass the legislation and might also have influenced the opinions of the Supreme Court justices. However, they also associated Roosevelt, against his will, with radical and totally unrealistic policies which alienated many potential New Deal supporters and voters.

Opposition from the conservative right

Overall, the opposition from the right, like the opposition from the left, was often. However, after 1936 this opposition became increasingly effective in preventing Roosevelt from carrying out his plans. An unofficial group of conservatives formed a 'conservative coalition' which could present a serious obstacle to any further radical changes. This group had powerful elements, including:

- Republicans in Congress and state governors and legislatures
- Southern Democrats in Congress
- the more prosperous professional classes largely unaffected by the Great Depression, who were frightened of labor union power, wage rises for their employees, reduced profits, regulation, higher taxes and lower dividends, and what they saw as too much support for African American people.
- substantial support from sections of the press.

Hoover and the Republicans in Congress

As mentioned earlier, the Republican Party was not always totally hostile to the New Deal. Its more liberal elements were in favour of developments such as the TVA and wanted the government to spend more money. However, a fairly large group of Republicans led particularly by former president Herbert Hoover, were fundamentally opposed to the New Deal. Hoover argued strongly that

Roosevelt was taking on 'dictatorial' powers and involving the government far too much in the management of the economy. Fortunately for Roosevelt, this group was not strong in either the Senate or the House of Representatives.

Southern Democrats in Congress

Members of the Democratic Party came to Washington DC from all over the United States, and represented very different interests and ideas. While some came from heavily industrialised states such as Michigan, or from urban, liberal, often immigrant-dominated states such as Massachusetts, others came from deeply conservative, largely rural and the more racist states such as Mississippi. The senators and representatives from many of the Southern states tended to be regularly re-elected, and consequently had great power in Congress. They were therefore in a position to either ignore Roosevelt's ideas or to join up with the more conservative Republicans and prevent much of the innovation suggested in New Deal legislation. These Democrats from the South were one of the biggest obstacles to innovation after 1936. They were both deeply conservative and strongly racist, and were keen to stop Roosevelt doing anything which might improve conditions for black people or in any way alter the domination of their states by whites.

Institutions: banks, business, unions and press

The New Deal brought a significant change to the role of the government, introducing regulation of, and intervention in, aspects of society that had largely been left to run according to free market and individualist principles. Institutions such as business, the press and trade unions offered varying degrees of opposition to Roosevelt's plan.

Inevitably, big business and the banks and those involved in the stock markets resisted and then opposed many aspects of the New Deal. They did not like the way Roosevelt and many New Dealers blamed them for causing the crisis. They felt that the New Deal violated their freedoms and prevented them from making profits. In their opinion, it was anti-capitalist, hindered business and probably did a lot more harm than good. They blamed the rise in unemployment in 1937, when the economy declined, on the New Deal. They argued that it was causing a lack of business confidence and was directly responsible for slowing investment.

178

Any organisation or person that might oppose Roosevelt – such as Alf Landon and some key senators and governors – received a great deal of financial support from this group:

> The New Deal is nothing more or less than an effort sponsored by inexperienced sentimentalists and **demagogues** to take away from the thrifty what the thrifty and their ancestors have saved and give it to others who have not earned it … And thus indirectly destroy the incentive for all future accumulation. Such a purpose is in defiance of all the tenets (basis) on which our civilisation has been founded.
>
> *From a pamphlet from the American Liberty League (founded by businessmen opposed to the New Deal), 1935*

KEY TERM

Demagogue: A leader whose power depends on their ability to stir up the emotions of crowds, usually at large public meetings or through their use of the media. They appeal to prejudices and not to reason.

Some labor unions were great supporters of Roosevelt and the New Deal. Others were not, and resented the government intervening in issues such as hours and wages, which they felt was their responsibility. Naturally, this group did not get on well with big business, so there was quite a degree of division within the opposition from these institutions.

Much of the press, both local and national, was highly supportive of Roosevelt in 1932. However, by 1935 a significant proportion of newspapers, which were very influential in the USA at the time, began to oppose the New Deal. They accused Roosevelt and the government of taking on unprecedented powers and making decisions that were not in the best interests of the country and its economic recovery.

Overall, this opposition reduced and modified much of what Roosevelt wished to achieve. However, it was unable to prevent his ambition to restore confidence in the economy of the United States, to radically reduce unemployment and to make a start in creating a welfare state.

Roosevelt's responses to opposition

Roosevelt made a mistake in his initial reaction to the Supreme Court's decisions to strike down some of his New Deal policies. He criticised the 'nine old men' who he thought wanted to take the USA back to what he called the 'horse and buggy era' and who failed to support his attempts to bring relief to the unemployed and hungry. However, amending the Constitution and modernising the Court would be extremely difficult. Congress had tried to change the Constitution in 1924 when it attempted to bring in an amendment to ban child labour. However, in 1937 Roosevelt's attempt to increase the number of Supreme Court judges angered both Congress and the public. There was opposition any major change to the nation's revered set of fundamental principles.

Roosevelt had to back down. While many people felt that it was not right for nine unelected and unaccountable old men to stop what both Congress and the public clearly wanted, the Court was still a respected institution. It was seen as a vital part of the 'checks and balances' which the Founding Fathers had built into the American system of government. Conservatives saw Roosevelt's 'Court Packing' plan as an attempt to increase his power. The Southern Democrats in Congress saw it as a threat to 'white' power in the South, and many liberals deserted him on the issue. It was a rare political mistake on his part.

Roosevelt was very good at spotting potential opposition and knew when not to provoke and when to compromise. He had experience from both federal government and state politics and knew that politics was very much 'the art of the possible'. This means "It's not about what's right or what's best. It's about what you can actually get done". He had a very good understanding of what Southern Democrats would oppose and what labor unions would support. He knew when he could appeal over the heads of politicians to their voters, and when to accept what he could not change. He also had the advantage of huge popular support, as his re-election in 1936 showed, and his opponents generally were badly divided. He had intended the Social Security Act, for example, to be more comprehensive in its coverage, but knew that Congress would not accept all of Frances Perkins' proposals.

Anticipation and avoidance was Roosevelt's successful strategy when it came to dealing with opposition. Sometimes he was fortunate, as was the case with the death of Huey Long. In other cases of opposition, such as Townsend, the unrealistic nature of what Townsend was asking for meant that Roosevelt could deal with him.

Roosevelt's New Deal: for and against

Arguments in favour

- It was intended to bring stability and security to the American people.
- Roosevelt held firm principles, but was prepared to experiment, adapt and innovate to stop the spread of the Depression and to alleviate poverty and unemployment.
- Unemployment did drop substantially, the banking system stabilised and the stock market recovered and rose steadily from 1933 onwards. Capitalists, consumers, workers, employers, pensioners, bankers and investors all benefited from his work. Only agricultural subsidies and pensions had long-term cost implications.
- He did not involve the government in the economy unless it was necessary. For example, the Securities and Exchange Commission brought in openness, sensible reforms and cost-free regulation to all stock markets which would benefit everyone. Other regulatory reforms, such as those for civil aviation, rail transport and communication, continued to be successful.
- Roosevelt played a major part in getting labor unions accepted and supported, and achieved an enormous amount in ensuring greater security in the workplace.
- The Deal brought sense and more stability into the housing and mortgage market.
- It made a start in tackling the terrible problems facing US agriculture – overproduction, excessive competition and tenant farming.
- It introduced regulation of vital utilities such as electricity and gas supplies.
- It did a great deal to encourage conservation and to protect the environment.
- Roosevelt modernised the US system of government, providing real leadership in an era of crisis. This enabled the country to face the serious challenges of the Second World War.

Arguments against

- Roosevelt could be inconsistent. At times, he was drawn towards those who supported huge spending by the federal government to encourage the economy; at other times, he wanted to cut spending. Sometimes he tried to cooperate with business; at other times, he attacked business leaders for their selfishness. At times, he favoured planning by the state; sometimes he favoured laissez-faire policies and market forces.

- He failed to resolve the effects of the Great Depression. Unemployment remained high until 1941. In the end, the Second World War ended the Depression. Roosevelt's inconsistent policies might have done more harm than good in some areas. Many of the programmes seemed impressive at a national level, but actually had little impact locally.
- He over-regulated and micro-managed by bringing the federal government into so many different aspects of American economic life. He actually harmed the economy, which would have recovered eventually. Government spending caused inflation, union demands bankrupted cities and companies, and the entrepreneurial spirit that had made America great was destroyed.
- The New Deal prevented the investment that was really needed to end the Great Depression. Taxation and regulation policies distorted the market and made it unclear.
- Roosevelt behaved unconstitutionally by acquiring more and more power for the president, and giving federal government responsibility for areas that the Founding Fathers intended states or individuals to deal with.

> The achievement of the new deal appears to be small. Relief there has been, but little more than enough to keep the population fed, clothed and warm. Recovery there has been, but only to a point well below pre-depression level ... there has been no permanent adjustment of agriculture ... very little has been done to iron out the problems of industry ... the money structure of the country is less under control ... however its achievement compared with the situation which confronted it in 1933, it is a striking success. Mr Roosevelt may have given the wrong answers to many of its problems, but at least he is the first president of modern America to ask the right questions.
>
> *The Economist, 3 October 1936*

There was much debate at the time on the pros and cons of the New Deal. The view from Wall Street was very different from that of dispossessed and hungry farmers and their families. In the years that followed the New Deal, conservatives attacked Roosevelt for introducing what they alleged was socialism, while liberals praised him for getting the federal government to solve the problems that Congress or the states could not. Some argue that all real economic gains made since 1945 have been the work of the government; others argue that all the crises faced since 1945 have been caused by the government.

> ●●● **THINK LIKE A HISTORIAN**
>
> Using the internet and a library, try to find a range of comments on the overall impact of the New Deal, both favourable and critical. Reflect on the authorship of those comments. Why do you think the authors held these views?
>
> Why has the New Deal aroused so much controversy among historians? Why do historians often make very different interpretations of the same issue?

Some more recent historians have said that the New Deal saved capitalism and allowed it to carry on exploiting workers and racial minorities. Others have argued that the New Deal was not a popular reform movement with great mass support. They say it was a movement by the rich to save themselves and their corporations – merely a movement to satisfy radicals. Some commentators have argued that the Great Depression was an opportunity for radical social and economic change, and that Roosevelt should be criticised for doing far too little. The debate will continue on this remarkable period in American history.

KEY CONCEPT

Changes and continuity

How much change and how much continuity have you noted in each of the following areas in the United States between 1900 and 1941:

- The role of the President in domestic affairs?
- The economy?
- The treatment of the poor?
- The Constitution of the United States?

What do you feel changed little in this period?

Exam-style questions

Source analysis questions

Read the four sources, then answer both parts of question 1.

SOURCE A

Chief Justice of the Supreme Court, Charles E. Hughes, ruling on the case against the NRA, 1937

Section 3 of the Recovery Act is without precedent. It supplies no standards for any trade, industry or activity. It does not undertake to prescribe rules of conduct to be applied to particular states of fact determined by appropriate administrative procedure. Instead of prescribing rules of conduct, it authorizes the making of codes to prescribe them. For that legislative undertaking sets up no standards, aside from the statement of the general aims of rehabilitation, correction and expansion described in section one. In view of the scope of that broad declaration, and of the nature of the few restrictions that are imposed, the discretion of the President in approving or prescribing codes, and thus enacting laws for the government of trade and industry throughout the country, is virtually unfettered. We think that the code-making authority this conferred is an unconstitutional delegation of legislative power.

Source: https://constitutionallawreporter.com/us-supreme-court-justices/charles-evans-hughes-2

SOURCE B

Roosevelt's fireside chat, March 1937

I am reminded of that evening in March, four years ago, when I made my first radio report to you. We were then in the midst of the great banking crisis.

Soon after, with the authority of the Congress, we asked the Nation to turn over all of its privately held gold, dollar for dollar, to the Government of the United States.

Today's recovery proves how right that policy was.

But when, almost two years later, it came before the Supreme Court its constitutionality was upheld only by a five-to-four vote. The change of one vote would have thrown all the affairs of this great Nation back into hopeless chaos. In effect, four Justices ruled that the right under a private contract to exact a pound of flesh was more sacred than the main objectives of the Constitution to establish an enduring Nation.

The American people have learned from the depression. For in the last three national elections an overwhelming majority of them voted a mandate that the Congress and the President begin the task of providing that protection – not after long years of debate, but now.

Source: www.presidency.ucsb.edu/ws/index.php?pid=15381

Figure 4.10: A cartoon commenting on Roosevelt's views on the Supreme Court, 1937

SOURCE D

From a magazine article by Senator Burton K. Wheeler, normally a keen supporter of the New Deal, March 1937

1   I agree with my friend that the Court has decided many cases contrary to his wishes and contrary to my views. I am one of those who has almost universally agreed with the minority views of the Court. Assuming that anything Mr. Landis says there is a wrong way and a right way to correct those evils. The wrong way is to pack the Court—the right way is to amend the Constitution.

2   The President of the United States, speaking at the victory dinner on March 4, implied that he could not insure the continuance of democratic institutions for four more years unless he was given the power to increase immediately the membership of the Supreme Court of the United States by adding six new justices and make it subservient to his will.

3   The picture of poverty, sweatshops, unemployment, long hours, back-breaking work, child labor, ill health, inadequate housing, poor crops, drought, floods, the

dust bowl, agricultural surpluses, strikes, industrial confusion, disorders, one-third of the population of the United States ill-housed, ill-clad, ill-nourished, was graphically painted to the American people not by the enemies of the administration, but by the President of the United States himself.

4   And all this, it is implied, was because of the Supreme Court, and because six men are over 70 years of age. We are led to believe that this Court was the instrument which had stricken down all of the legislation which the Democratic Party had enacted during the last four years and which it might enact to relieve the situation in the future.

Source: Burton K. Wheeler, Chicago Forum, *10 March 1937 (available at http://academic. brooklyn.cuny.edu/history/johnson/wheeler.htm)*

184

1   a   Compare and contrast the views on the Supreme Court in Sources B and D.

     b   'Roosevelt's decision to attack the Supreme Court in 1937 proved to be a mistake.' How far do Sources A to D support this view?

Essay based questions

Answer both parts of the questions below.

2   a   Explain why the financial system collapsed in 1929.

     b   'Hoover's policies to ease the Depression achieved little.' How far do you agree?

3   a   Explain why Roosevelt wanted a Second New Deal.

     b   How successful was the First New Deal?

Sample answer

How successful was the First New Deal?

The First New Deal, President Roosevelt's policies between 1933 and 1935, has had both supporters and critics. His supporters argue that he restored confidence in the American economy, ended the crisis of 1931–33 by his actions in the First Hundred Days, and made a start

on dealing with the problems that faced America. These ranged from mass unemployment, poverty, an unsound banking and stock market system, a weak farming system and a system of government which was unsuited to dealing with major national problems. He proved to be successful in these areas. However, he had many critics who argued that he was not successful. Some argued that his government interfered too much in the economy and slowed recovery. Some argued that he did not go nearly far enough in dealing with poverty and unemployment, and the New Deal failed too many of the American people. Americans had different views on whether it was successful or not.

> This is a good-quality beginning. The opening paragraph does not waste much time on background but gets straight to the point. It shows thought about what 'success' means in context. The main areas of discussion are set out in this paragraph and there is balance in the awareness of a case 'against'.

There is a very strong case for arguing that it was successful. In his First Hundred Days in 1933 Roosevelt was able to get passed through Congress a long list of Acts which showed his determination to help the American economy and its people. There was the Emergency Banking Act which helped stabilise the banks and keep them open. The Farm Relief Act started to assist farmers and showed a willingness by the federal government to intervene in agriculture. The CCC was created and soon created over 300 000 jobs, which showed that the federal government was going to help reduce unemployment. The Tennessee Valley Authority was set up to bring huge economic advantages through dams and flood control in a very poor area of America. A system was created to help those with mortgages keep their homes, and with the NRA a start was made in helping industry and jobs. The First Hundred Days helped restore confidence in the American system and its economy, and showed the people that this new government was determined to try and solve the many problems facing the USA.

> The second paragraph is also strong. The objective of the paragraph is made clear, a case 'for' is being developed. Several points are made, and they are supported with relevant and accurate detail. It is not a simple list. Details support points, but do not dominate.

After the initial Hundred Days, Roosevelt with his Brains Trust and cabinet started to deal with other major problems which faced America, with some real successes. An important part of the First New Deal was the Agricultural Adjustment Act, administered under the leadership of Henry Wallace. This act allowed the federal government to control both farm prices and the level of production, so the problem of oversupply was dealt with. Farm incomes rose for the first time since the First World War and steps were taken to help the heavy debts that many farmers faced. The rural unrest largely dropped away and the number of farmers who left the land and went to the cities also dropped. Conservation schemes were started and the TVA brought both jobs and real help to a large part of the South. Agriculture should be seen as a New Deal success story.

Another success was in banking and the stock market. The Federal Reserve Bank was given increased powers to regulate banks and stop banks from speculating with their customers' money, which had been a major cause of the Crash of 1929. The Securities and Exchange Commission was created to regulate the stock market which also helped prevent further crashes. Perhaps most important was the impact that the Federal Emergency Relief Administration had on poverty and unemployment. This organisation pumped over $4 billion into the US economy between 1934 and 1935 and it went to either helping the very poor directly or in providing jobs. Unemployment did drop by 1935.

> These paragraphs are again very good, as the structure is clear and reinforces the initial case made that the New Deal was a success. Clear points are made and are supported with relevant examples and accurate detail. Good knowledge and understanding is shown, and there is still a clear analytical focus.

However, from another point of view the New Deal was not successful. Unemployment was still high and some argued that if Roosevelt had not interfered in industry with organisations like the NRA, then recovery would have come sooner. Some, like Townsend and Father Coughlin, believed that he should have done more to get rid of poverty and that he did not go nearly far enough. There was little done for African Americans, particularly in the South, but Roosevelt was very dependent on Southern senators and Congressmen for getting his acts through Congress. Given the limited powers that presidents had over the economy under the Constitution, he did achieve a great deal.

> The penultimate paragraph shows balance and there are valid, and supported, points made. It is leading towards a conclusion.

Overall the First New Deal was a success. He prevented the crisis he inherited from getting any worse, and major steps towards solving the many problems that America faced were taken in the course of the First New Deal, especially in terms of farming, banking and the stock market. Jobs were created and the USA remained a democracy.

> The final paragraph concludes the response well. It summarises and does not repeat. An outstanding response might have reflected more on the criteria for 'success' in this context, and developed a stronger case either way. There was scope for more detail, perhaps on unemployment and the attempts to end poverty.

Summary

After working through this chapter, make sure you understand the following key points:

- the US economy in the 1920s and the causes of the Great Crash of 1929 and the debate around whether the Crash was caused just by greed and speculation, or by more underlying serious factors in the US economy

- the causes and the impact of the Great Depression and President Hoover's attempts to manage it. The debate about the links between the Crash and the Depression is also examined

- the First and Second New Deals and their impact on America and how successful they were

- the nature and extent of the opposition to the New Deal, together with the reasons for it and how much it limited what Roosevelt was trying to achieve.

Further reading

William E. Leuchtenburg, *Franklin D. Roosevelt and the New Deal* (New York, Harper Perennial, 2013). (This is quite an advanced text, but it has the most comprehensive, and readable, coverage of the whole topic. It is particularly useful for all events after 1932.)

Peter Clements, *Prosperity, Depression and the New Deal* (Banbury, Hodder Education, 2008). (This has a high level of comment on every aspect of the specification and is useful for dealing with questions which require analysis.)

M. J. Heale, *Franklin D. Roosevelt: The New Deal and War* (Abingdon, Routledge, 1999). (This is an excellent compact survey of Roosevelt's motives for, and management of, the whole New Deal process.)

One very good source of digital material is 'DocsTeach' which contains a variety of sources from the US National Archives relevant to the New Deal. They are laid out in a very student-friendly way.

If possible, ask your school or college to join the UK Historical Association. This organisation has a huge range of resources designed specifically for AS Level students, all available online. There is a very useful article on the impact of the New Deal and also podcasts on the Great Depression and the USA in the 1920s.

Chapter 5
Preparing for assessment

Learning objectives

In this chapter you will:

■   learn about the skills that you will develop by studying AS Level History

■   find out what types of question will test your skills and learn what other skills you will need in order to answer them

■   understand how your skills and work might be assessed and how you can study and revise most effectively.

5.1 Introduction

In order to achieve success at AS Level History, you will need to develop skills that, perhaps, were less important in courses you might have taken in the past. Generally, pre-AS Level assessments require you to demonstrate your knowledge and understanding of certain historical events. Now you will be required to analyse and interpret your knowledge in much greater depth.

This has implications for the way you study History at a higher level. Your teacher will provide the essential background knowledge, help you to develop the various skills you need in order to do well, and suggest the resources that you will need to work with.

It is essential at AS Level, however, that you are prepared to work and research independently and participate in discussion, which is essential for developing your own ideas and judgement. Your teacher cannot tell you what to think or what opinions to have, although they can help you learn how to think and how to form opinions. At AS Level, you will have far more responsibility for developing your own ideas, views and judgments. If you wish to aim for high-level grades at AS Level, you will have to put forward your own views on a subject and explain your reasons for coming to those views. To do this effectively, you need to acquire independent learning skills. In particular, this means reading as widely as possible around a topic so you can gain access to different interpretations of the same issues and events.

History is not a series of universally accepted facts, which once learned, will provide you with a detailed and accurate understanding of the past. Just as historical events were perceived in many different (and often contradictory) ways by people who experienced them at the time, so they have been interpreted in many different ways by historians who have studied them subsequently. Historical debates rage all the time, which make it very clear that historians often disagree fundamentally about the reasons for, or the significance of, certain key events.

You need to understand, for example, that there is no right answer to why the American Civil War broke out in 1861. Many great historians have researched this topic in great depth, and come to very different conclusions. You will need to learn to reflect on those conclusions, and come to your own judgement. This process of reflection will also give you an insight into the methods historians use to put across their ideas; you will be able to adapt these methods for your own use when answering historical questions.

History may seem to deal primarily with facts, but it is equally about opinions, perceptions, judgements, interpretations and prejudices. Many Americans in the 1930s felt that the Supreme Court should not have struck down New Deal legislation. Others believed it was the right decision because the New Deal was harming the American economy in the long term. Others felt that, while the Supreme Court was legally justified in revoking the legislation, it should not have done so on grounds of expediency. There are many diverse opinions from historians on this significant decision by the Court.

You will be asked for your opinion or judgement on an issue like this, and will have to make up your own mind. You need to study the evidence, reflect on what kind of evidence it is and then analyse what it proves. This will allow you to form an opinion. When asked for an opinion or judgement, you will need to back up what you offer with reasons and evidence. In this way, historians are like lawyers in court. You are making a case and then proving it. Sometimes your fellow learners and teachers might disagree with your opinion and be able to provide compelling evidence to demonstrate why. Sometimes they might convince you to change your mind. Sometimes you will be able to convince them to change or refine their opinions. Sometimes you might just agree to differ. It is this ability to see things in different ways, and to have the confidence to use your own knowledge and understanding to make judgements, form opinions and develop arguments, that makes History so interesting and challenging.

5.2 What skills will I develop as I study AS Level History?

It is worth stressing that, alongside your historical knowledge and understanding, a wide range of skills will

be assessed in the course of your studies. Most of these will be invaluable to you in both higher education and your working life. They include the ability to:

- acquire in-depth subject knowledge
- learn how to select and use knowledge effectively
- use independent research skills, which are critical for success, at AS Level and beyond
- develop independent thinking skills
- apply knowledge and understanding to new as well as familiar situations
- handle and evaluate different types of information source
- think logically and present ordered and coherent arguments
- make judgements, recommendations and decisions
- present reasoned explanations, understand implications and communicate them clearly and logically
- work effectively under pressure
- communicate well in English
- understand that information learned in one context can be usefully deployed in another.

All of these will be tested in some way in your History assessments. Merely learning a large number of facts will not enable you to achieve your best at AS Level History: you have to demonstrate a range of skills as well. Work on the principle that roughly half the marks awarded are for knowledge and understanding, and half are for your use of the skills listed above.

How can I acquire and demonstrate the key skills?

The skills listed above will form an essential part of the assessment process at AS Level. AS Level studies are not just about learning facts: you will also need to develop the skills to use them properly.

Acquiring in-depth subject knowledge

You need to find the most suitable way to acquire the knowledge you need and the most effective way of remembering it, so that you can use it when necessary. Often, it is a combination of reading, noting, listening, writing and discussing that helps to retain knowledge.

Selecting and using that knowledge effectively

Once you have acquired the right amount of subject knowledge, you must learn how to use it effectively. If you are asked a question on one of the many reasons why there was rapid industrialisation in the USA in the late 19th century, you should avoid writing about all of them: just focus on the one specified in the question.

Using independent research skills

The ability to research for yourself is vital. It would be virtually impossible for any teacher to give you all the information you need. You must be able to effectively use a library and other research sources and tools, such as the internet, to find out things for yourself.

Developing independent thinking skills

You must learn how to think for yourself and be able to challenge ideas. You will be asked for your view on a subject, for example whether Theodore Roosevelt or Woodrow Wilson did more to advance the Progressive Movement. Both men have a strong claim here, but which do you think was more effective and influential, and why?

Handling and evaluating different sources

You will learn to look at different sources and assess how accurate and useful they might be. For example, you may need to put yourself in the position of a historian who is writing about the Schecter Case. There are many contemporary sources which defend the Supreme Court's decision, and many which criticise it. Some may be from biased writers or cartoonists; others might be written by those who benefited or lost by the decision. Which is the most reliable and useful? Why? This is the sort of skill that might be useful in the present day – for example, if you are deciding which way to vote in an election after you have been presented with arguments from all sides.

Analysing and making judgements

This combination is a key skill. You will be asked for a judgement on, for example, whether the First New Deal was successful or not. First, you will have to work out for yourself what the criteria for 'success' is in this context. Then you will need to consider the grounds on which the New Deal might be seen as a success – in the role of defence counsel. Next, you should consider the grounds on which it might not be seen as a success. Finally, and this is the biggest challenge, you will have to weigh up the two sides, come to a conclusion, then be prepared to give clear reasons, and a defence, why you have come to that conclusion.

Explaining

You will need to explain quite complex issues clearly. For example, you could be asked to explain why mass immigration was so important to industrialisation in late 19th-century America, and have ten minutes in which to do it. You will need to summarise briefly what this immigration involved, and then in three or four sentences explain why this was essential to the process. Note that you will need to give sufficient focus to the 'so' word the question.

5.3 What types of question will assess my skills?

There are three types of question at AS Level. They will assess your:

- knowledge and understanding, and skills in communicating them
- analytical, evaluative and communication skills
- ability to read, evaluate and reach a judgement on a range of sources, demonstrating a range of skills as well as historical knowledge and understanding.

Understanding what a question is asking you to do

There are certain key words that appear in many AS Level History questions. These 'command words' are the instructions that specify what you need to do. They make it clear what is expected from a response in terms of skills, knowledge and understanding.

Source-based questions

Questions based on source extracts, might ask, for example:

To what extent do Sources A and C agree *on the impact of John Brown's raid?*

This type of question is looking for a firm *judgement* on the **extent** to which the sources **agree** (and disagree) on the impact of the raid. It is your *understanding* of those two sources that is key, and your ability to *identify the key points showing agreement and disagreement*. The question is also looking for *source analysis* and *contextual knowledge*.

Note that, in this instance, only the two sources specified should be used.

Compare and contrast *the views in Sources B and D on the robber barons.*

This type of question is looking for your ability to *identify the similarities and differences* between the views expressed in the two sources about the robber barons and, for example, their power and influence. A good response will comment on whether there are more similarities than differences, and why. *Contextual knowledge* and *source evaluation* will also be expected.

Again, only the two sources specified should be used.

'Lincoln provided outstanding leadership for the North during the Civil War.' **How far do Sources A to D** support this view?

What is looked for here is a clear *judgement* of **how far** *all four* sources (not just the two specified in the first two example questions) do, or do not, support the given view of Lincoln's leadership. One way of dealing with this response is by using the structure outlined in the next section for questions that highlight knowledge and understanding. You need to offer a *balanced argument* in addition to your judgement, and you should make careful use of all four sources and demonstrate contextual knowledge. The supporting paragraphs after your judgement are a good place to do this. Demonstration of *source evaluation* skills will also be expected.

To what extent *do Sources A to D support the view that Reconstruction was a failure?*

You can take a similar approach to this type of question as you did with the 'How far …' question about Lincoln. You need to make a firm *judgement*, with a good case made for this, on *how far* the sources back up the claim that the attempts at Reconstruction failed (not just a vague 'to some extent').

It is important to use all *four sources* and *contextual knowledge* when backing up your points. It is appropriate to quote the occasional phrase if you feel it is important to your argument, but avoiding copying out large sections of the documents. Demonstrating *source evaluation skills* will be crucial here.

Other questions that assess knowledge, understanding and analytical skills

The following questions give examples of the command words and key words that appear in questions that are not source-based.

Explain why *Franklin Roosevelt put through the Second New Deal.*

This type of question clearly requires an *explanation of why* Roosevelt saw the need for the Second New Deal. It is therefore your *ability to explain something clearly*

that is being assessed, as well as your *knowledge and understanding of the reasons* for the Second New Deal. It is not assessing your analytical skills, but your ability to *select and apply your in-depth knowledge effectively*.

'The Second New Deal was more successful than the First New Deal.' **How far do you agree?**

This type of question requires *analytical skills* as well as your *knowledge and understanding* of the New Deals. It requires a firm *judgement* on the *degrees* of success, or otherwise, that each New Deal had. You should reflect on what the *criteria for success* might be. Would either New Deal be considered a success if it just increased federal involvement in policy-making? Did it bring real benefit to the American people? You need to show that you know and understand what the New Deals involved and the impact of those strategies. An *examination of the nature and extent of the success* achieved should then lead to a concluding *judgement on the degree of success* attained.

This question is assessing your skill in analysing a topic you know a lot about, as well as your ability to come to a judgement on 'how far' you agree that the Second New Deal was a greater success than the First.

To what extent *had Franklin Roosevelt solved America's economic problems by 1939?*

This type of question is also assessing your *analytical skills*. It requires a similar approach to a 'how far' question. You should give a clear judgement on the 'extent', with evidence to show that you have:

- analysed Roosevelt's management of the economy in the specified period
- considered how far he did (and did not) succeed in solving the USA's economic problems.

You should then come to a conclusion based on the evidence.

How successful *were Progressive attempts to regulate industry?*

This type of question assesses your *analytical skills* as well as your *knowledge and understanding* of the Progressives' attempts to regulate industry. It requires a firm *judgement* on the *degree* of success, or otherwise, that the Progressives' achieved. Again, there needs to be some *reflection* on what the *criteria for success* might be. You should demonstrate your knowledge and understanding of the situation before the Progressives embarked on their various regulatory campaigns, and the situation at the end of the period studied. An examination of the nature and extent of the regulation achieved should then lead to a conclusion on the degree of success attained.

How effective *was the opposition to the New Deals?*

Note that the question specifies the 'Deals' and not just the 'Deal'.

A similar approach can be used here to the 'how successful' type of question. Some *reflection* on what **effective** opposition implies. Stopping the Deals' actions altogether? Making Roosevelt's government more cautious in putting forward the reforms they really wanted? The question requires an *examination of evidence* for where the opposition did prevent the New Dealers from doing what they wanted to, and also where it failed to. A good response will come to a *firm judgement based on the evidence*. Avoid vague responses such as 'It had some effect'. Argue your case strongly.

Questions that highlight knowledge and understanding

This type of question is assessing your ability to:

- understand the question and its requirements and keep a firm focus on that question alone
- recall and select relevant and appropriate factual material and demonstrate your understanding of a complex topic
- communicate your knowledge and understanding in a clear and effective manner.

An example of a 'knowledge and understanding' question might be:

'Explain why mass immigration was so important to US industrialisation.'

A good-quality answer to this type of question will:

- be entirely focused on the question: you should focus on mass immigration – you do not need to explain the causes of this immigration, but you must *explain the link* between immigration and industrialisation
- identify three or four relevant points and develop them with supporting detail

- indicate which of those points you feel are the most important, and why: this is vital in an 'explain why' type of question – there should be an emphasis on why immigration was 'so' important, explaining why industrialisation might not have happened without it.
- be written in as clear English as possible.

When answering, remember:

- Explain why.
- Answer the question that was asked and not spend much time on other factors.
- Do more than merely list facts which might or might not be linked to the question.
- Make specific points and back them up with relevant and accurate detail.

This type of question is testing understanding as well as knowledge. It is not just a case of explaining one relevant point. It is also very important to show that you understand its significance in context.

Questions that highlight analysis and evaluation

This type of question is assessing your ability to:

- understand the question and its requirements and keep a firm focus on that question alone
- recall and select relevant and appropriate factual material
- analyse and evaluate this material in order to reach a focused, balanced and substantiated judgement
- communicate your knowledge and understanding in a clear and effective manner.

Examples of these questions are:

1 'Reconstruction was a failure overall.' How far do you agree?

2 How effective were President Roosevelt's New Deal strategies?

Your answer to the first question, on Reconstruction, should contain a clear judgement or argument:

- It should be entirely focused on this question. It is not asking about the reasons for Reconstruction: it is asking if you think it failed, or not. Be careful not to write a narrative history of Reconstruction or just describe it.

- Demonstrate that you have thought about causative factors in general. What does 'failure' imply in the context of the USA in the 1860s and 1870s. What do you think are the criteria for success or failure in this case? Demonstrating that you have really thought about the implications of *failure* in this context, and what *success* might look like, helps to make a really high-quality analytical essay.

- Be balanced: demonstrate that you have considered both the case for it being a failure and the case against, and that you have considered the word 'overall' in the question (for example, that there might have been some successes, but that it did not, in the end, succeed in its main aims).

- Offer knowledge and understanding by backing up the various points you make with accurate and relevant detail.

- Include careful analysis: consider both the case for and the case against and come to a reasoned judgement. Do not simply lay out the case for and against and then leave it to the reader to reach a conclusion.

Remember:

- Avoid simply stating a case for and one against and leaving it to the reader to decide what the answer is. This is common error.

- Give a clear and developed answer. Make sure that your case is clearly laid out and developed carefully. Your reasons should then be followed up in subsequent paragraphs which contain the factual details to back up those points. Good responses usually contain an opening paragraph which sets out the answer clearly and gives the reasoning behind it. Later paragraphs – perhaps three or four of them – deal with the development of the case. In dealing with the case against, the strongest answers clearly explain, with supporting evidence, why you do not think it valid, demonstrating you are aware of alternative views.

- Show you have really thought about 'failure' in this context.

Tips for answering questions that ask 'How far do you agree?'

'The federal government must take full responsibility for causing the Depression of the 1930s.' How far do you agree?

Try thinking about this in terms of a scale, with 'I completely agree because …' at one end and 'I completely disagree because …' at the other:

1	2	3	4
Completely agree	Somewhat agree	Somewhat disagree	Completely disagree

Depending on where you are on the scale, The opening paragraph of a response might be similar to the following examples:

1. It was the imposition of tariffs, which damaged so much world and US trade and the failure of government to regulate industry, banks and the stock market, as well as ignoring national problems like the dustbowl droughts, that make the federal government primarily responsible. While there were other causal factors, such as … and …, they did not play nearly such an important part as the economic factors.

2. The federal government's failings did play an important part in causing the Depression, for the following reasons … But it was the impact of the First World War and the existing structure of the US banking system that were more important. These two factors were more important because …

3. The federal government cannot be seen to have played anything other than a minor role in causing the depression. It can be seen to have done too little in dealing with the effects of it. However the principal causes were the collapse of world trade and natural disasters such as the growth of the dustbowl. There were also severe limitations imposed on the government by the Constitution.

4. The federal government played an insignificant role in causing the Depression. Much more important were … and … as it was these two factors which …

Opening sections like these demonstrate thinking about the relative importance of causes, rather than just listing them. It shows analytical skills and understanding, not just knowledge. Remember that all three are being assessed at AS Level.

When writing a response to the second question, on the effectiveness of Roosevelt's New Deal strategies, you should bear in mind the following points:

- Focus on the effectiveness of the New Deal strategies. The question is not asking about the reasons for the New Deal, or whether Hoover's strategies were unsuccessful. Consider how 'effective' Roosevelt's were, on a scale from very effective to very ineffective.

- Demonstrate that you have thought about what an 'effective' strategy might be in the circumstances of the USA in the 1930s. Would it have reduced unemployment a little? Restored confidence in government? Rebuilt the US economy? Prevented a radical alternative strategy from the left or right? It is important to show that you are thinking analytically.

- Show knowledge and understanding by identifying the various strategies adopted by Roosevelt.

- Demonstrate your analytical skills by weighing up the identified strategies and commenting on the extent to which you consider them to be effective or otherwise. The focus should be on the effectiveness of each strategy, but you should also comment on their overall effectivenesss.

Another example of a timed essay-type question might be: 'Hoover's policies to ease the depression achieved little.' How far do you agree? Different students will take different approaches to this type of question, and you will find your own. While you are developing your techniques, you might find the following essay structure helpful. Even if you choose to organise your essay differently, it is important to note the strengths of this one and apply the same principles in your own writing.

Paragraph	Content
1	This needs to contain a succinct, clear answer to the question. Did Hoover's policies do much to ease the depression? An answer might be, for example: *They achieved little and in some cases even made it worse because* *(a) …* *(b) …* *(c) …* *although they did have some small impact for reasons (d) … and (e) …* This paragraph does not need not to contain much detail, just broad reasons, and should demonstrate that you are focusing on the question and thinking analytically. Avoid vague introductions or trying to 'set the scene'.
2	This could take point (a) and develop it in detail. Make sure that the objective of the paragraph is made clear from the start, for example: *The principal reason why Hoover's policies did so little was …* And then include three or four accurate and relevant facts to back up your point: the evidence. This section might also explain why you feel this particular issue was the most important point, demonstrating an analytical approach.
3	Point (b) could be developed here in a similar way. Again, take care to ensure that the objective of the paragraph is made clear: that you are clearly relating what you write to your statement that those policies achieved little. There is often a tendency to forget the purpose of the paragraph and simply list the facts. This often leaves the reader asking, 'So…?'
4	Again, make the objective clear and explain clearly why this point is of less importance than (a).
5	This is a good place to develop the case 'against' in points (d) and (e), to demonstrate the balance required in this type of response. There is nothing wrong with strong arguments, however, and if you feel there is no case 'against', say so and why. It might nonetheless be a good idea to start this paragraph with, for example: *Defenders of Hoover might argue that …* and bring out a possible defence of his work, however weak you might think it is.

Paragraph	Content
6	If you have developed your response as suggested above, this can be quite brief. Avoid repetition, and keep an analytical focus, perhaps emphasising the reasons behind your thinking. Remember to include an introduction as suggested in paragraph 1. Do not just indicate a case each way and leave all the analysis and answer to the 'conclusion'. That type of response is likely to leave you with insufficient time and to contain facts with no analysis or judgement. It merely presents the cases each way. Another failing might be that the case *for* is very long and detailed, while the case *against* is much briefer and undeveloped, and yet the brief conclusion is that the case against wins even though all the facts presented point the other way. In this case, there is just not enough analysis to fully answer the question asked.

Another example to consider is the following essay:

'The Progressives managed to bring about so much change in America.' How valid is this view?

One way of approaching this type of question is shown below:

Paragraph	Content
1	Identify the principal reasons why the Progressives did manage to achieve so much. Emphasise your response to the 'so' word in the question. It demonstrates that you are thinking analytically from the start. Including between three and five reasons shows good knowledge and understanding.
2	Take what you think was the most important reason for their success – for example, the support from presidents Roosevelt and Wilson – and develop this point in detail. Then develop the reasons why you do **not** think their success was the most important reason.
3, 4 and 5	Continue to develop in depth the reasons you have set out in your first paragraph, again making sure that your analytical thinking is clear and you are not merely listing reasons.
6	Avoid repetition. Focus on why you prioritised your reasons in the way you did, and show that you have thought very carefully about the why the Progressives achieved 'so' much.

Questions that highlight your ability to read, contrast, evaluate and judge a range of sources

Source-based questions are testing your ability to:

- understand a question and its requirements
- understand the content of a source in its historical context
- analyse and evaluate source content and the sources themselves
- reach a focused and balanced judgement based on evidence
- communicate your argument in a clear and effective manner.

A source-based question might contain, for example, four sources on the causes of the Great Depression and might ask:

1 Compare and contrast the accounts given of the state of US agriculture in Sources B and D.

2 How far do Sources A to D support the view that the United States government should take most of the responsibility for causing the Depression?

A response to a question such as Question 1 should include:

- evidence that you have really understood the points made in both sources and grasped their overall argument
- evidence that you have identified areas of both difference and similarity between the two sources
- contextual awareness, demonstrating your background knowledge on the topic
- evaluation of both sources and consideration of their validity and provenance. Which would you trust most and why?

When answering this type of question, remember that you do not need to provide a summary of the sources, or copy out large parts of them. You might need, however, to quote just a phrase or two to back up your points.

A response to a question such as Question 2 should include:

- evidence that you have fully understood all four sources (not just the two specified in the first question!) and grasped their overall arguments – demonstration of clear comprehension is vital for a high-quality answer
- evidence that you have clearly identified the extent to which each of the four sources does, or does not, suggest responsibility for the Depression should lie with the US government
- a focused and balanced judgement on the issue of responsibility
- contextual awareness – demonstrate that you have background historical knowledge and understanding and that you are not just relying on the sources for information
- evaluation of all four sources in this specific context (which is likely to differ from that of the first question) and consideration of their validity and provenance
- a firm, specific judgement: avoid merely saying, for example, 'The government was partly responsible – a more appropriate response might begin something like, 'The US government, through its foreign economic policies for example, must take some responsibility for the Depression. However, the actions of stockbrokers and speculators …'

Further guidance on source-based questions

In order to make judgements and form opinions about past events, historians need to gather as much information and evidence as possible. They use a wide variety of sources for this, including written extracts, speeches, photographs, cartoons, posters, film footage, oral records and archaeological finds. Much of the evidence historians find is contradictory, reflecting the many different perspectives and opinions of the people who produced the sources.

Documents and photographs, for example, can be altered by those wishing to create a more favourable view of themselves, or a less favourable view of others. Historians, therefore, need to analyse their sources very carefully in order to form their own opinions and judgements about the past, while avoiding a one-sided or biased study of an event or person.

Learning how to reflect on and evaluate the information you receive before you make up your own mind on a subject – whether this is who you might vote for or

which mobile phone you might buy – is an important skill to acquire. The feature 'Think like a historian' used throughout this book should give you an idea about how the skills you develop in this course are useful in other areas of your life.

In much the same way, you will be faced with a variety of different historical sources during your course. You will need to be able to analyse those sources in the light of your own subject knowledge. The key word here is *analyse*. This means going beyond just a basic *comprehension* of what a source is saying or showing. When answering source-based questions, you should avoid just describing or summarising the source. You should ask yourself questions about how reliable the source is and why it appears to contradict what some other sources seem to suggest.

Primary sources

A primary source is one that was written, spoken, drawn or photographed at, or very near, the time. It could also be a recollection some years later of an event or person. It is usually produced by someone who was directly involved in the event, or who was, in some sense, an eyewitness to it.

Primary sources tend to reflect the customs and beliefs of the creator and the time and place from which they come. You should not be critical of the contents of a primary source just because, for example, you do not share the same values. Opinions in the US today about equal rights, for example, are very different from those held by many people 150 years ago.

A primary source has many advantages to a historian:

- It provides a first-hand, contemporary account.
- It can offer an insight into the author's perceptions and emotions at the time.
- A source created by someone directly involved in an event might give detailed 'inside information' that other people could not possibly know.

Disadvantages of a primary source might be:

- The source only gives the reader the opinions of the person who created it, which might not be typical of opinions at the time.
- A source created by someone directly involved might contain bias: for example, in trying to convince an audience to agree with a particular line of argument.
- Eyewitnesses might not always be completely reliable. They might not have access to the full details of an event,

or they might be trying to impose their own opinions on the audience.

- The source might be based on the memory of an event or meeting which happened many years before, or could be over-reliant on the recollections of another person.

Different types of primary source you might be asked to use include:

- a speech
- a private letter
- a diary
- an official document, such as a Federal Government Act, an order from a minister to a civil servant, a report from an ambassador to the Secretary of State, a secret memorandum by an official, a legal judgement
- an autobiography
- a cartoon
- a photograph
- a newspaper report
- an interview.

A note on bias

The word 'bias' is often misused in History essays. A dictionary definition of bias is 'the action of supporting a particular person or thing in an unfair way by allowing personal opinions to influence your judgement'. Bias can be explicit and conscious: for example, politicians seeking election will naturally emphasise the good points about their record, and emphasise the bad points about their opponents. Bias can also be implicit and unconscious.

A note on hindsight

Hindsight is the ability to look back at an event some time after it has occurred, with a fuller appreciation of the facts, implications and effects. With hindsight, it is easier to understand the reasons why an event took place, its significance and the impact it had. It is important to remember that people living at the time of the event did not have the advantage of hindsight!

Assessing the reliability of sources

It should now be clear that historians have to be extremely careful when using sources. They cannot afford to accept that everything a source tells them is completely reliable or true. People exaggerate. People tell lies. People might

not have seen everything there was to see People have opinions that others do not share. People simply make mistakes.

Imagine you were out walking, lost in your own thoughts, when you suddenly hear a screeching of brakes and a thud behind you. As you turn in the direction of the sounds, you see a pedestrian fall to the ground, clearly having been hit by the car, which you see driving quickly away. You are the only other person around. Your first priority would be to try to assist the pedestrian and call the emergency services. When the police arrive, they see you as a vital eyewitness to the accident, and they naturally want to take a statement from you.

But were you really an eyewitness? Did you see the accident, or just hear it and see the result? You saw the car drive quickly away, but does that mean the driver was speeding or driving dangerously at the time? How might your sense of pity for the pedestrian affect your idea of what actually happened? Could you be certain the pedestrian was not to blame for the accident? Could the pedestrian have stumbled into the path of the car? Deliberately jumped? Could you describe the car in detail, or the driver? How far might your recollection of the event be influenced by your own shock? How and why might the statements of the car driver and the pedestrian differ from your own?

So, what can we do, as historians, to minimise the risk of drawing inaccurate conclusions from sources? There are a number of questions that need to be asked in order to determine how reliable a source is and to evaluate its provenance. These apply to all types of source, not just written ones:

- Who wrote it?
- When was it written?
- What is the context?
- Who was the intended audience?
- Why was it written? What was the author's motive?
- What does it actually say?
- How does it compare with your own subject knowledge and with what other sources say?
- What do you think the author might have left out?

Suppose, for example, that this is the statement given to the police later in the day by the driver of the car involved in the accident: 'I was driving carefully along the road well within the speed limit. Suddenly and without warning, a pedestrian jumped out in front of me from behind a parked lorry. I did not see him until it was far too late and it was impossible for me to stop in time and avoid hitting the pedestrian. In a state of panic, I did not stop. I drove away, in shock, but within minutes I calmed down and realised that I had to go and report the issue to the police. I had my children in the car, so once I had taken them home, I reported the incident to the police.'

- **Who wrote the source?** The driver of the car involved in the accident. Naturally, the driver would clearly not wish to be blamed for the accident, and therefore might have a very good reason for being less than honest.
- **When was it written?** Later on the same day as the accident. By this time, the driver would have recovered from the initial shock and understood that there was probably no option but to report the incident to the police. The driver might well have seen the witness and believed that the witness had the car's details and description. However, there would have been time for the driver to reflect on the incident and develop a version of events so that the responsibility for the incident can be placed on the pedestrian. Given the shock and what might have happened since, would the driver's memory be accurate?
- **What is the context?** The driver reporting to the police to admit involvement in the accident. The police would have to take such statements, as they might be needed if there was a prosecution in a court.
- **Who was the intended audience?** Initially the police, but also possibly a counsel who might have to decide whether or not to prosecute the driver, and therefore, a judge and a jury.
- **Why was it written?** What was the author's motive? The statement had to be written by law. It is possible that the driver accepted the need to report involvement in the accident. It is also possible that the driver, realising that the police would most likely catch up with him, was anxious to report the incident in order to clear his name by laying blame on the pedestrian.
- **What does it actually say?** The driver argues that he was not driving too fast or dangerously and that the accident was entirely the pedestrian's fault for jumping out suddenly into the road from behind a lorry, without checking for traffic. He admits to leaving the scene of the accident out of panic.
- **How might it compare with what other sources say?** The police are in a difficult position here. The driver might well be telling the whole truth and giving a perfectly accurate description. The driver might also have made up the entire story, as he was driving too fast and using his phone. Other witnesses might be able to comment on how fast the car was going at the time. There might be some CCTV footage of the accident of variable quality.

Mobile phone records can be checked. Marks on the road can be assessed. The driver mentions 'children' in the car. Would they be able to give a version of events? If so, would they just support their parent? If the parked lorry which hid the pedestrian from view had been moved, can an accurate picture of the whole event be made? The pedestrian might be concussed and not have an accurate recollection of events. If the police discover that the pedestrian had a long record of depression, might that not reinforce the possibility that he had 'jumped out' as the driver's statement alleges?

Finding the truth can be a very challenging task.

Now let's turn to an actual historical example: Lincoln's Gettysburg Address – one of the most famous speeches in American history. It was reported in full in the *New York Times* on 20 November 1863.

Four score and seven years ago our fathers brought forth on this continent a new nation, conceived in liberty and dedicated to the proposition that all men are created equal. Now we are engaged in a great civil war, testing whether this nation, or any nation, so conceived and dedicated can long endure. We are met on a great battlefield of that war. We have come to dedicate a portion of that field as a final resting place for those who here gave their lives that that nation might live. It is altogether fitting and proper that we should do this. But, in a larger sense, we cannot dedicate, we cannot consecrate, we cannot hallow this ground. The brave men, living and dead, who struggled here, have consecrated it, far above our poor power to add or detract. The world will little note, nor long remember what we say here, but it cannot forget what they did here. It is for us, the living, rather, to be dedicated here to the unfinished work which they who fought here have thus far so nobly advanced. It is rather for us to be dedicated to the great task remaining before us – that from these honoured dead we take increasing devotion to that cause for which they gave the last full measure of devotion – that we here highly resolve that these dead shall not have died in vain – that the nation shall, under God, have a new birth of freedom – and that Governments of the people, by the people, for the people shall not perish from the earth.

Source: Available online, for example at www.abrahamlincolnonline.org/lincoln/ speeches/gettysburg.htm

All sources need to be viewed critically, not just accepted at face value. To analyse this source effectively, you need to consider the same questions.

- **Who wrote (spoke) it?** The address was made by the President of the United States, Abraham Lincoln. It was a very short speech, just over two minutes long.

- **When was it made?** On 19 November 1863, with his potential re-election coming up in less than a year.

- **What is the context?** President Lincoln was speaking at the dedication of a national cemetery of war dead on the site of the vital Battle of Gettysburg fought four months earlier during the Civil War. The war still had not ended, and it was to become even bloodier and more bitter.

- **Who was the intended audience?** Certainly the people at the ceremony, a crowd estimated to be about 15 000. It was also aimed at the entire American people. Lincoln was well aware that there were plenty of journalists present and that his message would be widely reported across the United States.

- **Why was it written?** *What was the author's motive?* It was a remembrance for those soldiers who had died … It also restated the ideological purpose that the North was fighting for and attempted to maintain morale and possibly to demonstrate the importance of Lincoln's leadership.

- **What does the speech actually say?** It remembers those soldiers who died, making links to the country's Founding Fathers and stressing that the sacrifices of the war are being made for the country – for freedom and democracy.

- **How does it compare with other sources?** We know from other sources that Lincoln had taken enormous care over the speech and that he considered it to be sending out a very important message. Many reports at the time saw the speech very much as an attempt to encourage further support in the North. Since the war, however, it tends to be seen more as a fundamental statement of American values.

Questions that ask you to compare and contrast sources

One type of question you might face is 'compare and contrast'. Whenever you compare two or more things, you should draw attention to the similarities and what they have in common. When contrasting, you should draw attention to the differences.

A high-quality answer will show examples of the following skills:

- *Makes a developed comparison between the two sources, recognising points of similarity and difference.*
- *Uses knowledge to evaluate the sources and shows good contextual awareness.*

You are expected to do a great deal more than just give a summary of the two sources. You have to show that you fully comprehend them and can use your knowledge and understanding of them to answer the question. You also have to demonstrate contextual knowledge and show that you are fully aware of the provenance of the sources. You must evaluate them very carefully.

The two sources below present different views of society in the South of the USA.

SOURCE A

The natural manner of living in Slave States helps to cover up a multitude of Southern shortcomings – tobacco chewing, brandy drinking and other excesses of a like character which would otherwise without doubt render the masses of Southern people as fickle and unstable, as nervous and spasmodic as the masses of the North. God knows that dissipation and debauchery are rife enough over the whole land; and our opinion is neither the North or the South would be justified in casting the first stone at the head of the other. Such irregularities, however, are not so frequently committed by the gentlemen of the South as by a certain class of under bred snobs, whose money enables them to pretend to the character and standing of gentlemen but whose natural inborn coarseness and vulgarity lead them to disgrace the honourable title they assume to wear.

D.R. Hundley, Social Relations of our Southern States *(1860). Hundley was a Southern lawyer, but had had no training as a social scientist.*

SOURCE B

> The state of society in the South and their legislation exhibits a growing tendency to lapse back into barbarism. There are but few schools and the masses are growing up in ignorance and vice. Men resort to violence and bloodshed rather than to call discussion and courts of justices to settle their disputes and difficulties. All classes are impatient of restraint and indulge in a reckless and lawless disregard and contempt for all institutions of society or religion which obstruct the free exercise of their passion and prejudices … The Christian world rose up through just such a state of things to its present mild, moral, peaceable, humane Christian and enlightened standpoint. The South has already sunk three centuries back towards the age of barbarism.
>
> *An extract from an article in the* Milwaukee Sentinel, *a Northern newspaper, April 1861.*

In order to look at the similarities and differences between the two articles, consider the following points:

- **Who wrote them?** Source A is by a little-known Southern writer with legal training; Source B by an anonymous Northern journalist.
- **When were they published?** 1860 and 1861
- *What was the context?* Source A was published in 1860, before the secession crisis of 1861. B was published at the height of the crisis. It is important to stress this.
- **Who were the intended audience?** The readership of A is likely to have been the literate middle-classes of the USA. The newspaper article would probably have had a more local readership aimed at all classes.
- **Why was it written?** Source A gives a view of the South that emphasises both its good and bad points. It is clearly trying to present a balanced point of view and is trying to give a reasonable analysis of society in the South. The Northern journalist in Source B only emphasises what he believes to be the bad points, trying to stir up antagonism towards the South. Each is trying to convince the reader that his view is correct.
- **What do the texts actually say?** They are giving the authors' views on life and attitudes in the Southern states.

- **What is the context?** The differences between the North and South were widening at this time. The North was becoming increasingly industrialised, while the South remained primarily agrarian. Divisions widened after the election of Lincoln, and this led to many exaggerating what they felt were the worst features of the other side. Emotions were running high by the spring of 1861.
- **How reliable are the sources?** Source A is probably the more reliable, as the author is clearly educated, with legal training, and his comments do show some balance. However, he is likely to be appealing to the upper classes of the South, the ones most likely to buy his book. Source B, writing at a time of great tension, is appealing solely to a Northern audience, with no sign of balance at all, and is making sweeping assertions. There is no reason to see this as anything other than an attempt to criticise the South. It is an example of Northern prejudice.

A good way of comparing the views expressed in these two sources is to devise a simple plan once you have read them carefully, keeping the focus strictly on the causes of the revolution. For example:

Source A:

- argues that slavery helps to cover up a number of barbaric practices and that these are only carried out by some people, not by gentlemen
- claims that degeneracy and debauchery were widespread across the whole USA
- does not mention a return to barbarism
- seems to suggest, with the reference to the newly moneyed, that prosperity is coming to the South
- uses emotive language, such as 'fickle' and 'unstable', about the North.

Source B:

- does not mention slavery
- talks of barbarism in the South, but does not mention it in relation to the North
- makes no mention of class differences in the South, and instead claims that Southerners in general are barbaric
- also uses emotive language, including 'barbarism' and 'bloodshed'.

From this plan it is easy to see where the authors disagree and agree. To summarise:

- B sees Southern societies as barbaric; whereas A argues that such practices are probably confined to a small and untypical minority.

199

- A says that bad practices can be found in both North and South, while B maintains that they only happen in the South.
- B sees the North as enlightened and Christian, while A sees it as fickle and unstable.
- There is some agreement – of a limited nature – on the South, but none at all on the North.

Visual sources: posters

Visual sources should be analysed and evaluated in much the same way as written ones. Look at Figure 5.1, a McKinley campaign poster for the 1900 presidential election.

- **What is the message (in context)?** The current McKinley presidency has been a success for the USA in terms of economic growth and overseas power. On its left, the poster highlights the failings of the Democrats, with factories silent, people rushing to the banks to withdraw their money and allowing the brutal rule of Spain in Cuba. On the right, there are images of booming factories, a very different sort of 'run' on the banks and shows the takeover of Cuba by the USA. It also seeks to deal with the critics who saw the takeover of Cuba as colonialism, by saying that it had been done for 'humanity's sake'. Arguably it was done much more in the interests of US prestige and commerce.

- **Who is saying it?** The supporters of McKinley. There is obvious bias here, as it is a piece of propaganda. Arguably it was not correct to blame the earlier Depression on the Democrats, or the run on the banks, let alone the treatment by Spain of its Cuban subjects. Some might argue that many of the failings of the economy were really the responsibility of earlier republican administrations.

- **What is the context?** 1900, a presidential election year.

- **Who were the intended audience?** As wide as possible across the United States.

- **Why was it created?** To promote the Republican administration and party; to win votes.

- **What is the context?** It shows what the Republicans felt were the main issues at the time, and the fact that they won the election would suggest that they were right.

Figure 5.1: A Republican election poster highlighting the supposed failings of the Democrats and making claims for what would happen under a Republican administration

Visual sources: photographs

Photographs also need careful analysis and evaluation.

- ***What does Figure 5.2 tell us?*** It shows some shanty buildings within sight of the Capitol building in Washington on fire and a fire crew trying to extinguish the blaze. The most common caption seen in books is: 'Shacks put up by the Bonus Army on the Anacostia Flats burning after a battle with the military.' Another is: 'Shacks put up by hungry bonus marchers destroyed in brutal action by MacArthur's army.' So, when analysing images, attention needs to be paid to any possible bias in the accompanying captions. Although it is said that 'the camera never lies', altering photographs had been done for several years by 1932. Similarly, we only have the content framed by the photograph. The fire shown could have been the only one on the Flats, or it could have been one of many hundreds.

- ***Who took the photograph?*** As is the case with this photograph, the photographer is often anonymous. Was the photographer employed by the army or the government, and therefore anxious not to show his employer in a bad light? Was it taken by an independent photographer and published in a newspaper hostile to the government?

- ***When was it taken?*** It must be contemporary to the event, in this case 1932.

- ***What is the context?*** It was taken in a presidential election year, with the Great Depression well underway. Hoovervilles and their destruction, and the treatment of the Bonus Marchers, were highly controversial.

- ***Who were the intended audience?*** This depends on whether the photograph was published and where. In a radical newspaper, for example, it could be aiming at opponents of the government.

- ***Why was the photograph taken?*** It could have been taken as an accurate record of what actually happened or for propaganda purposes by either left or right.

- ***What is the context?*** You need to be aware of who the war-veteran Bonus Marchers were, the nature of their grievances and why they had come to Washington.

Like all sources, photographs can be very valuable to a historian, but they need to be used with care. Captions can be misleading and the action captured might even be a re-enactment.

Figure 5.2: Firefighters attempt to put out a blaze in a temporary shanty town in Washington DC. The Capitol can be seen in the background.

Visual sources: cartoons

Cartoons can be difficult to analyse. In most cases they are drawn and published for two reasons:

- To amuse and entertain
- To make a point and send a message.

To achieve either, or both, of these aims, cartoons employ symbolism and a subtle form of humour which might be easily understandable to people at the time, but which is less obvious to us today. Consider the following points:

- **Who is providing the information?** It was published in in *Punch*, a British satirical magazine which aimed to be both humorous and topical. It was known to support liberal causes.
- **When was it published?** November 1861, when the Civil War had been underway for six months.
- **What is the context?** The British cotton industry depended heavily on the imports of raw cotton from the Southern states. The South had placed an embargo (a ban) on exporting cotton to Britain in the belief that Britain would be forced to support the South in order

to get the raw materials needed to keep its vast textile industry going. The North had also imposed a blockade to stop Southern exports. This posed a real dilemma for the British. Many supported the North's anti-slavery views, but many thousands of jobs depended on getting in the raw materials needed for its factories. The Royal Navy was also in a position to break any blockade.

- **What is the message?** The cartoon uses symbolism, and depicts 'King Cotton' as Prometheus. Prometheus is a figure in ancient Greek mythology who was punished by the gods for giving fire to humans. His punishment was to have his liver torn out and eaten by an eagle (symbolising the North here) every day for the rest of eternity. As he was immortal, his liver grew back every night (only to be plucked out again the next day). King Cotton is not shown here in a sympathetic light.
- **Who were the intended audience?** *Punch* was known to support liberal causes, but it does set out the dilemma and the complex issues faced by both Britain and the US.
- **Why was it created?** To appeal to the mainly middle-class liberal readership *of Punch* in Britain.

When you study a cartoon like this, you need to reflect carefully how far your own subject knowledge supports or challenges the views represented.

Cross referencing between sources

A source should never be used in isolation. It needs to be interpreted in the light of information obtained from other sources, as well as your own knowledge. There are three main reasons why cross-referencing between sources is so important:

- We can only judge how useful and reliable a source is by comparing it with what we already know and what other sources say.
- Reading several sources can help us deal with apparent contradictions and other concerns we might have about the source.
- By using a combination of a sources, we can often deduce things that none of the individual sources would suggest by themselves.

Look at the following sources A–C. Analyse and evaluate them as indications of American public opinion on the issue of Cuba (then a badly-managed Spanish colony) in the 1850s.

KING COTTON BOUND;

Or, The Modern Prometheus.

Figure 5.3: The cotton industry shown as a modern Prometheus: the American Eagle starts to pluck a chained King Cotton, bound by a blockade

SOURCE A

It is clear that the annexation of the island of Cuba by the United States is regarded by the great mass of people as certain. If we are to have Cuba, let us buy it because we do not need it at the cost of war. There is no overwhelming necessity for acquiring Cuba. We are rich enough, strong enough and prosperous enough without it.

Source: New York Times, *October 1851*

SOURCE B

From the Ostend Manifesto, a secret document written to the US Government in 1854 by three US ambassadors to European countries. It was not intended for publication.

We are convinced that an immediate effort ought to be made by the government of the United States to purchase Cuba from Spain. It must be clear from its geographical position that Cuba is as necessary to the North American republic as any of its present members and belongs naturally to the United States.

Source: Available at, for example, www. historyofcuba.com/history/havana/Ostend2.htm

SOURCE C

It is said that Cuba naturally belongs to us on account of its position. After we get Cuba, the same claim can be used to acquire Jamaica, which is 90 miles from Cuba, while Cuba is 130 miles from out coast, and so on until we add all the West Indies to our possession and then, when there are no more islands to purchase or conquer, the discovery will be made that Mexico naturally belongs to us, and then, when we have acquired Mexico, it will be argued that we have a natural right to all the Central American states. And last of all,

Canada will be brought within the operation of this argument, and after that surely the Russian possession of Alaska.

Source: From a speech by Representative Royce of Vermont in the US House of Representatives, 15 February 1859

There is a contradiction between the information provided by these sources.

- In Source A, a newspaper, the *New York Times*, argues that the USA does not need to acquire Cuba. In Source B, the three authors of the Manifesto argue that it does. How can this contradiction be explained?
- The first thing to note is that Source A is written by a journalist in a New York newspaper in 1851. It was likely to try to appeal to its Northern, business, readership. Source B is an official, if secret, statement written three years later by three ambassadors, who may be commenting on the issue from an official, and European, perspective.
- Source C shows that there is agreement in Congress with the views expressed in Source A. He does not want further expansion.
- Source B is an example of irony – of someone saying one thing and meaning another. It could be argued that the author was in favour of the expansionism he describes. He does not seem to explicitly oppose it, but, in his use of exaggeration and unlikely examples, he indicates that he does.

In assessing how representative these sources are, both individually and collectively, it is important to evaluate each source. Source A is from a leading newspaper in the business-orientated North, where there were strong expansionist tendencies. Source B is by three senior and experienced government employees aware of the implications of a US takeover of Cuba. Source C is from the elected representative of a small Northern State. Arguably, none of the authors is particularly representative of either public or official opinion at the time.

By linking these three sources with your background subject knowledge, however, you can reach a conclusion. The USA did not invade or buy Cuba. The Ostend Manifesto, a key document at the time, was initially a private government paper. When it was eventually published it caused a serious political row. This suggests that Sources A and C were quite representative of opinion at the time, while the authors of Source B, from their position in Europe, were out of touch with much of opinion in the United States.

A summary on dealing with source-based questions

- Show that you have fully grasped what the source is saying. Try highlighting the key points. Remember that the key point can often be in the last sentence.
- Demonstrate that you have thought about provenance and reliability. You must not just accept what the source is saying. Think about what the author might have left out. You need to test a source's reliability by:
  - comparing what it says with what other sources say and with your own subject knowledge
  - looking carefully at who created it, when, why and for what purpose or audience.
  - establishing if there are any reasons to doubt the reliability of the source.
- Interpret. What can be learned from the source, taking into account your judgement on how reliable the source is?
- Be objective. Always look at a source objectively and with an open mind.
- Never make assumptions. For example, don't assume that a source must be biased because it was written by a certain person from a certain place at a certain time. These points might establish a motive for bias, but do not necessarily prove that a text is biased.
- Never make sweeping or unsupported assertions. A statement such as 'Source A is biased...' *must* be accompanied by evidence to show that you know exactly what bias is, as well as evidence and examples to demonstrate in what way it is biased, with reasons to explain why.
- Compare sources. If you are asked to compare and contrast two sources, make sure you analyse both sources carefully before you start to write your answer. Draw up a simple plan.
- Evaluate the sources clearly.
- Draw conclusions. What can you learn from your analysis of the sources? How does it enhance your knowledge and understanding of a topic or event?
- Include contextual knowledge.

5.4 How might my skills and work be assessed?

Revision techniques

Too often, students often think that the purpose of revision is to get information into your brain in preparation for an assessment. It is seen as a process where facts are learned. If you have followed the course appropriately, however, and made sensibly laid-out notes as you have gone along, all the information you need will already be there. The human brain, like a computer, does not forget what it has experienced. The key purpose of revision is not to put information into the brain, but to ensure that you can retrieve it when it is required.

Revision needs to be an ongoing process throughout the course, not just in the days or weeks before an exam. The focus of your revision should be on identifying the key points, on, for example, why the Great Crash happened in 1929. Once you have those key points clear, the supporting detail will be easier to remember. The notes you make during the course are very important, and you should ensure that they are presented effectively.

Copying lists of facts from a book can be a pointless exercise. You need to think about what you are writing, comprehend it and learn to analyse it. Make your notes in such a way that you are answering a simple question. For example: 'What were the most important aspects of Roosevelt's First Hundred Days?' Don't just write a list of the causes. Prioritise them with reasons. This will prompt you to study all the various events that happened in those days. You will think about which were the most important and why. Once you have identified the key points, make sure you note two or three relevant factors which show you understand *why* they were key points. These notes will help you deal with other questions such as: 'Explain why the First Hundred Days were so important,' and 'To what extent were the Hundred Days the most effective part of the First New Deal?'

Quality revision and plenty of practise in attempting questions under timed conditions are important. If you feel you have not done enough at school, you could ask your teacher to provide some questions you can practise on your own under timed conditions.

Exam preparation

This section offers some suggestions for how you could approach an examination. Some might seem obvious, but, under pressure, we are all capable of making mistakes. It is important to be aware of potential pitfalls.

The syllabus will include details of what you need to learn during your course and for the exams. You should be aware of the following points:

- What topics the questions can be about. This will be covered during your course.
- What form the questions can take. Your teacher can help you understand the types of task you are likely to face, and the syllabus will give details of wording. The different types of question in this book should help you become more familiar with exam-style questions.
- How long you will have to answer an assessment paper.
- Which parts of a question paper you can ignore. Some question papers might have separate sections for those who have studied different options, for example, Modern European History or International History.
- The equipment you will need for writing and what you may or may not bring into an exam room. There are very strict rules that do not allow, for example, mobile phones or smart watches. Check if you are allowed to bring water.

Rubric

All examination papers contain **rubric**. This provides you with essential information about how long a timed assessment will last, how many questions you have to answer and from what sections, and so on. It is surprising how many students make rubric errors each year, by answering too many questions or questions from inappropriate sections of the paper. These basic errors can really damage your chances of success.

> **KEY TERM**
>
> **Rubric:** This is the set of rules and instructions you must follow in an exam. They will usually tell you how long the exam will last, where to put your answers, how many questions to answer and from which sections.

Question selection

Sometimes, you may be required to answer all the questions in a paper. However, if you have an opportunity to choose, for example, two out of three questions, this advice might be useful:

- Read *all* parts of all questions before you make your selection.

- Avoid choosing a question just because it is about a topic you feel confident about. This is not necessarily a guarantee that you understand what the question is asking and can answer it effectively.
- Select by task – what the question is asking you to do – rather than by the basic subject matter. You might know about the topic generally, but might not have revised all the other factors required to answer the question comprehensively. Be careful!
- If questions consist of more than one part, make sure that you can answer all of the parts. Avoid attempting a question because you are confident about the topic in part (a) if you know very little about part (b).
- Decide the order in which you are going to attempt the questions. Perhaps you should not leave the question you feel most confident about until last if you are worried about running out of time.

Timing

Work out how long you have to complete each question or part of a question. Make a note of it and make every effort to keep to that timing.

Practising answering questions under timed conditions is something you can do on your own as part of your revision. Take care not to make the mistake of spending too much time on a question which you know a great deal about and leave yourself insufficient time for a question which might carry twice as many marks.

If you run out of time, you will not be able to answer all of the questions fully. If you have spent too long on your first question with its two parts, there might be a case for attempting the second part of the next question if it carries more marks.

Planning

There is always the temptation in an exam to avoid spending time on planning and instead just getting started. Without planning, however, you take the risk of including irrelevant information, or not fully explaining the relevance of information, when answering questions.

A useful plan for an 'Explain why …' question might be three or four bullet points identifying the main reasons for the event, in order of importance, with a couple of supporting facts for each. Effective plans for the longer essay-type questions, such as 'To what extent …', could be set out in 'case for' and 'case against' columns or as a mind map, which has a focus on thinking out an answer. A plain list of facts will not be much help as a plan. Use the plan to clarify your ideas about what the question is asking.

How much information should be included in a response?

This is not a straightforward question to answer. An important factor to remember at AS Level is that about 50% of marks are allocated to your knowledge and understanding of a topic, and about 50% to the skills used in applying them. In the example source-based questions provided earlier in this chapter, you have seen that it is important to bring in contextual knowledge to back up your source evaluation and the points you are making. A couple of factual points such as 'Wilson was making this speech in 1912, *which was a presidential election year*', is a suitable approach for the first part of a source-based question. For the second part, where you should develop a case, the points you make need to be backed up by clear references to the sources, and then by at least two factual points.

For questions in papers where there are no sources, the factual information plays a more significant role. However, use this to provide support to your explanations or arguments, and do not let it dominate. In an 'explain why' type of question, it is most important to identify the reasons why something happened, and then back up each of those reasons with two or three items of information. In essay-type questions, you should think in terms of bringing three or four factual items to support your points. Look on facts as support for your ideas: the evidence of your knowledge and understanding.

How much should I write?

There is no requirement to write a specific number of words in a response, nor to fill a certain number of pages. Aim to keep your focus on writing a relevant response to the question set and making sure that you are aware of the assessment criteria for the type of question you are dealing with. Don't worry if another student seems to be writing more than you are.

Past papers

Previous exam papers can be very helpful. They will give an idea of what types of question have been assessed in the past and provide plenty of opportunities for practise. If you use past papers, it is important to attempt the questions under the appropriate timed conditions. While tackling past papers is very good practice, attempting to memorise answers is very poor preparation. Students who produce ready-made answers are likely to be answering a question they might have expected, and not the one they are actually being asked.

The syllabus

The syllabus provides:

- details of the options to be studied at AS level
- how many options have to be taken
- how long each examination is
- what proportion of the overall marks are allocated to each paper
- the assessment objectives and the relationship between them and the different papers you take. It might say, for example, that:
  - 30% of the total marks at AS Level are awarded for Assessment Objective (AO) 1(a), which is knowledge and understanding in Paper 2
  - 30% of the marks are awarded for AO2(a), which is analysis and evaluation in Paper 2
- details of each of the papers, what form the questions take and how many questions there are in each paper; if there are sources, it will be clear how many there will be, what type of sources might be used and the maximum number of words in an extract, so you will know how much you will have to read
- the key questions; these indicate broad areas of history for study; all questions set in the exam will fit into one of the key questions. To use the International syllabus as an example, if a key question is 'Why was there a rapid growth of industrialisation after 1780?', then one of the AS Level exam questions might be something like, 'To what extent was improved transport the principal cause of the rapid industrialisation in the late 18th century?'
- key content; this suggests some of the areas which should be studied, but these are not all the areas to study for a key question; the fact that you are studying something which is not specified in the key content does not mean it will not be examined.

There are decisions to be made by your teachers when it comes to AS Level History. There might be a choice of areas of study – for example, between European history and American history. The choice might depend on the teachers' expertise and the range of resources available in your school. There may also be a choice of how many topics to study. Your teachers will decide whether to study all three topics, in order to give you a choice of question in the exam, or just study two, in order to focus on them and so build up additional knowledge and understanding.

There are real benefits to having the syllabus available in helping you know what to expect during your course and in the assessments.

Mark schemes

Mark schemes accompany the question papers and make it clear how your work will be assessed. They are in two parts. The first is a generic mark scheme, which lays out what is required from a response in general terms. This will specify the elements that make up a high-quality work, such as developed analysis, balance or source evaluation. The second part indicates the type of factual support expected and the principal points in a 'compare and contrast' question.

The mark scheme helps you to see what a good-quality answer looks like and you can use this to reflect on your own work and consider how it might be improved. The mark scheme makes it clear that just learning facts is not enough, you need to demonstrate a range of skills as well.

Assessment objectives

Assessment objectives cover the skills to be tested in the exams. The assessment objectives (AO) for AS Level History are:

- AO1: Recall, select and deploy historical knowledge appropriately and effectively.
- AO2: Demonstrate an understanding of the past through explanation, analysis and a substantiated judgement of: key concepts causation, consequence, continuity, change and significance within an historical context, the relationships between key features and characteristics of the periods studied.
- AO3: Analyse, evaluate and interpret a range of appropriate source material.

Index